Joy E

Kazantzakis

Politics of the spirit

PRINCETON MODERN GREEK STUDIES

This series is sponsored by the Princeton University Program in Hellenic Studies under the auspices of the Stanley J. Seeger Fund

Firewalking and Religious Healing: The Anastenaria of Greece and the American Firewalking Movement *by Loring M. Danforth*

Kazantzakis: Politics of the Spirit *by Peter Bien*

Kazantzakis

Politics of the spirit

PETER BIEN

PRINCETON UNIVERSITY PRESS
PRINCETON, NEW JERSEY

Published by Princeton University Press, 41 William Street,
Princeton, New Jersey 08540
In the United Kingdom: Princeton University Press, Oxford

This book has been composed in Linotron Bembo text and
Korinna Bold display type

Clothbound editions of Princeton University Press books are printed on acid-free paper, and binding materials are chosen for strength and durability. Paperbacks, although satisfactory for personal collections, are not usually suitable for library rebinding

Printed in the United States of America by Princeton
University Press, Princeton, New Jersey

Library of Congress Cataloging-in-Publication Data
Bien, Peter.
Kazantzakis : politics of the spirit / Peter Bien.
p. cm.—(Princeton modern Greek studies)
Bibliography: p.
Includes index.
ISBN 0-691-06786-4
1. Kazantzakis, Nikos, 1883–1957—Political and social views.
I. Title. II. Series.
PA5610.K39Z589 1989
889'.83209—dc20 89-8372

Contents

Preface

This is the first part of a projected two-volume study. It takes us from the start of Kazantzakis's career in 1906 to the publication of his epic *Odyssey* in 1938, when he was fifty-five years old. He still had nineteen years to live. Works composed after the *Odyssey*—including the novels that brought him international fame—will be considered in the second volume along with his continuing involvement in Greek politics.

The *Odyssey* is the natural place to end the present work because it forms a decisive watershed in Kazantzakis's career. On the one side it weaves into a single tapestry all his ideas and experiences up to the mid-thirties; on the other side its comprehensiveness left Kazantzakis with the frightening problem of what to do next (neither he nor anyone else could have predicted the solution he found). To end with the epic offers the double advantage, therefore, of bringing us to a culmination and of tantalizing us with regard to the best known portion of Kazantzakis's career.

Politics is a good way to approach all this because in Greece it stings everyone and everything. Nothing escapes. Language, the arts, religion, metaphysics, historiography, education, philosophy, even science and sports are subject to its inflammation. Thus the political approach, while providing a useful focus, need not be restrictive. Of Kazantzakis's diverse involvements, only one—his effort to enhance "demotic," the spoken language—will be excluded from this study, since I have already devoted a book to that subject.

In a review of Annie Cohen-Solal's *Sartre: A Life*, Stanley Hoffmann comments that there are at least four ways to write biographies, "especially those of writers as monstrously prolific as Sartre. One way is to try to deal both with the events in their private and public lives and with their writings. In the case of Sartre, this would require several volumes and an author who would feel competent to handle philosophy, epistemology, novels, plays, screenplays, politics, literary and art criticism and psychoanalysis." (All this applies word for word to Kazantzakis, of course.) Hoffmann continues: "Another possibility . . . is to try to find in the works the expression . . . of the writer's personal . . . traumas and conflicts." A third possibility is to discuss the works at least briefly and to show "their connection with the author's and the general public's concerns of the moment, without providing an extensive analysis of the content or indulging in psychological reductionism." Lastly, one can leave the work aside and concentrate on the life. "It is, of course, a debatable choice. What is Sartre without his books?" (Hoffmann 1987:3).

Hoffmann's survey defines my own choices. *Kazantzakis: Politics of the Spirit* is not a biography in the last sense, willing to sacrifice the works in order to ferret out every last detail of the life. For what is Kazantzakis without his books? Nor is this biography willing to discuss the works only briefly, without extensive analysis. On the other hand, it does not use the works primarily to indulge in psychological reductionism. Kazantzakis's inner life is present, of course—how can it be avoided?—but is treated more as a philosophical and religious pilgrimage than as a succession of traumas. This leaves Hoffmann's first way: to deal both with the events in Kazantzakis's life and with his writings—even though, like Sartre, Kazantzakis was monstrously prolific and also extensively involved in outward affairs.

Regarding those affairs: because I minimize psychological speculation I am able to concentrate instead on elements that can be better documented. Indeed, I perhaps border on pedantry in working so extensively from the voluminous resources that Kazantzakis left us in letters, glosses, notebooks, and essays, not to mention his imaginative writings themselves. Readers may find the parenthetical references cumbersome, especially since I take pains to give both the original Greek source and the English translation whenever such exists; but I hope that my scholarly motives will be appreciated, especially in light of the amount that has been written on Kazantzakis, pro and con, with little supporting evidence.

Of course I also allow myself the freedom (and joy) of interpretation. In particular I try to present a political reading of the works, although I realize that any such reading is partial. With regard to the life, I strive to comprehend its totality, aware that the result may incline more to mythopoesis than to history. Since my approach is organic and synchronic as well as chronological, certain events that belong to the span of this volume (for example, Kazantzakis's mission to the Caucasus) are deferred to the second part so that they may be considered together with the writings they influenced; similarly, certain early works (for example, the plays *Comedy* and *Christ*) are deferred so that they may be considered thematically alongside later works. As always in an approach that ranges forwards and backwards in an effort to demonstrate cohesion and the interrelationship of parts, the burden of perceiving chronological sequence is shifted somewhat to the reader, who in this case should employ the index to bring together scattered references to material that is out of chronological order.

Ideally, a literary biography should be comparative to some degree, showing how its subject relates to contemporaneous writers. Kazantzakis could be seen, for example, in relation to figures such as Dos Passos, Hesse, Barbusse, D. H. Lawrence, Sartre, Orwell, Rolland, Drieu la Rochelle, Thomas and Heinrich Mann, Shaw, Zweig, Musil, Bernanos, Aragon, and a host of other Europeans, not to mention Greeks. But *Kazantzakis: Politics of the Spirit* does not attempt such comparisons, even though it sometimes points out relationships in passing, or suggests a book where they can be further explored. The reason is simple: too much first needs to be said about Kazantzakis himself. My hope is that comparisons with his contemporaries will be undertaken in the future by other critics, aided perhaps by the present study. Suffice it to note here that Kazantzakis conforms to a familiarly romantic pattern seen in those whose formative years coincided with what appeared to be the death agonies of European civilization. Convinced that liberalism was bankrupt, contemputous of bourgeois values, he sought a mystical camaraderie rooted in the vibrancy of an all-embracing anti-intellectual myth that would solve his own and the world's malaise. Where to find this was the problem. In extreme nationalism? communism? fascism? But Kazantzakis also possessed an inborn fastidiousness that eventually made each of these solutions strike him as appalling. Thus, like so many of his contemporaries, he always returned to the central problem of filling his own emptiness. A comparative study might show the success with which he accomplished this. Unlike some others, he did not commit suicide, did not collapse into ideological rigidity or hypocrisy, did not employ politics as a screen to hide the exhaustion of his creative talent. Instead, with a noteworthy stamina and self-confidence, he continued to the very end of his long career to imagine, by means of literature, a viable replacement for the bourgeois, liberal culture he despised.

THE WRITING of this book has been greatly abetted by various institutions and individuals. I wish here to record my gratitude to the U.S. Educational Foundation (Fulbright program) for grants to Australia and Greece; to Dartmouth College for several faculty fellowships; to librarians at Dartmouth, at the Ethnikí Vivliothíki in Athens, where most of the research was done, at Harvard, the British Library, the Vikelaía Vivliothíki in Iráklion, the Historical Archives of the Benáki Museum in Athens, the New York Public Library, Woodbrooke College, and the universities of Birmingham, Cincinnati, Melbourne, Thessaloníki, and Uppsala. Among individuals, I am most indebted to six who have never minded being barraged by queries: Christos Alexíou, Yórgos Anemoyánnis, Chrysanthi Bien, Kimon Friar, Eléni Kazantzáki, and the late Pandelís Prevelákis. Eléni Kazantzáki has also allowed me access to her husband's unpublished notebooks, an invaluable resource. All quotations from Kazantzakis's published and unpublished works, letters, and notebooks are by her kind permission. Others who have helped in various ways are: Stylianós Alexíou, Tomas Anfält, Katerína Angheláki-Rooke,

Michael Antonakes, Martha Aposkítou-Alexíou, Roderick Beaton, Línos Benákis, Bertrand Bouvier, Inge Brown, John Burke, Sandra Cronk, Stámas Diamantáras, Bo-Lennart Eklund, Stathis Gauntlett, Michael Gelven, Yánnis Goudélis, Dimítris Gounelás, Yánnis Hasiótis, Yánnis Kakridís, Emmanuel Kásdaglis, David Kelsey, Maria Vertsoni-Kokóli, Bruce Lansdale, Evro Layton, Yánnis Láppas, Lily Macrakis, Theoháris Melissáris, Panayótis Moullás, Thanásis Papathanasópoulos, Yánnis Petritákis, Dia Philippides, Leftéris Prevelákis, Voúli Proúsali, Apóstolos Sachínis, Yórgos Savídis, Irving Shapiro, Anna Sikelianoú, Alki Soulouyánni, Yórgos Stefanákis, Peter Topping, Breck Trautwein, Valentíni Tselíka, Yánnis Vasilakákos, Speros Vryonis, Jim Warren, Bob Wessmann, and the students of my Kazantzakis seminar at Harvard in the spring term of 1983, when I tried out many of the ideas in this book. I also wish to record my thanks to Titíka Saklambáni, the curator of the Kazantzakis Museum at Varvári; to Andréas Kalokairinós, director, and Louíza Kalokairinoú, curator, at the Historical Museum of Crete in Iráklion; and to my editor at Princeton, Robert E. Brown, who oversaw the entire process with efficiency and concern.

All judgments, errors, and extravagances are of course entirely my own.

"Terpní," Riparius, New York — Peter Bien
26 June 1988

A note on documentation and transliteration

Abbreviations in the parenthetical references are limited to four: "Kaz." for Níkos Kazantzákis, "Eleni Kaz." for Eléni N. Kazantzáki (or Helen Kazantzakis or Eléni Sámios), "Prev." for Pandelís Prevelákis, and "Od." for *Odyssey*. Full bibliographical data for all works quoted, consulted, and mentioned are given in the alphabetical listing of "References." In sorting out Kazantzakis's numerous writings the reader will be aided by the index, and also by the List of Works, since each entry for a work in both places will include a cross reference to the rubric (e.g. "Kaz. 1958p") employed in the system of documentation. Let me add that in citing Greek in the bibliographical entries and elsewhere I employ the monotonic system except in exceptional instances where I might wish, for example, to emphasize a document's *katharévusa* idiom. When transliterating Greek I follow the *Journal of Modern Greek Literature* in favoring a system that aims to reproduce sound rather than spelling.

List of works

PRINCIPAL WORKS AVAILABLE IN ENGLISH TRANSLATION

(Date of composition appears at left, followed by the title of the work, its date of publication, and the rubric under which full bibliographic data can be found in the References at the back of the book.)

1906	*Serpent and Lily*, 1980	
	Ofis ke kríno, 1906 [Novella]	Kaz. 1906
1906	"The Sickness of the Century," in *Serpent and Lily*	
	"I arrósteia tu aiónos," 1906 [Essay]	Kaz. 1958d
1909?	*Comedy*, in *Two Plays*, 1982	Kaz. 1982
	Komodía, 1909 [Play]	Kaz. 1958t
1923	*The Saviors of God: Spiritual Exercises*, 1960	Kaz. 1960b
	Salvatores Dei. Askitikí, 1927 [Essay]	Kaz. 1927f
	Askitikí. Salvatores Dei, (2d ed. rev.) 1945	Kaz. 1962a
1924? 1926?	*Symposium*, 1974.	Kaz. 1974
	Simpósion, 1971 [Essay]	Kaz. 1971b
1925, 1927	*Russia*, 1989	Kaz. 1989
	Tí eída sti Rusía, 1928 [Travel articles]	
	Taksidévondas. Rusía, 1956	Kaz. 1965e
1926ff.	*Journeying*, 1975 [Travel articles on Italy, Egypt, Sinai, Jerusalem, and Cyprus]	Kaz. 1975
	Taksidévondas, 1961 [Travel articles on Italy, Egypt, Jerusalem, Cyprus, the Peloponnese]	Kaz. 1965d
1929	*Toda Raba*, 1964	Kaz. 1964f
	Toda-Raba, 1934 [Novel, written in French]	Kaz. 1962c
1926, 1933–	*Spain*, 1963	Kaz. 1963c
1934, 1936	*Taksidévondas. Ispanía*, 1937 [Travel articles]	Kaz. 1962b
1935	*Japan China*, 1963	Kaz. 1963a
	Iaponía-Kína, 1938 [Travel articles]	Kaz. 1964d
1936	*The Rock Garden*, 1963	Kaz. 1963b
	Le Jardin des rochers, 1939 [Novel, written in French]	Kaz. 1959b
1937	*Journey to the Morea*, 1965 [Travel articles on the Peloponnese]	Kaz. 1965b
	In *Taksidévondas*, 1961	Kaz. 1965d
1937	*Melissa*, in *Three Plays*, 1969	
	Mélissa, 1939, in *Théatro*, vol. 1, 1955 [Play]	
1925–1938	*The Odyssey: a modern sequel*, 1958	Kaz. 1958f
	Odíssia, 1938 [Epic poem]	Kaz. 1957
1940	*England*, 1965	Kaz. 1965a
	Taksidévondas. Anglia, 1941 [Travel articles]	Kaz. 1964c

1941–1943	*Buddha*, 1983	Kaz. 1983
	Vúdas, in *Théatro*, vol. 3, 1956 [Play]	Kaz. 1956e
1941–1943	*Zorba the Greek*, 1953	Kaz. 1953
	Víos ke politía tu Aléksi Zorbá, 1946 [Novel]	Kaz. 1959d
1948	*Sodom and Gomorrah*, in *Two Plays*, 1982	Kaz. 1982
	Sódoma ke Gómora, in *Théatro*, vol. 3, 1956 [Play]	Kaz. 1956e
1948	*The Greek Passion*, 1953 (In England: *Christ Re-crucified*, 1954)	
	O Hristós ksanastavrónetai, 1954 [Novel]	
1949	*The Fratricides*, 1964	Kaz. 1964e
	I aderfofádes, 1963 [Novel]	
1949	*Kouros*, in *Three Plays*, 1969	
	Kúros, in *Théatro*, vol. 1, 1955 [Play]	
1949	*Christopher Columbus*, in *Three Plays*, 1969	
	Hristóforos Kolómvos, in *Théatro*, vol. 3, 1956 [Play]	Kaz. 1956e
1949–1951	*Freedom or Death*, 1956 (In England: *Freedom and Death*, 1956)	Kaz. 1956a
	O Kapetán Mihális, 1953 [Novel]	Kaz. 1964b
1950–1951	*The Last Temptation of Christ*, 1960 (In England: The Last Temptation, 1960)	Kaz. 1960a
	O teleftaíos pirasmós, 1955 [Novel]	Kaz. 1955c
1953	*Saint Francis*, 1962 (In England: *God's Pauper, St. Francis of Assisi*, 1962)	Kaz. 1962d
	O ftohúlis tu Theú, 1956 [Novel]	Kaz. 1956d
1954	"Drama and Contemporary Man," 1976	Kaz. 1976
	"To dráma ke o simerinós ánthropos," 1954 [Essay]	Kaz. 1954
1955–1956	*Report to Greco*, 1965	Kaz. 1965c
	Anaforá ston Gréko, 1961 [Autobiography]	Kaz. 1964a

SELECTED OTHER WORKS

NOVEL

"Spasménes psihés," 1909–1910 (Broken Souls), Kaz. 1909a

POETRY

Tertsínes 1960 (Terzinas), Kaz. 1960c

PLAYS

"Ksimerónei," produced in 1907 (Day Is Breaking), Kaz. 1977d
O protomástoras, 1910 (The Master Builder), Kaz. 1910c
Nikifóros Fokás, 1927 (Nikiforos Fokas), Kaz. 1927g
Hristós, 1928 (Christ), Kaz. 1956c
Odisséas, 1928 (Odysseus)
Iulianós o paravátis, 1945 (Julian the Apostate)
O Kapodístrias, 1946 (Capodistria)

"Promithéas" [trilogy], 1955 (Prometheus)
"Konstandínos o Palaiológos," 1956 (Constantine Palaiologos)
"O Othéllos ksanayirízei," 1962 (Othello Returns)

ESSAYS

O Friderikos Nítse en ti filosofía tu dikaíu ke tis politías, 1909 (Friedrich Nietzsche's Philosophy of Law and the State), Kaz. 1909b, Kaz. 1959c
"I epistími ehreokópise?" 1909 (Has Science Gone Bankrupt?), Kaz. 1958h
"Ya tus néus mas," 1910 (For Our Youth), Kaz. 1910a
"H. Bergson," 1912 (H. Bergson), Kaz. 1912, Kaz. 1958b
"Omología pisteos," 1925 (Confession of Faith), Kaz. 1925a

PRINCIPAL COLLECTIONS OF LETTERS

Epistolés pros ti Galátia, 1958, 1984 (Letters to Galatea), Kaz. 1958a
Tetrakósia grámmata tu Kazantzáki ston Preveláki, 1965 (Four Hundred Letters of Kazantzakis to Prevelakis), Prev. 1965b
Níkos Kazantzákis, o asimvívastos, 1977 (Nikos Kazantzakis, the intransigent), Eleni Kaz. 1977, translated as *Nikos Kazantzakis, a biography based on his letters*, 1968, Eleni Kaz. 1968a

Chronology

1883. Kazantzakis is born on 18/30* February in Iráklion, Crete, then still part of the Ottoman Empire. His father, Mihális, a dealer in agricultural products and wine, is from Varvári, now the site of the Kazantzakis Museum. Much later, Mihális is to become one of the models for Kapetán Mihális in the novel *Freedom or Death*.

1889. Cretan rebels attempt unsuccessfully to win the island's freedom from the Turks. The Kazantzakis family flees to Greece for six months.

1897–1898. Another Cretan rebellion—this time successful. Nikos is sent for safety to the island of Naxos, where he is enrolled in a school run by French monks. This begins his love of the French language.

1902. Having completed his secondary education in Iráklion, Kazantzakis moves to Athens to study law.

1906. Even before taking his degree, Kazantzakis publishes the essay "The Sickness of the Century" and the novel *Serpent and Lily*; he also writes the play "Day Is Breaking."

1907. "Day Is Breaking" wins a drama prize and is produced in Athens, stirring up much controversy. The young Kazantzakis becomes instanteously famous. He begins his journalistic career and is initiated as a Freemason. In October he commences graduate studies in Paris, where he continues to write both journalism and serious literature.

1908. In Paris, he attends Henri Bergson's lectures, reads Nietzsche, and completes the novel "Broken Souls."

1909. He finishes his dissertation on Nietzsche and writes the play *The Master Builder*. Returning to Crete via Italy, he publishes his dissertation, the one act play *Comedy*, and the essay "Has Science Gone Bankrupt?" As president of the Solomos Society of Iráklion, a lobby advocating the adoption of the demotic language (that is, the language spoken by the common people) in the schools and the abandonment of the puristic language called "katharévusa," Kazantzakis writes a long manifesto on linguistic reform that is published in an Athenian periodical.

THIS CHRONOLOGY is based largely on the biographical summaries that Pandelís Prevelákis includes in the *Tetrakósia grámmata tu Kazantzáki ston Preveláki* (Prev. 1965b:3–16, 19–22, 125–127, 383–389, 531–541).

* The date is given as Old Style/New Style. This is because Greek dates prior to 16 February 1923 reflect the Julian Calendar. The Gregorian reform of the Julian Calendar, although accepted in most of southern Europe during the sixteenth century and by Britain and the United States in 1752, was delayed in Greece until 1923, when 16 February became 1 March. To convert Old Style (O.S.) to New Style (N.S.), add twelve days if the O.S. date falls in the nineteenth century and thirteen days if the O.S. date falls in the twentieth century.

1910. His essay "For Our Youth" hails Ion Dragoúmis, another demoticist, as the prophet who will guide Greece to new glory by insisting that it must overcome its subservience to ancient Greek culture. Kazantzakis and Galatea Alexíou, an Iráklion author and intellectual, begin to live together in Athens, without marrying. He earns his bread by translating from French, German, English, and ancient Greek. He becomes a founding member of the Educational Association, the most important lobby for demoticism.

1911. He marries Galatea.

1912. He introduces Bergson's philosophy to Greek intellectuals by means of a long lecture delivered to members of the Educational Association and later published in the association's *Bulletin.* When the first Balkan War breaks out, he volunteers for the army and is assigned to Prime Minister Venizélos' private office.

1914. He and the poet Angelos Sikelianós journey together to Mount Athos, where they remain for forty days at various monasteries. He reads Dante, the Gospels, and Buddha there; he and Sikelianós dream of founding a new religion. To earn a living, he writes children's books in collaboration with Galatea.

1915. Again with Sikelianós, he tours Greece. In his diary he writes, "My three great teachers: Homer, Dante, Bergson." In retreat at a monastery, he completes a book (now lost), probably on the Holy Mountain. He notes in his diary that his motto is "come l'uom s'eterna" (how man saves himself—from Dante's *Inferno* 15.85). He most likely writes the plays *Christ, Odisséas*, and *Nikifóros Fokás* in first draft. In order to sign a contract for harvesting wood from Mount Athos, he travels to Thessaloníki in October. There he witnesses the British and French forces as they disembark to fight on the Salonica Front in World War I. In the same month, reading Tolstoy, he decides that religion is more important than literature and vows to begin where Tolstoy left off.

1917. Because of the need for even low-grade coal during the war, Kazantzakis engages a workman named George Zorbás and attempts to mine lignite in the Peloponnesus. This experience, combined with the 1915 scheme for harvesting wood, develops much later into the novel *Life and Times of Alexis Zorbás* (*Zorba the Greek*). In September he travels to Switzerland, where he resides as the guest of Yánnis Stavridákis, the Greek consul in Zurich.

1918. He goes on pilgrimage in Switzerland to the sites associated with Nietzsche. He forms an attachment to another intellectual Greek woman, Elli Lambrídi.

1919. Prime Minister Venizélos appoints Kazantzakis Director General of the Ministry of Welfare, with the specific mission of repatriating 150,000 Greeks who are being persecuted by the Bolsheviks in the Caucasus. In July Kazantzakis departs with his team, which includes Stavridákis and Zorbás. In August he travels to Versailles to report to Venizélos, then participating in the negotiations for the peace treaty. Afterwards, Kazantzakis proceeds to Macedonia and Thrace to oversee the installation of the refugees in villages there. These experiences are used much later in *Christ Recrucified* (*The Greek Passion*).

1920. The assassination of Dragoúmis on 31 July (o.s.) dismays Kazantzakis. When Venizélos's Liberal Party is defeated at the polls in November, he resigns from the Ministry of Welfare and departs for Paris.

1921. He tours Germany, returning to Greece in February.

1922. An advance contract with an Athenian publisher for a series of school textbooks enables him to leave Greece again. He remains in Vienna from 19 May until the end of August. There he contracts a facial eczema that the dissident Freudian therapist Wilhelm Stekel calls "the saints' disease." In the midst of Vienna's postwar decadence, he studies Buddhistic scriptures and begins a play on Buddha's life. He also studies Freud and sketches out *Askitikí*. September finds him in Berlin, where he learns about Greece's utter defeat by the Turks, the so-called "Asia Minor disaster." Abandoning his previous nationalism, he aligns himself with communist revolutionaries. He is influenced in particular by Rahel Lipstein and her cell group of radical young women. Tearing up his uncompleted play "Buddha," he begins it again in a new form. He also begins *Askitikí*, his attempt to reconcile communist activism with Buddhist resignation. His dream being to settle in the Soviet Union, he takes Russian lessons.

1923. The period in Vienna and Berlin is well documented owing to copious letters from Kazantzakis to Galatea, who continues to reside in Athens. Kazantzakis completes *Askitikí* in April and resumes work on "Buddha." In June he goes on pilgrimage to Nietzsche's birthplace, Naumburg.

1924. Spending three months in Italy, Kazantzakis visits Pompeii, which becomes one of his obsessive symbols; then he settles in Assisi, completes "Buddha" there, and commences his lifelong discipleship to Saint Francis. Soon after his return to Athens he meets Eléni Samíou. Back in Iráklion, he becomes the guru of a communist cell of disgruntled refugees and veterans from the Asia Minor campaign. He begins to plan the *Odyssey* and he perhaps writes *Symposium*.

1925. His political involvements lead to his arrest, but he is detained for only twenty-four hours. He writes cantos 1–6 of the *Odyssey*. His relationship with Eléni Samíou deepens. In October he leaves for the Soviet Union as correspondent for an Athenian newspaper, which publishes his impressions in a series of long articles.

1926. He and Galatea are divorced; she continues her professional career under the name Galatea Kazantzáki even after she remarries. He travels to Palestine and Cyprus, again as a newspaper correspondent. In August he journeys to Spain to interview Primo de Rivera, the Spanish dictator; October finds him in Rome interviewing Mussolini. In November he meets Pandelís Prevelákis, his future disciple, literary agent, confidant, and biographer.

1927. He visits Egypt and Sinai, again as a newspaper correspondent. In May he isolates himself on Aegina in order to complete the *Odyssey*. Immediately afterwards he hastily composes scores of encyclopedia articles to earn a living, then collects his travel articles for the first volume of *Taksidévondas* (Journeying). Dimítrios Glinós's periodical *Anayénnisi* (Renaissance) publishes *Askitikí*. In late October Kazantzakis travels to Russia once again, this time as the guest of the Soviet government on the occasion of the tenth anniversary of the Revolution. He encounters Henri Barbusse. He delivers a bellicose speech at a Peace Symposium. In November he meets Panaït Istrati, a Greek-Romanian writer then very much in vogue in France. With Istrati and others he tours the Caucasus. The two friends vow to share a life of political and intellectual action in the Soviet Union. In December Kazantzakis brings Istrati to Athens and introduces him to the Greek public via a newspaper article.

1928. On January 11, Kazantzakis and Istrati address a throng in the Alhambra Theater, praising the Soviet experiment. This leads to a demonstration in the streets. Kazantzakis and Dimítrios Glinós, who organized the event, are threatened with legal action, Istrati with deportation. April finds both Istrati and Kazantzakis back in Russia, in Kiev, where Kazantzakis writes a film scenario on the Russian Revolution. In Moscow in June, Kazantzakis and Istrati meet Gorki. Kazantzakis changes the ending of *Askitikí*, adding the "Silence." He writes articles for *Pravda* about social conditions in Greece, then undertakes another scenario, this time on the life of Lenin. Traveling with Istrati to Murmansk, he passes through Leningrad and meets Victor Serge. In July, Barbusse's periodical *Monde* publishes a profile of Kazantzakis by Istrati; this is Kazantzakis's first introduction to the European reading public. At the end of August, Kazantzakis and Istrati, joined by Eléni Samíou and Istrati's companion Bilili Baud-Bovy, undertake a long journey in southern Russia with the object of co-authoring a series of articles entitled "Following the Red Star." But the two friends become increasingly estranged. Their differences are brought to a boil in December by the "Roussakov affair," that is, the persecution of Victor Serge and his father-in-law, Roussakov, as Trotskyists. In Athens, a publisher brings out Kazantzakis's Russian travel articles in two volumes.

1929. Alone now, Kazantzakis continues his travels across the length and breadth of Russia. In April he departs for Berlin, where he lectures on the Soviet Union and attempts to publish articles. In May he settles in a remote farmhouse in Czechoslovakia to write, in French, the novel first entitled "Moscou a crié" and then renamed *Toda-Raba*. This recounts his recent vicissitudes in Russia, only minimally disguised. He also completes a novel in French called "Kapétan Élia," one of the many precursors of *Kapetán Mihális*. These are his first attempts to develop a career in western Europe. At the same time, he undertakes a basic revision of the *Odyssey* in order to reflect his changed view of the Soviet Union.

1930. To earn money, he produces a two-volume "History of Russian Literature" that is published in Athens. The Greek authorities threaten to bring him to trial for atheism on account of *Askitikí*. Kazantzakis remains abroad, first in Paris, then in Nice, where he translates French children's books for Athenian publishers.

1931. Back in Greece, he settles again on Aegina, working on a French–Greek dictionary (demotic as well as katharévusa). In June, in Paris, he visits the Colonial Exhibition; this gives him fresh ideas for the African scenes in the *Odyssey*, whose third draft he completes in his hideaway in Czechoslovakia.

1932. Kazantzakis and Prevelakis plan a collaboration to alleviate their financial woes. This involves film scenarios and translations. The plan is largely unsuccessful. Among other things, Kazantzakis translates the whole of Dante's *Divine Comedy* into Greek terza rima in 45 days. He moves to Spain in an effort to make a career there. He begins by translating Spanish poetry for an anthology.

1933. He writes his impressions of Spain. He completes a terzina on his "general," El Greco—the germ of his future autobiography, *Report to Greco*. Unable to support himself in Spain, he returns to Aegina, where he undertakes a fourth draft of the *Odyssey*. After revising his Dante translation, he composes a set of terzinas.

1934. To earn money, he writes three textbooks for second and third grades. When one of these is adopted by the Ministry of Education, his financial woes are alleviated for a time.

1935. After completing the fifth draft of the *Odyssey*, he sails for Japan and China in order to write more travel articles. Upon his return he purchases some land in Aegina.

1936. Still attempting to establish a career outside of Greece, Kazantzakis writes, in French, the novel *Le Jardin des rochers* (*The Rock Garden*), drawing upon his recent experiences in the Far East. He also completes a new version of the Kapetán Mihális theme, calling it "Mon père." For money, he translates Pirandello's *Questa sera si recita a soggetto* (Tonight We Improvise) for the Royal Theater; he then turns out his own Pirandellesque play, "Othello Returns," which remains unknown during his lifetime. Next, he translates Goethe's *Faust*, Part 1. During October and November he is in war-torn Spain as a correspondent; he interviews both Franco and Unamuno. His home in Aegina is completed. This is his first permanent residence.

1937. In Aegina, he completes the sixth draft of the *Odyssey*. His travel book on Spain is published. In September he tours the Peloponnesus. His impressions are published in article form; later they will become *Journey to the Morea*. He writes the tragedy *Mélissa* for the Royal Theater.

1938. After the eighth and final draft of the *Odyssey*, he supervises the printing of the epic in a sumptuous edition. Publication takes place at the end of December. He suffers again from the facial eczema that occurred in Vienna in 1922.

1939. He plans a new epic in 33,333 verses to be called "Akritas." From July through November he is in England as a guest of the British Council. While residing in Stratford-on-Avon he writes the tragedy *Julian the Apostate*.

1940. He writes *England* and continues to sketch out "Akritas" and to revise "Mon père." To earn money, he produces novelistic biographies for children. Mussolini's invasion of Greece in late October makes Kazantzakis confront anew his ambivalence concerning Greek nationalism.

1941. As the Germans overrun mainland Greece and then Crete, Kazantzakis assuages his grief with work. He finishes the drama *Buddha* in first draft, revises his translation of Dante, and begins a novel originally entitled "The Saint's Life of Zorbás."

1942. Confined to Aegina for the duration of the war, he vows to forsake his writing as soon as possible in order to re-enter politics. The Germans allow him a few days in Athens, where he meets Professor Yánnis Kakridís; they agree to collaborate on a new translation of Homer's *Iliad*. Kazantzakis finishes the first draft between August and October, then plans a novel on Jesus to be called "Christ's Memoirs"—the germ of the future *Last Temptation of Christ*.

1943. Working energetically despite the privations of the German occupation, Kazantzakis completes the second drafts of *Buddha, Alexis Zorbás*, and the *Iliad* translation. Then he writes a new version of Aeschylus's Prometheus trilogy.

1944. In the spring and summer he writes the plays *Capodistria* and "Constantine Palaiologos." Together with the Prometheus trilogy, these cover ancient, Byzantine, and modern Greece. After the German withdrawal, Kazantzakis moves immediately to Athens, where he is offered hospitality by Téa Anemoyánni. He witnesses the phase of the civil war called the "Dekemvrianá" (the December events).

1945. Fulfilling his vow to re-enter politics, he becomes the leader of a small socialist party whose aim is to unite all the splinter groups of the noncommunist left. He is denied admission to the Academy of Athens by two votes. The government sends him on a fact-finding mission to Crete to verify the German atrocities there. In November he marries his longtime companion Eléni Samíou and is sworn in as Minister without Portfolio in the Sofoúlis coalition government.

1946. The uniting of the democratic socialist parties having occurred, Kazantzakis resigns his post as minister. On March 25, the anniversary of Greek Independence, his play *Capodistria* opens at the Royal Theater. The production causes an uproar, including threats by a right-wing nationalist to burn down the theater. The Society of Greek Writers recommends Kazantzakis for the Nobel Prize, together with Sikelianós. In June he begins a sojourn abroad that is meant to last only forty days but that actually lasts for the remainder of his life. In England he attempts to convince British intellectuals to join him in forming an "Internationale of the Spirit"; they are not interested. The British Council offers him a room in Cambridge, where he spends the summer writing a novel called "The Ascent"—one more precursor of *Kapetán Mihális*. In September he moves to Paris as a guest of the French government. Political conditions in Greece force him to remain abroad. He arranges for *Alexis Zorbás* to be translated into French.

1947. Börje Knös, the Swedish intellectual and government official, translates *Alexis Zorbás*, Kazantzakis, after pulling many strings, is appointed to a post at UNESCO, his job being to facilitate translations of the world's classics in order to build bridges between cultures, especially between East and West. He himself translates his play *Julian the Apostate*. *Alexis Zorbás* is published in Paris.

1948. He continues to translate his plays. In March he resigns from UNESCO in order to devote himself fully to his own writing. *Julian* is staged in Paris (one performance only). Kazantzakis and Eléni move to Antibes, where he immediately composes the play *Sodom and Gomorrah. Alexis Zorbás* is accepted by publishers in England, the United States, Sweden, and Czechoslovakia. Kazantzakis writes the first draft of *Christ Recrucified* in three months, then spends two more months revising it.

1949. He begins a new novel, *The Fratricides*, about the civil war then raging in Greece. Next come two more plays, *Kouros* and *Christopher Columbus*. His facial eczema returns; he goes to Vichy for treatment at the spa there. In December he begins *Kapetán Mihális*.

1950. This novel occupies him until the end of July. In November he turns to *The Last Temptation*. Meanwhile, *Zorbás* and *Christ Recrucified* have been published in Sweden.

1951. He completes the first draft of *The Last Temptation*, then revises it after reworking "Constantine Palaiologos." *Christ Recrucified* is published in Norway and Germany.

1952. Success brings its own problems: Kazantzakis finds himself increasingly occupied with translators and publishers in various countries. He is also increasingly bothered by his facial ailment. He and Eléni spend the summer in Italy, where he indulges his love of Saint Francis's Assisi. A severe infection in the eye sends him to hospital in Holland, where he studies the life of Saint Francis while recovering. His novels continue to be published in Norway, Sweden, Holland, Finland, and Germany—but not in Greece.

1953. He is hospitalized in Paris, still suffering from the eye infection (he eventually loses his right eye). Examinations reveal a lymphatic disorder that has presumably caused his facial symptoms throughout the years. Back in Antibes, he spends a month with Professor Kakridís perfecting their translation of the *Iliad*. He writes the novel *Saint Francis*. In Greece, the Orthodox Church seeks to prosecute Kazantzakis for sacrilege owing to several pages of *Kapetán Mihális* and the whole of *The Last Temptation*, even though the latter still has not been published in Greek. *Zorba the Greek* is published in New York.

1954. The Pope places *The Last Temptation* on the Roman Catholic Index of Forbidden Books. Kazantzakis telegraphs the Vatican a phrase from the Christian apologist Tertullian: "Ad tuum, Domine, tribunal appello" (I lodge my appeal at your tribunal, Lord). He says the same to the Orthodox hierarchy in Athens, adding: "You gave me your curse, holy Fathers. I give you a blessing: May your conscience be as clear as mine, and may you be as moral and religious as I am." In the summer Kazantzakis begins a daily collaboration with Kimon Friar, who is translating the *Odyssey* into English. In December he attends the première of *Sodom and Gomorrah* in Mannheim, Germany, after which he enters hospital at Freiburg im Breisgau for treatment. His disease is diagnosed as benign lymphatic leukemia. The young publisher Yánnis Goudélis undertakes to bring out Kazantzakis's collected works in Athens.

1955. Kazantzakis and Eléni spend a month in a rest home in Lugano, Switzerland. There, Kazantzakis begins his spiritual autobiography, *Report to Greco*. In August they visit Albert Schweitzer in Gunsbach. Back in Antibes, Kazantzakis is consulted by Jules Dassin regarding the scenario for a movie of *Christ Recrucified*. The Kazantzakis–Kakridís translation of the *Iliad* comes out in Greece, paid for by the translators because no publisher will accept it. A second, revised edition of the *Odyssey* is prepared in Athens under the supervision of Emmanuel Kásdaglis, who also edits the first volume of Kazantzakis's collected plays. *The Last Temptation* finally appears in Greece, after a "royal personage" intervenes with the government on Kazantzakis's behalf.

1956. In June, Kazantzakis receives the Peace Prize in Vienna. He continues to collaborate with Kimon Friar. He loses the Nobel Prize at the last moment to Juan Ramón Jiménez. Dassin completes the film of *Christ Recrucified*, calling it *Celui qui doit mourir* (He Who Must Die). The Collected Works proceed; they now include two more volumes of plays, several volumes of travel articles, *Toda-Raba* translated from French into Greek, and *Saint Francis*.

1957. Kazantzakis continues to work with Kimon Friar. A long interview with Pierre Sipriot is broadcast in six installments over Paris radio. Kazantzakis attends the showing of *Celui qui doit mourir* at the Cannes film festival. The Parisian publisher Plon agrees to bring out his Collected Works in French translation. Kazantzakis and Eléni depart for China as the guests of the Chinese government. Because his return flight is via Japan, he is forced to be vaccinated in Canton. Over the North Pole the vaccination swells and his arm begins to turn gangrenous. He is taken for treatment at the hospital in Freiburg im Breisgau where his leukemia was originally diagnosed. The crisis passes. Albert Schweitzer comes to congratulate him, but then an epidemic of Asiatic flu quickly overcomes him in his weakened condition. He dies on 26 October, aged 74 years. His body arrives in Athens. The Greek Orthodox Church refuses to allow it to lie in state. The body is transferred to Crete, where it is viewed in the cathedral church of Iráklion. A huge procession follows it to interment on the Venetian ramparts. Later, Kazantzakis's chosen epitaph is inscribed on the tomb: "Den elpízo típota. Den fovúmai típota. Eímai eléftheros." (I hope for nothing. I fear nothing. I am free.)

Kazantzakis

Politics of the spirit

CHAPTER ONE

Why Kazantzakis is not a political writer

> What Jesus established . . . is the doctrine of the freedom of the soul. Greece already had some fine thoughts on this subject; several stoics had discovered a way to be free under a tyrant. But in general the ancient world imagined liberty as connected with certain political forms. . . . [Jesus] revealed to the world . . . that . . . the individual human being is prior to and above the citizen.
>
> —Ernest Renan, *The Life of Jesus*, pp. 136–137

POLITICS OR METAPOLITICS?

No author who lives in Greece can avoid politics. But it is one thing for a writer to be personally interested in governmental affairs and quite another for him to be truly political. By this I mean someone whose basic concerns are societal: who focuses on how human beings rule themselves so that they may live harmoniously together and prosper. Kazantzakis did have societal concerns; he was involved in politics at every step of his career—sometimes by choice, sometimes not—and his books lose much of their density if we fail to see how they reflect political events. Nevertheless, it would be wrong to call him a political writer according to the above definition, for most basically he was not concerned with how masses of human beings achieve a viable existence through proper government. On the other hand, in denying that he was a political writer we must not call him apolitical, since he never ignored politics. How, then, can we speak about Kazantzakis and politics? We can do so by describing him as "metapolitical": involved in politics because of basic concerns that reach beyond politics to something more important.

If Kazantzakis's basic concerns were not societal, what were they? This question can best be approached via an anecdote. On 21 April 1967, the day of the Papadópoulos-Pattakós coup d'état, I happened to be in Athens. The next afternoon I visited a member of Kazantzakis's circle, a lady of poetic sensibility with whom I had made an appointment to discuss how the seventeen-syllable line of Kazantzakis's *Odíssia* sounds to cultivated native ears. We were pursuing this subject when the lady's nephew, a young man in his early twenties, entered the room. He sat politely in silence for a time, waiting for us to finish, but then suddenly rose and interrupted us with what developed into a tirade. "How can you chit-chat about prosody on this of all days?" he shouted. "And how can you be interested in Kazantzakis? For us [meaning the young], his work is dead and irrelevant!" Next, pointing to the street, which was still filled with tanks, he explained his anger: "Kazantzakis is a fake, a hypocrite. He presents himself as a great humanitarian. Political tyranny, social injustice, and economic exploitation draw huge public tears from his eyes. But when you see through the façade you realize that he couldn't care less about political problems because he is imprisoned inside his own egomania, oblivious of the fate of others, concerned only about abstractions like god and salvation. Why should we, the young whose future was cut off by yesterday's all-too-concrete events here on this earth, why should we be interested in such abstractions? And why should any Greek care about an egotistical, selfish writer who because of his other-worldliness, his introversion, his refusal to devote himself to the welfare of society, is un-Greek, outside Greek traditions, and therefore irrelevant to Greek reality?"

It is hard to refute tirades with logic, and even harder in this case because the young man was correct about Kazantzakis's basic interests. True, Kazantzakis's overwhelming concern was personal salvation; the proper motto for his work is the one he himself chose from Dante's *Inferno* (15.85): "come l'uom s'eterna"—how man makes himself eternal, saves *himself* from death and despair (Prev. 1965b:9; Eleni Kaz. 1977:76; 1968a:60). In all this the young man was correct. His mistake was to assume that Kazantzakis was a political writer who at the same time betrayed everything political: thus the charges of "fake" and "hypocrite." If he had really believed Kazantzakis to be irrelevant to Greek youth at a time of political crisis, he would have ignored him, not become incensed. The problem in this instance, as in similar accusations during Kazantzakis's lifetime, was an inability to distinguish between a writer who is political and one who is metapolitical. In addition, the problem was an inability to understand that Kazantzakis's metapolitical and political aspects are symbiotic. His critics have tended to analyze him into two separate persons, the religious seeker and the politician, failing to perceive that neither can exist independently of the other because the very method employed by Kazantzakis to win personal salvation is political engagement.

Kazantzakis must be seen in his totality. His politics grow out of his religious quest, his religious quest out of his politics. He does not leave one interest behind in order to proceed to the next, but carries his past interests with him while he accumulates new ones. The key word in his development is not "change" but "continuity." His nationalism is a continuation of his aestheticism, his communism of his nationalism, his anticommunism of the very ingredients that produced his communism.

And all his political and metapolitical positions are manifestations of certain continuing attitudes toward death, god, and the bourgeoisie; of certain psychological needs; and of a metaphysical system that added cosmological significance to his worldly activities. We are left with a paradoxical tangle that defies logic but that is the only genuine Kazantzakis.

Since the truth is this paradoxical wholeness, the worst way to refute Kazantzakis's accusers would be to split him apart, just as they do. By taking data out of context we could argue that he was truly political rather than metapolitical, but such a conclusion would warp the truth and serve only to perpetuate the misunderstanding that surrounds him. Instead of responding in this way, we should strive to comprehend him synthetically. If we at least try to do this, then perhaps we shall be justified in assigning priorities within the totality by claiming, as we have, that his basic concerns are god and his own salvation; conversely, perhaps we shall be forgiven occasional departures in which we consider Kazantzakis's politics as though they were a separate category. In any case, the important thing is to avoid the misinformation that has produced so many tirades against him in the past.

THE ESSENTIAL; THE ADVENTITIOUS; CONTINUITY

Kazantzakis's political involvements must be analyzed in a manner that separates the essential from the adventitious. Essentially, these involvements reflect the needs of his deepest, most creative level of personality. Seen in this way, he resembles his character Odysséas, who travels the road of participation in order to reach the destination of a meaningfulness that transcends participation. Essentially, political engagement was the means by which Kazantzakis actualized his nonpolitical potential. Adventitiously, on the other hand, his engagement reflects specific events in Greece and elsewhere—factors extrinsic to his deepest needs.

This was not always clear at the time. To many observers (and occasionally to Kazantzakis himself) he *appeared* to be essentially political: involved in the welfare of society as opposed to his own salvation. His activities affected his ability to publish, made him persona non grata at the National Theater (Prev. 1965b:498), sent him periodically into self-exile, and helped determine the subject matter of his works. Abused by both the left and the right, he exasperated all régimes by being too complicated. While the Greek communists called him decadent, idealist, bourgeois, mystical, incurably religious, and an advocate of war (which he was), the Chinese communists hailed him as an apostle of peace (which he was not), the Orthodox Church attempted to prosecute him for atheism, the monarchists considered him a Bolshevik rabble-rouser, and an official in the communist-controlled resistance movement suspected him of being a secret agent of British intelligence. As he himself realized, "There is no régime that can tolerate me—and very rightly so, since there is no régime that I can tolerate" (Eleni Kaz. 1977:475, 477; 1968a:401, 402).

But Kazantzakis was not the passive victim of these attacks; in many ways he encouraged them. The problem is that he often seemed to think of himself as a political writer, thus provoking others to expect him to behave like one. It is true that he hated propagandistic art and never condescended to write in the mode of socialist realism despite external pressure to do so; yet he denigrated art-for-art's-sake, considered beauty a luxury our age cannot afford, always felt that the artist must be committed—indeed, an agitator—and did not hesitate to express these views in public. In 1957, for example, when a radio interviewer questioned him about the relation between literature and politics, Kazantzakis replied: "It is shameful to remain unperturbed. . . . The writer . . . cannot repress his indignation or shirk his responsibility. He is duty-bound not to sleep; he must keep his people on the alert." "The writer today is a combatant if he remains faithful to his mission" (Eleni Kaz. 1968a:529; Sipriot 1957:3). Statements such as these make him vulnerable to charges of hypocrisy, especially when they are taken out of context (as this one is).

Another way in which Kazantzakis provoked the opposition was by confusing the adventitious with the essential insofar as he asserted (although he really knew better) that his life consisted of distinct stages each of which involved a new political allegiance. His life did consist of stages, but only circumstantially, never fundamentally. This confusion is seen in his autobiographical "novel" *Report to Greco* and also in his letters. In 1923, as he was entering his "Bolshevik stage" (adventitiously, not essentially), he wrote to Galatea, his first wife: "I have been a *katharevusiános* [linguistic purist], nationalist, demoticist, scholar, poet, socialist, religious fanatic, atheist, aesthete, and now none of these can fool me any longer" (Kaz. 1958a:184). The implication is that he had finally discovered himself owing to his new allegiance to Bolshevism. Thirteen years later, having renounced Bolshevism for metacommunism, he summarized his politics as follows:

> Until 1923, full of emotion and ardor, I passed through the nationalist camp. . . . From approximately 1923 to 1933, with the same emotion and ardor, I was part of the left wing. . . . Now I am passing through the third stage (will it be the last?). I call it freedom. . . . I have ceased to identify my soul's fortune—my salvation—with the fortunes of this or that idea. I know that ideas are inferior to a creative soul. (Prev. 1965b:464–465; 1961:160).

novella presents a theory of history central to Kazantzakis's later political thinking: the doctrine of the transitional age. This is difficult to discern in the text until we benefit from a gloss published in the same year. Whereas the text in vacuo might delude us into thinking that Kazantzakis sympathized wholeheartedly with his hero, the essay Ἡ ἀρρώστεια τοῦ αἰῶνος (The Sickness of the Century; Le Mal de siècle) shows him capable of standing outside his own decadent romanticism and seeing it ambivalently. Indeed, the essay suggests that he meant his young aesthete to exemplify a cultural illness diagnosed as romantic melancholy. The victims of this disease are trapped; their suicides, far from being heroic, merely confirm that no other solution exists for them. He explains all this by means of a cultural-historical theory, in the process transforming his essay from a lament into a manifesto. What we need to replace the decadent beauty-worship of our times, he asserts, is a virile, youthful, amoral paganism. He hails the ancient Greek civilization in which Apollo reigned, melancholy was unknown, and beauty could be pursued naïvely, unimpeded by either Christian or bourgeois morality. He then castigates Jesus as the destroyer of this pagan freshness. But what seems to be just an escapist call for renewed pagan spontaneity is actually an analysis of our impasse. The *mal de siècle*, says Kazantzakis, arises because we are caught in the middle. We can never return to paganism on account of Christianity's decisive influence on our culture; yet we can no longer be Christians because science has destroyed our belief in heaven, the basis of Christian hope. We are trapped between loss of spontaneous appreciation of this world and loss of faith in the world to come. Apollo is dead and so is Jesus. Melancholy victims of a transitional age, we vent our aesthetic instincts in the decadent, self-frustrating ways exemplified by the protagonist of *Serpent and Lily* (Kaz. 1958d).[3]

In order to appreciate the continuity of Kazantzakis's ideas throughout his long career, we should remember the ambivalence of this novella and its gloss. Together, they show that in his very first year as a professional writer he was already obsessed with the problems of death, freedom, spiritual fulfillment, and the transitional age. His future permutations—socialism, nationalism, communism, metacommunism, eschatological politics—were conditioned by these obsessions, for in every case he was seeking an exit from the trap set by the transitional age.

To explore such problems in the first year and a half of his career, he naturally drew from his limited education and experience. His materials were: love of ancient Greek culture; Darwinism's challenge to Christianity (Kaz. 1964a:139–144; 1965c:114–119); his platonic courtship of the unconventional bluestocking Galatea Alexíou (to whom *Serpent and Lily* is dedicated);[4] his clash with the bourgeois mores of provincial Iráklion, his birthplace, mores that had been rendered senseless in his mind by the removal of their only possible justification, reward in heaven. All these factors appear in his next major work, the Ibsenesque play Ξημερώνει (Day Is Breaking), written in 1906 and produced the following season with much fanfare, after having received high praise in a prestigious dramatic competition (although the judges refused to award it the official laurel because of its shocking immorality).[5] As in the novella, the setting here is domestic, not political. The heroine, Laló, falls in love with a romantic poet who happens to be her husband's brother. Her problem is whether she should go off with the brother, asserting her pagan right to be happy, or honor the anachronistic Christian morality that forbids adultery and commands her to maintain her dull marriage. Trapped by this predicament, she grows melancholy and chooses suicide as her escape. Throughout this sensational plot, Kazantzakis weaves a corresponding drama of clashing ideas. His own revolutionary views are represented by Laló's doctor,[6] who preaches the coming of a virile neopaganism that will make happiness a duty as well as a right and will allow neither bourgeois conventions nor flabby romanticism to threaten humanity's natural outlets. The threats come from Laló's mother and the romantic lover, respectively, the one an otherworldly Christian scandalized by the doctor's opinions, the other a gushy poet devoted to Heinrich Heine. Laló is thus tempted by two anachronistic falsehoods. If she stays, she capitulates to Christianity and bourgeois mores; if she goes, she embraces romantic decadence. The right way—the truth, the proper exit—is the doctor's virile defiance and joy, his sincerity, his strength. But although she knows what is right she cannot transform this knowledge into action—her soul is broken (Kaz. 1977d:208). Why? Because, born too early, she is trapped in a transitional age. Like the hoplite of Marathon, she "ran ahead of the others in order to proclaim the victory" and now must die for her pains (208). As she says in a doleful soliloquy: "I have arrived in time to tell you that the light is winning! The sun is rising, the sun is rising!" "Ξημερώνει!" she exclaims at the very end—"day is breaking" (210). But she herself will never see the complete daybreak (ξημέρωμα). She takes poison and expires, her strength leaving her just as she attempts to embrace the dawn.

This interesting play moves beyond Kazantzakis's *mal de siècle* pessimism to the qualified optimism of Laló's soliloquy. The sun is rising: we can at least announce the forthcoming victory whereby the night of Christianity, bourgeois morals, and romantic decadence will bow before the day of the doctor's pagan joy. However, we are still in the transitional age; this day has not yet arrived. We can wriggle ourselves out of the trap, but only in our imagination. Right thought is already possible in this transitional age even though right action is not. The truth can be known but not followed.

Here we should recall what I said earlier about Kazantzakis's romantic zeal for perfection: how it impelled him to dream about an ideal society but at the same time eroded itself through an opposite impulsion toward melancholy, since perfection is attainable only in thought, never in the finite world of objects. Established at the start of his career, the polarity between thought and action is useful in analyzing the remainder. At the height of his nationalistic and communistic enthusiasms, Kazantzakis was impelled toward a belief that right action is indeed possible. When he experienced frustration in his political endeavors, he returned to the more qualified optimism that we have seen in *Day Is Breaking*, creating a series of new Marathon runners who utter a cry (κραυγή) announcing the coming "day," and die as a consequence. However, these deaths, unlike Laló's, are no longer the result of weakness; the souls of these forerunners are not broken. Furthermore, the polarity between thought and action is no longer absolute. As always in Kazantzakis's development, a synthesis occurs—in this case one in which the proclamation of a thought by means of a freely chosen death becomes paradoxically the sole *action* by which these later protagonists can help bring the transitional age to an end. Nikifóros Fokás, Kapodístrias, Kapetán Mihális, Christ, Saint Francis, Manoliós, and Father Yánaros are no longer pinned mothlike to their fates; nor are they melancholy despite their failure to accomplish in the world of objects the right action that would have fulfilled their zeal for perfection.

Although many of these later situations are wholly or partially political, the basic ingredients determining their treatment derive from Kazantzakis's nonpolitical debut. I have emphasized the crucial obsession with the transitional age, the division between right action and right thought, the seesaw between pessimism and optimism, the central role of death as an exit from despair, and the conception of freedom as an escape from materiality. To these we may add other abiding motifs such as the hatred of bourgeois inertia, the exultation of pagan virility, and the valuation of passion as a good, indeed a duty.

Kazantzakis carried these concerns with him when he traveled to Paris in October 1907 and began his first intensely political phase, becoming a ferocious nationalist. Although his sojourn there lasted only twelve months,[7] its effect was extraordinary. As published evidence we have a series of newspaper dispatches, his doctoral dissertation on Nietzsche, the novel Σπασμένες ψυχές (Broken Souls), and the play Ο πρωτομάστορας (The Master Builder). In addition, Kazantzakis probably wrote a monograph on William James during this period, and he most certainly amassed the material for his 1913 lecture on Henri Bergson. The year in Paris left its mark on his entire personality, not just on his mind. Coming from the provincialism of Iráklion and Athens to a great European capital, he broadened his experience in many sectors—education, politics, culture, women, art—acquiring a sophisticated maturity previously lacking. For example, immediately after leaving Paris he could say scornfully of D'Annunzio, whom he had imitated only three years earlier: "He excites a few youths who, before knowing life, quite naturally seek from it very much more than it can give" (Kaz. 1958n:1292). This does not mean that he turned into a cynic. He remained a romantic dreamer but tried now to become a hardheaded one, spinning his visions from the stuff of reality (historical forces, realpolitik, biology, the nature of analytic reason) rather than from romantic poetry or fluffy, wishful thinking.

Matured in this way, he developed an increasing interest in action. At first he was especially impressed by the socialists led by Jean Jaurès.[8] In his earliest newspaper reports he describes their program of state ownership of land, asserting that this will be the beginning of the new society (Kaz. 1958g:1211). He then tries to view socialism scientifically with his new hardheadedness. The socialists address themselves to contemporary humanity, he says, because they base their program on the death of Christian otherworldliness. Since no subsequent life exists, they attempt to improve this one. They are the new apostles of the new religion that answers needs arising after the French Revolution (Kaz. 1958p).

There is no better illustration of duration and continuity in Kazantzakis's thought, for all this is simply a new way of approaching the old search for an exit from the impasse of our transitional age. The difference is that the juvenile enthusiasms of *Day Is Breaking* have been replaced by a practical interest in land ownership and economic reform.

The socialists did not appeal to Kazantzakis for long. He liked their atheism, to be sure; yet in other ways they failed to satisfy the interests he had brought with him from Greece. We should remember in particular his advocacy of a virile, amoral paganism. Confirmed in these inclinations by his readings in Nietzsche, he soon began to view the socialists as degenerately feminine. Whereas Nietzsche taught that the virility of a strong young nation is expressed by its expansion at the expense of weaker neighbors, the socialists were pacifists and internationalists; whereas Nietzsche preached passion, the socialists were rationalists; furthermore, insofar as they believed in the instincts, they invited license, abuse, and anarchy (Kaz. 1958p). In addition, Jaurès and his followers favored the parliamentary system whereas Kazantzakis's temperament was more attuned to Georges Sorel's open advocacy of violence as opposed to discussion (Sorel 1941:88, 121–122). What he missed in the socialists was discipline. In former times this had been provided by the Church through the fear of hell. Now this restraint was gone, replaced by an impotent substitute: scientific rationalism. Nations need the strength of an irrational faith. Accordingly, Kazantzakis began to inveigh in his newspaper dispatches against a France "made flabby by the premature and consequently criminal internationalism of various intellectuals" and to relate the feeling of Greek students in Paris that they must return home not as "socialist or internationalist windbags" but rather as youths who have learned "how fierce is the battle of life" (Kaz. 1958c:1285).

It is not surprising that his new allegiance to a virile, irrational faith in nationalism à la Carducci, Kipling, and Barrès (all of whom he invoked [1958c:1284])[9] should have pressed Kazantzakis to gaze increasingly away from France and back toward Greece. His articles grow more and more chauvinistic. He objects to the condescending attitude of gigantic France toward Lilliputian Greece, and he calls up the vision of "Great Hellas" (1958c:1285), the "Great Idea" of a revived Greek empire with Constantinople once more as its capital. All this is a new—yet at the same time familiar—search for an exit to humiliation and despair, a continuation, altered by circumstances, of his earlier paganism. Thinking specifically of Greece, he ferociously declares:

> Nations . . . must become egotistical and hard in order to trample the corpses of their opponents and to advance strong and happy in the sun-bathed, manly intoxication of life. The voice of our ancestors [presumably the Spartans] joins the voice of science [presumably Darwinism] in commanding us . . . to be beautiful and strong, to hate our enemies and . . . , released from the Christian ideals of the crippled and diseased, to hold high the selfhood of the race. (1958c:1285)

Kazantzakis's new ferocity led him to despise French artists—Debussy, for example—as displaying the "death-bringing smirk of thrice-delicate irony," the "tubercular, aristocratic grace of withering organisms," whereas in the barbaric primitivism of a Richard Wagner he saw individual rays of hope that, if only they could merge, would constitute the "great daybreak" (1958q:1287). Nor is it surprising that he should have begun to worship the iron-willed men of history: Napoleon, Cesare Borgia, Benvenuto Cellini, "all the hard and strong stalwarts (λεβέντες) who . . . left upon life the traces of their insatiable and rapacious desires." How magnificent, he sighs, were Florence's past rulers and how miserable are that city's "democratizing and socializing" children of today (1958n:1291).

These scattered remarks reveal the attitude that was to dominate the next decade of Kazantzakis's career. If this new stance must be given a label we can join Prevelákis in calling it aristocratic nationalism—aristocratic because of its Nietzschian assumption that leadership must come from figures whose sublime qualities distinguish them from the democratic herd. Yet I hope that by now we will interpret the new stance not as an essentially different one but as an allotrope of what preceded. Similarly, we should realize that Kazantzakis's nationalism was not essentially different from the allegiance that followed. When he aligned himself with the internationalist communists in the early 1920s, he appeared to make an about-face. If we spy beneath the surface, however, we see that his communism was simply one more allotropic expression of his concern about the transitional age, his search for an exit, his worship of pagan strength. This is why, to the chagrin of "real" communists, he could admire Mussolini at the same time that he admired Lenin. If we attach mutually antagonistic labels to his successive allegiances, his inconsistencies will make us angry; if we do not, we will realize that his seemingly contradictory enthusiasms were successive variations upon the same basic theme.

When, in April 1909, Kazantzakis reached Iráklion ready to proclaim the daylight of nationalism, he was neither a Marathon runner arriving ahead of the others nor an advocate of right thought born too early for right action. On the contrary, he returned to a Greece that, recovering from its defeat by Turkey in 1897, had already begun to develop the patriotic zeal that was to dominate intellectual as well as political circles for over a decade, swelling until it burst in the Asia Minor catastrophe of 1922.

The overall atmosphere that Kazantzakis entered is well described in a short essay on Kostís Palamás's play *Trisévyeni* (1902) by Basil Laoúrdas (Laourdas 1964). We cannot begin to understand what was happening in the remarkable decade 1901–1910, he argues, unless we recognize the crucial effect of the War of 1897. This humiliating defeat by the Turks stunned, but did not destroy, Hellenism's romantic dream of reconstituting Greece anachronistically as a revived Byzantine and/or ancient Greek empire. The immediate effects of the defeat were despondency, apathy, and a sense of emptiness. Before long, however, certain figures began to campaign for revitalization. The old ideals were not obliterated, only dormant; a man like Palamás knew that they would have to be adapted to changed conditions. Although he did not ignore the importance of the Greek past, he insisted that exclusive worship of former glory was a form of slavery. If Greece were to continue its heritage, it would have to achieve greatness in ways appropriate to modernity. In effect, he challenged his compatriots to enter the twentieth century.[10]

This call for rebirth and contemporaneousness was taken up by others, in particular by Ion Dragoúmis. He could not accept Palamás's optimistic view of Western science, nor could he avoid lamenting the disappearance of older forms of social organization; nevertheless, he demanded noble action in the present to make Greece a proud modern state and no longer a nation of rayahs (bondsmen). Toward this end (and at variance with his campaign against Western influence) he advocated an arrogant Nietzschian neoromanticism that despised the slavish herd and elevated above these rayahs the immoral, iconoclastic will of sublimely egotistic individuals, claiming that such egotism was paradoxically an altruistic force for social and nationalistic advance. As a model he offered Pávlos Melás, killed in 1904 in the Macedonian campaign, a paragon of energy, health, voluntarism, strength, youthfulness, bravado, patriotism, and self-sacrifice operating in the present in order to achieve a goal demanded by the past: the absorption into the Greek state of Hellenic populations under Turkish rule. Dragoúmis called upon the select few among his countrymen to emulate Melás by becoming heroic stalwarts among the rayahs. One of those who listened was Kazantzakis. Indeed, Dragoúmis—an intellectual who acted, a dreamer who possessed the discipline, knowledge, and self-knowledge to apply his dreams in the real world—typified Kazantzakis's ideal. No wonder that it was this man's shadow that Kazantzakis felt beside him as, "full of emotion and ardor," he "passed through the nationalist camp" (Prev. 1965b:464).[11]

Judging from Palamás and Dragoúmis, we may conclude that a despondent Greece was being challenged to move into the twentieth century as a means of recovering from the humiliation of 1897, but at the same time was being challenged to reach both regressively into the past and laterally into the contemporary cultural life of the rest of Europe—to form, in other words, a spatial amalgam of East and West, as well as a temporal amalgam of yesterday and today.

These ideas were operative in many spheres of Greek life—in educational and linguistic reform, for example, and in the arts. But their most spectacular (and eventually tragic) manifestations were in politics. The call for heroic stalwarts was answered by Elefthérios Venizélos, under whose guidance the Greeks emerged victorious in the Balkan Wars and later in World War I.[12] Their breasts, in Dimítrios Glinós's words, were "proudly swelled by colossal self-confidence. The bards of the race commenced grandiloquently to sing Hellenism's modern glories alongside the ancient" (Lambridis 1947:50–51).[13] What the poets and intellectuals helped to formulate was not a thoughtless expansionism but a sophisticated ideology that spoke to an entire generation of Greeks of all classes and all political persuasions. This was the revived Great Idea, the age-old dream of the enslaved Greeks of the Ottoman Empire, a dream that had always been modern Greece's consolation and hope, a psychological compensation for Hellenism in decline. The Great Idea, as described by Ion Dragoúmis in 1909, was "a memory that has remained deeply nestled in the soul of the Greek ever since the Turks captured Constantinople in 1453. It is the memory that Greeks, with Constantinople as their capital, ruled the East in the past" (Dragoumis 1909:6).

When Kazantzakis arrived home from Paris, this memory was yearning for practical application. No longer just a vague recompense for a nation in decline, the dream had become a force awakening the Greeks to the possibility of specific accomplishments. When Prime Minister Venizélos pleaded Greece's case at the Versailles Conference, he presented a table showing the distribution of the Hellenic nation. Only fifty-five percent resided in Greece; the remainder lived outside, chiefly in Thrace, Constantinople, Asia Minor, and the Caucasus (also in the United States, of course).[14] The Great Idea aspired to "liberate" these "enslaved" Greeks by acquiring the territories to which Greece believed it had rights. Furthermore, as an extension of this irredentist policy, it aspired to reinstate a Greek king at Constantinople and a Greek patriarch in Hagia Sophia.[15]

In sum, Kazantzakis returned to a country full of optimism. He soon formed decisive friendships with nationalistic figures such as Dragoúmis. Although he remained both a dreamer and—most basically—a philosophical pessimist, he was encouraged by the general euphoria of the times to behave *as if* he believed that the transitional age could be ended by right action. Specifically, he aided Hellenism by involving himself in demoticism and educational reform,[16] by volunteering for the Balkan Wars (he served in Prime Minister Venizélos's private office), and notably by heading a governmental mission to the Caucasus in 1919. The purpose of this last venture was to repatriate 150,000 of the Hellenic nation who were being persecuted by the Bolsheviks in retaliation for the Greek government's interference in Russia's internal affairs when Greece joined the Allies in sending an expeditionary force against the new Soviet régime. (We will consider Kazantzakis's activity in the Caucasus when we come to *Christ Recrucified* in the second volume of this study.)

Kazantzakis's new optimism had developed in Paris, as we saw. The novel and play he completed there document the change that had occurred. Both "Spasménes psihés" and *O protomástoras* are addressed to his fellow Greeks. The former begins with the protagonist making an Independence Day oration at Koraïs's grave, preaching an intellectual and moral revolution with Nietzschianism and evolution as its rallying cries. The protagonist's first name is appropriately Orestes—the world is out of joint and he is made to set it right, or so he thinks. But his surname is Asteriádis: the would-be avenger is just a stargazer (*astéri* = star) caught as usual in a transitional age and therefore unable to realize his dreams. Too flabby to extricate himself by suicide, he quickly descends from euphoria to despair, whereupon the novel becomes a study of generalized moral, physical, sexual, and intellectual frustration—hence the title "Broken Souls." Love is not a viable exit; nor is devotion to the ideals of ancient Greece, ancestor worship being satirized with especial cruelty. The problem is that Orestes and the other Greek expatriates lack not only the knowledge and self-knowledge that would enable them to base their dreams on reality, they also lack Spartan discipline.

The virile protagonist of *O protomástoras*, on the other hand, remedies these defects. Although he dreams, he does not overlook the Darwinian nature of life; although he is driven by passion, he controls and directs his impulses with ruthless logic. Accordingly, he conquers fate itself and is ready to move to the next practical achievement of the impossible (to recapture Constantinople perhaps?). The broken souls are modeled on certain flabby Greeks whom Kazantzakis met in Paris (Kaz. 1958r:1498) and also on his own past self. The master builder—dreaming yet knowing "how fierce is the battle of life"—projects his new self and by extension the newly virile Greek nation. It is hardly surprising that the play is dedicated to Ion Dragoúmis.

The intellectual center of *O protomástoras* is no longer a character spouting European ideals, as in *Ksimerónei*, but the famous folk song "Tis Artas to yofíri" (The Bridge of Arta), which provides Kazantzakis with a perfect metaphor for his own times. It might be even too perfect, for the political and moral allegory is so obvious that the play runs the danger of seeming schematic. The master builder is of course Dragoúmis's sublime voluntarist/egotist merged with Ibsen's Bygmester (master builder) Solness, that other compulsive engineer whose edifices rest on the ashes of his wife's happiness, and with a Nietzschian superman who despises slave morality. The wildly destructive river is fate, which our hero has the hubristic audacity to challenge. The bridge is Greece—the attempt of a society, here represented by the village, to build something useful, beautiful, and enduring over the ravages of nature and human nature. As Act I opens we learn that this bridge has already collapsed three times and has been rebuilt on each occasion. The chorus of villagers (Nietzsche's slavish herd; Dragoúmis's defeatist, demoralized rayahs) are certain that it will collapse again, and indeed it does begin to totter as soon as the river rises. But the master builder is not daunted; he has rebuilt it previously and will do so once more. He scorns the villagers, calling them "cripples" (Kaz. 1910c:19). When the women of the chorus invoke God Almighty, our hero's scorn only increases. Why prattle about God when *humanity* is omnipotent or could be? Actually, however, the master builder has a flaw that explains why the bridge has collapsed in the past. Yet this flaw is not part of his human condition; it is only a weakness of will—therefore remediable by a sublime assertion of will. Specifically, he has allowed dedication to his craft to be sapped by bodily passion: his love for the Archon's daughter, or rather his infatuation, since Kazantzakis has daringly made the relationship one of rut in both parties. This flaw is announced by the oraclelike witch of the village, who goes on to say that the bridge can be strengthened only if the master builder's hands are freed for absolute attention to his great mission—only, in other words, if he is willing to renounce personal happiness in the interests of duty. If the bridge is to be saved, he must sacrifice the woman who loves him by walling her up in the foundations. Said another way, he must bury his own heart in his great work if he wishes that work to stand. Utilizing the combined voices of Nietzsche, Dragoúmis, Pávlos Melás, Ibsen, and the folk song, Act I indicates to the Greeks of 1908–1910 that they are capable of overcoming defeatism and rebuilding their nation.

Act II shows them precisely how to proceed. After minimal hesitation, the master builder decides that it is better for the woman to be sacrificed than himself, since he is needed to strengthen the bridge. The girl, in her turn, announces her fornication without contrition. The master builder encourages her to accept immediate death by reminding her in public that one night of sex as experienced between herself and him is the equivalent of countless years in the lives of the others (1910c:42). The woman sacrifices herself bravely, whereupon the delighted chorus congratulate the master builder. Now the bridge will stand; the village will be saved. The hero moves on to his next challenge, and the play ends with a dance of triumph.[17]

Taken together, the two creative works composed in Paris in 1908—the serialized novel "Spasménes psihés" and the play *O protomástoras*—fuse in a new way the various concerns we have seen in Kazantzakis's early career: suicide, romanticism, love, the transitional age, the role of the exceptional man in history, and the need to sacrifice happiness to a great work. Most importantly, however, they lead us from a broken hero who is capable only of right thought to a virile one who proceeds ruthlessly from right thought to right act. Daybreak has become day.

Having said this, I must renew the caution voiced earlier. Whether we consider Kazantzakis's political writings or his direct participation in affairs, we should take care not to be deceived. Although it appears that he became truly political after his studies in Paris— that is, driven by an urge to mold reality so that an entire people might achieve a viable existence through proper government—he was acting not so much out of a belief that reality can actually be transformed as in spite of a belief that it cannot. His seemingly optimistic stance carried with it, and amalgamated, his earlier pessimism, which in turn was rooted in subjectivism.

For corroboration of this paradox we may turn to a piece that Kazantzakis published in 1910 ostensibly as a review of Dragoúmis's novel *Samothráki* but really as his own nationalist manifesto. It is called Για τους νέους μας (For Our Youth). In it Kazantzakis hails Dragoúmis as a leader of youth, the prophet who will guide Greek manhood to the faith that is needed to return Greece to glory. He goes on to praise Dragoúmis's voluntarism: the will is all-powerful, we can will ourselves to our manifest destiny, and so forth. On the surface, therefore, the manifesto is a ringing call to youth to join the good nationalist fight and support the Great Idea. But Kazantzakis undercuts himself (and at the same time demonstrates his intellectual honesty) by asserting that it makes no difference whether we support nationalism or its enemy, international socialism, since the former is no truer than the latter, both being "true" only subjectively. The world has no purpose; yet we can—we must!—give it a purpose. We should therefore choose whichever ideology suits our personality and then proceed *as if* we believed, remaining open-eyed and Olympian at the same time that we devote ourselves to the cause. The superior man, says our supposedly optimistic Kazantzakis, will "see the vanity of all things, and simultaneously . . . the need to clutch at various unbaptized ideas . . . and name them *truths*. And they really are truths—subjective ones" (Kaz. 1910a:236, 238). The emphasis here swings away from the group and toward the psychological needs of the person who is supposedly devoting himself to the group. He acts because he must save himself from his vision of universal vanity. The only "objective" good or truth becomes his own subjective willfulness that enables him to perform gratuitous acts with fervor and dedication. As Kazantzakis wrote seventeen years later, looking back on his "nationalistic" mission to the Caucasus: "The words 'Greece,' 'mission' and 'duty' are meaningless. But it is beautiful to sacrifice ourselves, willfully, for these nothings." "I believe that there is no religion more in accord with man's deepest hardihood than the cultivation of purposeless heroism" (Kaz. 1927b:364, 369).[18]

THE *KRAVYÍ*: A METAPOLITICAL "RIGHT ACT"

This metapolitical view, expressed so nakedly in 1927, was one of the foundations of Kazantzakis's "political" thinking as early as 1910, the fourth year of his long career. He embroidered this same motif of purposeless heroism into all his subsequent allegiances along with his other favorite, "come l'uom s'eterna." Although I will speak about each of these allegiances at the proper time, I would like to offer a brief preview now so that later, when we come to individual developments, we will be better equipped to see them not alone but embedded in the totality. Before beginning, however, I must stress once more that the positions I am about to summarize are allotropic variations upon an unchanging continuity composed of Kazantzakis's search for an escape from the transitional age. In addition, they are variations upon philosophical tenets that Kazantzakis had learned in Paris from Nietzsche and chiefly from Bergson; these we shall examine in the next chapter.

Kazantzakis's nationalism began to die in 1920 when Dragoúmis was assassinated. Observing his countrymen deal in such a barbaric way with a person who had fought so hard to resurrect them, and seeing them reject Venizélos himself at the polls several months later, Kazantzakis developed a scorn for Greeks—at least for "official" Greeks—and a determination to make his career elsewhere. These events symbolized for him the bankruptcy of Greek political life, which meant by extension the bankruptcy of the Great Idea (E. Alexiou 1966:119; Vrettakos 1960:63, 748). Politically, he replaced Dragoumian nationalism with communist internationalism (although he never renounced or forgot Dragoúmis[19]); he thought he saw in the Bolsheviks the same pagan energy, disciplined passion, and barbaric youthfulness that he had attributed to the Greeks a decade earlier. His new allegiance followed a predictable cycle. Starting with euphoric belief in the possibility of concrete action on behalf of others, it devolved into erosion of this sentiment on account of the philosophical pessimism that made him value the struggle itself as opposed to the goal. Whereas he at first hailed Russian communism as the daylight marking the end of the transitional age, by 1929 he had proclaimed the Russians to be merely a part of the transition: even this energetic society was not yet ready for right action. Furthermore, in projecting right action into some unspecified (and perhaps infinitely delayed) future, Kazantzakis naturally tended to conceive of such action in vague rather than concrete terms. Whereas he had originally spoken hardheadedly about specific educational programs, the abolition of hunger, and the like, he now invoked a post-Bolshevik age in which society would honor "spiritual values." He called his new hope metacommunism.

In due course we shall dwell on Kazantzakis's communism (if it can be called that) as well as on his difficult relationship with leftists in Greece and the Soviet Union. Suffice it to say here that from 1929 onward he could no longer place his faith in the Russians and that he therefore entered an extended period of political disorientation in which he fluctuated among empty recapitulations of the old communist line, attraction to fascism, and fascination with the emergent peoples of Africa and Asia.

His disorientation was terminated by a series of external circumstances—the Italian invasion of Greece on 28 October 1940, the Albanian campaign of 1940–1941, and the German invasion and ensuing occupation (1941–1944)—all of which revived his nationalism. But Kazantzakis never returned to the old Dragoumian mystique; instead, he developed what I like to call a mellowed nationalism stressing, rather than pagan vitality, Greek endurance under hardship—after all, he was no longer a Dragoumian youth. What he retained from his youthful past was the emphasis on fulfillment in some remote future; indeed, I characterize his final stance as "eschatological politics," a term that should help us realize the extent to which politics, for Kazantzakis, was subsumed beneath a religious vision. It would be wrong to call this vision Christian if in so doing we claimed that the author of *Christ Recrucified*, *The Last Temptation*, and *Saint Francis* returned in his final period to the faith whose central tenet, the promise of reward in heaven, he had dismissed as unscientific during his high school years and had cruelly satirized in his play *Comedy*, in which saints and sinners alike, awaiting judgment, discover that the Christian promise is a mockery.[20] He did not return to this faith. Yet he adapted Jesus' (metapolitical) politics. His mellowed nationalism is perfectly glossed by Ernest Renan's statement that "the idea of omnipotence through suffering and resignation, of triumphing over force by purity of heart, is indeed an idea peculiar to Jesus" (Renan 1867:141). Like Jesus, Kazantzakis increasingly assumed that the individual person is prior to and above the citizen, that true liberty is not necessarily connected with political systems, and that freedom of the soul is what matters—a freedom that liberates us even when we are outwardly subjected to political (or existential) tyranny.

After the Germans left, Kazantzakis still devoted himself in fits and starts to current affairs: in 1945 he led a minuscule socialist party that hoped to unify the noncommunist left; during the civil war (1946–1949) he favored the insurgents; in the 1950s, although embittered by his exile, he spoke out publicly in support of Greek aspirations in Cyprus. But, despite all this, the key words "future" and "spiritual" came to dominate his personal life as well as his writings. This is because he had finally reconciled himself to his own temperament and had consciously accepted the fate that made him not a man of affairs, directly molding contemporary reality, but a prophetic artist dedicated to man's infinite potential.

All this would seem to confirm the view expressed in the tirade cited at the opening of this chapter: that Kazantzakis is irrelevant to the concrete problems of the here and now, problems such as the tanks that rolled into the streets of Athens on 21 April 1967. Kazantzakis's pessimistic subjectivism, entrenched in him by his repeated failures and disillusionments in the political arena, prevented him, it is true, from confronting such problems on their own terms. Nevertheless, he considered himself a committed political writer and even an agitator. "The writer," we will recall him declaring, "cannot repress his indignation or shirk his responsibility." Taken out of context, this declaration seems hypocritical. It is not; Kazantzakis was truly committed. However, consistent with the world-view that he had developed as a graduate student in Paris, he was committed to the only things worthy of his *continuing* allegiance: the future and the spiritual. He insisted that this did not make him irrelevant to the present and the concrete. His work derives from his engagement with the political tendencies of his age. Its method, however, is prophetic. His procedure as a committed writer was initially to divine the nature of the present age, acting as its "most sensitive and responsible seismograph"

(Petros Haris 1945:511), then to formulate future "day" by creating archetypal embodiments of truth and heroism. As he himself once declared, "Driven by [my] duty as agitator, I compel myself in my work to set heroic models before the people. . . . They alone incarnate the claims and the hopes of the famished and the persecuted, and are capable of showing the people the way toward salvation" (Eleni Kaz. 1968a:530). In sum, the metapolitical writer can serve contemporary political reality even though he focuses on the future. By helping man's imaginative conceptions (the spirit) to stay out ahead like a bag of fodder in front of a horse, he inspires contemporary reality to catch up.

Kazantzakis's metapolitical politicism enabled him to reconcile the pessimistic and optimistic needs of his temperament. The purposeless heroism of his protagonists has a purpose after all, for these heroes are models of spiritual achievement, encouraging reality to reach them in some undefined (and constantly receding) future. In dying they voice a *kravyí* (cry) that will inspire others to live better and to construct more viable societies. Although intangible and spiritual, this *kravyí* is their right *act*, one that by definition will help bring an end to the injustice of the transitional age.

As far as Kazantzakis himself was concerned, this spiritual right act was the composition of plays, epics, and novels. Here was the freedom he invoked in 1936 as his "third stage." Each of his imaginative writings is a Kazantzakian metapolitical *kravyí* turned into a coherent *lógos* that, while constituting a riverbed into which future reality will flow, is also his own spiritual understanding of contemporary experience: the imposition of meaningfulness upon his outward life and thus his inward life's redemption. This is why his books are adventitiously political, essentially metapolitical. They trace the long way round taken in order to find the home of personal salvation; in them, Kazantzakis the political agitator fuses with the Kazantzakis whose basic concern is "come l'uom s'eterna." None of this may satisfy people who consider themselves truly political, believing in the establishment of justice and freedom for human society in the here and now. But Kazantzakis amalgamated his political urges with a temperament that from the start was devoted to the imagination. This is why he angered both the left and the right and was unacceptable to all régimes.

CHAPTER TWO

Philosophical studies in Paris

[Stephen's] essay was not in the least the exhibition of polite accomplishments. It was on the contrary very seriously intended to define his own position for himself.

—James Joyce, *Stephen Hero*, p. 76

Before moving ahead to consider the breakup of Kazantzakis's nationalism and the development of his "communism" and metacommunism, we must stop to examine his studies in Paris, for these, although not always directly political, governed his future thinking in all areas. He concentrated on three philosophers, William James, Friedrich Nietzsche, and Henri Bergson. The first was moderately important for his future development, the second very important, and the third most important of all.

WILLIAM JAMES

We know very little about Kazantzakis's relation to William James.[1] We do know, however, that when he lectured on Bergson's philosophy to members of the Educational Association in Athens in January 1913, he began by quoting "the great psychologist James," as follows:

> I never would have freed myself . . . and I would not have sacrificed the reason to something else superior to it and would not have removed it from the profoundest shrines of philosophy in order to place it in the only place where it has authority, in the world of simple human practicality, if I had not chanced to read Bergson. (Kaz. 1912:311; 1958b:13)

Judging from this citation,[2] we may conjecture that what Kazantzakis found attractive in James was an antirationalism that denies the intellect's power to solve ultimate questions (removing it from "the profoundest shrines of philosophy") but recognizes its efficacy in what Bergson calls the realm of clock-time ("the world of simple human practicality").

Beyond this we have nothing except the opinion of Pandelís Prevelákis that "the vitalistic theory of the American psychologist William James" is one of the sources of Kazantzakis's thought. According to this theory, writes Prevelákis, "every person ought to be consummated in his wholeness. . . . Moreover, individual experience and personal truth are more authoritative than rational knowledge. . . . In 1941–43 [Kazantzakis] personified James's vitalistic theory in the personality of Alexis Zorbás" (Prev. 1977:14; 1981:28–29).

It is likely that both Prevelákis's and Kazantzakis's conceptions of James are mediated by no less a scholiast than Henri Bergson himself, who de-emphasizes James's reliance on reason's efficacy in the realm of practicality in order to stress James's view that abstract reason has been overvalued. Traditional philosophy, Bergson insists,

> makes truth something anterior to the . . . person . . . who formulates it for the first time. . . . He *discovers* it. William James's conception is entirely different. . . . [I]t seems to him that truth, which can adhere only to what we affirm about reality, is created by our affirmation. We invent truth in order to utilize reality. . . . I think that one could summarize everything essential in pragmatism's conception of truth in a formula such as this one: *whereas for other doctrines a new truth is a discovery, for pragmatism it is an invention.* (James 1920:10–11)

Kazantzakis echoes not only this conception of truth but also the same language in a passage in Ταξιδεύοντας Ρουσία in which he affirms (through the mouth of a Soviet journalist) that truth "is not an abstract concept . . .; it is not anything ready-made, finished, outside of us, waiting for us to discover it. Truth is a compromise resulting from our everyday struggles with reality. It is not discovered. It is invented and created" (Kaz. 1965e:193).[3]

This strengthens my conjecture that what Kazantzakis appreciated in Jamesian pragmatism was its distrust of a priori reasoning. Let us, however, allow James himself to have the last word in this regard:

> Pragmatism represents a perfectly familiar attitude in philosophy, the empiricist attitude. . . . A pragmatist turns . . . away from abstraction . . . , from bad *a priori* reasons, from fixed principles, closed systems, and pretended absolutes and origins. He turns towards concreteness . . . as against . . . the pretence of finality in truth. . . . *The true is the name of whatever proves itself to be good in the way of belief, and good, too, for definite, assignable reasons.* (James 1955:45, 59)

FRIEDRICH NIETZSCHE

Our paucity of knowledge about Kazantzakis's relation to William James is not repeated when we come to Nietzsche. Indeed, although

Nietzsche is less central to Kazantzakis's world-view than Bergson, Kazantzakis wrote a great deal more about the former than the latter.[4]

These testimonies are valuable up to a point. The chapter on Paris in *Report to Greco*, in particular, conveys the sense of precious discovery felt by Kazantzakis at that "most critical, most hungry moment" of his youth (Kaz. 1964a:397; 1965c:331) when he was still searching for a systematic philosophy to replace Christianity: how he devoured Nietzsche's books in "divine, untroubled nights of work and study" (1964a:400; 1965c:334) and how, in the end, Nietzsche taught him "to distrust every optimistic theory":

> I began to feel that every religion that promises to fulfill human desires is simply a refuge for the timid. . . . I asked myself if Christ's way was the one leading to human salvation, or whether it was simply a well-organized fairy tale promising paradise and immortality with immense cleverness and skill. . . . I considered metaphysical hope an alluring bait that true men do not condescend to nibble. I wanted whatever was most . . . worthy . . . of the man who does not whine, entreat, or go about begging. Yes, that was what I wanted. Three cheers for Nietzsche, the murderer of God. It was he who gave me the courage to say, "That is what I want!" (1964a:404–405; 1965c:338)

Yet this and similar testimonies, despite their value in evoking the ardor of Kazantzakis's discipleship, give an incomplete version of what he actually learned from Nietzsche's writings during those months of graduate study in Paris. Fortunately, we also have his doctoral dissertation, completed in February 1909. Entitled Ὁ Φρειδερῖκος Νίτσε ἐν τῇ φιλοσοφίᾳ τοῦ δικαίου καὶ τῆς πολιτείας (Kaz. 1909b; 1959c; Friedrich Nietzsche's Philosophy of Law and the State), this provides a systematic statement of precisely what he found important in Nietzsche at the time. The dissertation was intended for submission to the Faculty of Law at Athens University so that Kazantzakis might receive a lectureship there.[5] But it was much more than a dry academic exercise; indeed, we can say of it as of much of the other work forced upon him by external circumstances, that it was undertaken so that he might define his own position. He was searching for a conception of life according to which he could regulate his writings and actions. This he saw as a duty for himself and every man. Although Bergson was ultimately the most important source for his overall world-view, in Nietzsche he discovered certain ideas that stood at the center of his subsequent political development.

Conversely, his attraction to Nietzsche reflects the political forces he encountered for the first time in Paris. Previously he had considered Nietzsche a decadent victim of the *mal de siècle* (Kaz. 1958d:695). But after his exposure in Paris to the hardheaded neopaganism of the political right, he was able to see in the German philosopher not primarily an exemplification of the age's sickness but precisely the opposite: an ally in his own crusade against that sickness. Rightist thinking convinced him that Nietzsche's apotheosis of the ego, his doctrine of universal struggle, even his so-called nihilism and his pervasive disgust, were not so much symptoms of the century's disease as homeopathic remedies. The world would be saved if it could only rid itself of the liberal/humanist/egalitarian ideals of the French Revolution and contemporary socialism. But if this were to be done, the whole structure of modern morality and law would have to be overthrown.

Emerging from all this are two important points, both of which are confirmed in the dissertation. The first is Kazantzakis's emotional discipleship. In Nietzsche he found not just a thinker whose ideas he could borrow but a full human prototype in whose joys and anguishes he could see his own struggles authenticated.[6] The second point is that Nietzsche's chief contribution to Kazantzakis's religious and political thinking was as a destroyer of the old. For a new world-view Kazantzakis turned primarily to Bergson. Nietzschianism was a negative factor reinforcing Kazantzakis's conviction that the old order must be evaluated, challenged, and overturned in the interests of developing a more viable culture.

The dissertation divides Kazantzakis's analysis of Nietzsche's thought into two large sections, the first treating the negative aspects and the second the positive.[7] The background to both is the intellectual history of Europe, ending in nihilism. Science, says Kazantzakis, has made our old value system irrelevant by revealing that nature is entirely unethical. The problem of value arises because of this wide gulf between ethics and natural reality. And science itself is of no help, for it explains the how, not the why. Darwinism, which appeared as a supposed answer to the eternal questions, actually thwarted all further hope; it demonstrated the mechanisms of evolution but was incapable of illuminating either evolution's cause or its goal. Attempts were made to establish new value systems to fill the ever-increasing vacuum created as knowledge eliminated God. Kazantzakis cites Kant's categorical imperative, the deification of reason in the Enlightenment, Comte's *culte de l'humanité* based on science and love, Marxism, Robert Owen's utopianism, Saint-Simon, Fourier, Feuerbach. But all these attempts have failed. Science itself has been increasingly undermined by philosophers such as Bergson who have revealed its ethical bankruptcy, with the result that advanced thinkers have been forced to confess that they know nothing. They cannot answer the great questions; instead, they admit that individual life is of no account, the world just a purposeless spark surrounded by darkness.

Nevertheless our age still clings to a leftover ethical system based on the Christian conception of a providential universe. We assume that there is justice, a purpose in life, and that human beings are the center of creation. We value truth over falsehood, morality over immorality, compassion over cruelty, kindness over malice—in sum, we embrace ideals that have no foundation in biology or physiology, and in which humanity can therefore have no deep, vital belief.

This condition in which mankind apprehends the antinomy between ideals and reality is a sickness, indeed *the* sickness of our age, the *mal de siècle.* It was perceived by Nietzsche even before it had advanced to its present critical stage; it forms the background to both the negative and positive aspects of his thought. The name of this sickness is nihilism. Notice that Kazantzakis presents Nietzsche not as the virus spreading nihilism but as the physician diagnosing it and attempting a cure. This should be remembered throughout our discussion of Nietzsche's negative aspects lest constant denial seem to overshadow his ultimate purposes of affirmation and healing.

Although Nietzsche wished to overcome nihilism, he may easily be thought part of the disease because his method of treating it was homeopathic. The problem is the discrepancy between scientific reality and our antiquated table of values. Nietzsche refused to cling to that table or to hide its inadequacy. He wished instead to increase the moral vacuum even more by completely destroying those values that were the cause of the disease: in order to cure nihilism he wished to administer drugs that produce the same symptoms as the disease itself. That such a method is dangerous and that Nietzsche was fully aware of the danger are facts acknowledged by Kazantzakis both in the dissertation and elsewhere (e.g. Kaz. 1958q:1286). Nietzsche had learned from Schopenhauer that one logical conclusion to nihilism is suicide. But he felt that this pessimistic nihilism need be a logical conclusion only for the weak. If he persisted in believing that the old table of values had to be destroyed, it was because a homeopathic injection of nihilism *in the strong* could produce something affirmative, indeed a cure. Such people, the optimistic (or Dionysiac) nihilists, might be led to a heroic acceptance of life-as-given, rejoicing at their deliverance from false hopes and at their opportunity to bequeath a purpose to life since of itself it has none. Nihilism administered as a homeopathic medicine, although hastening the death of some, might lead others back to life and health.

From all this Nietzsche arrived at his own role, which was to form the laws regulating human relationships in a way tending toward the triumph of Dionysiac nihilism. But in order to form these new laws he first had to clear away the old ones. His initial task was therefore to deny.

What values did Nietzsche deny? Kazantzakis tries to answer this question systematically even though he knows that Nietzsche's philosophy is not systematic. He assigns Nietzsche's negative thought to six large categories: man, the family, the state, religion, morality, and law. As I go through the specific items discussed under each of these headings we shall begin to notice, I trust, how thoroughly Kazantzakis himself embraced Nietzsche's negative teachings. Many of the attitudes encountered in this résumé of the master's thought reappear everywhere in the subsequent writings of the disciple.

Man (Kaz. 1909b:36–46). Our present table of values has the following as its three most important axioms: (1) man's existence has a purpose, (2) man's soul is immortal, (3) man possesses free will. All three axioms are false. Accordingly, whoever relies on them in this transitional age will fall into pessimism and nihilism. The solution is to destroy all three.

Regarding the purpose of man's existence, Nietzsche rejects any concept of a divine plan for humanity. Man is a product of evolution and in no way essentially different from the lower animals. Nor is there any purpose to evolution. Human evolution displays no progress; indeed, the higher types are incapable of dealing with life. Beauty is momentary, genius sterile, Caesar without a successor. Nature's formula, if anything, is to destroy the exceptions and allow the weak and mediocre to prevail.

Regarding man's supposedly immortal soul, Nietzsche insists that this axiom derives from the false distinction in the old table of values between man and the rest of nature, man being accorded a soul and the rest of nature denied one. He recognizes that *belief* in the soul (as distinguished from the soul itself, which does not exist) once served a useful purpose. Now, however, this belief leads to pessimistic nihilism. Hence Nietzsche is delighted that science has proved the soul and immortality to be false. He views this as a liberation, since we no longer have to worry about "eternal happiness" in the next world—a worry that prompts us to behave "correctly" in this world. Now we can afford to be wrong, indulging in "folly" and imagination. Instead of chaining our vitality to an inflexible dogma, we can open ourselves to all that experience has to offer.

Lastly, regarding free will, Nietzsche asserts that this has been placed in the table of values by the weak as a compensation for their inability to surpass the strong. In effect they declare that a man's worth lies not in the degree of power he commands but in his choice of how he applies his power. At a certain stage of human development the concept of free will was useful and indeed life-enhancing to the strong since it made them accept responsibility for their acts with a pride naturally denigrated as satanic by the weak. Now, however, free will must be stricken from the table of values. Modern studies of the influence of heredity and environment on personality completely deny free will. What we call freedom is really necessity. People differ from one another not because they choose to, but because necessity takes different forms in them according to their physical constitutions. The ethical, obedient person is such because he is not constitutionally subject to strong passions.

To these three most basic axioms under the category "man," Nietzsche adds one more that also needs to be destroyed. This is the belief in human equality. Nietzsche argues that the physical law of inequality is what spurs each organism to surpass the other. What is known today as equality is really the unjust right of mediocrities to crowd out all superior exceptions. As a result, the noble man recedes, hides, tries to live beyond good and evil. Because of his disappearance, we have ceased either to fear man or to entertain great hopes for him. This leads to pessimistic nihilism. Hence the axiom of equality must be stricken from our table of values.

Family (Kaz. 1909b:48–51). Having shown how man is distorted as an individual in Nietzsche's analysis, Kazantzakis proceeds to analyze how he is also distorted as a social being. He begins with the most intimate social relationship, the domestic one. If we examine the true nature of husband and wife, he says, and then compare this with the ideas of equality and feminine emancipation now prevailing, we will understand why the family today shows the same symptoms of decadence as does the individual. The first point that must be considered is Nietzsche's insistence upon the inequality of the sexes. The female's purpose in life is to marry and reproduce; husband and child are her occupation and her joy. The male's purpose is domination—to impose himself on the forces trying to suppress him. One way he does this is by marrying and reproducing, but sex is only a single episode in his life and if he devotes himself entirely to women he will become degenerate. In short, the female is a biological means for furthering evolution. Yet as soon as she attempts to hamper the male's vibrancy by tying him to the hearth, she becomes the greatest danger to his fulfillment and must be rejected. Nietzsche insists that men should marry out of a thirst for creation, ascent, the superman. They should not marry until they are able to control their physical desires; otherwise this need will be a cloak for bestiality or the fear of loneliness. And for truly vibrant men, women should not be a need at all but a kind of sport, the most dangerous kind. The true woman, in her turn, must be cunning and subtle, hiding a tiger's claw beneath the velvety foot—a worthy prey. But in these degenerate times the man has become a slave to the hearth and the woman has abandoned all her weapons, leaving herself without poetic mystery, rejecting as well the very qualities of tenderness, concern, and warmth that are distinctive in her and should differentiate her from the male sex. All this degeneration in family relations derives of course from the modern doctrine of equality. Feminine emancipation has produced the businesswoman with her financial independence and the learned woman—one of the saddest blemishes on today's civilization.

Marriage has been undermined because the man is afraid to say "I want" and the woman refuses to say "He wants." Both having distorted their true nature as individuals, the distortion is translated into social decline.

The State (Kaz. 1909b:46, 53–55, 60). Just as contemporary values exert a destructive influence on the male as husband, so, too, they influence him destructively in his capacity as citizen. Contemporary morality's political manifestation is democracy, which is at variance with nature because it advocates equality, compassion, and the rest. Democracy inhibits the male's natural need to dominate; its neglect of superior men threatens to extinguish all superiority because such men are driven to pessimistic nihilism. The natural political systems are aristocracy, monarchy, and tyranny. We must overcome the fiction that states are the result of a supposedly natural desire of all men for sociability. It is only the weak who flock together. Strong and healthy men tend to separate themselves out or, if they enter into social groupings, to do so in order to satisfy individual drives for power. States develop not because of the desire for sociability but as extensions of the individual will to power. They are the instruments of the strong; their laws are the means whereby these aggressive men may govern as they please. The state is the antithesis of equality and compassion, indeed of all morality. The actualization of undisguised strength, it exists so that men may do collectively what they would hesitate to do individually. It is implacably egotistic and cruel, without altruism, using any and all means to fulfill its need to expand, which is the natural need of every living organism. Insofar as it honors virtue, morality, or justice, it does so merely as an expedience to insure its own best interests. A nation that does not seek to expand, whether by war, commercial domination, or colonization, is atrophied and decadent—"ripe for democracy and the administration of grocers," which is what we see today. The contemporary state, with its object of insuring prosperity for the greatest number, is degenerate; it ends in humiliating its citizens instead of elevating them. This distortion of the state's purpose is one more source of today's pessimistic nihilism. Hence the democratic state must be abolished.

Religion (Kaz. 1909b:58, 63–66). From here, Nietzsche passes easily to a condemnation of the Judeo-Christian faith. The supreme examples of healthy, noble states are ancient Greece and Rome. But Greco-Roman civilization was undermined by the weak, that is, by the Jews and Christians, whose God demands repentance for sins and thus reduces everyone to the equality of worthlessness. This, together with an ethic of compassion, causes the degeneration of both the individual and the state. The admired ideals become mediocrity, abstinence, timidity, and obedience instead of strength, beauty, and superiority.

A people creates its gods in its own image. While the Jews were strong they had a strong god; when they began to decline they conceived of a new god and new values. The strong, nationalistic Jehovah turned into the weak, cosmopolitan Jesus Christ. At a time when the Jews were subjugated and could not maintain a state they invented a god who censured nationalism, forbade military service, abolished the distinction between native and foreigner, and preached heaven as the only true kingdom. In reality, all this was disguised scorn for life's aggressive strength; it was a craving for annihilation.

Yet Christianity still prevails. Its sickly hatred of the noble and superior together with its vaunting of compassion and equality form the basis of contemporary morality, law, and the degenerate, democratic state. All this must be overturned. Since the Judeo-Christian faith is a product of weakness, it should be erased from the table of values.

Kazantzakis is careful to note, however, that Nietzsche is not opposed to all religions or to religion per se. He esteems gods who arise from eras of strength as projections of human superiority.

Morality (Kaz. 1909b:36–37, 44, 68–70, 75–77). Like everything else in his philosophy, Nietzsche's ideas on morality follow from the assumption that our basic drive is the will to power. All human activity, including ethical behavior, manifests this drive. In a healthy person or society, moral values develop as an instrument for self-assertion. Only late in history do they become separated from self-assertion, at which time they appear altruistic and seem to possess independent validity apart from their utility. Goodness and compassion are now mistakenly thought to reside in the very nature of things, which they do not. This objectification involves a perversion of our life-instincts and must perforce accelerate decadence. Whereas a man should say, "I live to satisfy life's basic instincts and I therefore seek the good, true, and beautiful insofar as they are useful for this satisfaction," he now says, "It is blasphemous to seek these values because they are useful to me; I must seek them because they have independent worth."

In other words, morality teaches us to make war against our nature. To be virtuous is to curb the will in the interests of pleasing conscience. This cheapens man. When morality tells him to sacrifice himself for others it is telling him in effect to dry up his own wellsprings of energy, desire, passion, and egotism. Worst of all is the modern religion of compassion preached by utopian socialists and deriving from the Jewish democratic ethos, which killed off the aristocratic ethos of the Greeks and Romans. This is an indication of how emasculated we have become, afraid not only to experience pain ourselves but to mete out punishment to others. We see here a perversion of the life-instinct and a transgression of the laws of selection, which rule that the weak should be eliminated; we see as well a refusal to acknowledge that pain, for the healthy man, is the great teacher, the incentive to almost every noble action. The ethic of compassion is a conspiracy against health, making misfortune contagious. Since the degenerate, wretched, and impotent are now placed on the conscience of the strong, the world's misery is multiplied.

Our present table of values has led to slave-ideals. Christian morality has forced man to deny his most virile qualities, robbing him of the self-respect that in a healthy ethos is the source of all virtue. It has eroded the life-instinct by stigmatizing joy and pleasure as sinful, by exalting mediocrity, by preaching the irreverence of self-respecting egotism, and by objectifying moral norms so that they become divorced from the will to power. The result is an unchecked momentum toward pessimistic nihilism.

Nietzsche attacks contemporary morality in one further way. According to today's table of values an act can be moral only if freely willed by the individual in question. But this has not always been the case. In prehistoric times an action's worth was judged first according to its results and only afterwards according to its generating principle. It was easy then for this generating principle to be confused with intention. Nietzsche insists that the so-called freely willed intention is just a mask for the will to power, which is the generating principle. He calls for the destruction of a morality based on free will since such a morality rests upon nonexistent foundations. Instead, we must judge actions according to (a) their results and (b) the strength of their generating principle. In the new morality, an action will be "good" if it issues from a strong, vital life-instinct and "bad" if it issues from weariness or defeat.

Law (Kaz. 1909b:47, 73). As we have seen, equality for Nietzsche is extrinsic to man's nature. Consequently, true justice must be not the guarantee of equal rights to all but rather the unequal distribution of unequal rights and obligations among unequal beings. What we have now is a legal system that reflects (1) Judeo-Christian morality in its reluctance to punish and (2) the myth of free will in its emphasis upon intention and premeditation. Law, on the contrary, should concern itself with the one thing that matters most: transgression against the life-instinct. But whether it does so or not, such transgressions cannot be made with impunity. Because modern societies have transgressed, they are being punished with pessimistic nihilism and dissolution. The remedy, once more, is to overturn the false table of values.

In connection with the foregoing résumé of Nietzsche's negative thought under the categories man, family, state, religion, morality, and law, we must recall once again that the denial of reigning values is a negativism in the service of a desired affirmation. Kazantzakis insists throughout that Nietzsche's alleged immorality is in the interests of a new and better morality. It would seem, therefore, that the lengthy section devoted to Nietzschian nihilism should be but prelude to an even fuller treatment of the positive aspects of Nietzsche's thought, and indeed the dissertation's next section is devoted to these positive aspects. But they occupy only eleven pages (Kaz. 1909b:79–90), whereas the negations require forty-six. It is clear both from this scant treatment and from comments made by Kazantzakis at the time and afterwards that he did not find Nietzsche's positive ideas as congenial as his negative ones.

The positive features that Kazantzakis does discuss are four: the will to power, the superman, morality, and society's hierarchical divisions. Everything derives from Nietzsche's insistence on flux. Life is movement; a vibrant man needs eternal unrest. However, this movement is not at random; it is directed toward self-overcoming. Life's desire to surpass itself is discernible in all organisms and species. If an organism is healthy it will seek to fulfill its appointed role by imposing itself upon the surrounding organisms. Therefore the form of eternal unrest required by the vibrant man is self-extension. His purpose is to conquer other organisms by asserting his superiority and ultimately by striving to such a degree that he surpasses himself, producing a new species more in accord with the natural laws of motion and self-overcoming. Hence Nietzsche's new table of values has as its foundation the will to power and superiority.

The hypothetical result of self-overcoming will be the superman, by definition he who heroically discards the present table of values and—rejecting previous consolations such as religion, the afterlife, and free will—develops man's qualities to the utmost, placing as the central purpose of his existence the goal of surpassing his own being. Because war is the leading incentive to progress and selection, he will preach cruelty instead of compassion. Repose, for him, will be preparation for new conquests. By seeking trials of increasing danger and heroism, he will stamp his ego on the age. But he will be harsh toward himself as well as others. He will renounce all luxury, rest, peace, and happiness without becoming discouraged. Grateful for sorrow as well as for joy, he will bless life in its entirety.

The new decalogue that the superman fashions will involve an ethic passing beyond good and evil. The very term "evil" is a leftover from the old decalogue. In the new one, as we saw when discussing Morality, "good" will be everything that contributes to the strength and progress of life, "bad" everything that exhausts life.

Finally, the new decalogue can exist only for the elect. Nietzsche realizes that the old concepts of ethics, religion, the state, and law will continue to be needed for the weak. Thus he divides society into two groups. The lower includes the bourgeoisie, workers, farmers, and scholars—all those who are content to limit themselves, who do not or can not exert their will to power. These people will maintain the higher group, which will be subdivided into (a) warriors and (b) creators and lords. The new morality will apply to this group alone.

Of the four positive features discussed in the dissertation, the only one that meets with Kazantzakis's wholehearted approval is the new morality. Regarding society's hierarchical divisions, he complains about Nietzsche's arbitrary differentiation of men into slaves and lords (Kaz. 1909b:88). How will this be accomplished? What criteria will be used? This is the vulnerable part of the system. (Yet in his utopian city in the *Odyssey* Kazantzakis divides society more or less according to the Nietzschian formula.) Although these objections are not voiced in the dissertation itself, Kazantzakis's essay "For Our Youth" shows that he harbored them as early as 1910. They derive from the Bergsonism that he embraced in the latter part of his Parisian sojourn. We will hear more about this philosophy in a moment. Suffice it to say here that Bergson convinced Kazantzakis that the most fundamental natural law of the universe is not the will to power but the transubstantiation of flesh into spirit. If life realizes itself most perfectly by striving to escape materiality in order to achieve pure motion and freedom, then the goal can be accomplished only when all embodied (hence compromised) forms of motion and freedom have been surpassed. Life's fulfillment comes not in the superman but in the abyss of pure disembodied spirituality.

Kazantzakis felt that the superman derived from Nietzsche's cowardice. Although scorning weaklings who cling to a chimerical hope in the face of life's overwhelming cruelty, Nietzsche himself succumbed to precisely such a hope after his anguished reflection that while matter is limited, time is illimitable (Kaz. 1964a:390; 1965c:325–326). Even Nietzsche then "gave way to terror for an instant. Eternal recurrence struck him as an interminable martyrdom, and out of his fright he fashioned a great hope, a future savior, the superman. But the superman is just another paradise, another mirage to deceive poor unfortunate man and enable him to endure life and death" (1964a:406; 1965c:339). Kazantzakis himself insists that life's culmination is achieved not in the superman but paradoxically in the annihilation of materiality.

In "For Our Youth," written shortly after his return from Paris, he reiterated his quarrel with the positive aspects of Nietzsche's thought: "Nietzsche . . . ended by elevating the peculiarities of his own constitution to a new decalogue. . . . If anything remains from Nietzsche it is only a rhythm that can guide us most logically . . . to heights completely contrary to the Nietzschian superman" (Kaz. 1910a:237). Many years later he added: "I loved [Nietzsche] for the questions he asked, . . . not however for his answers, which were not good" (Jouvenel 1958:102; 1962:1580).

What, then, did Kazantzakis learn from Nietzsche? It would be an oversimplification to say that he embraced most of Nietzsche's negations and few of his affirmations. Nevertheless, the postulates that he considered the negative part of Nietzsche's teaching were the ones that remained most prominently in his philosophy. Generally, Nietzsche convinced him that nihilism could be a homeopathic weapon for the cure of contemporary decadence and not just a symptom of that decadence. He taught him that this negativism would help to accelerate the dissolution of a table of values no longer consistent with our scientific knowledge of ourselves and our universe. Specifically, he encouraged Kazantzakis to make war against democracy, pacifism, and feminine emancipation; against man as "God's darling"; against free will, immortality, Christian meekness and compassion—all in the interests of renewed vigor for the individual, the family, and the state.

IT IS MY HOPE that the foregoing account will enable us to approach Kazantzakis's Nietzschianism with some precision. It should help us to breathe specific content into certain broad statements that Kazantzakis made about Nietzsche in later life and to distinguish between what is specifically Nietzschian in those statements and what is merely a generalized existentialism saturating the air in Europe between the two world wars. Typically, the burden of such statements is "heroic pessimism": the ability of the strong individual to accept a meaningless world and to bequeath to that world a meaning spun out of his own entrails:

> [Nietzsche] taught me . . . that you never need to have a conception of life that allows you hopes, rewards. You are a free man, not a mercenary. . . . To struggle without deigning to seek reward, [that] is true freedom. . . . (Jouvenel 1958:102; 1962:1580)

> What did he tell us, above all, to do? He told us to deny all consolations—gods, fatherlands, moralities, truths—and, remaining apart and companionless, using nothing but our own strength, to begin to fashion a world that would not shame our hearts. . . . What is the most valiant joy? To assume complete responsibility! . . . Together with him I had begun my own battle to match the unmatchable—to reconcile utmost hope with utmost despair, and to open a door beyond reason and certainty. (Kaz. 1964a:394; 1965c:329)

Statements such as these do little to identify the specific ideas that Kazantzakis learned from Nietzsche. But they alert us to the personal part of Kazantzakis's indebtedness: the emotional discipleship that I stressed earlier.

We remember Kazantzakis saying in 1910 that if anything remains from Nietzsche it is only a "rhythm." The word ρυθμός means more in modern Greek than it does in English; perhaps "style" would be a better translation. What Kazantzakis wishes to say is clarified at the end of his dissertation when he remarks that Nietzsche gave old ideas a new radiance. He was to Kant what Ferdinand Lassalle was to Marx, spilling out into passion, indignation, visions, irony, sarcasm, ecstasy. This radiance is the Nietzschian "rhythm" that so impressed Kazantzakis and that he desired to emulate in his own writings.[8] The ideas are secondary. Kazantzakis makes this his final point in the dissertation. Even though Nietzsche's system is in part arbitrary and fantastic, he concludes, its sincerity and élan are noble.

HENRI BERGSON

Bergson's influence on Kazantzakis was entirely different from Nietzsche's. What Kazantzakis valued in Bergson was an intellectual program as opposed to any "radiance." Nietzsche had prepared him for Bergson by insisting that our value system must be based not on a chimera but on the true nature of the circumambient universe. This does not mean that Kazantzakis wished to rely on empirical science as his guide to truth. On the contrary, ever since his allegiance to the Christian worldview had been eroded by Darwinism, he had nonetheless yearned for a vision that passed beyond scientific boundaries. Here now was Bergson with "proof" that the force driving the universe is an ever-creative vitality that transubstantiates flesh into spirit. This was mysticism, to be sure, but at the same time sufficiently scientific (or pseudoscientific) in its presentation to respond to Kazantzakis's need for a post-Christian worldview that would be religious yet not at odds with modern thought. As he wrote to Dimítrios Kaloyerópoulos about Bergson in January 1908, only three months after his arrival in Paris:

> At present I am studying philosophy and literature at the Sorbonne, the Collège de France, and the Ecole des Hautes Etudes.
>
> I want to formulate an individual, personal conception of life, a theory of the world and of human destiny, and then, in accord with this, systematically and with a specific purpose and program, to write—whatever I write.
>
> Fortunately I am auditing the celebrated psychologist Bergson here and I feel that I am not wasting my time. (Markakis 1959b:35)

As always in Kazantzakis's development, there is continuity. Bergsonism was not an abrupt turn for him; it was the systematic culmination of intellectual convictions and spiritual drives already manifest. Christ had murdered Apollo; Darwin had murdered Christ; mechanism was no more acceptable than teleology; subjectivism had to be rescued from nihilism and converted into a positive value. Responding to these needs, Bergson supplied Kazantzakis with a perfect new god.

TO DISCOVER the nature of this god we must first pose certain cosmological questions—precisely those that Kazantzakis asked and answered under Bergson's tutelage. They are the "where?" questions: Where have we come from? Where are we going? The answers appear in the prologue to Kazantzakis's Ασκητική, *Salvatores Dei* (Kaz. 1962a; 1960b), the book in which he eventually attempted to expound his Bergsonian ideas with Nietzschian radiance. "We come from a dark abyss [and] we end in a dark abyss." Life is a luminous interval between two black voids. These formulations take Kazantzakis's earlier doctrine of the transitional age and expand it into a cosmological principle. The entire universe is now a transition from one void to another.

The next question involves the relation of the luminous interval to the abysses at either end. These might seem to annihilate life, rendering all evolution futile. Bergson taught Kazantzakis otherwise, however. Since the so-called voids are absolute freedom and spirituality, they paradoxically fulfill life's strivings rather than negate them.

Bergson's argumentation in support of these conclusions is complicated, but we will have to examine at least some of it now if we wish to understand Kazantzakis's post-Christian theology. (When we treat Kazantzakis's 1913 lecture on Bergson later in this chapter, we will encounter additional proofs.)

Bergson posits a pre-existent life force (*élan vital*), a pure energy that wills to become alive. To become alive it must collaborate with matter. Not that matter is anything separate; life, Bergson writes, is the vital current "loaded with matter, that is, with congealed parts of its own substance" (Bergson 1911:252; 1907:260). Once the life force has created life, it tends to divest itself of its congealments in order to return to pure energy. Creating a "machine that triumphs over mechanism" (1911:278; 1907:286), life advances toward increasing spiritualization by means of transubstantiation. Rocks evolve successively into plants, animals, and humans; sensation develops into instinct, intelligence, and finally self-consciousness. But then change moves toward inertness, heterogeneity toward homogeneity. Our solar system, says Bergson, is "ever exhausting something of the mutability it contains" (1911:257; 1907:265). Yet this does not negate all the "desires" of the cosmos; rather, it leads to a consummation that the life force itself brings about. Both life and death are willed by the same "god." The black abyss at the end of life is not an arbitrary, unjust negation of life; it is the logical conclusion of the very process it seems to nullify. Death is life's crown because the sloughing off of matter releases the primal force from the weight of its own heterogeneous congealments, enabling its vitality to be unencumbered once more in its will to become alive. Annihilation equals fulfillment. The material universe, in sum, is "a *creative action that unmakes itself*" (1911:261; 1907: 269).

We have almost reached the point where we can begin to discuss the new god that Kazantzakis found with Bergson's help. First, however, we must realize that although Bergson posits a monism in which matter is a congealed form of energy, in practice he speaks dualistically of energy and matter as distinct entities. Thus he pictures (a) the life force surging upward toward creativity, motion, heterogeneity, and consciousness, and (b) matter pressing downward toward stability and homogeneity. Life is the meeting of the two. Kazantzakis echoes this definition in the prologue to *Askitikí*: "In the temporary living organism, these two streams collide: (a) the ascent toward composition, toward life, toward immortality; (b) the descent toward decomposition, toward matter, toward death." He adds, however, that "both streams well up from the depths of primordial essence" and goes on to state that "it is our duty . . . to grasp that vision which can embrace and harmonize these two . . . indestructible forces." Precisely here, in this synthesizing vision, Kazantzakis found his new god. Seen monistically, *god is the entire evolutionary process*: the primordial essence that first wills its own congealment into life and then wills the unmaking of that creative action.

THIS IS the complicated deity that satisfied Kazantzakis's needs. The basic ideas are all Bergson's even though in our exposition of Kazantzakis's version of the system I have included terminology employed in *Askitikí*. This is because Kazantzakis's approach to the new religion remained empirical only temporarily. His mystical temperament, his aestheticism, and his intellectual quarrel with science all kept impelling him increasingly toward intuitional rather than scientific language, faith rather than proof.[9] In 1908 he was able to make his alter ego Orestes in "Spasménes psihés" devote his Independence Day oration at Koraïs's grave in the Montparnasse cemetery to a new religion that is a hodgepodge of neopagan joy, Nietzschianism, and evolution, all based "on the granite of Science" (Kaz. 1909a:6 September, pp. 6–7). At the same time, however, Kazantzakis's doubts about science are evident in his satirical treatment of this same speech: he has Orestes' bombastic harangue cut off in the middle by a downpour (1909a:13 September, pp. 4–5). Later he makes Orestes himself question science's validity after reading Spencer, Kant, and Moréas (1909a:1 November, pp. 2–3).

Kazantzakis articulated his quarrel with science in November 1909 in the important essay Η επιστήμη εχρεωκόπησε; (Has Science Gone Bankrupt?), taking his title from the pronouncement by Ferdinand Brunetière[10] that science is indeed bankrupt as an ethical force (Kaz. 1958h:1377; 1958l:1082). Reacting to Jules Henri Poincaré's *La Valeur de la science* (1905), Kazantzakis begins by recapitulating the limits placed on reason's powers by Kant. He then proceeds to Kant's conclusion that one of the few realms in which absolute truth may still be discovered is mathematics (1958h:1375). But now Poincaré "completes what Kant commenced more than a century earlier"; he proclaims "that even mathematical truth is relative." On the other hand Poincaré has declared: " 'The search for truth is the only mission worthy of our intellect' " (1958h: 1376). Kazantzakis now attempts to escape this dilemma in which we are meant to devote our intellects to the discovery of the undiscoverable. To do so he says that science is indeed bankrupt if we expect it to produce happiness and progress, that is, if we require it to have an ethical purpose and result. It is not bankrupt, however, if we approach it aesthetically as "*the marvelous instrument . . . through which the spectacle of life perpetually spreads itself out and shifts in front of [our intellects]*" (1958h:1377; the italics are Kazantzakis's). Indeed, our inability to discover absolute truth is a blessing instead of a curse because "the spectacle thus becomes interesting" in its extreme variety, and science becomes a "superb, magical lens [that] reveals with ever-increasing clarity the perpetually unfolding cinematographic sequence of the phenomena of life" (1958h:1378).

In effect, Kazantzakis declares in this essay that he will be scientific only on his own terms, which have become increasingly intuitional. Although he never mentions Bergson, the peroration about life's perpetually unfolding cinematographic sequence is Bergsonian in both substance and expression. The essay indirectly affirms Kazantzakis's determination to be aesthetic in relation to Bergson's "scientific" conclusions.

Just as Kazantzakis adjusted his attitude toward science following his sojourn in Paris, so, too, he strengthened his attachment to philosophical pessimism. Bergson's faith in life's eternal power had initially swept him along—we see evidence in *O protomástoras* and also in the important essay-review on Jean Moréas, published in 1910, in which Kazantzakis espouses the *fact* of Bergsonian voluntarism as opposed to "systems such as Buddha's . . . [and] Tolstoy's, which deny life . . . , are contrary to the élan of physical laws, and consequently subjective and ephemeral" (Kaz. 1910b:356–357; Yalourakis 1978:86–87). In 1914–1915, however, owing partly to the influence of Angelos Sikelianós, with whom he traveled to Mount Athos and then throughout the Peloponnesus, and partly to the interruption of Venizélos's premiership, Kazantzakis spent considerable time in ascetic contemplation in various monasteries and concurrently became attached to Tolstoy,[11] whom in 1910, as we just saw, he had condemned as a life-denier. This does not mean that he now renounced Bergson; on the contrary, it means that he moved forward by finding that previous antagonists could be collaborators. Thus on 1 May 1915 he noted in his diary: "The great teachers: Homer, Dante, Bergson," and on the next day: "All of my new development I owe (a) to my excursions: Mount Athos, Mystras, Delphi; (b) to my recent readings: Dante, Rodin, Bergson, Claudel; (c) to my companionship with Sikelianós" (Prev. 1965b:8; Eleni Kaz. 1977:72; 1968a:58 [misdated 19 March]).

What Kazantzakis accomplished in these years following his initial exposure to Bergson was to assimilate the new philosophy into his preexisting temperamental, intellectual, and spiritual concerns, emerging with the amalgam that received its most important expression in *Askitikí* in 1922–1923. We shall treat this definitive credo in its proper place, emphasizing once again its debt to Bergson. Here, however, I want to look even further ahead in order to cite part of a much shorter credo composed by Kazantzakis in 1953, since this text indicates so clearly how the "scientific" philosophy he learned in 1908 from Bergson was transformed in 1914–1915 into a revelational faith:

> I tried many different roads by which to reach my salvation: the road of love, of scientific curiosity, of philosophical inquiry, of social regeneration, and finally the difficult and solitary path of poetry. But I saw each time that the road I had taken led to the abyss. . . . Finally, in despair, I sought refuge on Mount Athos. . . .
>
> There . . . I began a new struggle. . . . Finally one night I sprang up in great joy, for I had seen the red ribbon left behind him in his ascent . . . by a certain Combatant; I saw clearly his bloody footprints ascending from inorganic matter to life and from life to spirit.
>
> Then suddenly a great light shone within me: the transubstantiation of matter into spirit. This was the great secret, the red ribbon followed by the Combatant. (Kaz. 1958f:xxiii–xxiv; 1958s)

This statement is characteristic in that, like "Has Science Gone Bankrupt?" it never mentions Bergson. Furthermore, it suggests that Kazantzakis's discovery of the doctrine of transubstantiation of matter into spirit occurred at Mount Athos (presumably in 1914) rather than in Paris in 1908. Yet the "Combatant" here invoked is none other than Bergson's *élan vital*; the "red ribbon" left behind by the warrior's "bloody footprints" is Bergson's "continuity of genetic energy" realized because life is "*like a current passing from germ to germ through the medium of a developed organism*" (Bergson 1911:28–29; italics in the original); transubstantiation of matter into spirit is evolution's march from corporeality to consciousness.

The 1953 credo confirms Kazantzakis's assimilation of Bergsonism into a mystical belief capable of expressions such as "come l'uom s'eterna." This, in turn, perhaps explains his relative silence regarding Bergson's influence. We have noted that he barely mentions the French philosopher in *Report to Greco* whereas he devotes an entire chapter there to Nietzsche.[12] All I can find in addition—except of course for the 1913 lecture that we shall examine momentarily—are a few words of praise in *Le Jardin des rochers* (Kaz. 1959b:28, 76; 1963b:28, 65) and two brief affirmations of indebtedness, both in interviews: "You know that I am a follower of Bergson" (Jouvenel 1958:102; 1962:1580) and "[Bergson was] a marvelous spiritual guide who profoundly influenced my life. He answered questions that had been bothering me for a very long time" (Sadoul 1955). In no case is there any analysis or expansion.

On the other hand, Bergson is an unacknowledged presence in many of Kazantzakis's formulations not only of his own world-view but also of his political position—formulations that typically eschew scientific language. I have already spoken of *Askitikí* in this regard, but will add here that while writing that work in Berlin Kazantzakis importuned Galatea, who was still in Athens, to mail him the volume of Bergson that he had lent to an acquaintance (Kaz. 1958a:124). Another example from the same period concerns Kazantzakis's effort to justify his allegiance to the Bolsheviks even though he harbored no illusions about what they were doing to the pure conception of communism. "The Idea," he wrote in 1922 "is like God—amid unbelievable crimes . . . he nevertheless advances slowly, . . . ascending. . . . Our duty is: to try to discover the rhythm of his march and when we have found it to adjust the rhythm of our own small, transient lives as much as we can to his. Only thus do we mortals succeed in accomplishing something eternal, since we collaborate with some Immortal" (1958a:116). This is merely Kazantzakis's way of saying—via the theological language he preferred—what we heard Bergson saying earlier: that the essential thing is the invisible progress on which each visible organism rides during its short interval on earth. Kazantzakis aligned himself with communism at this time not for a Marxist reason but for a Bergsonian one: because he considered the Bolsheviks the "developed organisms" best suited to allow life's continuity of genetic energy to pass like a current from germ to germ in its ascent toward consciousness or supraconsciousness—considered them the organisms best suited during that particular transitional age to help reality become "productive of effects in which it expands and transcends its own being" (Bergson 1911:55; 1907:56). But of course he could not say it in this way.[13]

THE ONLY OCCASION on which Kazantzakis developed his Bergsonian thinking systematically, at length, and in "scientific" language was in the lecture he delivered to members of the Ekpaideftikós Omilos on 30 January 1913.[14] This seems to have been the first formal presentation of Bergson's thought to have taken place in Greece, although intellectuals well read in French culture already knew something not only about Bergson himself but about various schismatic disciples and also about opponents of Bergsonism such as Julien Benda.[15] I have postponed consideration of this lecture until now because I wanted first to convey Kazantzakis's Bergsonism in language more appropriate to the theological mysticism that appealed to him most—language that he did not apply to Bergson's teachings until a few years after his lecture, as we saw earlier. In the case of Bergson as in that of Nietzsche, however, if we desire to know precisely what Kazantzakis learned in Paris we must rely on the early treatise as opposed to subsequent formulations.

Kazantzakis's 1913 lecture consists of a short introduction, four main sections, and a recapitulation. Since this important document has never been translated, nor even published in book form in Greek, I shall summarize it here at some length, adding cross-references to Bergson's writings at various key places.

The introduction begins as follows:

> Bergson advances one step further than Kant. Kant said: the human intellect can discern only phenomena, not noumena—"things-in-themselves." He established in this way the boundaries of human reason and rendered impossible any further metaphysics *based on intellect.*
>
> Bergson diminishes the worth of the human intellect even more. The intellect can conceive of extensity and quantity only, never of motion, intensity, or quality. As soon as the intellect confronts a phenomenon it immobilizes it, taking away its motion and life. This is why the intellect has absolute authority in mathematics, in abstract concerns. It is however absolutely incapable by nature of knowing the phenomena of life and of evolution.
>
> Yet while Bergson diminishes the intellect's worth in this way, on the other hand he nevertheless enlarges the worth of the total human being. Humans have, besides intellect, other faculties that are able to know motion, life—in other words the essence of reality, the "thing-in-itself."
>
> Thus a new metaphysics becomes again possible and justifiable, one based no longer on the intellect alone but also on the other capacities for knowledge that human beings possess. . . . (Kaz. 1912:310–311; 1958b:12)

Section 1 (1912:311–316; 1958b:13–16) offers a radical critique of the intellectualism that has dominated Western philosophy since Plato and has led to the erroneous conclusion that true reality consists of essences as opposed to phenomena (cf. Bergson 1911:332ff.) The intellect does this because of its invincible inclination toward simplification. Confronted with life's chaotic prodigality it prefers "to omit much, to illumine little, and in this way to impose a certain harmony and order on the chaos of sensations" (Kaz. 1912:312; 1958b:14). As an example, Kazantzakis offers Bergson's celebrated analysis of motion whereby the intellect, in its futile effort to comprehend, merely succeeds in converting time, without which there is no motion, into space, thereby defining motion as an infinite number of immobilities (cf. Bergson 1960:98–117). What intellect accomplishes, in other words, is to deprive us of an accurate perception of reality. If, however, recognizing intellect's proper limits, we do not expect it to discern truth, we may value it pragmatically, since human activity requires a system of thought "that places phenomena in unshakable relation one to another," enabling them to be governed by laws. "For a practical system such as this, immobility is indispensable" (Kaz. 1912: 313; 1958b:14–15).

The result is an incurable clash between our thoughts and our innermost experience. This is what Bergson studies; and although he goes beyond Kant in denying the intellect's ability to comprehend phenomena, he acknowledges the unquestioned prestige that the intellect enjoys in the area of practical affairs.

Kazantzakis next expands on Bergson's proofs, invoking the latter's differentiation between homogeneity and heterogeneity, his example of the astronomer predicting an eclipse (an argument that left Kazantzakis open to challenge in the *Anayénnisi* controversy when he repeated it in 1926 in his "Sizítisi m' énan arhigó"), the metaphor of cinematographic stills misrepresenting flux (cf. Bergson 1911:321–323), and so forth. He ends the first section with a paragraph on the limits of science.

Section 2 (1912:316–324; 1958b:17–22) is devoted to Bergson's treatment of the problem of free will—more precisely, to the errors that the intellectualist method has committed in this area and, contrariwise, to a "true" understanding of freedom. It is based chiefly on Bergson's *Essai sur les données immédiates de la conscience* (1889; official English translation under the title *Time and Free Will: An Essay on the Immediate Data of Consciousness*). Kazantzakis's résumé constitutes the single most important gloss we possess on his treatment of psychology in his imaginative works.[16]

He begins with Bergson's discussion of erroneous approaches in the past. Both sides in the debate between free will and determinism base their arguments on what precedes a choice; their common mistake is to convert previous time into space and consequently to convert heterogeneity into homogeneity, quality into quantity (1912:317; 1958b:17–18; cf. Bergson 1960:173–176, 183–186). To be correctly understood, freedom must be sought not in the relation of a choice to something previous but simply "in the *quality* of that act" (1912:317; 1958b:17). A free act is "the external manifestation of [our] internal state . . . since it expresses the entire self" (1912:322; 1958b:21), and our internal state—our truest, completest self—is not governed by the homogeneity and quantity of spatiality but instead by the heterogeneity and quality of temporality: of creative evolution. "Our inward psychic states [are] continually in flux, metamorphosing, escaping every measurement" (1912:323; 1958b:22). In the "creative evolution of our internal world, . . . moments are of dissimilar form and are spaceless"; hence in our internal state "a cause can never again bring the same effect for the simple reason that a cause can never return exactly the same" (1912:324; 1958b:22). This explains why it is of no use to try to argue the case either for free will or for determinism on the basis of what precedes a choice. Our acts are free insofar as they stem not from our external involvement in the practical world of homogeneous extensity that is predictable, subject to law, and therefore convenient for our social arrangements, business affairs, and scientific investigations; they are free in the rare moments when this "thick crust that covers our personal sentiments . . . bursts" (1912:323; 1958b:21–22; cf. Bergson 1960:169). The resulting act will then be a "faithful and complete expression of our true self"—in other words, free, free because of its quality, free because of the intensity of feeling that overcomes predictability and other intellectual considerations, which by definition apply only to the external realm of extensity, quantity, and homogeneity.

Section 3 of Kazantzakis's lecture (1912:324–329; 1958b:22–27) is devoted to theories of evolution. It extends the psychological considerations of Section 2 by placing freedom in the much larger contexts of biology, chemistry, and physics. As before, Kazantzakis begins with the errors perpetrated by intellectualist methods, which are bound to go wrong because the intellect can never comprehend the fluid state of living organisms. The two equally erroneous explanations offered by intellectualism are the mechanistic and the teleological. After rehearsing Bergson's arguments against both (drawing on Bergson 1911:20–21, 37–42), Kazantzakis concludes that since the intellect in each case removes from evolution precisely what it aims to elucidate, namely motion, we must therefore refer to the faculties of instinct and intuition if we are to comprehend life's "incessant creation, the leap upward, the *élan vital*" (1912:326; 1958b:24).

On the other hand, although the scientific investigation of living beings is not sufficient, it does provide a beginning. This is why Bergson relies on empirical data in order to seek out the historical manifestations of creative evolution even though the eternal causes are revealed only by intuition. What he finds is the following:

> The *élan vital* divided itself into various directions. . . . The first division is that between plant and animal. . . . However, the same vital energy that pushed plants to manufacture chlorophyll also pushed animals to acquire nerves and brains . . . [Kaz. 1912:327; 1958b:24–25; cf. Bergson 1911:120; 1907:124; also 1911:112, 114–115, 119].
>
> The direction toward the animal was torn in its turn into a multitude of paths . . . only two of which were successful, those of the arthropods and the vertebrates, which result in two marvelous instruments: instinct and intelligence. . . . Instinct knows phenomena, intelligence the relations among phenomena [cf. Bergson 1911:141–142, 149–150, 156, 161–163].

Evolution's failures are many, the most obvious being the bees and ants, which are ossified into complete automatism. "It was in the *human being* that this automatism was conquered for the first time." "The difference between humans and apes is no longer one of quantity but of quality; something new was born, not the perfection of the already existing instinct but something entirely new that employs inanimate matter and makes it its tool and subordinate. The whole history of life until the human being was a gigantic effort by the *élan vital* to raise matter up in order to create a being liberated from the inflexible mechanism of inertia . . ." (Kaz. 1912:328; 1958b:25–26; cf. Bergson 1911:278–279).[17]

> But we must not therefore consider man to be something completely isolated in nature. Just as the smallest grain of sand is indissolubly bound up with the solar system, drawn along with it in matter's inverted evolution toward decomposition, so all organic beings from the humblest to the most elevated, in all places and times, constitute one and only one *élan vital* upward, the inverse of the movement of matter [cf. Bergson 1911:285; 1907:293]. Both streams, those of matter and of life, move. But they move in contrary directions, the one toward composition and the other toward decomposition. Bergson imagines the *élan vital* to be a jet of steam that in its upward surge condenses into drops that fall.[18] These drops constitute matter, that is, something that does not open out in an upward direction toward creative evolution, in time, but decomposes, in space. Organic beings, on the other hand, are continually taking on *élan vital* and assimilating it, that is, are continually being created, are adding something new to their existence,

> whereas the vital energy of inorganic matter is radiated, as the chemists say. Inorganic matter decomposes; no further creativity is possible for it. Consequently it falls perfectly within the jurisdiction of our intellect's mathematical calculations. (Kaz. 1912: 328–329; 1958b:26).

Kazantzakis ends his section on evolution by citing three reinforcements of Bergson's theory arrived at independently by Gustave Le Bon. Although two of these merely repeat elements discussed by Kazantzakis himself, the third adds an important corrective since it stresses the monism underlying what may easily appear dualistic: "Matter and energy are substantially one and the same; there is no dualism. Matter is simply energy's condensation, its stable equilibrium" (Kaz. 1912a:329; 1958b: 26).

Kazantzakis proceeds now to his fourth and final section (1912a:329–332; 1958b:27–29), which treats the method of the new metaphysics.

Bergson once defined metaphysics as "the science that claims to dispense with symbols" (Bergson 1946:58), by which he meant that metaphysics "seeks intuitive vision of the real beyond the distorting forms of conceptual thought" (Alexander 1957:15). Kazantzakis, at the very end of his section on the method of metaphysical knowledge, shows that the symbols disparaged by Bergson are not the images of art but rather the symbolizations that science inevitably employs as a consequence of its basis in conceptual thought. On the other hand, art and even philosophy (that is, Bergson's kind of philosophy), since they "both rely on intuition," are able to enter "into unmediated communication with the cosmic flux" (Kaz. 1912a:332; 1958b:28–29).

This is Bergson's conclusion regarding the method of the new metaphysics. The preceding material in Kazantzakis's Section 4 summarizes Bergson's ways of distinguishing among the various terms involved. Instinct "is able to put us in unmediated communication with life." Intuition is "the instinct of the educated person."[19] Intellect and intuition are mankind's two faculties for knowledge. "We are aware of the intellect's shortcomings and advantages: it can apprehend only material phenomena and only the relations among phenomena. . . . But it has at its disposal an instrument of utmost importance: language. Instinct, on the other hand, has the advantage of penetrating life's essence—of sensing motion [and] creativity—but it has the greatest of shortcomings: it cannot express itself clearly. . . . The philosophy that aspires to . . . discover the essence of phenomena . . . can work only with instinct, with intuition. . . . [Yet] we must be able to formulate our conclusions and to harmonize them with all the data provided by science. Only thus will philosophy differ from ecstasy and dream. Hence intuition must collaborate with intellect" (1912a:329–330; 1958b:27).

We should by no means reject our scientific investigations, continues Kazantzakis. On the contrary, we should extend them. But we will always face the problem of the intellect's inability to "render faithfully the mobile depth of reality." The solution is to find a nonscientific means of intellectual expression equal to the task of translating what we have discovered via intuition. The one means presently at our disposal is the image, which is "able to impart rhythm, . . . to render quality and present flux" (1912a:332; 1958b:28).[20] All this helps us to understand the kinship between art and intuitive philosophy. The purpose of both is to lift the veil of deception that the intellect, because of its practical needs, places before us, and to reveal the "profound and pulsating soul of phenomena." But art differs from philosophy in that it is not subject to verification by the intellect whereas philosophy is. When all is said and done, however, philosophy and art, since both rely on intuition, stand over against science in their capacity for metaphysical insight (1912:331–332; 1958b:28).

Kazantzakis concludes with a short recapitulation (1912:332–334; 1958b:29–30):

> Such, most generally, is Bergson's philosophy.
>
> He combated intellectualism . . . and limited the authority . . . of science solely to material phenomena. He introduced a new concept to philosophy, *durée réelle*, that is, real duration, creative evolution. He demonstrated the deceptions into which mankind has been misled by the confusion between *durée réelle* and homeomerous[21] space. In *psychology* this confusion made the problem of free will unsolvable, obliging Kant to resort to the *deus ex machina* of the thing-in-itself by assigning freedom to the noumenal realm, that is, beyond reality and human experience. In *biology* the same . . . method, by treating life as though it were matter, . . . reduced evolution to solidified fragments, analyzing motion into an infinite number of motionless points.
>
> [Bergson] based his biological hypothesis of the *élan vital* on the reliable deductions of science. . . . He separated the organic world from the inorganic, intellect from instinct, science from philosophy.
>
> Bergson . . . determined not only philosophy's content but also the means by which it attains its goal. He was the first to demonstrate . . . that the boundaries of the human intellect are narrower than what Kant posited but that the boundaries of humanity are wider than Kant imagined—he raised up intuition . . . , deter-

mined its strengths and weaknesses, and was the first to call for the collaboration of intuition and intellect in philosophical inquiry.

NOW THAT WE have seen two accounts of Kazantzakis's Bergsonism, the first in the religious language that Kazantzakis applied to this philosophy during his period of monastic retreat in 1914–1915 and brought to fruition in *Askitikí*, the second in the "scientific" language employed in the lecture delivered to members of the Educational Association in January 1913, we are in a better position to evaluate the reason I gave earlier for Kazantzakis's extraordinary devotion to Bergson's teaching.

We know that Kazantzakis was searching for a theory of the world and of human destiny in accord with which he could regulate his life and work. What I claimed earlier was that he considered teleology and mechanism equally unacceptable as world-views and at the same time could not be fully satisfied with the negativism of subjective nihilism. Bergsonian vitalism provided him with a perfect exit from each of these impasses. While unteleological in its denial that vital evolution serves any purpose or design outside of itself, Bergsonism nevertheless gives the human species a purposefulness and an orientation toward the future that provide emotional substitutes for Christian hope. While unmechanistic in its assumptions (a) that the whole in biology is greater than the sum of its parts, (b) that this nonmaterial whole persists in every living thing despite changes of material constituents (see Schubert-Soldern 1962), and (c) that vital processes cannot be explained by the uniform, predictable behavior of homogeneous elements on analogy with particles of inorganic matter, Bergsonism nevertheless roots its mysticism in the precision (or at least pseudoprecision) of scientific investigation. In addition, it steers a middle course between chance and determinism as governing principles, positing in evolution a creative—that is, indeterminate—purposefulness. Lastly, while it provides a strong antidote to nihilism and despair, it is compatible with Nietzsche's antirationalism and his attack on the central beliefs of the Western tradition.

For all these reasons Bergsonian vitalism enabled Kazantzakis to avoid a ninety-degree turn and instead to extend previous directions such as his yearning for the conquest of matter by spirit (*Ofis ke kríno*), his renunciation of romantic dreaming (*Ksimerónei*, "Spasménes psihés"), and his desire to pay homage to science in pragmatic areas. As always, the method enabling him to extend previous directions was synthesis—in this case the synthesis of biology's empirical precision with metaphysics' visionary imprecision. Bergson appealed to Kazantzakis for the same reason that Ignatius Loyola and the Alhambra did when he visited Spain in 1926, because the saint and the edifice each proved that "a metaphysical idea is able to be formulated no longer in terms of romantic figures of speech and idealistic vagueness but in terms of mathematics and geometry" (Kaz. 1962b:121; 1963c:133).

Earlier, I held that Bergson supplied his disciple with a new god. In other words, what Kazantzakis discovered as an auditor of Bergson's lectures was not just a philosophy but a religion. Clifford Geertz has defined religion brilliantly as "(1) a system of symbols which acts to (2) establish powerful, pervasive, and long-lasting moods and motivations in men by (3) formulating conceptions of a general order of existence and (4) clothing these conceptions with such an aura of factuality that (5) the moods and motivations seem uniquely realistic" (Geertz 1966:4). It is in this sense that Bergsonian vitalism became for Kazantzakis a creed that he would henceforth confess with a convert's fervor.

The question of Kazantzakis's Bergsonian "orthodoxy" has been raised. Nikos Pouliópoulos, the central figure in the small socialist party of which Kazantzakis was the nominal head in 1945, asseverates that Kazantzakis was not a blind follower of Bergson any more than he was a blind follower of Nietzsche or Buddha. He argues at some length that Kazantzakis was more of a rationalist than Bergson, less of an ecstatic and mystic, more of a believer in practical action for social amelioration (Pouliopoulos 1975:56–62). I think that he is wrong, indeed that we have here an instance of special pleading in which Pouliópoulos is attempting to make Kazantzakis more compatible with Pouliópoulos's own socialist ideology. But I also think that the question of Kazantzakis's orthodoxy or heterodoxy vis-à-vis Bergsonism is unimportant. Kazantzakis did not worry about maintaining the purity of his Bergsonian ideas even though he valued them in their own right. Certain Bergsonian dogmas of course remained with him for life, but they were always subject to adjustments in emphasis or expression as he encountered other thinkers, whether fully compatible (like Sorel and Shestov), somewhat compatible (like Schopenhauer), or incompatible (like Marx).[22]

What is important is not the question of whether Kazantzakis was an orthodox Bergsonist but rather the extraordinary degree to which Bergsonian vitalism as he conceived it pervades his discursive and imaginative writings. Among the former I have already mentioned *Askitikí*, of course, and the pieces connected with the *Anayénnisi* controversy, all of which I shall discuss later. Among the imaginative writings, the *Odyssey* may best be described as a series of images meant to suggest a creative action that unmakes itself. Consistent with Bergson's own method, Kazantzakis attempts here (as elsewhere) to excite in the mind of the reader the intuition of duration; not surprisingly, he states in a letter that in writing the *Odyssey* he was driven by "an entirely anti-intellectual flame . . . , an *intuition mondiale*" (Kaz. 1977a:187). Izzet's sense of the kinship between *Alexis Zorbás* and Bergson has already been noted; it is explored further by

Friedman (1967) and also by Poulakidas (1972). Izzet finds Bergson's presence as well in *The Last Temptation*, where Jesus, he claims, "est le symbole de la création toujours créatrice . . . , la manifestation la plus pure de la 'réalité toujours jaillissante' de l'éternelle création."[23] My own view is that Bergsonism's most subtle presence occurs in *Christ Recrucified*, where it governs the very structure of the plot since the refugees—forever moving, forever producing effects by means of which their own reality expands and transcends its being—are the developed organisms through whom the continuity of genetic energy passes like a current, upwards, toward composition, whereas the established citizens who resist them in the village represent matter's inverted evolution toward decomposition. The meeting of these two streams is the luminous interval called life, the interval between the one dark abyss from which the refugees enter the book at the start (as energy longing to express itself via materiality) and the other dark abyss into which they pass out of the book at the end, defeated in materiality but with their creative potential intact. If we allow the images to guide us to an intuition of duration, as both Bergson and Kazantzakis desire, we will appreciate the degree to which this remarkable novel is governed in its deep structure by a vitalistic theory of the world and of human destiny.

Of course there are critics who acknowledge Bergsonism's centrality to Kazantzakis and then proceed to claim that this centrality is precisely the trouble—that Kazantzakis was attached too exclusively to a single world-view and was too obsessive about that attachment. To answer such critics we have to know the exact basis of their complaint. If they feel that creative writers, whatever their personal faith or ideology, should confront life's variety as uncommitted observers, then we can reply that Dante, Milton, and Dostoevsky—not to mention lesser figures such as Camus, Malraux, and Lawrence—do not fit this mold, although it is admittedly filled to perfection by Shakespeare or Homer. If on the other hand they object to Bergsonism per se, claiming that it is eccentric, trivial, or untrue, we need to address each complaint in its own right.

Although Bergson has been out of fashion wherever the academic orthodoxy is A. J. Ayer's empiricist philosophy[24] or some other form of logical positivism, and has been especially neglected in England and America, he has continued to be discussed on the Continent, especially in France. Far from being eccentric, he comes out of one of the central streams of European philosophy—not the Cartesian to be sure, but the Hegelian (the treatment of history as evolving psychic awareness), Kantian (the limitations placed on reason's powers), Schopenhauerian and Nietzschian (will as the prime impetus behind evolution). Moreover, he forms a link between these and subsequent developments such as process theology (which in Berdyaev, for example, is based on a Bergsonian differentiation among different kinds of time[25]), indeterminism (which in

Karl Popper is based on an opposition to scientific determinism, that is, to the doctrine that any future event can be rationally predicted if we possess all the past data [see Popper 1982]), holistic biology as opposed to the reductionist biology that carries on the assumptions of Cartesian rationalism (see Rose 1980), and of course existentialism in general, not to mention the animistic vitalism of Teilhard de Chardin.[26]

Even if Bergsonism is not eccentric, it may still be trivial in the eyes of some. To this the best counterargument is the serious consideration accorded vitalism by an impressive list of nontrivial figures of modern literature. Proust is the most obvious, the central purpose of his great novel being to provide its hero with intuitions of *durée réelle*. George Bernard Shaw is a vitalist, as are D. H. Lawrence and Virginia Woolf.[27] Dylan Thomas's "The force that through the green fuse drives the flower / Drives my green age; that blasts the roots of trees / Is my destroyer" hymns an *élan vital* whose action unmakes itself. This same *élan vital* is the motivating principle of Joyce's *Finnegans Wake* ("Promptings by Elanio Vitale" [Joyce 1947:221]), in which the river Liffey ("Life") is the vitality energizing everything else, and the unpredictability of creative evolution's precise turns is epigrammatically summarized as the "agnosis of postcreate determinism" (262). In form, the book playfully mimics the life force's unstanchable flow by immersing us in a flood of images and deliberately nonlogical language meant concertedly to awaken in us an intuition of duration. As for *Ulysses*, the dramatic conflict there is between intelligence and intuition, with due respect accorded the former (as in Bergson) but ultimate homage paid to the latter in the person of Molly Bloom, into whose *durée réelle* in the final episode the fragmented, analytic reality that preceded is fully subsumed.

Bergsonian vitalism may be neither eccentric nor trivial; yet the problem of its truth remains. Its opponents have argued vigorously that it is not only a deceptive doctrine but an insidious one (e.g. Lewis 1927). In 1913, eager to convince himself and others that Bergsonism was true, Kazantzakis took care to speak of the "indisputable deductions of science" and the "latest chemical investigations" that allegedly verified Bergson's hypothesis (Kaz. 1912:332; 1958b:29). At one point it did seem that the scientific determinism of classical physics might give way to indeterminism in conformity with the Heisenberg uncertainty principle and quantum theory; yet molecular biology and in particular the discovery of the role played in the hereditary process by DNA have tipped the scales back in favor of the Cartesians to the detriment of the vitalists. As Jacques Monod wrote in 1969:

> In order to survive as a point of view, vitalism requires that in biology there should remain, if not actual paradoxes, at least certain "mysteries." Developments in molecular biology over the past

> two decades have singularly narrowed the domain of the mysterious, leaving wide open to vitalist speculation little other than the field of subjectivity: that of consciousness itself. One runs no great risk in predicting that in this area as well, for the time being still "off limits," such speculation will prove just as sterile as in all the others where it has hitherto been practiced. . . . (Monod 1971:29)
>
> Bergson . . . beheld in evolution the expression of an *absolutely* creative force, in the sense that he imagined it as bent on no goal other than creation in itself and for its own sake. . . . Bergson could not help being alive to the stunning richness of the biosphere and the amazing variety of forms and behavior it displays, which seem to bear almost direct witness indeed to an inexhaustible, completely untrammeled creative prodigality.
>
> But where Bergson saw the most glaring proof that the "principle of life" is evolution itself, modern biology recognizes, instead, that all the properties of living beings rest on *a fundamental mechanism of molecular invariance*. . . . And so one may say that the same source of fortuitous perturbations, of "noise," which in a non-living (that is, nonreplicative) system would lead little by little to the disintegration of all structure, is the progenitor of evolution in the biosphere and accounts for its unrestricted liberty of creation, thanks to the replicative structure of DNA: that registry of chance, that tone-deaf conservatory where the noise is preserved along with the music. (Monod 1971:115–117)

What effect, if any, should all this have on our evaluation of the "truth" of Kazantzakis's Bergsonism? I think very little. The reason is that Kazantzakis himself, despite his dutiful obeisance to scientific verification in the 1913 lecture (rarely later), did not conceive of truth in this rationalist, empiricist manner. Even in 1913 he ended his lecture with the following peroration:

> If you wish to understand Bergson's system it is not enough for you to be persuaded by the psychological, biological, or philosophical arguments that he adduces. It is always likely that you will find various obscurities or insufficiencies. You must forget the one-sidedly intellectual method that we have followed until now in connection with our desire to know a philosophy, that is, an explanation of life's totality, and must place yourself inside the philosopher's flowing, evolving thought, joining intuitional capabilities to your intellectual ones. . . .
>
> . . . We must *feel* these verbal fragments—these words, thoughts, images—of which [reality] is composed, must blow a breath of life into them. For how do you expect to understand the

> totality solely by means of the intellect, which was given us for other purposes and which is just one part of the world's evolving energy? It is the same as wanting to include the whole in a part . . . (Kaz. 1912:333; 1958b:29–30)

According to Kazantzakis, the truth of Bergson's system when all is said and done cannot be proved or disproved scientifically; it can only be felt. If the system is espoused with sufficient intensity by the entire self—that is, by that which is governed not by spatiality's quantifiable homogeneity but rather by temporality's qualitative heterogeneity—then the system will take on for that believer the "eternal truth" of a religious creed and be able, as Geertz says, to clothe its conceptions of the general order of existence with an aura of factuality.

Kazantzakis became, and remained, a believer. Although in many other respects he reacted throughout his career like a weather vane, changing direction at every new wind, in his Bergsonism (and his demoticism) he always stood firm. William James's pragmatism was for him an extension of Bergson's teaching that we must honor the intellect's role in practical affairs but recognize that the most important truths are those that are felt and lived before being thought. Nietzsche constituted the prolegomenon, the antecedent fury at the world's degradation; he was the wild forerunner heralding the tranquil teacher. By following all three philosophers, but primarily the last, Kazantzakis worked out in Paris a theory of the world and of human destiny in accord with which he was henceforth to write what he wrote, systematically and purposefully, in collaboration—he firmly believed—with some Immortal.

CHAPTER THREE

Development of Kazantzakis's (meta-)communism

> I belong to the lost intelligentsia. My sympathies are with the Left on paper and in my soul. But not in my heart or my guts. On paper—yes.
>
> —Louis MacNeice (copied by Kazantzakis into his notebooks)

Kazantzakis's next phase after the breakup of his nationalism was a similar foray into politics followed, as before, by disillusion and withdrawal. The difference this time was that international communism replaced ethnocentric Hellenism.

We have seen that he dated his new allegiance from 1923: "Until . . . 1923, I passed through the nationalist camp. . . . From approximately 1923 to 1933, I was part of the left wing . . ." (Prev. 1965b:464). The year 1923 seems late when we know that he had already hoped to collaborate in the publication of a communist periodical in Athens at the end of 1920 (Kaz. 1958a:11) and was surely in the communist camp by May 1922 when he wrote to Galatea from Vienna, "Now with our *new perception*, you can't imagine how moved I am when I see people here suffering from hunger and despair. . . . Better the world be destroyed, the firmament be purged of the disgrace of contemporary life!" (1958a:18–19; italics added). Nevertheless, 1923 is still a meaningful date, for it reminds us that Kazantzakis's "new perception," although predating the Asia Minor disaster, was in large measure a reaction to that event. Having begun to lose his faith in Greek nationalism owing to the murder of Dragoúmis in 1920 and the subsequent defeat of Venizélos at the polls,[1] he was ready to embrace a new ideology with vigor when the horrendous events of 1922 in Asia Minor signaled the total collapse of the Megáli Idéa.

THE ASIA MINOR DISASTER AS THE STIMULUS FOR KAZANTZAKIS'S IDIOSYNCRATIC COMMUNISM

What happened between Venizélos's defeat in November 1920 and the sack of Smyrna in September 1922 by the victorious Turks of course can not be described adequately in a few paragraphs, but I must nevertheless attempt a crude outline. Greece—once more a kingdom after the plebiscite that recalled King Constantine—feared for the Hellenic population of Asia Minor, especially after Mustapha Kemal established a nationalist parliament in Ankara. Despite a depleted treasury, the Greek General Staff pressed for immediate occupation as the solution. After all, it was 1921, the centenary of the 1821 Revolution; the nation dreamed that the present king, conveniently named Constantine, would soon be crowned emperor in Hagia Sophia. But the campaign was doomed from the start owing to incompetent leadership, difficult terrain, lack of foreign support, and an enemy fighting on its own soil under the direction of a military genius. At first the Greeks did well enough. But Mustapha Kemal was meanwhile gaining time, forming his army, and luring the invaders to a battle ground of his own choice—the line of the Sakharia River. When he counterattacked in late August, the Turkish offensive

> rapidly turned into a Greek rout, with the Greek forces retreating in disarray to Smyrna and the coast. On 8 September the Greek army evacuated the city, which the Turkish army entered the following day. Initially the Turkish occupation of the city was relatively orderly but on the evening of the 9th outbreaks of killing and looting began. This was followed by a full-scale massacre of the Christian population, in which the Armenians suffered the greatest casualties. Some 30,000 Christians perished, and in the great fire that ensued the Armenian, Greek and Frankish quarters were very largely destroyed. . . . A quarter of a million people fled to the waterfront to escape the inferno. . . . Within a few days the last Greek troops had abandoned the soil of Asia Minor and withdrawn to the Greek islands and mainland. A 2500-year Greek presence on the western littoral of Asia Minor had been abruptly terminated in conditions of total disaster. (Clogg 1979:117–118)

As if this humiliation were not enough, the Greeks now took vengeance on the leaders of the Asia Minor expedition in a way that shamed the nation in the eyes of the international community. A junta headed by Colonel Plastíras demanded the abdication (for the second time) of King Constantine, who complied. The revolutionary government then sentenced three ex-premiers, two ex-ministers, and the former commander-in-chief to death. Despite protests from the British and from Venizélos, the victims were lined up against a wall and shot. Such was the ignominious end of the Megáli Idéa.[2]

The political, economic, social, ideological, and literary repercussions following these events cannot be overemphasized. From the turn of the century until 1922 the Greeks did not have any ideological problem to solve. The Megáli Idéa had cut across boundaries of political allegiance, education, and class, promising the nation new accomplishments in every sector. When all this crashed into ruin, people obviously attempted to adjust, but a permanent wound remained, together with "a painful yearning for something that could replace the lost ideal, fill the vacuum" (Theotokas 1958:1). This yearning was particularly imperious in Kazantzakis. Already disillusioned with Greek political life, he became increasingly open to Soviet Russia and Leninism as he experienced not only the Greek debacle (at a distance) but also the horrendous postwar conditions in Vienna. The sputtering extinction of his nationalism is evident in the letters he wrote to Galatea between May and December 1922. Having just traveled from Athens to Belgrade, he commented: "Here too is humanity. . . . How horrible all these borders so filled with hate and blood. . . . What unity among animals . . . ! How much better they serve the unknown purpose . . . ! I think of Turks, Bulgarians, everyone we were taught to hate" (Kaz. 1958a:16; 1979a:46). The day after the Greek army evacuated Smyrna, he reacted as follows:

> I wonder if the wretched Greeks will put some sense into their heads now. I wonder if this disaster will be the inception of a rebirth. This is how I take it and accept it—with gratitude.[3] Given the present régime, victory would have been fatal for Greece. It would have laid a foundation for today's villains and have drugged the common people, which is exactly what they want. Now, however, the great misfortune will either brace or annihilate them. . . . This is how Russia and Germany were reborn: through disaster. France, through her victory, reached the summit of villainy, because victory stabilized the capitalist régime that governs her. (1958a:77–78; 1979a:57)

And he concluded: "Greece's bitter trial today increases our responsibility and makes an intensive propaganda campaign more imperative."

As the subsequent events unfolded he refused every chauvinistic temptation, applauding for example Galatea's decision not to sign a protest against Turkish atrocities because the protest did not condemn Greek atrocities as well. "At this stage," he commented, "we are interested in humanity, without labels. Turks and Greeks dishonored humanity in Asia Minor" (Kaz. 1958a:97; 1979a:61). As for the execution of the Six, he stated bitterly:

> They should have been killed by the common people, but still it was fine that Plastíras was found to say a brave word. It's better we destroy ourselves playing a tragedy than remain alive playing an operetta. Here [Berlin], all Europe is aroused by the barbarity. And for the 50,000 homeless and the thousands of Turks killed by the Greeks they remain totally impassive. I'm glad because I think

> that only now the Greeks will realize that something important is happening . . . (1958a:114–115; 1979a:69).

In the next paragraph, he continued: "For the first time in my life I'm interested equally in my own and all other peoples. Indeed . . . the sincerest representatives of the human race for me today are the Russians. They strike me as today's bearers of divinity."

He was ready to embrace communism as a way of filling the ideological void. However, the particular concept of communism that he favored even at this early stage included ingredients from his previous orientation. For example, in the same letter of 9 September in which he reacted to the defeat in Asia Minor and called for a propaganda campaign, he advised Galatea that they should feel compassion not for individual human beings, who are wretched and insignificant, but for humanity in the abstract (1958a:77; 1979a:56). This theme is continued in a long communication written at the end of the year:

> Chérie, . . . No one despises the . . . *contemplateur* more than I do (because that's what I used to be). When I say that the end of our activity must not be our country, I say it not so that we'll fold our arms and view the spectacle of the world's peoples from on high . . . , but so that we'll shift our activity . . . to a wider circle of the struggle: to humanity, to humanity without labels of Turk or Greek. . . . Now we have to fight . . . to teach . . . all peoples to breathe outside of borders and to suffer and be glad when folk in China or Russia suffer and are glad.
>
> . . . Great perspicacity of mind is required for us to know what each people has contributed to the common struggle and how each nation must educate and arm itself . . . in order to . . . take its place, like a mosaic stone, in the icon of the god that is being created.
>
> This last need—perspicacity of mind—makes us understand what a large task each intellectual must assume for his nation. . . . But struggling in this way for his nation (to which he must direct his initial efforts), he will know what he is working for: that his nation is a means and not an end, and he will really know this now, because he will have liberated himself from the iron collar of exclusive patriotism. . . .
>
> So, what is the Greek intellectual's action for his nation going to be? . . . My own view, for example, is that our national virtues are exhibited only outside of state régimes. As a politician the Greek is horrible. As Odysseus—wandering, working, trading, thinking, without his own state system, like the Jews—he is unique in the world. (1958a:138–140; 1979a:79–81)

Similar statements confirm the degree to which Kazantzakis's communism continued his previous political mentality. Prevelákis is wrong when he speaks of a *tabula rasa*, claiming that the Asia Minor disaster "cleaned away all of [Kazantzakis's] previous beliefs" (Prev. 1965b:xlvii). Instead, we have an old body draped in new clothing.[4]

If we look for additional evidence for the continuity of Kazantzakis's thought, it is easy to find, thanks to the invaluable letters to Galatea in which he was constantly explaining himself, since he knew that his wife disapproved of his idiosyncratic form of communism. He took pains, for instance, to fuse his new perception with his old heroic pessimism. "The complete change of front cannot take place," he wrote in July 1922. "So, no salvation. Will we at least be given a chance to be killed somewhat heroically . . . ? I strongly doubt it. But let's wait. You won't believe it, but if this hope were lacking I would have killed myself recently" (1958a:46). By the end of the year this same stance had become less personal and more philosophical: "Where are we headed? No one knows. . . . Maybe we're not headed anywhere. . . . So much the better! This is how we conquer the last and greatest temptation—hope. . . . We work, and there is no boss to pay us our wages at the end of the day. We are despairing, calm, and free. This is true heroism, man's supreme exploit . . ." (1958a:117; 1979a:71). Various other ingredients of his abiding mentality evident in the same letters are: antirationalism (1958a:152–153), elitism (1958a:100,221; 1979a:62,100), vitalism (1958a:222; 1979a:100), and antimaterialism (1958a:216). These last elements are what Prevelákis had in mind when he wrote that "Lenin won Kazantzakis over—Lenin, not Marx":

> Marxism inherits the tyranny of rationality called into question by Bergsonian philosophy; Lenin, on the other hand, represented that impetuous and uncontrollable flight from logic, that "world-begetting power which converts us humans . . . into its carriers, . . . and which moves hastily along as though it had a purpose . . ." [Kaz. 1965e:10; 1989:3]. What attracted Kazantzakis to the Soviet Union was not a political theory, and still less a philosophy of history; it was an inexplicable passion. (Prev. 1977:21–22; 1981:36–37; cf. 1965b:xlvii)

Prevelákis adds in a footnote—perhaps superfluously—that "the reader will recognize in the phrase 'world-begetting power' none other than Bergson's *élan vital*. . . ."

Ironically, the very factors that enabled Kazantzakis to embrace "communism" were the ones that prohibited him from ever becoming a communist. He was aware of the discrepancy from the start, but sometimes in the heat of his initial enthusiasms he veiled this discrepancy with rhetoric. On balance, however, the passages quoted above should convince us that he was never self-deceived.

We, in our turn, must be wary of the schematization suggested by Kazantzakis himself in his letter to Prevelákis whereby a clear demarcation is placed between a nationalist period and a leftist one. We must also beware when we find a similar demarcation in *Report to Greco*, which makes Kazantzakis's days in Vienna seem dominated by Buddhism while those in Berlin are dominated by a communism requiring the renunciation of Buddhistic withdrawal. Conversely, we must be wary of a further schematization suggesting that Kazantzakis's unsuccessful attempts to act as a communist sent him back to the Buddhistic world-view as evidenced by the *Odyssey*. There is enough truth in all of these dichotomizations to make them appear plausible; yet we should always remember Kazantzakis's declaration in 1927: "I am a monist. Most deeply, I feel that matter and spirit are one" (Kaz. 1965d:82; 1975a:78). Kazantzakis's development was Bergsonian in its avoidance of impenetrable cell walls separating past, present, and future. There was always osmosis, always the interpenetration of apparently antagonistic views. Just as his communism carried forward attitudes seen in his nationalism, so too his Buddhism carried forward his Christian/Schopenhauerian/Parnassian revulsion against the vanity and ugliness of the "world of objects," dressing that revulsion in new clothes. As for the future, he did not renounce his Buddhism in favor of communism but attempted to fuse those opposites in the monistic vision proclaimed in *Askitikí*. Still later, he did not suddenly disavow communism owing to his experiences in Russia; the essential incompatibility of his position and the communists' had been present from the start.

VIENNA: POLITICAL YEARNINGS VERSUS BUDDHISM

On the other hand, as Kazantzakis admitted at the same time that he affirmed his monism, once we try to explain things we are obliged to use reason, which means that we necessarily "separate that which by its nature is inseparable." This is what I too shall do in the next few chapters as I attempt to sort out Kazantzakis's permutations during the years 1922–1929, confident that we shall keep remembering that apparent shifts in essence are only adventitious shifts in emphasis.

Let us return now to Vienna, where Kazantzakis lived for a little more than three months in 1922, from 19 May until the end of August. The account in *Report to Greco* emphasizes his facial eczema there and his immersion in the Buddhistic world-view. The letters to Galatea, however, reveal more diverse activities; the sojourn was a characteristically "monistic" one in which Kazantzakis easily combined worldly with spiritual interests. His reading extended far beyond the Buddhist scriptures. He dipped into Freud, Rathenau,[5] and Japanese art (Kaz. 1958a: 24,38,34). He bought a pile of books on Russia as well as on Asian civilization, and sent home for his copy of Theocritus (1958a:62). Besides attending lectures by the theosophist Rudolph Steiner, he went to concerts, museums, and the theater—despite his increasing conviction that art was a luxury unless it functioned as propaganda preparing the revolution (1958a: 23,41,29). Nor did he neglect his own writing. He completed a novella called "A Year of Solitude" (now lost) and began to develop ideas for a new work that was to be "purely theological," announcing to Galatea on 9 August that he had already "planned out its skeleton" and that it would be "very difficult" (1958a:63)—obviously the future *Askitikí*.[6]

But Kazantzakis's interests in Vienna were not just cultural, artistic, mystical, and theological; they were also political, as we already know. His very first impression was of frightful poverty and despair in counterpoint to the shamelessness of the rich stuffing themselves with beefsteaks (1958a:26, 39; 1979a:49, 52). The sight of a destitute woman in the gutter (1958a:19)—an experience included in the chapter on Vienna in *Report to Greco* with interesting elaborations—moved him, as we have seen, to call for the firmament to be purged of the disgrace of contemporary life. He arrived in the midst of the runaway inflation that followed World War I. At the end of June he lived through a general strike, then experienced huge demonstrations with red flags waving (1958a:50). The capitalist system had evidently ceased to function in Austria just as, according to Kazantzakis, it had in Greece. In his opinion the cause was France (1958a:21), the solution communist revolution. Seeking out the local Bolsheviks, he reported approvingly to Galatea the enthusiastic declaration of a "famous communist, Jewish naturally," who had visited him in his room: "The knife has cut to the bone, heaps of people will start dying, deliverance is at hand. Revolution!" (1958a:26,28). As the general strike loomed, he repeated for Galatea the current communist slogan: "Better a terrible end than terror without end" (1958a:37).

How was all this reconciled with his concurrent interest in Buddha? It was and it was not.

It was not insofar as he protested to Galatea that the play he was then writing on Buddha constituted "the last artistic temptation" that was going to lure him (1958a:80). Nor was it insofar as he moaned, even after tearing up all 3,000 verses of the original version and recasting it along lines more "wild and bitter" in order to please Galatea, that first he had to unburden himself of the poetic metaphors weighing on him if he were to be ready afterwards to do his duty, that is, to "become absorbed in today's unrest, and to hope and work henceforth not with words but with people" (1958a:99, 95, 105; cf. 183).[7]

On the other hand, Kazantzakis's political yearnings *were* reconciled with Buddhism insofar as the play itself constituted an attempt to justify action in light of Buddhistic knowledge. We of course do not know if this was the case, since all the early versions are lost, but we are tempted to speculate along these lines because of a remark to Galatea: "*Buddha* is advancing . . . , becoming contemporary; the barbarians are intervening, Buddha is growing broader" (1958a:206; 1979a:99). What we do know for certain is that the published version, written twenty years later, examines the conflict between action and Buddhistic withdrawal in a way that draws the contending opposites together into a monistic framework. As always in Kazantzakis's development, thesis and antithesis coalesce in synthesis.

BERLIN: BOOKISH AND OTHER INFLUENCES; EDUCATIONAL REFORM

The direct evidence for Kazantzakis's desire to reconcile action with withdrawal is *Askitikí*, completed during his sojourn in Berlin, which extended from the end of August 1922 to 18 January 1924. He had to work out to his satisfaction why his Bergsonian world-view demanded action and why the communists were models for correct action at that particular moment in history. What he accomplished in Berlin was a systematic investigation of communism from a metaphysical perspective.

Berlin at this time is well described by Victor Serge, about whom we shall hear more later.

> Bemedaled cripples from the Great War sold matches outside night-clubs in which girls . . . danced naked among the . . . flower-decked tables of the diners. Capitalism was running riot . . . and accumulating immense fortunes in the midst of insolvency. . . .
>
> Permanent conspiracies of various sorts went on in limitless ramifications. . . . In philosophic language, Oswald Spengler proclaimed the Decline of the West. . . . The portraits of Oskar Kokoschka palpitated . . . with a cosmic neurosis. . . .
>
> Germany was bled white. Nobody there had any real confidence in the future, and practically nobody had any idea of the public good. . . . Energy, when it was divorced from reason, took refuge in the military leagues; where it was coloured by dogmatic reasoning, it gathered around the Communist Party. . . .
>
> Seen from here, the Russian Revolution appeared as a superb exploit. It preserved almost all its halo of newly-arisen justice and organization, as well as of unprecedented democracy. . . . (Serge 1963:159–160)

Kazantzakis's outward experiences in this extraordinary atmosphere duplicated those he had undergone in Vienna: poverty, hunger, demonstrations, communist ferment, runaway inflation. Unlike Vienna, however, Berlin made Kazantzakis share some of its privations; his wife, when she visited, found him wrapped in blankets and wearing thick woolen gloves as he wrote (Galatea Kazantzaki 1957:183). But the chief difference was the people he met. Berlin was full of "the most extraordinary Russians: communists, dancers, singers—lots and lots of activity, so much that a Russian wrote the other day: 'Berlin is a beautiful city, except that it is full of Germans!' " (Kaz. 1958a:72). In addition there were circles of Jewish communists, and German intellectuals of all sorts. In sum, Kazantzakis moved to Berlin because he considered it the "center of the whirlpool" and admired in general the "momentum of the German mind today" (1958a:62). Immediately upon his arrival he threw himself into this whirlpool with characteristic energy, supplementing his previous orientation with intensive reading and also with personal contacts.

The major new influences upon him in Berlin were Oswald Spengler and Lev Shestov. He purchased the enlarged edition of Spengler's *Decline of the West* published in 1922–1923, carrying it back to Greece when he returned (Prev. 1958:106; 1961:61). Having experienced (a) what seemed the end of Greek strength, hope, and youth and (b) what seemed the breakup of the Austro-Hungarian Empire, he was receptive to Spengler's theory that every culture "passes through the age-phases of the individual man. Each has its childhood, youth, manhood and old age." A culture "dies when [its] soul has actualized the full sum of its possibilities in the shape of peoples, languages, religious systems, arts, states, sciences" (Spengler 1922–1923:I, 145,144; 1980:I, 107, 106; cited by Prev. 1958: 105–106; 1961:60). At this point it yields its place to a young culture.

Spengler gave Kazantzakis historical data for the doctrine of the transitional age. Although reconfirming the latter's pessimistic assurance that all is vanity, he simultaneously strengthened Kazantzakis's optimistic assurance, based on Bergson's theory of evolution, that a young organism will always appear, and that our task is to help it appear all the sooner. Spengler thus encouraged Kazantzakis to place specific political manifestations such as the decline of the Austro-Hungarian Empire and the ascent of Russia within a framework large enough to be called (loosely) metaphysical. His importance is indicated by the quotations from *Der Untergang des Abendlandes* that Kazantzakis copied into his notebooks and by his adoption of Spenglerian terminology, especially in reference to degenerate Greeks, for example,

> Papaïoánnou described to me the life of his friends in Paris. . . . I was horrified by these young people, who desire to live in such a

> sterile way. Like the scum (ξεφυσίδια) of some decadent nation. . . . Spengler is right to call us Fellahenvolk. (Eleni Kaz. 1977:196; 1968a:155; cf. Prev. 1965b:56)

> Will the spirit come [to Castile] again, I wonder. Does the spirit come twice to the same nation in the same place? Fellahenvolk! This cruel name that Spengler applied to peoples who created great civilizations only once—Egyptians, Assyrians, Persians, Indians—frightens me . . . (Kaz. 1962b:31; 1963c:36)[8]

It is important to remember that Kazantzakis was truer in the long run to Spenglerism (and also of course to Bergsonism) than to communism. As we shall see, he soon began to view the Bolsheviks, too, as the end of a culture rather than the beginning, and therefore to look forward to a *meta*communistic society.

Shestov, whom Kazantzakis called "Russia's greatest contemporary philosopher" (Kaz. 1958a:116; 1979a:70), was an equally important influence. The affinity of the two minds becomes obvious when we listen to Albert Camus's distinction between Shestov and those who subscribe to the absurdist view of the universe: "To Chestov reason is useless, but there is something beyond reason. To an absurd mind reason is useless and there is nothing beyond reason" (Camus 1964:35). What lay beyond reason for Shestov is identified by D. H. Lawrence: " 'Everything is possible'—this is his really central cry. It is not nihilism. It is only a shaking free of the human psyche from old bonds. The positive central idea is that the human psyche, or soul, really believes in itself, and in nothing else" (Shestov 1920:10). Reading Shestov's aphorisms in his *Apotheosis of Groundlessness* is like reading a Kazantzakian anthology. Here are three examples:

> The habit of logical thinking kills imagination.

> The root of all our philosophies lies, not in our objective observations, but in the demands of our own heart, in the subjective, moral *will*.

> Is not the very conception of truth, the very assumption of the possibility of truth, merely an outcome of our limited experience . . . ? Truth . . . is only *limitness*. . . . Until the contrary is proved, we need to think that only one assertion has or can have any objective reality: *that nothing on earth is impossible*. (Shestov 1920:37, 126, 240–241)

Standing much closer to Kazantzakis's heart than communism ever did, Shestov's open-ended irrationalism, his voluntarism, and his mystical faith in the soul helped, like Spengler's theory of historical transitions, to foster the metacommunist position that became the principal fruit of Kazantzakis's stay in Berlin.[9]

To supplement these bookish influences, Kazantzakis cultivated active contacts with two groups of Berlin intellectuals, those engaged in educational reform and those dedicated to communist revolution. His involvement with the former extended an interest dating back to his days as a graduate student in Paris (Kaz. 1958g:1210) and continuing in his work with the Solomos Society in Iráklion and the Educational Association in Athens. During his seventeen months in Berlin, education was the only area in which he actually applied his political principles. He began on 1 October 1922 by attending the *Tagung Entschiedenen Schulreformer* (Congress of Resolute School Reformers), whose leaders he greatly admired and came to know personally (Eleni Kaz. 1977:104; Kaz. 1958a:92–93, 101; 1979a:62). By December he was associated with a radical group called the League of the Resolute, a "marvelous, militant association of people, chiefly teachers, who seek the complete reformation of the school system—a change not just in the methods of education but in the purpose. They're all communists and extreme socialists. . . . I'm a member of this League and among the most extreme" (1958a:172; 1979a:85). What he meant by this is evident in a speech he gave at one of the meetings: "Reform must begin with society's foundations, where the school system starts. In order to help society to advance, we must free it from its rotten roots—must free humanity from the obstacles that prevent it from becoming free" (Eleni Kaz. 1977:112; 1968a:90). He also turned his attention to the schools themselves, writing out blueprints that he intended to compile in a book on educational reform to be entitled "Letters to My Wife" (Kaz. 1958a:194), a "totally revolutionary" work meant "exclusively for Greece. . . . I'll discuss what should be included in the curriculum of the contemporary Greek school, the nature of our age and of Greek reality, how we should bring up and prepare the new generation. A book totally communistic, without a single compromise, a revolutionary manifesto using the school problem as a pretext" (1958a:190–191; 1979a:93).[10] As examples of his educational prescriptions we have the following:

> Schooling must prepare the child for contemporary life. What is contemporary life? The end of one civilization, the creation of a new civilization. Consequently, we need to prepare fighters in our schools, fighters who will hate the crumbling régime and will battle to overthrow it and to create a new one. (1958a:194–195)
>
> School today must not be a refuge, an island of beauty in the ocean of contemporary ugliness. . . . It must not be far away in a forest. . . . The school today . . . must be in the common, ugly

> environment where the student is destined to live and work as he grows up. The students and their teacher must observe this environment well, must hate it, attempt to change it. . . . And I would say as well: . . . The students should learn to experience injustice and to resist it and protest. They should not have regular meals but should often go hungry and thirsty, should suffer. Healthy bodies—not, however, because they become beautiful in this way, but because they become strong. And to what use will their strength be put? . . . to destroy the old world (the world of their parents) and create a new one. (1958a:173–174; 1979a:86)

> Each person in his given area must destroy, must preach hate, must prepare [future] generations: . . . One-sidedly, consciously, inexorably, irreconcilably. . . . [T]he world is divided into two: good and bad, up and down, God and anti-God. We are God's soldiers, which means that our duty is to hate one half of the world's direction and to love the other half. Later . . . (after our victory, in other words) let people be taught to be harmonious, universal, and tolerant. (1958a:182–183; 1979a:89–90)

All this is relevant to our concerns not only because it shows Kazantzakis attempting to apply his principles to the active life by participating in congresses and making speeches, but also because its one-sidedness, inexorableness, irreconcilability, and intolerance (to turn his own rhetoric against him) paradoxically had to be reconciled, in *Askitikí*, with a totally opposite viewpoint.

If we ask what made Kazantzakis appear so ferocious in Berlin (for he was not so by nature), the answer is undoubtedly the women he met there, especially Rahel Lipstein, with whom he cohabited for a time. They are described in Chapter 25 of *Report to Greco*, so we need not dwell on them here, except to note that they were hushed over in the letters to Galatea! However, the initial encounters with Rahel are narrated with gusto in entries from Kazantzakis's diary that have been printed by Mrs. Kazantzakis (Eleni Kaz. 1977:104–110; 1968a:84–88). These authenticate what we find in the autobiography (Kaz. 1964a:433; 1965c:361), which repeats the following, among other things, with interesting changes:

> "What is your Weltanschauung?" I asked her, and I grasped her shoulder blades, as is my habit, and massaged her skinny shoulders. She bent over to escape, letting out a cry of pain. And then she said: "That we should demolish the world, brother! Hate, brother!" (Eleni Kaz. 1977:106–107; 1968a:86)

Living with such a woman, Kazantzakis, too, became ferocious. Perhaps his admiration for Lipstein and her circle was a psychological compensation for the moment in 1918 when he reacted in a "stereotypically bourgeois way" to the sight of Rosa Luxemburg harranguing a crowd. A man next to him commented: "She must be hysterical. I would marry her off, so she'll calm down." "And I laughed," Kazantzakis recalls with chagrin. "Never in my life had I fallen so low, committed such a great sin. She was crying out. . . . But then we were not listening" (Kaz. 1958e:174). Now Kazantzakis was listening.[11] Later, he melded Luxemburg and Lipstein to create the characters Rahel in *Toda-Raba* and Rala in the *Odyssey*, as well as Mei Ling, the revolutionary female in *Buddha*, and Li-Te in *Le Jardin des rochers*. Lipstein also must have been the original for Noemi in *Kapetán Mihális* and for the Jewess in *Christ Recrucified*. She was one of Kazantzakis's greatest influences.

ASKITIKÍ

The fruit of these intellectual and practical experiences was Kazantzakis's *Salvatores Dei*. *Askitikí*, as he called it when it was first published in the periodical *Anayénnisi* in 1927 (he reversed the title to *Askitikí. Salvatores Dei* for the revised version, issued in 1945). The importance of this work in relation to Kazantzakis's career cannot be overstated. Nikifóros Vrettákos reminds us that it ended a period of over a decade (1910–1923) during which Kazantzakis had published nothing except a few secondary items "of no special interest" (Vrettakos 1977:36). Terminating this relative silence, *Askitikí* was honored by Kazantzakis from the time of its composition until the end of his life as his definitive "credo," the impetus behind all of his subsequent poetry and prose.

The first version (we must keep in mind that the ending was revised in 1928) was begun at the close of December 1922, after Kazantzakis had destroyed the 3,000 verses of his initial attempt at *Buddha* and had commenced a second draft of that play, in prose. But the credo's earliest sketches go back, as we know, to the conclusion of his sojourn in Vienna, when he desired to concentrate on a purely theological work (Kaz. 1958a:63). By the end of March 1923 this work was ready (Mitsotakis 1972:106; Kaz. 1979a:41), although Kazantzakis expected as usual to revise the manuscript many times (Kaz. 1958a:197). The style was a new departure for him, influenced perhaps by the poetic prose of his second try at *Buddha*, perhaps by Nietzsche's *Thus Spake Zarathustra*, Shestov's aphoristic method, and/or the prophetic books of the Old Testament. In any case, afterwards he characterized *Askitikí* as his "lyrical attempt" (Kaz. 1927f:599). It was a lyrical attempt affected as well by the *Spiritual Exercises* of Saint Ignatius of Loyola, which Kazantzakis definitely knew,[12] and, if Prevelákis is correct, by the militant invective of Lenin himself (Prev. 1965b:xlviii). *Askitikí*'s style, in sum, is a mélange of many important influences on Kazantzakis.

If this is true of the style, it is even more true of the contents. Kazantzakis brought together here, and twined, numerous threads from his past—not just the ones he had acquired in Vienna and Berlin. These include the lively awareness of the abyss/Nada/silence so dramatically evoked in *Comedy*;[13] Poincaré's view, invoked by Kazantzakis as early as 1909 (1958h:1378), that life is a brief incident between eternities of death, consciousness a lightning flash between two endless nights; Dragoúmis's "first I must sense my self somehow or other; as soon as I analyze this well, I shall also sense my nation more deeply. From my nation I arrive at the other nations; afterwards I return to myself and see humanity" (Dragoumis 1926:124); Pascal's "Le silence éternel de ces espaces infinis m'effraie," copied by Kazantzakis into his notebook; Kant's *Critique of Pure Reason*, first summarized by Kazantzakis in 1909 in his essay "Has Science Gone Bankrupt?" (1958h:1375); Nietzsche, of course—his call for a new table of values aimed at regulating the state; Schopenhauer's subjectivism;[14] Bergson in abundance; Buddhism's vision of the phantasmagoria of nothingness;[15] Sorel's conviction that mythic consciousness, far from inhibiting action, fosters it, and his concurrence with Vico's view that "the barbarism of reflection" signals contemporary Europe's decline (Sorel 1941:98); Shestov's groundlessness; Spengler's prediction, based on historical "law," that the transitional age would be ended by "a new element of inwardness," a "second religiousness" starting with "rationalism's fading out in helplessness" (Spengler 1980:I, 424; II, 310).

Askitikí is normally treated as a philosophical or religious work, which it surely is (in part). Philosophically it may be described as a lyrical exposition of subjectivism. The subjectivist bias is confirmed in *Le Jardin des rochers*, where Kazantzakis defines the ασκητής as he who "masters the rebellious forces of nature and gives them the form decreed by his mind" (Kaz. 1959b:53; 1963b:48). Religiously, the work is theological in the sense that it discusses the nature that god will assume in his "future appearance" (Eleni Kaz. 1977:214; 1968a:171). Unsurprisingly, the future god discovered/invented by Kazantzakis is none other than Bergson's *élan vital*. Explaining his faith to Galatea, Kazantzakis declared:

> I firmly believe in the nobility and power of a Spirit that passes through plants, animals, humans, and is now consciously struggling inside me, wanting to surpass me, to free itself from my unworthy nature. . . . (1958a:222; 1979a:100)

Since this god evolves creatively as opposed to fulfilling a teleological plan, he (she? it?) is "not omniscient, all-good, omnipotent" (1958a:223; 1979a:101) but instead must struggle to escape his defects. In this struggle—this creative evolution of the cosmos—humans play an essential role; indeed, they save god instead of being saved by him:

> This struggle of his I feel inside me; I am one of his minor military camps. . . . And to the degree that I struggle, he struggles too; to the degree that I ascend, he ascends. . . . The ascent is endless. I shall die in the middle of the journey, but my spirit will unite with his Spirit and will leap to all bodies and continue the march. (1958a:223; 1979a:101)

> My god . . . does not save us. We save him. Salvatores Dei! What does this mean? From the ephemeral clay that is our existence, we rescue the eternal spirit; we transubstantiate flesh, air, water. . . . Out of matter we manufacture Spirit in this bodily workshop of ours, freeing god. Our lives have no other purpose. (Mitsotakis 1972:97; Kaz. 1979a:38–39)

This conception of god's nature dictates a specific form of behavior. As in other religious systems, the key in Kazantzakis's is service: "I struggle to serve this Spirit because I know that it—and not this sack of bones, flesh, brain, and passions that I carry round—is the essence of my soul" (Kaz. 1958a:222; 1979a:100). But service, at least for the high priests of the faith, requires previous understanding, or perhaps one should say "initiation"; hence Kazantzakis's spiritual exercises, like Loyola's, are a systematic training for the ascent to a knowledge of god. "I am currently writing 'Askitikí,' " he informed Galatea, "a mystical book where I lay out the method by which the soul ascends from one circle to the next until it reaches the supreme Contact. There are five circles: self, humanity, world, universe, god" (1958a:133; 1979a:78). An alternative formulation, this one dispatched to Papastefánou, lists four steps, the number employed by Loyola: "I have started . . . a new book, totally mystical: Salvatores Dei. Its purpose is to teach the method of salvation briefly, in simple words. It is divided into four successively wider circles: (1) exodus from the self, (2) exodus from humanity and the world, (3) exodus from the universe, (4) exodus from exodus. Each circle has its decalogue, its spiritual training (άσκησις), its virtues" (Mitsotakis 1972:94; Kaz. 1979a: 36–37).

Religiously, *Askitikí* is a gospel ("good news") containing a theology, a method of initiation into the knowledge of god, and a prescription for behavior. In other words, it contains a doctrine, a ritual, and a morality. And, like other gospels, it is meant to be spread.

Voices that cry in the wilderness do sometimes attract occasional listeners. Kazantzakis had gathered unto himself his Berlin cell group and also (he hoped) Reverend Papastefánou in Ohio, to whom he wrote:

> Here I've found a nucleus . . . who received our religion ardently, and whose lives have been changed. . . . I'm aware of you, far away, struggling in your own right and calling out. . . . Without fail we must found churches in various places. . . . I am impatient to finish *Askitikí* and to send it to you for your comments . . . before I have it translated (into Hebrew and Russian to begin with), printed, and secretly distributed to the catechumens.
>
> . . . [A]s soon as I can I'm going to leave for Russia. . . . If only I had your warmth . . . ! I think I'd be able to proclaim a new crusade against contemporary civilization and to flood Europe with millions of starving, divinely-inspired Russians. . . . Lord, the world has gone rotten. We must plant a new one. . . . What is lacking? Seed! I feel that I am holding the seed in my palm, just like a hand grenade. Oh, if only—jumping over the hurdle of reason—I could toss it into humanity's fields! (Mitsotakis 1972:95–96; Kaz. 1979a:37–38)

It should be evident by now that *Askitikí*, although rightly treated as a philosophical and religious tract, should also be viewed as a political one. The world seemed truly rotten to Kazantzakis, requiring a "new perception." Thus one of his purposes in *Askitikí* was to formulate his ideas on communism (Eleni Kaz. 1977:224; 1968a:179). Yet he was not so naïve (despite the extraordinarily naïve letter to Papastefánou just quoted) to overlook his distance from the communists of his day—witness his use of the term "metacommunist" in the prefatory note to the 1927 edition (see Kaz. 1960b:22). At this point it would be well to know precisely what he meant by that term. In January 1927 he published a lengthy and rather diffuse article on the subject under the title "Crucified Russia." We will encounter this in Chapter Five. Meanwhile, here are two other formulations that are more precise. The first constitutes an ideally succinct definition while the second offers a helpful gloss on that definition:

> [1] Metacommunism is the second stage of communism—the creative stage. The first stage is the destructive one. (Darakis 1935)

> [2] Marx gave [the masses] a faith. What are this faith's chief characteristics? Two: (1) materialism; (2) worship of the machine. Soviet Russia's ideal is America. . . . Communism's mission is not the creation of a new civilization but the dissolution of bourgeois civilization. Communism is the end, not the beginning. It has all the symptoms of the end: unadulterated materialism, hypertrophy of rationality, fatal dissolution of every faith that surpasses the five senses, deification of practical goals. . . . We must . . . intensify all of communism's tendencies to the extreme so that salvation

> may arrive that much sooner. What salvation? The destruction of this world and the beginning of the creation of another . . . in which the worship of the machine, of rationality, and of practical goals will be considered unworthy. . . . (Prev. 1965b:154–155)

Summarizing all this, I would say that when Kazantzakis called *Askitikí* his metacommunistic credo, he meant a theology of activism justifying the destruction of capitalism's decadent remains in the interests not so much of economic or social justice (materialistic progress) as of a vital inwardness higher in the spiritual scale than either capitalism or communism—in the interests, more precisely, of an inwardness capable of discovering and honoring the Kazantzakian world-view! For Kazantzakis, the aim of revolution was to raise human beings sufficiently in the evolutionary scale to make them understand what he himself had understood about ultimate reality.

NEEDLESS TO SAY, this did not appeal to the communists of his day.[16] As a Greek critic commented in 1977, "the Nouveau Philosophes . . . of contemporary France would have shuddered with delight [at Kazantzakis's metacommunism]; however, in 1922 or 1927 metacommunism could be translated only into anticommunism" (Frangopoulos 1977:56). *Askitikí* was vulnerable to attack by Marxist rationalists as being far too mystical. But it was also vulnerable to attack for precisely the opposite reason: as being far too theoretical. Although Kazantzakis purported to be inveighing against rationalism in favor of myth, as Sorel and others had taught him, his book was clearly a product of the very reflectiveness that Sorel scorned as decadent. If he had been as important as Georg Lukács, who in 1922 wrote *History and Class Consciousness*—a book similar to *Askitikí* in its "messianic utopianism" and its stress on "the overcoming of artificial separations between activity and consciousness"—and if, furthermore, Kazantzakis's book had been read by Lenin, as Lukács's was, the verdict would presumably have been the same: "too 'contemplative' ": in short, "theory incapable of generating a real practice" (Hitchens 1971).

On the other hand, we should honor Kazantzakis's independence. Although writing at a time of revolutionary euphoria and before the barbarities of Stalin, he disdained to follow the party line. As Frangópoulos comments, he preferred to "remain always in no-man's land"; his refusal to engage in the way expected of him should be a lesson for those who perhaps are in too much of a hurry to take sides today (Frangópoulos 1977:56). Kazantzakis "does not offer solutions" (Anghelaki-Rooke 1977: 133). As he was to say in self-defense in 1930 or 1931, "I wanted . . . to enlighten as many as possible—communists and bourgeois. . . . Therefore I satisfied neither the communists nor the bourgeois. No matter. My aim was not to satisfy anyone, but to tell the truth. I am neither a narrow-minded denier nor a superficial panegyrist. This is because I am not a man of practical activity but someone who has set as his life's goal the effort to think and to articulate his thought" (Prev. 1965b:229).

So Kazantzakis's consciously contemplative metacommunistic credo is probably incapable of generating a real practice. Nevertheless, let us not forget its monistic aspiration to fuse contemplation with action, theology with practicality. We know that Kazantzakis, less sober in 1922 than in 1930 or 1931, was sufficiently swept up in the revolutionary euphoria of Berlin to believe that he was writing a political as well as a religious document. The major importance of *Askitikí*, I repeat, is the way it manages by prestidigitation to be a theology of activism, incorporating recipes for political action within a pessimistic world-view.

IT WOULD BE WELL, accordingly, to dwell on this fusion some more. Despite his convictions about ultimate futility, Kazantzakis preached neither a Buddhistic search for nirvana nor a Greek Orthodox quest for ataraxia, the imperturbation of noninvolvement.[17] After informing Papastefánou about the four circles of his *Salvatores Dei*, all of which are exoduses from everyday practical contacts in the interest of an ultimate Contact with the nonmaterial essence, he added, surprisingly: "From the highest circle the highest initiates descend to everyday life, act with mankind, live, work, get married—but with an altogether new light" (Mitsotakis 1972:94; Kaz. 1979a:37). I emphasize once again that Kazantzakis's aim was not to lead contemplators permanently away from involvement but rather to send them back into the world furnished with his own understanding of ultimate reality. This is why, in *Le Jardin des rochers*, he calls the god proclaimed in *Askitikí* the anti-Buddha, insisting that this god "believes in matter": "endeavors, sweating, to transform a little flesh into spirit," as opposed to Buddha, who craves either "absolute annihilation or else eternal union with the universe" (1959b:222, 219; 1963b:186, 185, 183). And this is why, in the part of *Askitikí* called "Action," the final section in the credo's original form, before the 1928 revision, he includes the anti-Buddhistic, antisubjectivist statement that this world "is not a deception, a multicolored phantasmagoria of our mirroring mind," but instead the visible sign of what is in effect Bergson's *élan vital* in its struggle with the descending force that wishes "to come to a standstill, to die" (1927f:628; 1962a:84; 1960b:119). All this explains Kazantzakis's ability to defend his metaphysic to Galatea as "a tool, a plough for this earth, a weapon for today's struggle" (1958a:205; 1979a:98) and to insist to Elsa Lange that his method as he expounded it in *Salvatores Dei* "does not involve a denial of spirit and body, but rather aims at the conquest of them through the prowess of spirit and body" (Eleni Kaz. 1968a:125–126).

If we ask in what precise way Kazantzakis's method achieves the goal of amalgamating activism and nihilism, the answer will involve factors with which we are already familiar. His god can evolve only through matter; thus we, the visible signs of the *élan vital*'s struggle upward through matter toward dematerialization, can and must help god in his progress. The only way we can do this is by avoiding the stagnation that strengthens Bergson's descending force. Hence we must act energetically to increase the world's motion or, in the Kazantzakian cliché, to transubstantiate flesh into spirit, flesh being in Bergson's system characterized by inertia, spirit by freedom. The morality of Kazantzakis's spiritual training thus becomes all too simple: "The greatest sin is satisfaction" (1958a:223; 1979a:101). Whatever fosters change and instability is good; whatever abets the status quo is bad.

But these prescriptions are still too general. Kazantzakis knew that to provide a precise formula for vital, creative action would be a contradiction in terms, since creative evolution must be nonformulaic. To escape this dilemma he had recourse to the doctrine of the transitional age. The ways of saving god are many. In various ages men and women as diverse as Jesus, Genghis Khan, Lenin, Zorbás, Buddha, and Rosa Luxemburg have been saviors of god, each in his or her own way. But not all paths are applicable in a given era. For each transitional age there is a dominant method for fighting stagnation and liberating the flame. There is also a dominant group that applies this method. Kazantzakis's nonformulaic formula is that we must seek out the group in our own age that seems to have the greatest and sincerest vitality, the group whose actions most effectively enhance motion, creativity, and freedom, thereby bringing new, open-ended possibilities as opposed to completion. In our own age, he concludes, the way chosen by the ascending spirit is communist revolution. The successive steps in the logic leading to this conclusion are clarified in various glosses, among which we have one that is contemporaneous with the writing of *Askitikí*:

> Every day now I feel that the highest form of the idea is action. . . . Thus, enlightened by the supreme investigation of God's struggle, I must see what this era in which I was born is, and how I, in this era, can help God in his ascent to the best of my ability. I am interested neither in what humanity's duty was in bygone eras ("duty": that is, *the form that was taken by mankind's assistance to God*) nor in what it is going to be in future eras. The only duty I look at is my own in a depleted era that cries out as it engenders a new world. . . . Every day the features of my God be-

> come stabilized into those of an austere . . . general in the contemporary battle between opposing forces that are eternal. More specifically, today my God leads the dark proletarian masses who are fighting to win their freedom from bourgeois abomination and injustice. . . . His former allies, having lost their momentum, nobility and creative spirit, have become obstacles; my God clutches at the class that, in pain, wishes—and is able—to engender children. He will abandon this class as well, like the others, as soon as it, too, becomes an obstacle. (Mitsotakis 1972:107–108; Kaz. 1979a:41–42)

Since for Kazantzakis the highest form of the idea is action and since his theological initiates are meant to descend to everyday life and re-establish contact with struggling mankind after their supreme Contact with essence, Kazantzakis ends his program for spiritual training (in its unrevised form) with three concluding beatitudes that no longer appear in the version available to us today but are printed in Greek in the Τετρακόσια γράμματα του Καζαντζάκη στον Πρεβελάκη (Prev. 1965b:l–li) and in English in Kimon Friar's useful preface to his translation of *Askitikí* (Kaz. 1960b:32). After the fifth verse-paragraph of the final exorcism or incantation—"O Lord, you cry out: 'Help me! Help me!' You cry out, O Lord, and I hear"—the first version ends with:

> Blessed be all those who hear, because they shall be saved, by fighting.
>
> Blessed be all those who are saved, because they free God, by creating.
>
> Blessed be all those who on their shoulders bear the Supreme Responsibility.

Having climbed the philosophical circles of initiation higher and higher, at their summit we are brought back down to earth via our duty to assist God by becoming (in this particular transitional age) revolutionary communists.

I HAVE PURPOSELY explicated *Askitikí* up to now with the aid of external glosses because these glosses, exempted as they are from the text's lyricism, tend to be more straightforward than the text itself. Now that we possess what I hope is an adequate familiarity with *Askitikí*'s basic ingredients, I want to begin again from the beginning in order to offer a running commentary. If I risk becoming tedious, I do so because *Askitikí* is of such central importance in Kazantzakis's work and because many readers even today find its ideas difficult to follow.

Askitikí's basic ingredients are everything that we have been discussing:

the two abysses, the luminous interval between, the relation of that interval to the abysses, god's nature, our duty to save him, and how to do this in our own transitional age. Not willing simply to tell us the conclusions of his philosophical quest, Kazantzakis leads us through the systematic training (áskisis) necessary for enlightenment. Like W. B. Yeats in *A Vision*, he fits one set of gyres within another set that points in the opposite direction: while one spiral progression proceeds in a Bergsonian way from the broadest circle of awareness to the precise point that is our person, the other progression begins with this personal center and proceeds outward ever more broadly to the whole.

But enlightenment, no matter how attained, presupposes a theory of knowledge. Accordingly, after a brief prologue that announces the two abysses and the luminous interval between them, then dismisses both the Buddhistic response and the Christian in favor of the Bergsonian,[18] Kazantzakis begins with an epistemological section. Called Η προετοιμασία (The Preparation), this is an abbreviated Kantian critique of pure reason. Dividing reality into phenomena and noumena, it insists that the mind (meaning the ratiocinative faculty) can deal only with the former, although even when concerned with phenomena it merely forces them into the Procrustean bed of its own categories: "I impose order on disorder and give a face—my face—to chaos" (Kaz. 1927f:600; 1962a:12; 1960b: 48). Epistemologically, our first duty is to recognize these limitations of the human mind. As for the noumenal realm, with luck this can be known too—not by the ratiocinative faculty, of course, but by Bergson's intuitive faculty, which Kazantzakis here calls the heart. Our second duty is to attempt to pierce to this unified essence beyond appearances. Let us skip the crucial third duty for a moment, since in the psychology of spiritual questing this can come only after, not before, the next two exercises. In the first of these, Η πορεία (The March), Kazantzakis describes rationality's attempt to understand phenomena; in the second, Το όραμα (The Vision), he describes intuition's attempt to understand noumena. The march employs the method of expanding consciousness; it is a journey through phenomena beginning with the self-centeredness of the infant and ending with the universal awareness of the sage. Although this awareness can tell us only of the relationships among phenomena, it can provide an intimation of the unity underlying the visible world. Thus it prepares us for the heart's vision, which is the next step. Psychologically, this step involves an intuitive awareness that pierces through the divisiveness of clock time to the succession without distinction that characterizes Bergsonian duration: a "momentary eternity that encloses everything, past and future" (Kaz. 1927f:619; 1962a:59; 1960b:94). What is perceived behind time and phenomena is of course primordial energy (Bergson's *élan vital*, as always), struggling painfully upward via matter and transubstantiating that matter into spirit.

Now that the mind and heart have done their work, the next logical step is the third duty, although this will again be held in abeyance, as we shall see in a moment. The mind, which hopes to impose order on the phenomenal realm, imposes on it nothing but relationships derived subjectively from its own categories; the heart, which hopes to apprehend the noumenal realm, apprehends merely a human meaning, a human myth, and imposes this on the unknowable. The third duty, therefore, is to conquer the mind's hope to understand phenomena and the heart's to understand noumena. We abolish these dualities in a joyously monistic acceptance of the meaninglessness of our existence: "Where am I going? Do not ask! . . . Life is good and death is good. . . . I surrender myself to everything. . . . It is your duty . . . to say 'Nothing exists!' " (1927f:604–605; 1962a:24–25; 1960b:58–59).

This would seem to nullify all that went before, but it does not. The final acceptance of meaninglessness, although overriding the previous attempts to discover meaning, does not reject those attempts. Just as the Bergsonian god can achieve the goal of noncongealment only by the laborious process of evolution through congealment, so the acceptance of meaninglessness can be achieved only after a previous conviction that meaning can be found. Only when the mind and heart have labored futilely in pursuit of their respective chimeras do we have the right to proclaim universal futility. This proclamation cannot nullify the previous efforts since those are its own ineluctable precondition. Kazantzakis is telling us that the mind and heart must burn themselves out through aspiration if the freedom of nonaspiration is ever to be achieved. He is telling us, furthermore, that this is the "rhythm" ("course," "process," or "style") followed by the universe itself.

We must remember that Kazantzakis was toiling to discover/invent a rationale for action while remaining within the framework of philosophical pessimism. His conclusion is that we are meant to try to make the world a better place not in spite of the twin abysses but because of them. This is his metacommunistic credo.

Accordingly, the spiritual exercises end (in the original version) with a section on practical behavior. The third duty must be held in abeyance until we have burned ourselves out. Kazantzakis passes directly from "The Vision" to Η πράξη (The Action), reminding us that once we have discovered "the rhythm of God's march" (1927f:620; 1962a:62; 1960b:100), our responsibility is to adjust the course of our small and fleeting lives to that larger course. This section begins with a metaphysics of action, specifying the proper relationship between man and god; it proceeds to a morality of action, specifying a relationship between man and man in which behavior is based on groundlessness and good and evil are defined, respectively, as "whatever surges upward and hastens to God's aid" and "whatever moves downward and hinders God's ascent" (1927f:623; 1962a:72; 1960b:108). The final section insists that our actions should push nature forward in the evolutionary process, reminding us that each person must do this in his or her own fashion. Kazantzakis follows this (in the original version) with a recapitulation of the third duty but then concludes positively with a call to everyone to shoulder the "supreme responsibility" of saving god in the world of objects, here and now.

How was *Askitikí* received? Kazantzakis had it translated into German at the end of 1923 (Kaz. 1958a:231) and sent it off in this form to the Soviet Union. Two months later he heard that some readers there were so profoundly moved that they wished to invite him to come and instruct them (1958a:248). Generally, however, his credo was ignored. In cases where it was not, it was praised for the wrong reasons (with a few notable exceptions) or condemned.[19] Kazantzakis was dismayed: "It's a question of whether three souls can be found here to agree with it" (Eleni Kaz. 1977:207; 1968a:165). "Greece is smothering me. No one here is my comrade; no one is capable of sensing my spiritual anguish. They all . . . treat *Askitikí* as a work of art, no one as a cry of searching and terror—because no one has that cry inside him" (Eleni Kaz. 1977:207). He concluded, "*Askitikí* . . . will be heard after my death. At this point people understand only the poetic form" (Eleni Kaz. 1977:214; 1968a:171).

Truly, during his lifetime (and after his death as well) the book had very little effect on the Greek reading public, although it did acquire a small circle of admirers (Evelpidis 1958:240).[20] The situation is well analyzed by one of the most sensitive of Kazantzakis's critics, Nikifóros Vrettákos:

> I was a high school student [in 1927] when *Askitikí* came out in book format. . . . I took hold of it then with great expectation, but it gave me the impression that . . . we were dealing with nothing but style. I . . . was in no position to discern his *kravyí* and to relate it to the times and to its author. Later, I viewed *Askitikí* differently, within the totality of his *oeuvre*. . . .
>
> *Askitikí* did not enjoy the response that Kazantzakis expected. . . . There were two reasons for this practically indifferent reception. When you subtracted the poetic elaborations . . . , it did not say anything new, philosophically. Beyond this, his narrowly personal nihilism . . . could not find acceptance . . . because the allure of life—especially here in Greece—as a rule restricts nihilism to the intellect, leaving the heart and soul untouched. . . . He wanted to say cosmogonic things and instead

> uttered nothing but a *kravyí* which his readers at that time, if they failed to hear it, did not miss. (Vrettakos 1977:38–40)

Thus Vrettákos concludes his bitter analysis, or all but concludes it, for in a final paragraph he goes on to declare: "Kazantzakis's own consciousness of [the public's indifference] incited him to march with even greater anguish toward the work generated out of his despair, the *Odyssey*."[21]

It is understandable that Vrettákos should wish to lead us directly from Kazantzakis's disappointment in 1927 to his engagement with the epic voyage of Odysséas. The *Odyssey* is truly *Askitikí* writ large, as though Kazantzakis were proclaiming to his indifferent public, "You failed to notice my brief exposition of mind, heart, and soul; now, by god, I'll translate it into something so gargantuan that to fail to notice it will be impossible!" Yet Vrettákos is also misleading, because what came after *Askitikí*'s poor reception was not the *Odyssey*'s first draft but its second, in 1930, and also because much intervened between 1927 and 1930. The second draft was incited not just by Kazantzakis's failure to be appreciated in Greece in 1927 but by a quite different failure there in 1928 and by still another failure in Russia itself that convinced him that the Soviets were not ready for metacommunism. These repeated disappointments in the area of application drove him away from the life of direct participation in mankind's struggles. The highest form of the idea was action, but if action met only with frustration, the idea could always be elaborated once again on paper.

All this concerns the second draft. In its initial draft, the epic was begun in the winter of 1925, before *Askitikí*'s publication, and was completed in 1927 on the precise day (22 September) on which Kazantzakis complained that everyone was treating *Askitikí* as a work of art, no one as a cry of searching and terror. In a loose sense, Vrettákos is still helpful, because the connections between *Askitikí* and the second draft hold true as well for the first draft in that this, too, (a) elaborated *Askitikí*'s philosophic system and (b) reacted to a failure in application.

This prior failure is what we must now examine.

CHAPTER FOUR

The Iráklion incident and the *Odyssey's* first draft

Men can only be happy when they do not assume that the object of life is happiness.
—George Orwell (1961:248)

ITALY: BUDDHA, SAINT FRANCIS

Having completed his metacommunistic credo, Kazantzakis thirsted to apply his doctrine. But the question was how and where. In Berlin, the few who listened to his preaching were Russians and Poles, not Greeks (Kaz. 1958a:121; 1979a:73). We have seen that he dispatched *Askitikí* to the Soviet Union; although he claimed to have no illusions about the Russians, he felt that on balance "their souls are the deepest, darkest, most luminous, most God-bearing in today's world. In other times it was the Indians, Greeks, Arabs, Europeans—today it is the Russians" (Kaz. 1958a:179). On another occasion he announced that he had determined to live in that "divine, horrible, and excellent chaos" (Kaz. 1958a:115; 1979a:70). In sum, he was apparently clear about what should happen next:

> I've made up my mind to leave for Russia. I don't know when. I have to get ready. I'm learning Russian now, and in a few days I'm going to go to a craftsman here [in Berlin] who has a shop, to learn a trade—carpentry. In this way I'll work three hours a day in Russia, making the rounds from village to village. There I'll test the Word I bring. (1958a:120; 1979a:72)

But things were not so simple. First of all, in the back of his mind Kazantzakis always felt Greece to be his proper place, despite his scorn for Hellenes and Hellenic civilization; even at the height of his enthusiasm for the plan to settle in the Soviet Union he envisioned himself writing revolutionary books in his homeland, perhaps while languishing in jail (1958a:195). Secondly and more importantly, he never conquered his basic aversion to the active life. His activism was forced, not natural. It arose in part out of a kind of panic that—like Orestes in "Spasménes psihés"—he had accomplished nothing in his life. His problem was the fate that had made him ineluctably an intellectual: someone condemned to see the complications in human affairs and consequently to be caught in the middle when one-sided conclusions were required: "I have no illusions—unfortunately. That's the source of all my weakness. If I had illusions I would conquer ridicule, . . . I would become a man of action" (1958a: 127; 1979a:75).

It is hard to say which of these two—panic or lack of illusions—displayed the bitter truth to Kazantzakis in a dream at the start of January 1924, precisely at the transition point between his sojourn in Berlin and whatever was to come next. This is how he recorded the dream in his notebook:

> There was a war going on and the general looked at me and said: "Don't go away! Come and fight with the rest of us!" A slight horror visited my body. Fear. In my dreams, whenever I dream that I'm going to war or being exposed to danger, I'm always overcome by shudders of fear, whereas in my waking life I've always appeared brave every time I've had the occasion to be tested. However, since I'm not [brave] in my dreams, I think that down deep I'm a coward. Yet because I'm ashamed of myself, I manage out of pride to control my fear and to be brave. I stood there trembling, resolved to fight. The general thought a bit and added: "But you can't fight on the right, because you look also to the left. Nor on the left, because you look also to the right. So you'll carry ammunition right and left, to both camps." (Eleni Kaz. 1977:124–125; 1968a:103)

The tensions revealed so interestingly in this dream presumably help to explain the repeated bouts of melancholy, indecision, and self-laceration recorded in Kazantzakis's letters to Galatea, for example:

> Last night as I lay down to go to sleep I was so sad I couldn't hold back the tears. . . . I write, read, listen to music, and nothing consoles me. I'm working on a plan to go to Russia, and I know what awaits me there and am unable to give myself over entirely to the joy and illusion of the new journey. (1958a:132–133; 1979a:77)

> If I could only make the "leap," could only leave my writings and poetry behind me on the opposite bank and speak to mankind, without judging, without feeling ashamed, without weighing [pros and cons]. . . . If I could only speak and incite people regarding the problems of their daily life today. . . . Everything is clear and complete in my mind, but I lack the strength to jump the fence and conquer ridicule. . . . (1958a:150)

Again we must wonder about the real cause of such agonizing. Negatively, I have suggested panic; positively, intellectual integrity. To these I wish now to add mythomania, a concept we shall encounter again at the very end of volume two when we consider Kazantzakis's so-called autobiography, *Report to Greco*. Kazantzakis in Berlin in 1923 seems remarkably like his early characters in *Serpent and Lily* and *Day Is Breaking* since both they and he are caught in a trap. Author and characters alike crave an exit, a therapy for the world-weariness symptomatic of the *mal de siècle*. His earliest fictional creations found no exit save death. A later one, the Master Builder, displayed the resolute voluntarism that Kazantzakis had learned from Dragoúmis and that he himself had been attempting at that time to channel into nationalistic endeavors. Now, revolutionary communism had replaced the previous two "solutions." But the psychological basis in all cases, including the last, was the same—the burden of entrapment in wearisome meaninglessness: "Theory has value only as a preparation; the crucial struggle is the active one. . . . We must find a task that all of us . . . can devote ourselves to. . . . *Only thus will we conquer life's tedium*" (Kaz. 1958a:171; 1979a:85; my italics).

This confession issuing from Kazantzakis's days of fervent communism unmasks the psychological continuity of similar motivations operative in supposedly different periods. But just as the motivations were essentially similar, so too were the diverse therapies for curing ennui: these were allotropic states of the same basic element: mythomania. What this means is that Kazantzakis's real solution in each case was not the power to change the world but rather the power to change the eyes with which we see the world. In each case he invented an imaginative substitute for reality and then attempted to act in terms of that chimera as if it were real. The earliest example, in *Serpent and Lily*, is of course obvious; the novel's main point is that mythomania brings salvation. Regarding nationalist endeavor, Kazantzakis's subjectivist assumptions are articulated in his essay on Yánnis Stavridákis, the man whom he considered the prototypical nationalist. In this essay, he makes Stavridákis subordinate patriotism to the requirements of Kazantzakis's own heroic pessimism. "Greece, mission, and duty are meaningless. Yet it is proper for us willfully to sacrifice ourselves for that nothing. . . . I think that there must be no higher religion . . . than the cultivation of purposeless heroism" (Kaz. 1927b:364, 369). If the tensions, misgivings and self-lacerations evident in the communist period seem missing in the nationalist one, perhaps the reason is that the Stavridakian mythomania was not so far out of step with "reality" since the entire nation had fallen prey to the chimera called the Megáli Idéa. To apply one's subjectivism in the Russian context was not so easy. The Soviets' problem according to Kazantzakis was lack of vision: they were positivistic to a fault. But quite aside from the exacerbation in this instance, Kazantzakis's difficulty always arose from a fundamental contradiction. His only hope to escape life's tedium came from the successive chimeras manufactured so readily by his mythomania. Yet these, because unreal, could never be applied to life without causing further difficulties that only increased his anguish. In short, the solutions became problems in their own right. Nevertheless, Kazantzakis was typically unwilling (except in *Report to Greco*) to turn his back on reality and make a virtue of his mythomania per se. Behind the immediate question of how and where to act lay this fundamental difficulty.

This knowledge should mute our surprise when we learn that his next project was to complete his play *Buddha* (Kaz. 1958a:261) at the same time that he continued his revolutionary dreaming.[1] He was now in Italy, having failed to arrange either to travel to Russia or to connect with the revolutionary movement in Germany (Prev. 1965b:li). But most of his attention during the Italian sojourn was directed toward Saint Francis. Given Kazantzakis's aspiration to combine theology and politics, Francis was a compatible figure, someone who, while obviously a religious genius, was at the same time, in Kazantzakis's opinion, "a great, idealistic communist" who saw "that the source of every evil is private ownership and forbade . . . his disciplines to have any property whatsoever, small or large" (1958a:258; 1979a:106). Reviewing the extent of Francis's accomplishment against overwhelming odds, Kazantzakis reaffirmed his conviction that "nothing can happen without faith" and vowed to follow, like Francis, "this road that renews life." Specifically, he wished to use the power of faith "to create a soul different from the bourgeois one" and then to "act entirely differently from the bourgeoisie" (1958a:260; 1979a:107).

So Francis, despite Kazantzakis's simultaneous attention to Buddha, was not a detour away from politics but merely a delay: one more imaginative mask donned to fortify him against the moment when action would indeed be demanded.

IRÁKLION: PRAXIS

At precisely this time, an opportunity presented itself—moreover, an opportunity to act in Greece. We remember Kazantzakis's vision of himself writing revolutionary books in his homeland, perhaps while languishing in jail. This was in May 1923. He could not have suspected then how close to fulfillment this vision was going to come a year and a half later, when he was summoned to trial for illegal political activity, spent a night in prison,[2] and composed a succinct defense of his revolutionary thought.

I call this episode the Iráklion incident. It haunted Kazantzakis for the rest of his life, entering *Víos ke politía tu Aléksi Zorbá*, for example and, more fundamentally, Ο Χριστός ξανασταυρώνεται.[3] Its immediate effect was to launch the *Odyssey*.

We first hear of the problem in question in a letter to Galatea posted from Assisi sometime between 1 March and 13 April 1924. The veterans from the disastrous Asia Minor campaign who had returned to Iráklion were publishing a newspaper called Φωνή του Εφέδρου (Voice of the Reservist). Galatea had sent Kazantzakis an issue containing a communication from her to the editor in which she counseled the veterans to hate and be inflexible—suggestions that Kazantzakis in his reply praised as "corresponding perfectly to my soul." He promised to write in his turn in order to "encourage them." They must be "simple folk made fools of by Iráklion's 'intellectuals,' " he continued; "so it's a good and brave deed for the two of us to stand by their side." But then, as a foretaste of what was to ensue when he actually established himself as a guru for these "simple folk," he added in a Sorelian vein: "I'll write them about the need for all this struggle to be transubstantiated into the unshakable faith that we shall win. We shall win not because it is 'just' and 'ethical' for the common people to be relieved of suffering, but above all because—whether we like it or not, realize it or not—this is the invincible course of human history" (Kaz. 1958a:256–257; 1979a:105). In short, his purpose was to gain new initiates for his myth.

At this point he was not aware of the problem's ramifications. And it is difficult for us, too, to acquire a precise knowledge of what was happening, since Kazantzakis's letters and diaries describe only his own involvement. Fortunately, however, there are other sources. From Elli Alexíou we learn that the veterans had returned to find their homes in ruins whereas people who had not served their country had meanwhile prospered (Elli Alexiou 1966:297). Stérgios Spanákis, secretary in 1924–1925 of the Central Union of Reservist Combatants and Army Casualties (*Nea Efimeris* 24 Dec. 1924:3), a communist organization, reminds us that many of these veterans had been continuously under arms since the Balkan Wars of 1912–1913 and that they had returned to Iráklion in 1922 accompanied by floods of refugees from Asia Minor. Once home, they found an acute shortage of employment as well as housing and farmland. The government failed to satisfy their needs; the reservists decided to organize; the government attempted to suppress the movement—and into the eye of the storm stepped Kazantzakis (Spanakis 1962:49). Still further information is contained in *Toda-Raba*, which helps us to understand the government's fear. Evidently the reservists were not alone in their discontent. In the novel's opening chapter we find (a remarkably Kazantzakian) Géranos still in Crete, where "men exploit men" but where "there are some men who suffer and struggle and do not forgive [cf. Galatea's advice to hate and be inflexible]: some tobacco workers . . . , longshoremen, sailors, and poor cripples from the war" (Kaz. 1962c:11; 1964f:15). This working-class solidarity is confirmed by other sources. It suggests that the fear of a general uprising among the unemployed, exploited, and dispossessed is what put the authorities on edge. The same passage goes on to tell us how Géranos approached these "simple folk": he "understood all this suffering, but he endeavored to isolate it above the individuals who were suffering, and to discover a *metaphysical synthesis* of these earthly struggles" (italics added)—to discover, we may surmise, a Bergsonian metacommunistic explanation rather than the Marxist-sounding "invincible course of human history" that Kazantzakis had planned to reveal to the reservists when in Assisi he first learned of their difficulties.

So far, none of these sources has openly specified another principal factor in the Iráklion imbroglio—communism. Fortunately, one of Iráklion's daily newspapers, *Néa Efimerís*, covered the situation extensively, opening its columns to all viewpoints, including Kazantzakis's, although the editor, Elias Dialinás, was firmly anticommunist. A perusal of the paper from the autumn of 1924 to the winter of 1924–1925 alerts us to this other factor and to many additional ones in an extraordinarily complicated situation. In December, for example, Dialinás in his lead article was saying that Iráklion's few communists should realize that they were becoming ridiculous in the eyes of most of the city's inhabitants, who ignore them because their "intellectual disease presents so little danger" to the great majority. At the same time, he described the German communists' success in exploiting the desire of the masses for reform, and warned his readers that communism was the "supreme brutalization of the human being" since communists deny precisely those attributes that constitute our humanity, namely "worship of God, esteem for the family, obedience to law, love of country, and respect for the institution of private property" (*Nea Efimeris*, 12 Dec. 1924)—a litany that will be heard again in *Christ Recrucified*. Two months later, however, things had flared up in Iráklion to such an extent that the communists could no longer be dismissed so easily. The igniting spark was the temporary expulsion of the Ecumenical Patriarch from Istanbul, an event that had roused Greece to a frenzy of bellicose patriotism. *Néa Efimerís* for 7 February 1925 describes how the local communists came out into the open in order to incite the reservists to oppose a new war against Turkey, arguing that the veterans should not go to fight "ya éna paliopappá ke ya mía pórni patrída" ("for a lousy old priest and a whore-motherland"). The same article explains that Emmanuel Kakoudákis, chief of Iráklion's communist youth, having failed to find other supporters after 1922, "insinuated himself into the masses of upstanding reservists, who unsuspectingly followed as he organized them into reservist societies for the purpose of claiming their rights." It notes as well that Kakoudákis "propagandized the reservists through the *Foní tu Efédru*, now identified as the organ of the young communist league. A later article (31 March, p. 1) describes how the local communists were attempting to "help" (that is, seduce) workers, farmers, reservists, and Asia Minor refugees through International Red Aid.

These testimonies assist us in comprehending how broadly based was the unrest that Kazantzakis discovered in Iráklion when he returned there, and how central was the role of the city's communist cadre in bringing things to a boil. The testimonies also give us sufficient background to begin to follow Kazantzakis's involvement in some detail, insofar as the surviving records permit.

Kazantzakis left Italy at the end of April, spent the next two months in Athens, where he met Eléni Samíou for the first time, and traveled to Crete on 5 July. The new relationship with the young Miss Samíou, who remained in Athens, accounts for some long letters that reveal Kazantzakis's very mixed emotions upon returning to his provincial birthplace after experiencing so much of interest in sophisticated Vienna and Berlin. Mrs. Kazantzakis informs us that he already had two antithetical plans in mind: "to meet the cadre of the Communist Party with the hope of offering them his experience, and to shut himself away somewhere in absolute solitude so that the floodgates might open and the *Odyssey*, which was about to drown him, pour out" (Eleni Kaz. 1977:26; 1968a:24). Perhaps it was the discouraging reunion with his immediate family and his relatives that sent him so quickly to the city's communists:

> . . . Mother [asked] . . . why I'd lost weight . . . [and] when I was going to stop. The relatives started to arrive: the female cousins as fat as can be—provincial fat—the male ones fat, millionaires. A gulf between us; they viewed me as a peculiar, incomprehensible fruit of the family tree. . . . I think of Berlin, the fever there of human anguish . . . , my cruel duty to reject mother and father, to go far away from them, against them, against their morality, religion, social prejudices, economic endeavors. Last night I talked to my father about Bolshevism a little. He flew into a rage, fell silent, rose, and went upstairs to his room—his greatest possible expression of indignation. (Eleni Kaz. 1977:27–28; 1968a:24–25)

An entry in his diary for 15 July, which he also copied out and dispatched as a letter to Samíou in Athens, records that each day he met "secretly with the leaders of the communist movement" in order to draw up "the plan of the future battle."

> There are about ten of them, simple, uneducated, strong minds, warm ardent souls . . . like a woman in love waiting expectantly for the spirit to descend upon them in the form of a man and fructify them. The whole sea, the whole vision of solitude and eternity, is still in my eyes—the whole "Circle"—and suddenly [when

> I am] among these poor, simple "fishers of men" there leaps up inside me the ephemeral, flaming love for humanity, this despairing frenzied age in which I happen to have been born, and the full Circle contracts into a fiery point—immediate action.
>
> I say: These comrades constitute the lowest, the first, degree of initiation in my religion. They rush forward to be saved—they themselves—from injustice and poverty. They are insects who believe that the honey of flowers was created so that they could eat and be filled.
>
> The second degree is: We do not fight for ourselves but for humanity. We must save humanity, not our insignificant ephemeral selves.
>
> The third and highest degree is: We fight neither for ourselves nor for humanity. All of us, whether we like it or not, realize it or not—plants, animals, humans, ideas—are fighting for the salvation of God.
>
> This is the complete, firmly planted Askitikí. It does not issue from the whim of a single person but from the soil, like an oak. I am glad that it was my good fortune to put down the roots of my God here in this paternal soil. . . . I have to plough this group well, to adapt it to today's needs, to employ this local form of contemporary worldwide discontent, . . . and to find today's simplest, most compelling expression for my mystical theogony. Today, willy-nilly, the first degree of initiation is communist revolution. "Let this world be destroyed. Let it be destroyed by force. Let us be ready!" These are the three articles of faith I gave to my Cretan comrades.
>
> Oh, if only my flesh were equal to my mind! Sometimes African lightning bolts pass across my sight and I shout: Yes, I am ready! But then they fade. . . . We'll see . . . (Kaz. 1924a)

Much of this sounds familiar: once again we see Kazantzakis agonizing over his reluctance to act. But this time he screwed his courage to the sticking-place. A few days after writing the diary entry just quoted, he went out to Varvári, the "ancestral village" (now the location of the Kazantzakis Museum), choosing it as the first stop on a projected campaign throughout Crete. "I went," he says, "in order to set it on fire—to cast our Idea on it as a flaming seed so that it might burn and be saved. . . . Let us rouse those who are serene, make them unserene, show those who are humbly satisfied that they are miserable, toss lighted coals into the courtyards of every peaceful home . . . so that the world will not rot in tranquility and stagnation, the soul not rot in prosperity and patience" (Eleni Kaz. 1977:32–33; 1968a:28). This is the same Kazantzakis who as a schoolboy founded a Friendly Society "to make uncompromising war on falsehood, servitude, and injustice" (Kaz. 1964a:135; 1965c:111)—but with one difference. Then an older voice was needed to balance illusion with disillusion; now his own voice assumed this role as well, and indeed spoke even before he had tilted against very many of these new windmills. In the same letter in which he described to Eléni Samíou his new campaign, calling it "our difficult, heavy, supreme duty," his Buddhistic side cried out with the usual anguish:

> My heart is filled with unbearable bitterness. I have no illusions and that is precisely why I am fighting without respite—despairing and free. I know that as soon as this abominable, vapid bourgeois class falls, the proletariat will come, will contribute whatever thought and beauty it can, will become abominable in its own turn, will become vapid, the Great Spirit will depart from above it and another class will come—and so on without cease until the earth grows totally dark and life is exterminated like a parasite from the crust of this insignificant planet of ours. (Eleni Kaz. 1977:31; 1968a:27–28)

As expected, Kazantzakis was still struggling to amalgamate his antithetical drives toward contemplation and revolution. Meanwhile, however, the "supreme responsibility" to act had to be carried further (although he allowed himself a summer holiday reading Homer, Aeschylus, Goethe, and Shestov with Eléni and Galatea [Eleni Kaz. 1977:33–35; 1968a:29–30]).[4] The next we hear is that, after arranging to get away from his parents and occupy a house outside the city in order to begin the *Odyssey* in solitude, he was engaged in preparing a deposition for the police. The date is 7 October.

> All day long today I was composing my defense. I was summoned because of a revolutionary article I'd written and was given twenty-four hours to defend myself. Oh how abominably petty is life in this place! . . . If it were somewhere else I'd run the risk—the hope—of being killed. Here, they won't even put me on trial and give me a chance to see if I'm brave. If only I were a Russian! . . . (Eleni Kaz. 1977:37; 1968a:32)

We hear nothing more about this. Perhaps, as happened several times in Kazantzakis's subsequent career, the judicial proceedings were quietly forgotten: we should remember that as late as 12 December the communist menace was not being taken very seriously in Iráklion. Perhaps for this very reason Kazantzakis counseled escalation. At all events, mass meetings, demonstrations and protest marches formed the next stage. The most immediate issue at this point was the reservists' demand to be allowed to take over agricultural lands owned by the monasteries (*Nea Efimeris*, 18 Dec. 1924:2). On 21 December the authorities refused permission to the Cretan branch of the Panhellenic Union of Combat Veterans, officially part of the Communist Party (*Nea Efimeris*, 7 Feb. 1925), to hold a mass meeting, whereupon the members gathered anyhow and marched to the Town Hall to protest (*Nea Efimeris*, 22 Dec. 1924:2). This or a similar series of events in December led to arrests; in the trial that occurred the following July four reservists were sentenced to six weeks in jail and several others were acquitted (*Nea Efimeris*, 15 July 1925:1).

The next stage in escalation is what sent Kazantzakis briefly to jail. The new spark, as noted earlier, was the expulsion of the Ecumenical Patriarch from Istanbul. On 30 January 1925 the committee organizing the exchange of Greeks and Turks in the aftermath of the Asia Minor disaster published its decision that Constantine IV was no different from any other Greek priest on Turkish soil, hence should be part of the exchange (*Anorthosis*, 31 Jan. 1925:4). On the same day, the Turks escorted him by force to the border (*Anorthosis*, 1 Feb. 1925:1); on 31 January he reached Thessaloniki, where he received a tumultuous welcome (*Anorthosis*, 3 Feb. 1925:4). Relations between Greece and Turkey were of course at the breaking point owing to this final humiliation imposed upon the already humiliated nation. The next day, 1 February, the citizens of Iráklion were called to display their patriotism, the newspaper *Anórthosis* greeting them with a headline in capital letters: "TODAY'S MASS DEMONSTRATION OF PROTEST AGAINST THE EXPULSION OF THE ECUMENICAL PATRIARCH IS RELIGIOUS IN CHARACTER. NO ONE SHOULD BE ABSENT."

We can imagine how Kazantzakis and his cadre of young communists and disgruntled reservists viewed these developments. We know Kazantzakis's disgust at Greek political life and his conviction that nationalism was bankrupt; we know his resolve to escape his parents' religion with its bourgeois values. In Germany he had been initiated into the communists' internationalist perspective: their view that the common people of one nation must not fight against those of another but should unite to overthrow their respective oppressors. The present crisis—adding nationalism and religion to the previous problems of unemployment, land, and housing—offered a perfect opportunity for transforming principles into action. And this is what happened.

First, at the demonstration "of a religious character," which of course was a demonstration in favor of war with Turkey (*Nea Efimeris*, 4 Feb. 1925:3), someone shouted "Peace!" someone else "Down with war!" An army major who was on the scene indicated later in his deposition that the provocation was sufficient "to make the patriotically impassioned crowd turn upon the supporters of communism who were present in order to maltreat them; however, the undersigned arrived in time to take charge of two of the most lively among them and to remove them thence in order to protect them from possible danger" (*Nea Efimeris*, 4 Feb. 1925:3).

Secondly, to complement this challenge to the state, the dissidents vented their spleen more directly against religion following the arrest of their leader for fomenting civil disorder (*Nea Efimeris*, 7 Feb. 1925:2). On 5 February, about forty to fifty communists gathered in front of the cathedral, Saint Minas's. While some broke down the door to the belfry with axes and stones, ascended, and rang the chimes, others down below shouted antiwar slogans (*Anorthosis*, 6 Feb. 1925:3; *Nea Efimeris*, 6 Feb. 1925:2 and 7 Feb. 1925:2). The reaction among the bourgeoisie was severe. "The general topic of conversation yesterday in all the coffeehouses," reported *Néa Efimerís* on 7 February (p. 2), "was the communists' vandalism against the Holy Temple of the city's protector, Saint Minas, which the Turks did not dare to touch during the period of Turkish tyranny. . . . Public opinion is exceedingly indignant against the impious communists who insulted the Christian religion so sacrilegiously through their acts of vandalism. . . ." On the other hand, there was also a comic side to this episode, something that is important to note, for it makes the events in Iráklion seem flaccid by comparison with what Kazantzakis had experienced in Germany and indeed with what was happening elsewhere in Greece.[5] After the police had expertly dispersed the demonstrators in a manner "inspiring absolute confidence among peace-loving people," the communists regrouped outside the precincts of the cathedral and "attempted to move in one body to the police station where their comrades were being held; however, . . . a heavy rain started to fall, and since most of them did not have umbrellas they retired to their own homes" (*Nea Efimeris*, 6 Feb. 1925:2).

Dialinás editorialized on 8 February that the communists' effrontery had reached the point where it proved itself a threat to the established social order. Yet, despite an announcement by the district's military command that "severe measures" would henceforth be taken "to safeguard civic tranquility" (*Nea Efimeris*, 8 Feb. 1925:2), the communists held an antiwar rally on this same day (*Nea Efimeris*, 9 Feb. 1925:1). The rest of that week there were more arrests, as well as a bill submitted by the Minister of the Interior in Athens meant to prohibit propaganda for communism (*Nea Efimeris*, Feb. 1925:2). On 14 February the newspaper reported (p. 2) the "recent arrival in Iráklion of the public prosecutor of the Court of Appeals to inaugurate interrogations regarding the communists' improprieties during the past week." And on the fifteenth (p. 2), under the headline RELEASE OF PERSON UNDER ARREST, we read:

> . . . the day before yesterday the scholar Mr. Nikos Kazantzakis of this city, who was suspected of directing the communistic sub-

versive activity here, was arrested and detained for 24 hours at the police station.

Yesterday, having been sent to the public prosecutor, he was released after declaring his innocence.

What happened on 14 February is that Kazantzakis went to the public prosecutor armed with the defense he had written the previous October. We know this because he proceeded to publish it two days later in *Néa Efimerís* (Kaz. 1925a)—bravely, despite the reigning political climate. It was one of the rare times in his life that he lived up to his own expectations regarding political daring. Since this document has never been translated into English and is difficult to find even in Greek, I shall cite it almost in full (with emphasis added):

To the Editor:

. . . In these days in which the free citizen is terrorized, I consider it my simplest duty to set forth . . . my ideology.

If this ideology is considered dangerous to our current régime, I shall calmly await my prosecution and punishment.

Confession of Faith

I. I believe that today's bourgeois status quo has rendered itself incapable of arranging henceforth for the contemporary needs and anxieties of society as a whole.

ECONOMICALLY—It is based on the unequal distribution of wealth, on the shameless exploitation of the working classes by rapacious, strongly organized capitalism.

SOCIALLY—Within the bourgeois status quo, the continuously crumbling moral foundation of relations between individuals paralyzes every possible effort to make the individual, domestic, and social life of mankind rest on moral principles.

POLITICALLY—The . . . practically exclusive catering to the ruling class by each successive group holding political power, to the detriment of the great majority of the people, makes every change of personnel or law inadequate and superficial.

In my opinion these are always symptoms of the decline of a class. The bourgeois class produced what it could in thought, art, science, action. . . . Having . . . carried out its destiny, it is beginning to decompose . . .

Such has always been the course of history. . . .

I firmly believe that we are experiencing the end of the bourgeois social class.

II. What class will succeed it? The working class, whether they be laborers, farmers, or intellectual producers. A century ago, this class . . . attempted to arouse the sentiments of philanthropy and justice in the bourgeois classes . . .

However, it quickly perceived that class war is an unavoidable historical law. . . . No class has remained in power for ever. . . .

This realization constituted the beginning of a . . . more profound conception of the working class's rights and obligations. For the first time it was understood that this class had a duty to organize, to become educated, and to articulate a specific program since, having been summoned by historical necessity, it would supplant today's ruling class, the bourgeoisie, sooner or later.

The two opposing camps are already arrayed in this way, consciously, constrained by the course of history.

The outbreak of the world war unexpectedly accelerated this course. This war altered people's psychological atmosphere . . .

This postwar psychological anxiety—the acute feeling that there is already a need to discover some way of deliverance from this economic, social, political, and intellectual abomination—constitutes today's MAJOR worldwide REALITY.

III. Compared to this major worldwide reality we have the minor . . . reality of Greece.

What is this Greek reality, and what relation necessarily emerges between the major and minor realities?

Only if we answer this question clearly will we be able to comprehend our contemporary duty as Greeks and as human beings.

In Greece the class war still does not possess . . . the clear design that exists in other countries that are more developed industrially or intellectually. However, given today's means of communication, . . . an idea cannot be confined to one country. . . .

Because of this, whether or not we want it, whether or not we are sufficiently mature for it, this worldwide Idea that has already begun in many countries to change into colossal power will lure Greece as well *without waiting for our country to mature* industrially or intellectually. The localized minor reality will be lured by the major reality.

What is our duty, then? I profoundly believe that the duty of those in power, if they are to influence our land whether in the field of thought or action, is this: *to adapt our minor reality to the major reality*. How? By educating the populace, enlightening them, strengthening the higher ethical principles that still remain, demonstrating henceforth not just the rights belonging to a class bound to assume responsibility, but also that class's obligations.

Only if we prepare the populace in this way will we be in a position, when the inevitable critical moment arrives, to adapt today's worldwide momentum for renewed creation to the special conditions of our land, the specific psychology of our people's history.

The struggle as I conceive it is not just economic. Economic emancipation is only a means leading to mankind's psychological and intellectual emancipation. We do not seek to overturn religion, family, and country, but to give a higher, deeper content to religion, family, and country.

All of us who feel compassion for humanity have a duty (a) to refuse any longer to tolerate the injustice and immorality of today's social, political, and economic life, (b) to preserve and strengthen the common people's right to want to improve their situation—and not just the right but also the power to raise the level of all aspects of their lives.

Our goal is to create a higher morality, to bring justice to the world, to give a profounder meaning to virtue, to honor, and to mankind.

N. KAZANTZAKIS

For whatever reason, the authorities chose to ignore Kazantzakis's provocation; his forthright statement involved him in nothing worse than an extended public discussion, as we shall see in a moment. Nor did Kazantzakis ever achieve the martyrdom of an extended jail-sentence either now, or when threatened in 1928–1930 with prosecution for his Alhambra Theater speech about the Soviet Union, or again in 1930–1931 for having published *Askitikí*, the charge in this third case being "derision of the Orthodox Church and disturbance of its peace" (Glinos 1930). In the last two instances, the impending trial was postponed and eventually canceled. In one or both, however, Kazantzakis had recourse to his 1924–1925 "Confession of Faith," which he revised, keeping the same general outline but expanding the statement in order to make it (a) reflect more recent developments such as the emergence of nationalism in African and Asian colonies, (b) reflect his current position, after his visit to the Soviet Union, and (c) show him to be a man of thought, not action.[6]

The public discussion stimulated in 1925 by the "Confession of Faith" should interest anyone following Kazantzakis's career because it reveals so unmistakably his position vis-à-vis Christianity and the Church, therefore providing valuable background for *Christ Recrucified*, not to mention the scene in the *Odyssey* (21.1116–1370) when the hero debates the fisher-lad, the type of Christ.

The area of debate was shifted to Christianity by Dialinás, who on 17 February—the day after Kazantzakis's defense appeared in *Néa Efimerís*—published a reply under the heading "To Kinonikón Próvlima" (The Social Problem). Dialinás agreed with Kazantzakis's contention that society was sick but he differed regarding the remedy. Instead of hunting for new theories, "why shouldn't we follow the principles of Christianity to the full? . . . Instead of becoming socialists, communists, and heaven knows what else, let us all become perfect Christians . . ." (Dialinas 1925, 17 Feb.).

Kazantzakis's answer appeared on the nineteenth (Kaz. 1925b):

> 1) The basic difference between our perceptions lies in this: you think that I am proposing medicines to cure the injustice and immorality of the degenerate postwar world. But I am not proposing any medicines; I am simply articulating a historical law that . . . governs human history: A class dominates with its own morality . . . , loses its faith and disappears. Another class—always *a lower one*— . . . succeeds it . . . and passes through the same . . . stages of creativity and decay.
>
> 2) We are living at the critical moment when a world is turning rotten. . . . Naïve ideologues have always been found to suggest medicines for rebirth and salvation . . .
>
> Thus today, too, many ideologues and moralists suggest that the only salvation is for us to return to past simplicity, to revive Christian ethics, to put an end to infamy. They forget just one thing: that life does not turn back and that the height of infamy is the indispensable prerequisite for future virtue. This is because only when infamy reaches its height does it cause the extermination of the rotten organism that gave birth to that infamy, in that it forces the common people, who are the victims of that infamy and who suffer, to break out in indignation and wrath, and to call for justice.
>
> 3) The class that is being treated abominably today and is suffering is, as always, the *mass of working people immediately under the dominating class*. . . .
>
> We are living in a transitional age in which one class has turned rotten yet still keeps its organization strong . . . while another class . . . is conscious of its power but is still not completely organized. . . . The fate of our generation . . . is not peace, reconciliation, the flowering of the new civilization, but rather war, hatred, the spasmodic agonies, antinomies and brutalities of the civilization that is in the process of being born.
>
> 4) A new morality is never the offspring of the imagination or heart of a social reformer and ideologue. It derives from the profoundest psychological and material needs of a new totality.
>
> Whoever struggles today to convince the bourgeoisie to return

> to Christian morality is nothing but a naïve dreamer. The bourgeoisie will not be convinced. Morality, i.e. the system of precepts governing human relationships within the social totality, is always the image and likeness of the class that dominates . . .

Concluding, Kazantzakis challenged Dialinás to refute the above four points clearly and calmly, so that the discussion might proceed.

Dialinás picked up the challenge in an article that appeared on the following day, the twentieth. Kazantzakis had called for clarity and calm; these were observed. Perhaps the best way to appreciate the elevated level of this debate is to compare it with what was appearing concurrently in Iráklion's other daily, *Anórthosis*, where a series called "Communist Ideology" warned against the "danger of . . . Jew-communism . . . ," which insults "the world's most sacred sentiment, the sentiment of *Motherhood*," etc. (*Anorthosis*, 19 Feb. 1925:1, 2 and 21 Feb. 1925:1). By contrast, Kazantzakis was attempting to influence his countrymen by means of argumentation as opposed to slogans. Dialinás's rebuttal on the twentieth set his interlocutor up for the next round by contending, in response to Kazantzakis's challenge, that human history would have been different if people had chosen to do unto others as they would have others do unto them (Dialinas 1925, 20 Feb.).

Kazantzakis replied with another long essay (Kaz. 1925c): Yes, history would have been different if mankind had evolved differently. But we must pose two queries. The first is, "*Could* human history have followed a different course?" Only if human nature had been higher, which was not the case. "The organism . . . that matured . . . in order to liberate itself from the monkey and ascend . . . to self-consciousness was man, i.e. a beast together with an angel, a mixture of . . . the impulse to rise and the dark instinctive return toward the depths. . . ." The second query is, "*Should* human history have followed a different course?" Responding, Kazantzakis directs a rhetorical question at Dialinás: "What does 'should' mean? Does it mean that it would have been more fruitful spiritually and ethically if mankind had taken the tranquil, peaceful course that you invoke, without struggle, passion, injustice, and hatred?" He then answers his own question, as follows:

> . . . without struggle, there would have been no progress; without wickedness, there would have been no virtue; without darkness, light would have had no meaning. . . .
>
> Our lives are not an idyll. . . . Dark waves full of gore undulate rhythmically across the centuries. The only light that foams, white and ephemeral, at the crest of these heavy seas is the mind.
>
> If that light is to be lit, dark forces must come to blows. If hope

is to be created, despair must be at work for ages along with suffering and injustice. . . .

One of the principal causes of our disagreement, Mr. Editor, is connected with this point. I recognize this universal rhythm and accept it as the creator of divine counteraction and impetuosity. You recognize it but condemn it as the creator of every sin.

But both of these questions—"could it?" and "should it?"—are valuable only theoretically. . . . We exist in an intellectual chaos and a chasm of ignominy. What has to happen? In other words, what is the duty of each of us? That is the interesting question.

You say that we should return to the great principles of Christianity and base our entire social existence on the maxim of the great Chinese philosopher of practicality, Confucius: "Do not do unto others what you would not have others do unto you." Unfortunately, this maxim goes against life's essence: Every complete organism . . . does not hold a scale to calculate gram by gram what others have done to it and what it is doing. Inside it is an impetuosity pushing it to implant its roots as deeply and broadly as possible, to do wrong, to seize in order to dominate, to transubstantiate as much of its own and others' materiality as it possibly can, turning that materiality into spirit. On this earth, this is the sole method followed by all organic beings in order to deliver themselves from inertia, tranquility, and prosperity, and to throw themselves into danger, adventure, and unexpected success.

Having concluded this outline of Nietzschian and Bergsonian vitalism, Kazantzakis brings his sermon to a close with a peroration directed at every believer. The duty of each of us is: "Hate. Merciless war . . . against . . . the bourgeoisie. . . . This hate is the only means whereby we can reach the broadest possible love . . ."

Fortunately, the debate now petered out; each side was beginning to resort to *idées fixes* and to repeat itself. All that Dialinás offered in reply the next day (23 February) was the observation that the real difference between Kazantzakis and himself was Kazantzakis's acceptance of Darwin's theory of evolution, which, because it ignored Divine Power, he—Dialinás—found unacceptable. Man was created in God's image: perfect. He freely chose to fall. Now his only salvation is to choose to follow the dictates of Christianity . . .

It was time to stop. What came next was a spate of letters to the editor—one from G. Manáris, leader of the Cretan branch of the Social Democrats, agreeing that Christian principles were the best but reminding his readers that these principles needed the proper political party to implement them (*Nea Efimeris*, 27 Feb. 1925:1); one from a certain Papadákas congratulating Dialinás on his adherence to Christ as the only true guide (*Nea Efimeris*, 28 Feb. 1925); and a huge vituperation from the Greek-who-hated-the-Greeks, arriving in May from Tanga, East Africa, in which—quoting Schopenhauer profusely—he glossed the Dialinás-Kazantzakis debate with apothegms such as "Man is a 'brute' and will remain such for ever. . . . Communism turns him into a 'consummate pig.' " "It is . . . exceedingly strange for Mr. Kazantzakis to write about *spirit* and mind, while the entire '*world-view*' of . . . Engels, Marx, and Lenin is absolute, unadulterated, and utterly grim '*materialism*' " (Karabasis, 16 and 17 May 1925).

By this time, however, Kazantzakis was deep into the first six cantos of the *Odyssey*. We know that he had begun to compose the epic as soon as he settled all alone into a house by the sea in the Iráklion suburb of Poros—that is, by mid-October 1924.[7] There were interruptions to deal with reservists, public prosecutors, and zealous newspaper editors, as we have seen. Nevertheless, by the end of March 1925 he was going strong again:

> I'm writing you from a deserted seashore near Kástro [Iráklion] where I've been living for months now and writing. Never has my soul been so assured and fertile. I'm writing a large work that will last for years. It will be my life's work, my greatest effort to save my soul. . . . (Mitsotakis 1972:112)

But we also know something else thanks to Prevelákis, who has printed a few paragraphs appended by Kazantzakis to the long entry in his diary for 15 July 1924, quoted earlier, in which he described his secret meetings with the simple folk who were the rank and file of Iráklion's communist movement. This addendum, added soon after Kazantzakis's debate with Dialinás, consists of a final judgment on the Iráklion incident that, while unexpected, is not inconsistent with Kazantzakis's "system":

> Around March 1925 I arrived at the following conclusion:
>
> The communists are not the ones who will create the new culture.
>
> The lowest classes as a totality . . . have never carried an entirely new seed. Only ameliorations, etc. to the old system.
>
> They have always perfectly carried out (1) the negative, (2) the anticipatory mission: they have cleared the ground, subverted the rotting structure, and have proclaimed the need for "new life."
>
> The positive, creative role has always been taken by the "barbarians." Only they possess the seed. Today's barbarians—the Asiatics once more, and specifically the Russians. But Russia's current

leaders are disregarding their true mission and looking to Europe for seed: materialism, Marx, etc.

The world will not experience a renaissance until the Russians (today's vanguard for the barbarians) comprehend wherein lies their power and their mission. (Prev. 1965b:159–160)

IRÁKLION: ART

This addendum brings the Iráklion incident to a close and also serves as a convenient fulcrum shifting us ahead to the *Odyssey*. It does not say anything theoretically new—despite Kazantzakis's assertion to Eléni Samíou on 2 May 1925 that he had "recently advanced to some unexpected conclusions regarding communist ideology, leaving behind my old theories" (Eleni Kaz. 1977:150; 1968a:120). Rather than leaving old theories behind, it merely restates them on the basis of new experience, namely Kazantzakis's discovery during the Iráklion incident that communists are materialists deaf to metacommunism and therefore at best only forerunners for the barbarians (whom he eventually assumed would come from darkest Africa).

Kazantzakis's addendum serves as a fulcrum shifting us ahead to the *Odyssey* not only because disillusion with workers in favor of barbarians is one of the *Odyssey*'s motifs but because, marking the conclusion to the Iráklion incident as it does, it helps us realize that the epic's entire first half is in many ways an imaginative recreation of what Kazantzakis experienced in his home town during the eight months from his arrival there on 5 July 1924 until the end of February 1925. Again I must stress that the Iráklion incident did not furnish him with new ideas—the ideas were already on paper in *Askitikí*. It translated those ideas into disillusioning experiences, confirming what he already knew, namely that his own role was as a manipulator of words, not people. I conclude that it was the Iráklion incident coming on top of the theoretical formulations in *Askitikí* that enabled Kazantzakis to launch his *Odyssey*.

In any case, the epic's first half in its most general outline (discounting the wish-fulfillments) clearly duplicates what happened to Kazantzakis after he returned to Iráklion: (1) In real life, he had come home after many travels and a long absence (he begins his 7 July 1924 letter to Eléni Samíou: "The *second Odysséas* has returned to his home town" [Eleni Kaz. 1977:27; 1968a:24, italics added]). The epic begins daringly where Homer's ends, at the point where the second Odysséas returns home after many travels and a long absence. (2) In real life, he was dismayed by what he found in Iráklion after the excitement of European capitals. Similarly, Odysséas, after he dispatches the suitors, is dismayed by the pettiness and dullness of his provincial home; he too determines to reject father, wife, and son, sensing a gulf between himself and them. (3) In real life, Kazantzakis of course remained home in a physical sense, but in a metaphorical one he abandoned the values of his parents and fellow citizens, uniting himself with a nonestablishment group determined to overthrow those values. Odysséas, after uniting himself with a group of vagabonds and misfits, leaves in a physical as well as a metaphorical sense, and proceeds to join various movements aimed at overthrowing established values. (4) In real life, becoming disillusioned with the workers as potential restorers of civilization, Kazantzakis looked to the barbarians. Odysséas chooses barbarians over workers in a contest; then, having collaborated with a group clearly modeled on the leaders of Bolshevism, heads down the Nile to find the barbarians of darkest Africa . . .

There is of course much much more than this to the *Odyssey*, a poem that we know only in its final form, after it underwent numerous revisions reflecting experiences subsequent to those in Iráklion,[8] but the general congruence between the Iráklion incident and the skeletal framework of the epic's first half should be evident.

Kazantzakis managed to draft only the initial six cantos in his house by the seashore near Kástro. These show Odysséas's resolve to abandon family and home; his gathering of a crew of ne'er-do-wells; his voyage to Sparta, where he develops an antipathy toward his own class and a sympathy for both workers and barbarians; his subsequent choice of undisciplined, violent barbarians over impotent workers; his abduction of Helen in conscious defiance of the morality of his class; his crossing to Crete, where he experiences the decadent ruler's desperate and obscene stratagems to remain in power while his oppressed people die of starvation and rebellious elements join with blond Dorian barbarians from the north in planning a revolt; finally, Odysséas's complicity in their plans to slaughter the overlords and burn down the palace.

The seventh and eighth cantos, in which this wish-fulfillment is enacted; the ninth through eleventh, in which Odysséas attempts to overthrow still another decadent régime, in Egypt; the twelfth through fourteenth, which describe the exodus to the source of the Nile; the city-building in Canto 15; and the entire contemplative Nostos ("Return") occupying cantos 16 to 24—these had to wait almost two years, until the summer of 1927, to be committed to paper. But the scheme, surely of the first half in detail, and also of the second half at least in broad outline,[9] was in Kazantzakis's mind concurrently with his involvement in the affairs of Iráklion's disaffected reservists, and was influenced by his failure then to achieve the political victories in real life that he so easily made the second Odysséas achieve in the life of the imagination.

CHAPTER FIVE

Russia

> Russia does not interest me in the least . . .
> —Letter to Pandelís Prevelákis, 16 February 1929

The years between the first draft of the *Odyssey*'s initial cantos in 1925 and the epic's reworking during the winter of 1929–1930 constitute a new cycle in Kazantzakis's life, one that repeats the previous pattern whereby artistic and philosophical endeavors at the desk give way to political endeavors in the marketplace, then to disillusion, and lastly to the resumption of artistic endeavors at the desk.

In coarse outline, the cycle consists of Kazantzakis's experiences in Russia, which sent him back to the *Odyssey* with his Buddhistic side strengthened. In fine outline, however, this straightforward route becomes devious. His active engagement was neither steady nor confined to Russia. At various times during 1926 and 1927, his career as a journalist sent him on assignment to Spain, Italy, Cyprus, Palestine, Egypt, and Sinai. He also attempted to participate in Greek political life once again in January 1928 by lecturing in Athens about the accomplishments of Soviet communism. Nor did he slacken as a writer during these supposedly activist years. Ταξιδεύοντας. Ισπανία. Ιταλία. Αίγυπτος. Σινά (Traveling. Spain. Italy. Egypt. Sinai) came out in 1927; the articles from the second and third sojourns in Russia[1] were collected in two volumes issued in 1928 as Τί είδα στη Ρουσία (What I Saw in Russia); we already know that he took a rest from action between these two trips in order to complete cantos 7 through 24 of the *Odyssey* in first draft; during the fourth trip to Russia (April 1928–April 1929) he revised *Askitikí* by adding Η σιγή (The Silence); finally, between May and June 1929, almost immediately after his return from the Soviet Union, Kazantzakis dashed off *Toda-Raba*, a fictionalized evocation of his failure to act and his rejection of the Soviet system. All this—but chiefly the fulfillment of his yearning to live among the Russians and the ensuing disillusionment—furnished grist for the *Odyssey*'s second draft.

SYMPOSIUM

Before following Kazantzakis on his second trip to the Soviet Union and examining the political repercussions in Greece of two articles resulting from that experience, I wish to mention Συμπόσιον. This work, which he never attempted to publish, may belong to another period in Kazantzakis's career; on the other hand, an educated guess tells us that it was written sometime between 1924 and 1926.[2] The symposiasts are Arpagós (= Kazantzakis), Kosmás (= Ion Dragoúmis, the man of action), Pétros (= Angelos Sikelianós, the devotee of beauty), and Míros (= Myron Gounelákis, a frustrated metaphysician turned merchant).[3] The interchange among these speakers reflects Kazantzakis's effort to transcend the naïve activism that believes in goals so that he may subscribe instead to a theory that encases positive engagement inside a pessimistic world-view. Subjectivized activism denying goals is the first step in this progression. Yet Arpagós challenges Kosmás (which means that Kazantzakis challenges the activist part of himself) to advance to a still higher step in which the goal (or nongoal) is correctly recognized as the abyss but is understood in a Bergsonian way to be the achievement of total freedom through dematerialization of the *élan vital*, hence not just an ending but simultaneously the beginning of a new cycle of creativity.

The interchange also reflects Kazantzakis's effort to escape the aestheticism represented in *Symposium* by Pétros and in Kazantzakis's life by Sikelianós, whose influence during the former's precommunist days vied with Dragoúmis's.[4] Thus Arpagós denounces Pétros's view that the world is a Troy burning for Homer's sake (Kaz. 1971b:34; 1974:37). He, on the contrary, seeks to stand not on Beauty but on firm ground—namely, the "source of . . . universal life and the justification of endeavor." He does not care what they call it: religion, God, chimera, poetry, or delusion. *He* calls it salvation (1971b:40; 1974:42).

Having disposed of Kosmás and Pétros, Arpagós now responds to Míros, the failed metaphysician.[5] He does this in his "confession," much of which reminds us of *Report to Greco* because it covers some of the same ground: parents, childhood, sexuality, Christian renunciation, political action. Although clearly unfinished (a fact suppressed by the publishers, translators, and editor, who offer *Symposium* as a completed work, which it is not), the confession in its incomplete state exposes enough of Kazantzakis's central plan for *Sympósion* to allow conjectures regarding the whole. His charge is to reveal his vision of the absolute. We know in advance that this absolute is bound to be the *élan vital*; we are not surprised, therefore, to find Bergsonism's two principal streams, the upward and downward, announced near the start, treated as male and female:

> Two voices began . . . to struggle inside me.
>
> One shouted: "I want freedom! . . . To transcend nature, conquer law, deny my father and mother. I am the chimera, the gateway out of life besieged, the essence of the male penis."
>
> The other voice resisted, replying: ". . . I . . . receive the seed, and stay in place to feed it. . . . I want to . . . descend to the ani-

mal, fall back to the tree, become immobile. I am tired. I hate life, strength, hope, the ascending flame . . ." (1971b:52–53; 1974:53)

The remainder of the confessional fragment presents variations on this Bergsonian theme. The opposing forces are always the same, although they are presented in different forms such as action versus contemplation, action versus aestheticism, and contemplation versus springtime, with its universal urge to reproduce. In the course of all this we are given not only childhood and family memories reminiscent of *Report to Greco* but also Kazantzakis's fullest account of the method of spiritual exercise that he was taught at Mount Athos, and finally a strong evocation of his father, Kapetán Mihális, as a force bludgeoning him into an activism contrary to his contemplative nature.

What the confession in its fragmentary nature fails to provide, but what its central plan allows us to divine, is Arpagós's ultimate vision of the absolute. We can conjecture that this would have been the same as the one that Kazantzakis was projecting concurrently in his epic: a justification for all forms of endeavor (sexual, political, philosophical, artistic) as necessary steps in a progressive initiation leading to the discovery—and acceptance—of the Abyss/Silence/Salvation/Freedom that negates but at the same time fulfills and renews. The absolute is not the concluding abyss but rather the entire cycle that brings us from one abyss to another across the luminous interval called life—in a word, it is the plot of the *Odyssey*.

Kazantzakis was right not to publish *Sympósion*. It is a digressive, rambling work needing rigorous revision, quite aside from its incompleteness. And the prose, despite its metaphoric wealth, is embarrassingly gushy in the manner of *Serpent and Lily*. What, then, is *Symposium*'s value, especially in the context of this study? Its value lies, I believe, in the confirmation given to our suspicion that, even at the height of his political activism in Iráklion, Kazantzakis was not a *zoon politikon* but instead a *zoon metaphysikon* for whom politics were subordinate to (yet necessary for) a contemplative effort to discover the ultimate meaning of life and death. We should keep this in mind throughout the period between the *Odyssey*'s first and second drafts whenever we encounter Kazantzakis's further attempts at activism.

SECOND TRIP TO THE SOVIET UNION; THE *ANAYÉNNISI* DEBATE; "CRUCIFIED RUSSIA"

Kazantzakis was eager to go to Egypt in connection with Odysséas's descent down the Nile. He accomplished this desire, but not until later. Unexpectedly, on 10 October 1925, came "a great piece of news. I'm leaving for Moscow in three days! Everything was ready for my trip to Africa, but at the last minute I was given the chance to go to Moscow and I seized it with delight" (Eleni Kaz. 1968b:131; 1977:161; 1968a:128).[6] In 1925 no one in Greece knew at first hand what was happening in the Soviet Union. Everyone had expected the Bolshevik régime to collapse; it had not, and curiosity regarding its tenacity was increasing (Markakis 1959a:40). Kazantzakis's chance to go to Russia and to report his findings in the newspaper *Eléftheros Lógos* possessed a significance transcending the personal.[7]

Leaving on 13 October by ship, he found himself reacting in a "non-Greek" manner as he gazed at the lights of Istanbul three days later:

> My heart does not pound at all as I see the city "of Greek longings." I feel that I have given nationalism the slip. . . . I experience the full struggle of human beings apart from their national labels. . . . I sense the hopes and energies of the Young Turks; I'm with them, a human being like them . . ." (Eleni Kaz. 1977:162; 1968a:129)

His first stop in the Soviet Union was Odessa, from where he dispatched an ingratiating letter to his father, whose morose reaction to Bolshevism we saw earlier:

> Dear Father,
>
> I'm writing you a few words to tell you that I arrived in Russia and am fine, so don't worry.
>
> It's cold but I bought a marvelous fur coat and the cold doesn't bother me. Tomorrow I'm going by train to Moscow, where I'll stay three months and will write you regularly. . . .
>
> The Russians are very kind people and I'll live among them easily. I like Russia and always wanted to come and stay a little. . . .
>
> With much love and reverence.
>
> I kiss your hand.
> Nikos
>
> (Goudelis 1978:24–25)

On 30 October, *Eléftheros Lógos* printed a photo of Kazantzakis (p. 3) followed by the headline, "Starting Sunday in 'Eléftheros Lógos' the First Greek Journalistic Investigation in Bolshevik Russia." The ensuing article explains that Kazantzakis had indeed arrived in Moscow and would be writing about all aspects of Soviet life: social, economic, political, intellectual. "Until now," it continues,

> we have known about the situation in Russia only through descriptions and studies by foreigners—pro-communist or anti-

communist. Mr. Kazantzakis was sent in order to see the situation OBJECTIVELY and to report to us the bad or good accomplished by Bolshevism, to give us a picture of the life of the cities and the muzhiks, to describe people and things. In short: to inform us what communist Russia is like today.

Kazantzakis's series commenced on 1 November, under the headline "A Great Journalistic Mission . . ." Running until 27 December, it consisted of twenty-four articles. What Kazantzakis actually did in Moscow we can follow owing to a list of visits and experiences compiled by Preveläkis from his friend's diary entries between 5 November 1925 and 25 January 1926—for example, dance school, revolutionary theater, trade school, prison, children's theater, Ministry of Social Welfare and Health, Jewish theater, Orthodox liturgy, opening of an electric generating plant, speech by Trotsky, gynecological hospital, school in the forest, Tolstoy Museum, Dostoevsky Museum, Byzantine Library, asylum for vagrant children (Prev. 1965b:15–16). The impressions and conclusions resulting from this potpourri of experiences may be seen of course in the articles themselves,[8] some of which are reprinted in *Taksidévondas. Rusía* (Kaz. 1965e; 1989), but also in several letters sent to Eléni Samíou in November and December. These voice familiar refrains:

> What moves me in Russia is not the reality they have reached but the reality they desire and do not know that they cannot reach. The total value of mankind nestles in the chimera; it is worthwhile acting and dying for this intoxication. To be happy, to eat better, and to be enlightened are of course worthy human goals for the masses—workers, peasants, women; but I consider all these things petty, practical illusions . . . (Eleni Kaz. 1977:165; 1968a:131)

> I've been talking with various "leaders" here in Moscow. Only their action, their *élan*, their holy smoke-filled fire, has value; their thought strikes me as extremely naïve. (Eleni Kaz. 1977:167; 1968a:132)

But the same letters also contain at least one surprise: "This trip came just in time—at the moment when I was struggling to free myself from the bewitchment of art. I have accepted it and am experiencing it as one of the fruits of my arduous and prolonged áskisis" (Eleni Kaz. 1977:165; 1968a:131). Kazantzakis had accused the Russians of naïveté, but he himself possessed a childlike enthusiasm that swept him up into the activity of the moment despite his better judgment. Remembering his devotion to the *Odyssey* so shortly before, as well as his denigration of activism in *Symposium* and his desire to travel to Africa in order to enrich his art, we now wonder how all this could metamorphose so effortlessly into another period of activist yearning. Yet it did—until the pendulum swung the other way again (but not definitively) in 1929. (On a deeper level of understanding, however, these oscillations can all be comprehended as subtending from Kazantzakis's subjectivism, as I hope we shall see shortly when we reach the *Anayénnisi* debate.)

The articles were evidently received in the spirit in which they were intended: as objective reporting of the good and the bad.[9] In any case, they did not cause any trouble, and a dozen or so were reprinted the following August and September, together with a few additional pieces (Katsimbalis 1958a:20). However, three additional essays based on this trip brought Kazantzakis into open conflict with both the left and the right. The first, published in the inaugural number of Dimítrios Glinós's periodical Αναγέννηση (Renaissance), was called Συζήτηση μ' έναν αρχηγό (Discussion with a Leader); it prompted rebuttals from Greek Marxists. The second, Η νέα Πομπηία (The New Pompeii), and the third, Η σταυρωμένη Ρουσία (Crucified Russia), helped to provoke a memorandum from a bishop to the Synod of the Greek Orthodox Church attacking these essays along with *Askitikí* as antireligious (Athanasios of Syros 1928).

"Discussion with a Leader" is an expansion of Kazantzakis's comment to Eléni Samíou that we saw a moment ago, in which he characterized the Soviet leaders' ardor as valuable but their thought as naïve. What this article does is to expose and correct instances of such naïveté in communist thought. The doctrine that Kazantzakis offers in opposition is of course metacommunistic vitalism, with its belief in things unseen.

He begins with Bergson's famous distinction in *Time and Free Will* between clock time and psychological time, in order to rebut the Bolshevik's assurance that the social sciences have the potential to become as accurate as the physical sciences, which explains why the communists are "studying social phenomena today and are gradually subjecting them to law." "I disagree," objects Kazantzakis. "Vital phenomena, unlike physical phenomena, do not unfold in homogeneous time, which, like space, you can reduce as much as you wish and sum up in a mathematical formula. Vital phenomena unfold and mature in psychological time" (Kaz. 1926b:19).[10]

The Russian concedes that we "cannot predict a revolution with as much accuracy as we can predict a solar eclipse." He insists, however, that the social sciences can at least explain the past and, on this basis, give better predictions of the future than are possible by any other method. Kazantzakis bombards him with Bergsonian objections: Yes, sociology can interpret the past, because the past is dead; but the future is alive and creative, that is, unpredictable. What if Napoleon had been drowned as a child? Would the French Revolution have metamorphosed into the dream of empire? Could that have been predicted?

This makes the Russian concede every inch of ground except "one ironclad law governing human society: the law of economic causality. . . ."

Now it is Kazantzakis's turn to concede, but not for long. Yes, your point possesses a grain of truth, he tells the leader. "But you generalize [from this truth] so broadly, loading it with so many claims, that it ends up false. . . . First of all, the law you formulated is not an absolute law. Economic causes are not always the greatest forces that set populations into motion . . . ; very often other factors as well . . . determine the way a people evolves" (1926b:21–22). This leads to his final point: "Even the most fanatical Marxists admit that economic causes are the means, not the end. . . . There is some other human need that is stronger and deeper. Humans fight for this whether they know it or not. . . . In order for the masses to . . . create great epochs, they need a divine folly each time, a faith. That is why I consider your sociological theories not only intellectually defective but also incapable in practice of creating a great, fertile movement in human history" (1926b:23).[11]

At this point the Russian gives up. Discussion degenerates into (good-natured?) threat as he comments that if Kazantzakis wishes to stay in Russia spreading such ideas, he will order that he be hanged!

Yet Kazantzakis still considered himself an adherent of communism, at least of a communism possessing "the broad psychological meaning" that he attached to the term (Eleni Kaz. 1977:194; 1968a:154). At precisely the time that the Greek communists were calling him a heretical mystic on account of this article and "The New Pompeii," he felt that in about three years he would be ready to stand for Parliament as a communist candidate from Crete. This would give him the opportunity "to talk to the poor and hungry, in simple words. It's the modern way to preach our religion" (Eleni Kaz. 1977:194; 1968a:154). Evidently his discouraging experience with the "simple folk" of Iráklion had not cured him. To be accurate, however, we must recognize that his primary mission was to preach not to the masses but to Marxist intellectuals.[12]

They answered him publicly, thanks to the forum provided by Glinós, who in the September issue of his periodical had invited discussion of Kazantzakis's first article and had repeated the invitation in the October issue, which had published "The New Pompeii,"[13] stressing that *Anayénnisi* would not reject a priori any viewpoint expressed in a scholarly manner, that is, based on research (*Anayennisi* A:117). Subjectivism and partisan rhetoric were excluded. Glinós's dream was to raise the level of intellectual debate in Greece in order to encourage those ideas that showed the way to a "radical regeneration of contemporary civilization" at home and abroad.

All this explains the elevated level of discussion (especially compared to the mud-slinging that Kazantzakis endured in the 1950s on account of his novels) that commenced in the November 1926 issue. Kazantzakis led off with a "Prosisagoyikó simíoma" (Introductory Note) in which he effectively placed himself hors de combat. For a student of Kazantzakis's complicated politicism, this document is especially useful since it so clearly proclaims the author's subjectivism, reminding us that when Kazantzakis stepped back onto the stage of political life he was consciously performing a fiction and thus not forsaking his artistic/religious self but merely expressing it in "living theater" as opposed to novels, credos, or ascetic practices.[14] Here, then, is the substance of his subjectivist manifesto:

> In order for the . . . discussion set in motion by *Anayénnisi* on the occasion of my two articles to have fruitful results, we first of all have to agree, I believe, on several fundamental notions. . . .
>
> I divide people who want to solve philosophical problems not into *materialists*, *idealists*, *positivists*, etc., but into two large categories:
>
> 1) Those who accept the words *matter*, *spirit*, *God*, *life*, *soul*, *ions*, *electrons*, etc. as a satisfactory answer. I place materialists, idealists, positivists, etc. in this category.
>
> 2) Those who find these words unsatisfactory. . . . They are aware of (no, not simply aware of: they *experience*) the terrifying dark forces behind this bulkhead of words. This second category is divided into three classes:
>
> a) All those who tremble and do not dare to step beyond these words. . . .
>
> b) All those who advance with certainty beyond these words. They have discovered Mystery's eternal, real form, and have outlined its substance, activity, and relation to humanity in irrefutable dogmas.
>
> c) All those who . . . advance beyond the words and give a *consciously* transitory form to the unknown forces, but a form that helps us advance.
>
> In this second category, the first group strike me as more "thunderstruck" than is proper, the second as more naïve than is proper. It is to the third—call them what you will—that I belong.
>
> But in order for this third class to be adequately defined, we must . . . distinguish the following two notions: *hypothesis* and *fiction*. A hypothesis claims to discover the Truth (with a capital T);

> it wants to conform to Reality (with a capital R) as faithfully as possible. A fiction makes no such naïve claim; it is a useful means commensurate, in a *fruitful* way, with mankind's need to integrate the fragmented details of its observations and theories. A fiction helps us (1) to advance, (2) to avoid self-deception. . . .
>
> In other words, *a hypothesis discovers, a fiction invents.*
>
> The means used by people in the third class of the second category in order to advance beyond the words "matter," "spirit," etc. are not "hypotheses"—they are "fictions." (Kaz. 1926a)

Not having the benefit of this subjectivist declaration in advance, Messrs. Karoúzos and Kordátos, who had responded immediately to Glinós's invitation for commentary on "Discussion with a Leader," took Kazantzakis in that article at his word. Karoúzos's "Answer to Mr. Kazantzakis" was published in November, Yánnis Kordátos's "Physical and Social Laws" in December, and his "The Critics of Marxism" in January. Others then joined the debate, as we shall see. I of course cannot reproduce all these articles, some of which are lengthy, but I do wish to offer several summaries.

Karoúzos begins provocatively by declaring, "In *Anayénnisi*'s first issue, Mr. Kazantzakis published a lyrico-philosophical prose-poem" (Karouzos 1926:137). He proceeds to refute Kazantzakis's Bergsonism, claiming that it is arrogant of Kazantzakis to distinguish natural life from the life of human societies, which are governed by laws and therefore subject to scholarly investigation and prediction. Indeed, scholarship has discovered the basic factor of historical evolution, namely economic determinism (139–140). In sum, Mr. K's "foggy, mystical, undisciplined, and anarchic" conclusions demonstrate only this: "It is one thing for the poet to hallucinate the 'integral circle' . . . and quite another to understand the historical development of human society" (142).

Kazantzakis answered briefly in a "Déftero simíoma" (Second Note), beginning: "We've made a mess of it." The subject is supposed to be "Are physical and social laws the same?" which really means, "What are the limits of the human intellect and consequently of science?" (Kaz. 1926e: 203). Karoúzos expresses the "faith that reached its zenith in the mid-nineteenth century, that science has absolute sovereignty over social as well as physical phenomena," as well as the "faith that reached its zenith in the Middle Ages, that there is an objective reality outside of humanity and that the purpose of science is simply to discover the laws that exist in nature independently of mankind" (203–204). If this discussion is going to have any value, he continues, we must stick to the topic, which means answering the following questions: "1. Can the human intellect conceive of 'what really is' (Τὸ ὄντως ὄν, the thing-in-itself), or only of phenomena? 2. Of all phenomena, or only of materialistic ones? 3. Of materialistic phenomena, or only of the relationships among them? 4. Are these relationships real, outside of mankind, or only human? 5. Are the only possible ones human, or just the most convenient ones?" He ends with the pessimistic opinion that nothing new will be added to this philosophical investigation. "But let's at least be lucid" (204).[15]

At this point, Glinós intervened editorially, picking up Kazantzakis's parting thrust and also Karoúzos's recourse to ad hominem tactics in his insinuation that Kazantzakis was merely a poet hallucinating foggy conclusions. Greek discussants are probably not capable of adding anything to the topic, concurs Glinós, but this does not matter:

> In this kind of discussion, even the errors of the discussers are most instructive. But for the matter to proceed in a suitable way, all of us must first speak with cool and sober self-control, without even a trace of personal innuendo. . . . The gain will be immense if once and for all in Greece we can have a discussion that does not end in personal insult. . . . (*Anayennisi* A:204)

Glinós then goes on to say that Kazantzakis's second note fails to get to the heart of the matter. The central question is, "Does there exist a *science of ethical phenomena* in the same way that there exists a science of physical phenomena?" (*Anayennisi* A:204–205).

We will appreciate, I trust, Glinós's effort to shed light on basic principles that might determine one's stance vis-à-vis communism, as well as Kazantzakis's role in stimulating responsible debate. Happily, Yánnis Kordátos's first article fulfills *Anayénnisi*'s expectations by sticking to the topic and by arguing from a broad knowledge of history. Without innuendoes against anyone, it comes directly to the point: "Does that which happens in nature . . . also happen in the life of [human] societies?" Objective investigation of every historical era shows various phenomena recurring. "We can therefore say that in social life there is no *irregularity* whatsoever, i.e. nothing happens by chance" (Kordatos 1926:200–201). "It is true that the professor of political economy cannot forecast an industrial or commercial crisis" with the same accuracy with which the astronomer can predict an eclipse. "However, this does not mean that social laws are not firm, but only that our knowledge is still limited. . . . All human acts, efforts, desires, and feelings have a specific cause. They are not independent, incoherent phenomena, the products of free will; they are determined" (203).

It is noteworthy that Kordátos never once refers to Kazantzakis's article in this first part of his response; he saves that for the second part, entitled "I epikrités tu Marksismú" (The Critics of Marxism). Kazantzakis, unlike others who censure Marxism, he says here, "does not begin with . . .

aphoristic dogmatism. He discusses; he offers examples; he thinks. He is neither a 'conservative' type nor an 'apologist' for contemporary social institutions. What he wants is precisely to be 'a friend of the new Russia,' and also a revolutionary man of letters. . . ." However, influenced "solely by Bergson, he finds no other suitable philosophy to meet his expectations. This is why he is impelled to suppose that 'fictions' and imaginary 'myths' are an innermost human need, a position that brings him close to Sorel's syndicalistic anarchism. . . . He is therefore thoroughly *anti-materialist* and *anti-dialectical*. This explains his quarrel with Marxism. Marx's dialectical materialism rejects metaphysical acrobatics . . ." (Kordatos 1927:260). We are told by Kazantzakis that the "materialistic conception of history . . . is *one-sided*. . . . We do not say that in a given historical period nothing but economic phenomena played a role, but that the basic origin of historical change was economic causes. . . . Ideas . . . have great influence, but their origin is not from on high, they are not pure and unexpected *creations* of the 'spirit' " (264).

Kordátos's second article brought the *Anayénnisi* debate to a close, in effect. The controversy should teach us that Kazantzakis, even at this stage in his leftist allegiance when he still viewed the Soviet Union as mankind's hope, (a) promulgated his heresies publicly without hesitation, (b) was not appreciated by the Greek left, (c) yet was important enough to make leftist intellectuals notice him rather than look the other way. Furthermore, the controversy should teach us that in this kind of presentation Kazantzakis was neither a careful scholar nor an original thinker, but a clever journalist using the trappings of logic on the one hand and poetic rhetoric on the other to capture his audience from both sides, so to speak. I do not mean that he was "slick"; I believe that he was sincerely pursuing an educational mission. But as his high-handed "Second Note" demonstrates, he was not always prepared to *discuss*. He tossed his intellectual grenades and let the shrapnel scatter, without waiting for his opponents' next move.

In this instance, when Kordátos's rebuttal appeared in January 1927, Kazantzakis was already enjoying his previously postponed journey to Egypt and Sinai. After his return from Moscow he had traveled first to Palestine and Cyprus, then in the late summer to Spain, and in October to Italy. All these trips were sponsored by newspapers and resulted in articles subsequently collected as additions to *Taksidévondas*; all were political in ways we must consider. Last but certainly not least, much of what Kazantzakis encountered helped him in his imaginative writings. Egypt enters the *Odyssey*, as we know; Mussolini (whom he interviewed in Rome) is one of the models for the Big-Jawed Man in *Toda-Raba*; the topography of Palestine appears in *The Last Temptation*.

But we must take care not to get ahead of ourselves. I still wish to show the aftereffects of Kazantzakis's second trip to the Soviet Union, which means that we must consider yet another essay, "Crucified Russia," the one cited along with *Askitikí* and "The New Pompeii" by Bishop Athanásios of Syros in his anti-Kazantzakian memorandum to the Church. Kazantzakis was already placing himself in a no-man's-land between the left and the right, a situation much exacerbated as his career unfolded. He knew this and did not attempt to avoid it by capitulating in either direction; instead, he cherished his position as a lone voice crying in the wilderness, scorned by all.

"Crucified Russia" appeared in the January 1927 issue of *Anayénnisi* and was later incorporated in *Taksidévondas. Rusía*, considerably condensed. An attempt to define metacommunism, it is the piece to which Kazantzakis was referring, I believe, when he shared the following fears with Eléni Samíou on 13 December 1926: "I've finished the essay on metacommunism that I wrote you about. . . . It will be published later—because it is a decisive step in my life and I have to ponder over it very much. It's a big rupture with communism—not in a backward direction, of course, but terrifyingly forward. All my communist friends will be furious; those who agree will misinterpret again . . ." (Eleni Kaz. 1977:196; 1968a:155). The provocation begins with the opening paragraph:

> One day I was leaving a workers' meeting. . . . The workers had been . . . arguing among themselves . . . , their brains . . . blinded by two or three correct, coarsely wrought doctrines [Kaz. 1927c:271].
>
> O! the spirit, I was thinking . . . How many of these will be enlightened . . . ? Very very few. . . .
>
> "Well, comrade, I said with a laugh to my friend . . . , what are you thinking?"
>
> "I detest people—that's what I'm thinking. The idea is degraded as soon as it touches them. . . . For three years I wrestled with the god-awful . . . factory, trying to do as much good as possible. . . . Eventually I felt that . . . the state system was to blame [272]. I sided with the workers. . . . They too thirsted for light, justice, love—like me. That's what I kept saying. I battled to organize them, . . . to displace the center of their struggle from the belly to the brain. Useless! . . . How can you expect the rebirth of the world from such masses?"
>
> ". . . The idea follows dark underground pathways and its feet are covered with mud. . . . What do you expect here on this muddy earth with its lewd beings all with belly, penis, and uterus? [274] . . . You want everyone to be enlightened first and then to rise up and revolt. But a revolution was never made by the major-

ity. The few always . . . organize as many as they can with the lure of an immediate hope . . . [275]. *Blood and crime are the indispensable initiation.* . . . 'God'—let us give that name to the dark forces—is not the kindly family-man we thought. He is cruel, he does not care about individuals. . . . He descends . . . and catches hold of what he wants—of humanity's belly, penis, mind. *The first moment of his descent is called Chaos. . . . Justice and happiness are moments of somnolence contrary to life's sublime nature.* . . . Today Russia is the world's vanguard, opening a path amid blood and hunger. . . . But from the innumerable deaths will remain just a kravyí. . . . Even the greatest Russian forerunners . . . assumed they were bringing justice, peace, and love. . . . But a spirit higher than them blows down upon them, leaving them behind and mobilizing everyone." . . .

"Do you think, then, that the overthrow of the Russian régime and everyone's turmoil will take on . . . a religious meaning? But people can no longer believe in hopes after death. . . . They want this life . . ." [277].

"There is only one way for us to enjoy our ephemeral moment keenly . . . : *To subject ourselves to a rhythm higher than ourselves.* . . . Faith . . . has always been the most ardent method for humanity to experience . . . *not the next world, the future one, but this terrestrial world.* The masses can become elevated only through faith. And what does 'elevated' mean? It means to subject their needs and desires to a *supra-individualistic, i.e. a more profoundly human, rhythm.* . . . Even if the lógos does not come to save Russia's inarticulate kravyí, the kravyí will keep working tirelessly on the generations of mankind, until it becomes a lógos. . . ." . . .

"What are we supposed to call this heretical way you look upon communism? With such positive means you are struggling to reach such a mystical goal. . . . What you are talking about is not communism!"

"What value do names have? . . . However, so that your mind may rest at ease, give it a name, call this heretical opinion of mine not communism, but *metacommunism.*"

This diffuse essay does not represent Kazantzakis at his incisive best. Nevertheless, it is easy to see why Bishop Athanásios of Syros, Tinos, and Andros read "I stavroméni Rusía" with horror. Indeed it is the first text he cites in his memorandum regarding the communist infection and antireligious currents being transmitted to Greek society. He alerts his Synod, "In this article (p. 275) we read 'Blood and crime are the indispensable initiation.' And: 'You see, "God"—let us give that name to the dark forces—is not the kindly family-man [οικογενειάρχης] we thought. He is cruel, he does not care about individuals. He kills, gives birth, kills again' " (Athanasios 1928:84). After quoting copiously from *Askitikí*, with a side glance also at "The New Pompeii" and Elli Lambrídi's assertion that Christianity was good in its own time but must be replaced today by a new religion, he goes on to condemn Greek booksellers for their ever-increasing trade in translations of Marx, Lenin, Trotsky, and Renan. This, as I noted earlier, was the beginning of a wrestling bout between Kazantzakis and ecclesiastical authorities (supported by other conservative elements)[16] that would culminate in efforts to excommunicate him and deny him Christian burial (both unsuccessful), not to mention the placement of *The Last Temptation* on the Roman Catholic index of forbidden books, which of course greatly aided its sales throughout the world.

But the Church and Kazantzakis did not come to serious grips until the 1950s. In the 1920s, continuing into the 1930s, his more problematical relationship was with the communist and noncommunist left. This went from bad to worse. Despite his continued usefulness to the left owing to his journalism (a new series on the Soviet Union published in January 1928) and his fiercely pro-Russian lecture in the Alhambra Theater in that same month, his basic mentality was "heretical" in ways that his critics in the *Anayénnisi* debate made clear in reference to "Discussion with a Leader" and that they would have been even more emphatic about had "Crucified Russia" also been under consideration. But even they were in for a surprise. This is because Kazantzakis's heretical mysticism, idealism, subjectivism, "as-if-ism," Sorelism, Shestovism, and Bergsonism were soon to be joined by something even more antipathetic to the far left: an attraction to fascism. The seed is already in "Crucified Russia," perhaps because this essay was written shortly after Kazantzakis's visits to Primo de Rivera's Spain and Mussolini's Italy. This seed, although unnoticed by his critics, is easy to discern in hindsight. I am referring to his insistence that our lives, if they are to have immeasurable meaning, must be subjected to a rhythm higher than ourselves—to something supra-individualistic. Of course this was not the first time he had voiced such a sentiment; furthermore, he was thinking of communism, not fascism, when he did so. But in fascism he discovered another "supra-individualistic rhythm" that seemed to have great power. Thus he dared to suggest that there were similarities in the two ideologies, at least similarities of means if not of ends, in defiance of the communist line that considered fascism a bitter rival in every respect.

This new interest is something we must discuss both now and later. First, however, so that we may properly round off the 1925–1926 trip to the Soviet Union, I wish to mention one more article published by Kazantzakis in *Anayénnisi*—the final one, which also served (with significant revisions) as the conclusion to *Taksidévondas. Rusía.* Called Επισκόπηση της Σοβιετικής Ρουσίας (Survey of Soviet Russia), it consists of ten conclusions that may be summarized as follows:

1. We live in a time of crucial change. The World War brought one age to a close; the Russian Revolution inaugurated another age (Kaz. 1927d:349).

2. This change did not occur peacefully. That is always what happens in history.

3. The proletariat wanted to realize its ideals all at once. But this was impossible.

4. Lenin understood that accommodation was necessary (350).

5. Within Bolshevism itself there were two opposing tendencies: the uncompromising version of the communistic ideal and the accommodating version. Russian communism is not an inflexible system but an organic one with left and right wings that contend and strike various balances.

6. The old table of values has been broken; the new one is not yet engraved. But the first direction is: submission of the individual to the social totality.

7. "Like every living organism, the Bolshevik idea has a tendency to spread. . . ." (351)

8. "*It is inevitable that bourgeois actuality and the Bolshevik idea will come to blows.* The later this happens the better the interests of Bolshevism will be served. Time is its ally. . . . A second, even greater danger is that half-savage tribes are being roused. . . . Who will regulate the new descent of the barbarians? Will Russia, which threw them the spark, be able to discipline these irascible dark forces when the explosion comes?"

9. We are entering an extended time of . . . vicissitude. Later, our period will perhaps be called a middle age, when one civilization is dying and a new one being created. But nothing is certain; the new tendency may succumb to disaster or compromise.

10. "*What is our duty? It is to discern the historical moment in which we live and consciously to assign our small efforts to a given camp.* One current rushes forward, another resists. . . . *The more you are in phase with the current that is moving forward, the more you aid the difficult evolution . . . of mankind.*" Where is this ascending current headed? Toward what goal? No one knows—"not even 'God,' because he too advances with us, groping, in danger, struggling. *Our duty is not to ask, but to advance and work*" (Kaz. 1927d:352; cf. 1965e:267–270).

CHAPTER FIVE

ITALIAN FASCISM

Having seen these conclusions based on the 1925–1926 trip to the Soviet Union, we can return now to Kazantzakis's interest in fascism, always remembering, however, that the major problem for him between 1925 and 1929 was his relation to Bolshevik communism. Of course it is wrong when discussing Kazantzakis to oppose the two interests, because communism and fascism in his view were not an either/or. What attracted him was their similarity, and also their symbiotic relationship. For example, although there is no mention of Italian fascism in the "Survey of Soviet Russia," not even in conclusion no. 8, where he speaks of time as Bolshevism's ally, Kazantzakis was aware that fascism might be a factor delaying the inevitable clash between capitalism and the left,[17] with Mussolini serving as "nothing more than the harsh forerunner, in Italy, of Lenin" (Kaz. 1965d:30; 1975:24). If this were true, then the two ideologies, so bitterly antagonistic on the surface, might "involuntarily and unknowingly, [be] faithful collaborators" (*Eleftheros Tipos*, 28 Feb. 1927: 1[a]z. 1965d:28; 1975:22).

As in his attraction to communism, so in the new attraction to Italian fascism Kazantzakis carried forward older positions from his nationalistic days, finding yet another bottle for more or less the identical wine. In the same article in which he speaks about the faithful collaborators, he analyzes Mussolini's power by invoking Napoleon, one of his favorites from the "discontinued" phase, and he summarizes Il Duce's strengths in terms that are Dragoumian: "His central core is not an idea but a faith." His "supreme duty is *élan*, vitality, mobilized faith" (Kaz. 1965d:26, 28; 1975:20, 22). As I suggested previously, in fascist Italy Kazantzakis encountered people who had found a way to subject their lives to a supra-individualistic rhythm.[18] On the lowest level this could be expressed through the organized energy he had admired in the German *Jugendbewegung* in Berlin: "You should see these young people . . . , how they sing, how they go on excursions, how they work, how they dress . . ." (Kaz. 1958a:101; 1979:62). More deeply, supra-individualism was valued by Kazantzakis as a manifestation of Dionysiac oneness. In short, he viewed Italian fascism (as he did everything else) in a way more religious than political, admiring its conscious and unconscious ritualism as well as its harsh realism about life's cruelties, which for Kazantzakis meant its allegiance to an ascending "god" totally unlike a kindly father.

We should remember that he had tasted Mussolini's Italy briefly in the winter and spring of 1924, just after he left Berlin. Then he had suspected that Mussolini was greater than people were accustomed to think, that fascism was much more than just a political current, and that some day he would like to study all this further. His chance came when the newspaper *Eléftheros Típos* sent him as a correspondent to Spain (then under Primo de Rivera) and subsequently to Italy six months after his return from Moscow. The series of articles on Italian fascism appeared throughout the month of February 1927, immediately after "Crucified Russia" and simultaneously with the "Survey of Soviet Russia." For those on the far left, they constituted, as I suggested earlier, an unexpected addition to the accumulating evidence of his heresies.

There were fifteen articles in all.[19] Of particular interest is Kazantzakis's assertion that whether one likes Mussolini or not, one cannot be indifferent to him. There is not just order in Italy, he assures us, but something deeper: "discipline . . . a rhythm . . . that cannot derive from external pressure" (6 Feb.). Furthermore, Italian fascism and Russian communism are "the two central points . . . from which today's human drama will unfold" (7 Feb.). "The essence of both [fascism and Bolshevism] is faith, i.e. something . . . beyond logic. . . . Socialism starts with class war and sets as its goal the triumph of the proletariat. Fascism starts with rivalry among the various productive classes; its idea is cooperative effort by all classes for the good of the nation" (11 Feb.). "At first the intellectuals . . . were the greatest enemies of fascism [because] fascism's basis was not theory but action. . . . *Intellectuals are always the last to be swept away by a new faith*" (21 Feb.).

Kazantzakis's interview with Mussolini is strange because in most of it Mussolini is interviewing Kazantzakis. I have already indicated the attributes that Kazantzakis found compelling in Il Duce, whom he presents as a perfect carrier of the *élan vital*, a man dedicated to the assault as opposed to the victory.[20] Kazantzakis ends the interview by emphasizing once more the main point he wished to make in his series on Italy: that fascism and Bolshevism are secret collaborators. He does not overlook the differences in goals. Unlike communism, fascism "inflates the patriotic sentiment and backs Catholicism. It respects private property and fights with dubious means to regulate the class struggle" (Kaz. 1965d:29; 1975:23). But the similarities, even if they lie in the area of means more than ends, are much more striking:

> The violence used by both to subjugate the individual slavishly to the whole. The strict limitations on individual liberty. The implacable control over economic production and consumption, as well as political and social expression. The hatred of the parliamentary system and of liberal democratic ideology. Order, security, immediate suppression of all resistance. A pitiless rhythm. (1965d:29; 1975:23)

Beyond these outward expressions, the two supposedly antagonistic ideologies are similar in the "religious" ways I noted before. Their supra-individualism makes history move; the direction does not matter. Even if they push history backward, this is good because it "obliges the life force that is moving in the other direction . . . to rage all the more" (1965d:28; 1975:22).

Despite Kazantzakis's italicized aphorism, "Intellectuals are always the last to be swept away by a new faith," he himself was an intellectual attracted to Mussolini's fascism for intellectual reasons. In judging him, we must remember first of all that the time was still only 1926–1927 (on the other hand, Kazantzakis's attraction lasted throughout the 1930s). Secondly, we must remember his disgust with liberal democracy because of the shambles it had made of Greece. Thirdly, fascism's program in the early days possessed a leftist flavor to some degree.[21] Fourthly, Kazantzakis was not alone. There was Stravinsky, for example, whose "attraction to the strong-armed government of Mussolini, beginning in the mid-1920s, is understandable," writes Robert Craft, considering "the chaos of the last years of Imperial Russia."[22] Croce was attracted at first; the favorable stance of Eliot, Lawrence, and Yeats is well known; Sorel was able to lavish equal praise on Mussolini and Lenin. . . .

But to get to the heart of Kazantzakis's attraction we must not dwell on any of these considerations but rather return to his intellectualism. Despite his pronouncements advocating radical change, and also despite his devaluation of intellect and his corresponding exaltation of voluntarism and faith, Kazantzakis was primarily a disinterested observer attempting to understand intellectually what others, blinded by immediate needs or goals, could not understand. He was attracted to fascism primarily because of his intellectual excitement at discovering what others had overlooked or had preferred to deny—namely, the "secret collaboration" between ideologies as apparently antagonistic as fascism and communism. The one place where he confesses this intellectualism unmistakably is not in the articles on Italy but in those on Primo de Rivera's Spain, which were written after his return from Italy and thus reflect the latter experience as well as the former. The article printed in *Eléftheros Típos* on 18 December 1926 begins, "One of the greatest pleasures of the human mind is to hear one side, to hear the other also, to acknowledge the relative value possessed by all . . . points of view, and to attempt to create an integral synthesis out of fanatically opposed ideas. Men of action are necessarily always one-sided and narrowminded. Otherwise they would be ridiculous amateurs, powerless to impose a direction on practical life and to assume responsibility." With that as general prologue, he proceeds to the case at hand:

> The two camps are lining up. When the inevitable clash takes place, and when, after the havoc, the new period of creativity be-

> gins, then the men of action will see for the first time that the two enemies were collaborators . . .
>
> I repeat—the pleasure of the human mind that gazes to the right and to the left, removed from action, is this: immediately . . . to discern in the enemies faithful collaborators united in an integral synthesis.

Kazantzakis, I submit, was using the two camps as a laboratory in which he could test his intellectual convictions. Needless to say, this did not endear him to either side.

EGYPT AND SINAI

The next publication to appear in this busy period of Kazantzakis's life was the series on Egypt and Sinai: nineteen articles running in the newspaper *Eléftheros Lógos* from 3 April to 3 May 1927.

The long-desired journey to Africa had materialized at the end of the previous January[23] after vigorous efforts initiated by Kazantzakis almost immediately after his return from Italy. He had originally craved this experience for the *Odyssey*'s sake, a motive that continued to be primary.[24] But the articles on Egypt also have a political interest. In them Kazantzakis continues his leftist bias insofar as he looks toward the Soviet Union as the embodiment of the future; at the same time, he continues to offer his mystical philosophy as a stumbling block between himself and the Marxists.

Regarding Soviet Russia, he situates her in the larger context of eastern nations. The discussion is concentrated in the chapter of *Taksidévondas. Eyiptos* called "Contemporary Life," where he treats Egypt's difficulties as a colony awakening to nationalism but consequently incurring new problems such as mimicry of the West (Kaz. 1965d:69; 1975:65–66). The dilemma is whether to renounce the West and remain economically backward or to learn from the West and become a mere imitator, losing the distinguishing aspects of native culture. As a radical answer to this dilemma Kazantzakis offers the dissolution of European civilization: "Only . . . then will the Oriental world be able to give once more to Europe what it has always given—new seed" (Kaz. 1965d:70; 1975:66). He predicts that this will happen soon: "The new World War that is coming will probably destroy [Europe] completely . . . Then the entire fate of the world will be displaced from the West to the East. And when I say the East, I include Russia" (1965d:77; 1975:73).

The clash between his mysticism and the Marxists is encountered in the description of a banquet given him on the eve of his departure from Alexandria and also in the "Letter to Mudíta" (Elli Lambrídi)[25] that is appended to the original articles to form their conclusion in *Taksidévondas*. At the banquet a young man approaches Kazantzakis with the abrupt challenge, "Much of what you wrote in *Anayénnisi* we do not accept." The banquet must have been held in February 1927; hence the Alexandrian leftists would have seen "Discussion with a Leader," "The New Pompeii," and perhaps even "Crucified Russia." Kazantzakis then sets up a debate, turning the affair into a true symposium with himself as a latter-day Socrates. People side with one political faction or another, but before long there are two major camps: those who assert that economic causes are the prime movers of history, and those who disagree. When Kazantzakis's turn comes, he divides life into matter and spirit, preferring to speak of matter as "hunger" and spirit as "passion"—all this after first declaring himself a monist. With these and other qualifications behind him, he summarizes his position as follows: ". . . Hunger—the economic cause—is the prime motive in normal times, i.e. most of the time. But in critical times . . . the prime motive is passion" (1965d:83; 1975:79). The "Letter to Mudíta" extends the activist side in an important new direction: toward the "barbarians" of the third world. He declares here that the contemporary god must don the mask of the worker who is hungry and in revolt. He must no longer be the chief of a single tribe, like Jehovah, but of the entire human race. "The 'Exodus' from the land of bondage has begun. . . . The peoples of the East are getting into rank, interchanging passwords, and setting out. . . . All the Asiatic and African peoples sense their brotherhood, and this is the greatest event of our times. In the lead with them are all the peoples of Europe and America who are oppressed and in revolt . . ." (1965d:140; 1975:139). On the other hand, he declares with equal conviction:

> We are on an island. Everything that we create with our senses and think with our minds is a tiny island consisting of human brain and flesh in the midst of a boundless, barren, all-dark ocean. No matter where we begin, we always find the abyss at the end. We weep, shout, curse, turn back, try another route. We say: Finally, this road is one that will continue forever. But at the end we always discover the abyss. (1965d:139; 1975:138)

None of this is new. What is new in *Taksidévondas. Eyiptos*, besides the extension of his political vision to Africa and Asia, is the discovery of two splendid symbols: the Nile for human effort, and the desert for the force which, bordering that effort on all sides, will swallow it up:

> Never will I forget how one day, from the highest point in Heliopolis, suddenly I glimpsed the desert through the cool green leaves of a banana plant—close by, lying in wait, glistening like a

> rose. My heart skipped a beat because I sensed that this terrible tiger would win out, sooner or later. In vain does the Nile cover a narrow, insignificant ribbon of sand and make it fruitful. For how long? Wretched half-naked people draw up water, dig irrigation ditches, sow seed, hoe, struggle. The moment the Nile shrinks—and it will shrink—everything will fall back into the calm, gray, unconquerable sand. (1965d:40–41; 1975:34–35)

An island in a boundless sea, the Nile surrounded by desert, or Odysséas headed for Antarctic ice—the metaphors are interchangeable. They are what the *Odyssey* is all about: this double vision of biological vitality coexisting with eternal annihilation. Elsewhere in *Taksidévondas. Eyiptos* he explains that two criteria helped him to deal with this antinomy or, as he says there, to subject the disordered vision of human life to an ordered hierarchy. These were: (1) the relative criterion, the human one, which filled him with indignation at the suffering and poverty of the Egyptian felaheen; (2) the absolute criterion, the inhuman one, which "views all these human undulations without being deceived by any theory or hope . . ." (1965d:46; 1975:41–42). Most starkly, the Nile and the desert—Egypt's green face and her sandy gray one—are the great Yes and No, both of which, Kazantzakis asserts, he profoundly loves (1965d:47; 1975:42).

All in all, *Taksidévondas. Eyiptos* is a particularly felicitous expression of a total political vision in which communism and Buddhism are somehow forced to cohere.

ODYSSEY; THIRD TRIP TO THE SOVIET UNION; PANAÏT ISTRATI

When Kazantzakis returned from Egypt and Sinai, he remained in Athens temporarily in order to draft his articles. His great wish, however, was to settle somewhere else and resume the *Odyssey*. Paris was his first choice, since Eléni Samíou was living there at the time, but all his machinations to convince *Eléftheros Lógos* to send him abroad came to nothing, and he decided instead to retreat to the nearby island of Aegina (Eleni Kaz. 1977:205; 1968a:163).

There, in peace, from 19 May to 22 September, he worked from 5 A.M. to 8 P.M., determined to finish all twenty-four cantos of his colossal Οδύσσεια. In Athens the gossips were busy. One periodical wrote in June, "Goethe could not complete an analogous epic. Will Kazantzakis have the stamina?" (Eleni Kaz. 1977:206; 1968a:164). But Kazantzakis never lacked stamina. "My desire is as extreme as can be; so is my perseverance," he declared in the same month to his new friend Pandelís Prevelákis (Prev.

1965b:27), whom he had met in Athens several months before his departure for Egypt. In August, he was still going strong: ". . . In three or four days Canto 17 will be finished. . . . I think that these months have been the best of my life" (Prev. 1965b:33).

In late August, when Kazantzakis had almost completed Canto 20 and the end was in sight, he had already begun to worry about the immediate future. The accustomed rhythm was asserting itself: he was ready to return to activism but craved non-Greek companions and still wished to settle in Paris near Eléni Samíou. Toward this end, he attempted through Venizélos's influence to gain an appointment to the Institute de Coopération Intellectuelle Internationale, without success (Prev. 1965b:38–39; Elli Alexiou 1966:238). He had to be content temporarily with a contract that Preveákis arranged for him with the Eleftheroudákis Encyclopedia for an extensive series of well-paid articles, starting with Buddha, Gandhi, and Lenin.[26]

At this point, his choices seemed to be either to manage to live in Paris thanks to hack work for the Encyclopedia, or to found an intellectual retreat center in an abandoned monastery outside of Athens—something that depended on the government's willingness to turn the building over to him (Prev. 1965b:30, 32, 50; 1958:67–68; 1961:40–41). Fortunately, fate intervened: "As you know, 8 November [*sic*] is the anniversary of the Russian Revolution," he wrote to Eléni Samíou at the end of September:

> Extra special celebrations will take place in Moscow now, on the tenth anniversary, and the Russian government has invited one or two people from each country. They invited only one from Greece and it happens to be me. . . . Perhaps I'll publish a series of articles. . . . I'm extremely moved at the prospect of seeing Russia again. . . . I'll take some copies [of *Askitikí*] in English translation to give to people I find in Moscow. It's a bit dangerous for me to make propaganda for metacommunism, which the communists hate so much, but I must . . . (Eleni Kaz. 1977:208; 1968a:165)

He still expected to be in Paris in December, not foreseeing that this third journey to Russia would lead quickly to a fourth. The immediate problem was to take advantage of the opportunity at hand. He feared that the Greek government would not allow him to go (Prev. 1965b:53). In addition, he was pessimistic about convincing an editor to dare publish the resulting articles because of the "vehemently anti-communist current" in Greece. Finally, at the last minute, he persuaded Η Πρωΐα to accept ten articles.[27]

On 20 October he departed, again by ship through the Dardanelles to Odessa. He remained for two months, until 22 December. Thus we find him—after the "diversions" to Egypt, Sinai, Spain, and Italy (not to mention Palestine and Cyprus),[28] and the intense interlude devoted to completing the *Odyssey*'s first draft—traveling once again along the major route that determined his direction between 1925 and 1929, namely the renewed attempt to act in the Soviet context and also to continue his service as an evangelist in Greece for the new faith.

The excitement of the tenth anniversary celebrations is well conveyed in Chapter 26 of *Report to Greco*, and also in Kazantzakis's letters to Samíou and Prevelákis. What is omitted in these sources is his own participation. All we see is (1) his resolve to play an active role in the congress (Prev. 1965b:58), and (2) his curt entry in his diary for 12 November: "Congress. I spoke" (Eleni Kaz. 1977:215; 1968a:171). Fortunately, we possess other sources. From these we learn that the congress was a grand affair with more than one thousand delegates from all over the world. It opened with an account by Aleksey Rykov, the Soviet premier, of the Revolution's first ten years (Prev. 1958:212; 1961:130). The main topic was how to avert the attack that the Russians expected momentarily from bourgeois nations. When this came under discussion, Kazantzakis went to the podium and delivered a ferocious oration whose contents we know because he summarized them in the article published on 10 January 1928 in *Proïa* under the heading "The Moscow Congress." "I am convinced," he told the delegates,

> that we are heading inevitably toward a new capitalist war. Peace propaganda is superficial and dangerous. Life is not an idyll but is profoundly tragic and has never obeyed reason or the goodwill of mankind. Among other things, it is excessively optimistic to hope that we shall be able to organize the masses of workers in a way that enables us to avert war at the crucial moment. This may lead to disaster. Bourgeois régimes will never allow us either the means or the time to organize our forces. The moment is critical. What is our duty?
>
> We must look the problem in the face. With harshness and lucidity we must propagandize the masses with this slogan: "Capitalist war is inescapable because for a war to occur is in the interests of the capitalists, who lead you by the nose. There is only one salvation: you must prepare for a socialist war."
>
> This conception of the goal is not a mere nuance. The prevailing view today is this: Let us proclaim to the masses that they will be able to escape the war if they organize. I suggest: Let us proclaim to the masses that capitalist war is inescapable.
>
> There is a profound difference between the two conceptions. In the first, we urge the peoples of the world to be optimistic, which may make them feel secure, again fatally. With this optimism, the

> peoples will find themselves embroiled again in war, which in their naïveté they thought they could escape. In the second, the masses are no longer lulled by delusion and their aim is no longer negative and chimerical—that they will escape war—but positive and realistic: When the capitalist war comes, they will convert it into a socialist war (Kaz. 1928d).[29]

This outspoken pronouncement made him fear that his passport would be taken away if he returned to Greece (Eleni Kaz. 1977:215, 219; 1968a:174–175); but it endeared him to Panaït Istrati, the person who was destined to become the major factor in the ensuing segment of his career. Istrati sent him an invitation the very next day. "They'd told me you were a mystic," he commented in his idiomatic Greek, according to Kazantzakis's account,

> "but I see that you've got your act together and need more than fresh air to fill your belly! . . . You laid it into them all right—those idiotic Europeans. They think they're going to prevent the war with their little pacifist penholders, or, if war does break out, that the workers, supposedly enlightened by their propaganda, will revolt and throw down their arms! Bullshit! I know the workers all too well. They'll go off to the slaughter again and kill. You said it right. Like it or not, a new World War is going to break out, and we might as well be ready!" (Kaz. 1965e:236; 1989:228; cf. 1964a:488; 1965c:406).[30]

It was an impetuous friendship just like the one between Kazantzakis and Sikelianós in 1914, and destined to travel the same road of estrangement followed by reconciliation. Istrati's importance in Kazantzakis's life is best summarized in the letter to Preveläkis dated 12 October 1936 that we have already seen more than once, in which Kazantzakis, listing his political allegiances, names nationalism first and then the "left wing (never a communist . . .)." The "pale shadow" he felt by his side during the latter allegiance, replacing Dragoúmis, is cited as Istrati (Prev. 1965b:464–465) even though Istrati did not enter the picture until long after Kazantzakis had begun to look to Bolshevik Russia for "salvation." In any case, Kazantzakis's leftist aspirations and activities now became linked with Istrati's in ways we shall see. This changed all his immediate plans.

Who was Istrati? As Prevelákis says, writing in 1958, "thirty years ago that question would have been out of place" (Prev. 1958:213; 1961:130). In the 1920s Istrati had charmed all of Europe with his autobiographical roman-fleuve *Les Récits d' Adrien Zograffi*, starting with volume one, *Kyra Kyralina*, in 1924. Karl Kerényi reminds us that he was the first to awaken European interest in the Balkans, in this sense paving the way for Kazantzakis's great success with *Alexis Zorbas ou Le Rivage de Crète* in France a quarter of a century later (Kerényi 1959:43). Indeed, Istrati was "Zorbatic" in his own right. Born in Rumania the illegitimate son of a Rumanian peasant and a Greek smuggler, he ran away from home at age fourteen to wander through the East—Constantinople, Port Said, Jerusalem, Damascus, Alexandria—working as a baker's assistant, grocer, waiter, blacksmith, house painter, stevedore, and itinerant harvester, sleeping under bridges, reading Russian novels, and soaking up folktales. After a short time back in Rumania as a pig farmer and a new convert to socialism, he found himself a "vagabond philosopher" in Switzerland at the age of thirty-two, and there discovered the marvels of the French language. Reading Romain Rolland's *Jean-Christophe*, he determined to become a writer. He inscribed a twenty-page letter to Rolland detailing his misery and aspirations. Rolland did not answer. In 1921, in despair, Istrati cut his throat in the Parc Albert in Nice, where he was working as a photographer on the beaches. This was his great good fortune, because a farewell note addressed to Rolland was discovered on him and forwarded, whereupon Rolland rushed to his bedside, intrigued by the fact that the desperate letter of an immanent suicide was twice interrupted by humorous anecdotes of his past adventures. Rolland told him to write books instead of letters, and got Eugène Ionesco to encourage him as well. Istrati recovered. He completed *Kyra Kyralina* while working as a photographer on the beaches of Normandy and Brittany.

It was an instantaneous critical and popular success. Rolland hailed him as the "Gorky of the Balkans." Additional fictionalized accounts of his childhood, wanderings, and adventures came rapidly from his pen. "These vigorous tales, colorful, alive, charged with a human emotion totally new and yet as old as the world," established his career (Talvart and Place 1950:11; Kaz. 1927e:1; Istrati 1931:7–8; *Monde*, 14 July 1928). Yet Istrati continued to lead a pitiable existence, preferring further adventures to affluence. Thus in an indignant article in *L'Humanité* called "Peuple écoute" (4 May 1927), he bid a disgusted farewell to Western civilization in its state of decomposition and, in Kazantzakis's words, "took refuge in the new land where he will henceforth live and work—Russia. At the height of his glory . . . Istrati is cutting all of his ties with the West, abandoning all the small certainties, and throwing himself into a new, supremely high adventure in vagabondage—into the great uncertainty of Russia" (Kaz. 1927e:2).[31]

Kazantzakis's account is part of a newspaper article meant to introduce his new friend to the Greek public and in the process to explain why he was so drawn to the Gorky of the Balkans. He goes on to assure his readers that "Marxist theory and official communism do not constrict Istrati's soul in the least. He is going to work in Russia; to try to see and express her bright, bloodied features without Procrustean bias and without excessive, superficial hope" (Kaz. 1927e:2). This last prediction was to turn out false. What Kazantzakis's article discovers (or invents) is the Istrati whom he saw before him in those early months of the friendship—the Istrati who would become the accompanying shadow during his own new adventures with the Soviet Union and communism.

The unexpected encounter with Istrati made Kazantzakis resolve to change his plans about going to Paris. His aim now was to settle permanently in Russia. Only four days after the encounter, he reported to Prevelákis: "Various Russian periodicals here have proposed that I write articles for them, 50 rubles (5 pounds) each. One can live on 200 rubles a month. The large state publishing house wants to bring out a book of mine; so there may be a way . . ." (Prev. 1965b:59). These prospects eventually solidified into an economic plan that Kazantzakis hoped would keep him afloat, enabling him to bring Eléni Samíou to Russia from Paris and allowing him to maintain his independence from the Soviet government, which he suspected would not appreciate his heterodoxy. Besides the sources of income mentioned above there would be the continuing revenues from the Eleftheroudákis Encyclopedia, and a series of scenarios for the Russian cinema (Eleni Kaz. 1977:224; 1968a:179). The long-term plan was for him and Istrati to travel around Russia and write: "A grand, difficult life lies before me—together with Istrati. . . . Articles, books, organizing, propaganda for abroad" (Eleni Kaz. 1977:221; 1968a:176).

He and Istrati had already begun a tour of the Caucasus; their immediate itinerary included a brief visit to Greece, after which they would resume their Russian activities: "I'll try to put down roots here, giving an abrupt turn to my life" (Prev. 1965b:61).[32] It is important to realize the role played in all this by Istrati, especially considering the reversal that took place later. "My only joy," Kazantzakis wrote Eléni Samíou from Baku, "is Panaït Istrati, who is with me and who will be, I have a premonition, a faithful, warm, and productive companion for the rest of my life. We'll go to Greece together, I'll give lectures, then he'll . . . return to Moscow. We're talking about buying a four-room house to be ready in February. He'll occupy two rooms, I the other two, and I expect that we're going to experience a thousand delights" (Eleni Kaz. 1977:218; 1968a:174).

GREECE: THE ALHAMBRA SPEECH AND ITS CONSEQUENCES

The two friends traveled to Greece together as planned, arriving in Athens on 30 December. They also returned to Russia as planned, but not until February in Istrati's case and April in Kazantzakis's, for their desire to bring the light to Greece involved them both in heaps of trouble, fulfilling Kazantzakis's wish as he approached his homeland: "I'd like to be able to suffer by going hungry, by loving someone hopelessly. . . . Everything comes to me opportunely and I'm ashamed" (Eleni Kaz. 1977:222; 1968a:177).

They did not waste a moment. The day after their arrival, *Proïa* carried Kazantzakis's article introducing Istrati to a curious Greek public (Kaz. 1927e).[33] This, the lecture he intended to give, and the travel articles for *Proïa* had been written on shipboard during the journey home (Eleni Kaz. 1977:221; 1968a:177). Kazantzakis also lost no time in signifying his changed status to Preveläkis by the symbolic act of delivering to him, wrapped in a red cloth, the mask of Nietzsche that had hung over the door of his cell for years—he now possessed a new guru (Prev. 1958:101; 1961:132). Istrati's debut, a public meeting on 11 January in the Alhambra movie theater off Omónoia Square, was arranged by Dimítrios Glinós as part of the series of lectures conducted by the Educational Association. Elli Alexíou, who was present, remembers the crush. A huge audience—"the answer to persecution" (*Anayennisi* B:236)—packed the aisles and sat on each other's laps in the seats (Elli Alexiou 1966:287). The crowd shouted, sang songs, applauded with ever-increasing enthusiasm (Vrettakos 1960:140). Istrati constituted the principal attraction; Kazantzakis was meant to introduce him—which he did, but not before presenting his own lengthy analysis of Soviet problems followed by a call for responsible action, all couched in the "sober intoxication" he liked to affect in his polemical utterances. We know what he said because the full speech was published in *Anayénnisi* under the title "Tí yínetai sti Rusía" (What Is Happening in Russia). Here is a summary:

"Recently the Revolution celebrated its tenth anniversary in Moscow. Forty-three nations of the world sent representatives—manual and intellectual workers. They saw three things: (1) the external vision of Russia, (2) the formidable effort, (3) the great new dangers" (Kaz. 1928b:193).

Under (1) Kazantzakis vividly described the excitement and grandeur of the celebrations—briefly, because what interested him more was part two: Russia's formidable effort from 1921 onward, after hostilities had ceased, to reconstruct its economy. "What we see today is truly a miracle. In minimal time, six years, Russia has managed to raise herself up . . ." (194). He then passed to the great dangers, citing two: one internal, the other external. The internal danger comes from kulaks, nepmen, and bureaucrats, that is, the new bourgeois classes. After explaining the origin of the problem, Kazantzakis proceeded to two possible solutions, Trotsky's and Stalin's (196).[34] The external danger is a world war. Despite his speech at the congress, Kazantzakis now supported the Stalinist policy that Russia's best course for the present was to avoid any provocation that might endanger world peace. "The position of the two opposing worlds is tragic. One still has not matured and seeks the allowance of a few years of peace. The other, which is over-mature and has almost disintegrated, understands . . . how devastating peace may be for it and how equally devastating war may be." Kazantzakis concluded his analysis by invoking Russia's superiority in the "force that is imponderable and inexplicable, the force that we superficially call Idea or Faith because we do not know what else to name it" (197) and by reminding his audience of their duty to "desire salvation . . . at this critical moment for the world" (197–198).

At this point he shifted to Istrati, holding him up as a model because he had renounced the West and fixed his hopes on Russia while being neither a communist nor a bourgeois but simply a human soul fighting for freedom (198).

Istrati's speech—delivered in French and translated extemporaneously half by Prevelákis and half by Kazantzakis (*Anayennisi* B:459; Prev. 1965b: 66)—was published the following day, preceded by the customary editorial disclaimer. Entitled "Social Theories: Between the West That Is Dying and the East That Is Being Born," it was divided into three sections: (1) the collapse of the older world; (2) the "reserves of the new life," that is, the hordes of the hungry and dispossessed "who will step into rank on the front line tomorrow when the need arrives for a new social class to be created"; (3) views of the new world that will have a place "for every healthy being, every moral being" (Istrati 1928a).

"The lecture became an apotheosis. Apotheosis of Istrati and of the humanistic ideal" (*Anayennisi* B:236). What actually happened afterwards, as reported by the conservative newspaper *Proïa*, is that about three hundred communists in the audience "descended on Omónoia Square in a procession, chanting the anthem of the Third International" (*Proïa*, 12 Jan. 1928:6). As if this were not sufficiently provocative, Istrati had also visited imprisoned communists and had made some declarations about the appalling conditions in the Sotiría Tuberculosis Sanatorium (see Istrati 1929a:125–126), which he exposed as a national disgrace especially when compared to the luxurious life of Athenian high society, which he had observed at first hand in the salons that had opened their doors to him, little expecting such ingratitude.

A storm of abuse against Istrati broke out in the conservative press, and he was ordered to leave Greece within a week. But Alexander Papanastasíou, the socialist leader who was then Minister of Agriculture, came to his rescue in the Ministerial Council meeting of 14 January, brandishing Romain Rolland's tribute before the members. He convinced a majority to vote for annulment of the decree of deportation (*Proïa*, 15 Jan. 1928:6; Istrati 1929a:125), whereupon he invited Istrati to tea. But this did not stop the public prosecutor from subpoenaing Istrati, Kazantzakis, and

Glinós for "insulting the state and disturbing civic tranquility" (Vrettakos 1960:140).[35] Nor did it stop the conservative press from continuing its assault against Istrati. This led to the publication of a protest—signed by K. Paráschos, Kóstas Ouránis, Kostís Bastiás, F. Polítis, G. N. Polítis, Alkis Thrýlos, P. Pikrós, N. Lapathiótis, and F. Kóndoglou, among others—against the newspapers in question for "insulting the intellect, and the civilization of this land . . . , about which, at least until now, we were able to boast" (Vrettakos 1960:752–753). The trial, after several postponements, finally took place from 7:30 P.M. to 3:30 A.M. on 1 June, with only Glinós in the dock since Kazantzakis and Istrati had already left the country (*Anayennisi* B:380). Glinós's attorneys were Alexander Svólos and Pericles Rállis. Papanastasíou was among those who testified in his defense (*Anayennisi* B:451–460). He was acquitted.

But Kazantzakis, and especially Istrati, were not forgotten while the trial was pending. On 23 January they were both subpoenaed to defend themselves for allegedly urging the patients in the Sotiría Sanatorium to abandon it and install themselves by force in the fancy villas of Kifissiá! The accused insisted that they had "merely . . . expressed their indignation" at the miserable conditions in the sanatorium. They were released without being charged (*Proïa*, 24 Jan. 1928:6). The next day *Proïa* carried the news that conditions in the Sotiría would be improved by the addition of two hundred additional beds (*Proïa*, 25 Jan. 1928:6).

Meanwhile, the chief of police, despite the government's decision, kept calling for Istrati's deportation, now on the pretext that he had allegedly invited Maxim Gorky to visit Greece (*Proïa*, 29 Jan. 1928:6). Matters became worse when it was bruited abroad that Istrati had accompanied the Minister of Agriculture (or that the Minister had accompanied Istrati) on a visit to Lávrion to hear the grievances of the workers there. This incited a curious debate in Parliament on the morrow.[36] Four days later, on 3 February, the government fell. When a new government was sworn in on 8 February, Papanastasíou was not retained as a minister. An order of deportation was duly served on Istrati, who requested an extension owing to his tubercular condition (*Proïa*, 18 Feb. 1928). Marís, the Minister of the Interior, refused any extension (*Proïa*, 19 Feb. 1928), and Istrati seems to have departed by rail on 21 February (*Proïa*, 21 Feb. 1928). Recalling his Greek experience later, he wrote bitterly:

> I left behind me there sufferings that could find a place worthy of them only in a great epic of our age of horrible terror. Why speak of civilization when, at the foot of the Acropolis, men are thrown on the rocks of islands uninhabited except for a few miserable shepherds who are ordered to let these exiles die of hunger—these communists, these men 'who sleep with their sisters' and who af-

> firm that the Virgin Mary was only 'an ordinary woman'? Why speak of science, pity, help for the sick, when, near to Athens, Sotiría is nothing but a row of death chambers where hundreds of patients in every stage of tuberculosis spit in each other's faces, fight rain and cold, eat worse than pigs ever ate, pursue vermin and rats, vainly howl their ghostly despair, and lamentably await the hour of their supreme deliverance?
>
> Why not, then, . . . wish to burn up this world and prove oneself able to create a better one? . . .
>
> The sight of terrorist Greece made me force down into the bottom of myself the few Soviet evils that I knew at this time, the start of 1928. I applied myself more than ever to the Bolshevik program. . . . I brought my companion [Bilili Baud-Bovy] there. [With] the Cretan and his woman we . . . would compose a bloc of four consciences serving the same ideal. (Istrati 1929a:126–127)

Again, I have recounted events in considerable detail. My motives here, as in the Iráklion incident, have been double: (a) to establish the facts so that further discussion may be based on them and not on conjecture or error,[37] (b) to convey some of the flavor of the political life that Kazantzakis was forcing himself to share. Knowing this flavor, we may better understand the revulsion and withdrawal that were his typical reactions whenever he played the man of affairs. At the end of December, just before leaving Russia, he had determined to give an abrupt turn to his life, bequeathing it a "fierce, extremist expression" (Prev. 1965b:61). Now, six weeks later, and only three weeks after the Alhambra speech, he wrote to Prevelákis from Aegina:

> Here, once again, I've found tranquility, . . . the sea, mountains—and myself. How superficial, how external to my nature were the commotions in Athens, the Sotiría, the examining magistrates, and the ersatz spunk [ψευτοπαλικαροσύνες] of the communists! (Prev. 1965b:65)

In contrast to these commotions, he was reimmersing himself in poetic concerns, trying to learn more about the scansion of the seventeen-syllable iambic line he had chosen for his *Odíssia* (Prev. 1965b:65), and revising one of the most metaphysical of his works, the play *Hristós*. Even more tellingly, he had begun to look beyond the projected activism in Russia: "O! when will our service in Russia be over and we be able to retreat to a quiet hermitage near a huge city? O! how ready I am now for the second draft of the *Odyssey*!" (Eleni Kaz. 1977:226; 1968a:180). At the same time, he was still awaiting trial, preparing his defense, hoping to escape a jail sentence, and deploring the public prosecutor, who "has purchased whatever I have in print in order to prove that I want to destroy religion, morality, fatherland, etc. It's a disgrace for someone to live under the same sky with such creatures . . ." (Eleni Kaz. 1977:226; Kaz. 1968a:180).

Putting all this together, we see the cycle familiar to us from previous years, whereby Kazantzakis screwed his courage to the sticking-place, acted, found difficulties or frustrations, and immediately invoked his "true self," the ascetic, aesthetic, and metaphysical one. In addition, we see once again the Olympianism that so angered all sides. On the one hand he laments the anticommunist atmosphere in Greece; on the other he scorns the communists themselves. As always in Kazantzakis's personality as well as in his works, we are forced to confront this bewildering conjunction of opposites; his "positions" are not positions but temporary shifts of emphasis—swings toward either pole of a duality explicable only in terms of his deepest allegiance, which was to Bergsonian monism.

The trial, as we know, was repeatedly postponed. Istrati had gone to Yalta to await Gorky and "the Cretan," his fellow Dioscuros. Kazantzakis decided to leave, but with mixed emotions. As much as he craved an exit from Greece ("I hope it is years before I see her again" [Eleni Kaz. 1977:228; 1968a:182]), he felt no joy in his heart on the eve of departure: "What I'd like now above all else would be to remain quietly in one spot and to work. And later on, to travel . . ." (Eleni Kaz. 1968a:182). Nevertheless, he sailed on 19 April and five days later reported that he was in Kiev, where Istrati had settled with Bilili, "a thousand plans boiling" (Eleni Kaz. 1968a:183).

FOURTH TRIP TO THE SOVIET UNION; REVISION OF *ASKITIKÍ*

Kazantzakis's fourth and final trip to the U.S.S.R. lasted exactly a year (April 1928 to April 1929) and turned out to be one of the most crucial periods in his development, concluding the cycle begun in 1925, dampening his activism for fifteen years, reaffirming his subjectivism, which vented itself in the revised ending to *Askitikí*, and greatly affecting the second draft of the *Odyssey*, commenced in 1930, after he had laid the ghost of his Soviet activism in the novel *Toda-Raba*.

Although he doggedly pursued the plans developed before he and Istrati had gone to Greece, the Alhambra experience and its consequences had altered his mentality, as we have seen. His letters from Kiev (e.g. Eleni Kaz. 1977:236; 1968a:189; Prev. 1965b:69) show the *Odyssey* to be the only project that mattered to him now; his hopes for active involvement were mere leftovers, those of a man who could not abruptly halt a previous momentum.

Istrati's instability complicated the thousand boiling plans, the most likely of which at this point was a journey throughout Siberia resulting in a co-authored book (Eleni Kaz. 1977:229; 1968a:184). Meanwhile, Kazantzakis was trying his hand at film scenarios. When Istrati and Bilili finally went off to Moscow in early May, he felt greatly relieved: "I'm working quietly in my room, not talking, not seeing anyone. At last I've found my own rhythm. . . . Ever since Istrati left it's as though I'd escaped a stupefying noise" (Eleni Kaz. 1977:231–232; 1968a:185).

His involvement with film led him back to Buddha. "I have done a great deal of thinking about the cinema," he wrote to Eléni Samíou from Kiev on 26 May 1928, "and I'm glad that I chanced to have this experience, too. . . . It's useful for the *Odyssey* (which is going to constitute my life's purpose until 1933) . . . because I feel a most bitter, Buddhistic pleasure in creating passion, love, and conflict out of shadows and then in seeing them suddenly disappear, mutely, like ghosts. Isn't the vast screen of the universe the same?" (Eleni Kaz. 1977:237; 1968a:189). In an almost identical letter sent to Prevelákis the day before, he added that this "harsh pleasure in the huge surge and the abrupt disappearance characterizes what I have written to date," after which he expressed his impatience to begin a projected scenario on Buddha himself, "who . . . plays with shadows, knowing that all things are ephemeral creations of the ephemeral . . . human camera. The idea that a motion picture cannot last more than two or three years and afterwards is erased from the film would fill Buddha with delight" (Prev. 1965b:73).

But his real goal, as indicated above, was the *Odyssey*. Interestingly, in the ensuing months his desire to return to the epic became increasingly obsessive in direct proportion to his growing disgust with the Russians in particular and with mankind in general:

> . . . I'm writing articles for various periodicals here; life is intense and interesting, but I'm scarcely able to speak and write here because the people are naïve and require a few rough-cut dogmas, and their spiritual anguish is detestable.
>
> . . . This life I'm leading here cannot continue longer than a year more. I must confront the *Odyssey* again. . . . (Prev. 1965b:91)

> . . . I'm coming more and more to detest the beast called "man." . . . I'll subdue a few more humane qualities in me and will realize the "type" that is the ultimate point of my being: the "monster." (Prev. 1965b:88)

> What interests me, as you know, is not mankind but that which I so imperfectly call "God." (Eleni Kaz. 1977:237; 1968a:189)

> I'm sorry that I wasn't in Greece to go and see [the earthquake damage in] Corinth. I feel no sorrow, only anger and scorn for

> both the material forces that kill and the humanity that is killed. When I contemplate such spectacles, I find the farcical nature of life unbearable. I shall attempt . . . to express the *spectacle* in consummate lines of verse. (Prev. 1965b:69–70)

> Every day I verify more profoundly that there is something inhuman in me. Somebody inside me converts human desire and tendencies into something dark, cruel, insatiable, and despairing. Istrati is human, a good human being—and he is totally unable to sense this black alchemy. (Prev. 1965b:80)

What we see here as the activist cycle edges toward its anti-activist sequel is the compensatory role played in Kazantzakis's life by art. This was his sole recourse for the resolution of contradictions that he could not resolve by interaction with other human beings. In this instance, the *Odyssey* became the only way he could escape the psychological crisis that developed during this fourth trip to Russia, a crisis arising from his perspicacity in recognizing the contradictions within himself and from his sincerity in admitting his revulsion against establishing meaningful contact with individuals or pitying their sufferings.

The contrast with Istrati is particularly important because Kazantzakis increasingly measured his own "inhuman" tendencies against the opposing "human" ones of his friend, until the Roussakov affair precipitated a complete rupture at the end of the year. Already in May 1928, however, Kazantzakis foresaw the parting of the ways. On the seventeenth, while he was still in Kiev and Istrati was away in Moscow, he dispatched to him an ultimatum in which, as he explained to Prevelákis, he "set out the two roads ahead with inhuman clarity and great, warm sympathy, telling him which road I have taken. Let him come if he can; if he cannot, let him get over the illusion that we are traveling together . . ." (Prev. 1965b:69):

> Dear Panaït,
>
> . . . To "succeed," for me, means to "achieve a great work." . . . Neither you nor I has any more time to squander his strength in the pursuit of aims inferior to his soul. . . .
>
> Panaït, I love you too much to neglect doing everything I can to bring you back . . . to your soul. So far we've done nothing. . . . We're at the peak of the human curve—let's escape the decline!
>
> . . . Personally, I have resolved to concentrate all my powers on transforming the curve into an arrow. If you abandon me, I shall try to "succeed" alone; if we strive together, the task will not be easier, but it will be deeper and richer. . . . (Eleni Kaz. 1968b:194–195; 1968a:187–188)[38]

All these factors—revulsion against activism after the Alhambra imbroglio; alienation from the Russians because of their blindness to anything beyond practical goals, and from Istrati because of his petty formulas for "succeeding"; Olympian scorn for human suffering; involvement with the cinema's Buddhistic ephemerality; the aestheticism/subjectivism that values life as a spectacle; obsessive interest in the "god" that cruelly, indifferently plays with the human soul—combined to induce Kazantzakis to revise *Askitikí* on 11 June 1928, after he had rejoined Istrati, in the interests of shifting the emphasis to the transience of all endeavor.

As originally conceived, we will remember, *Askitikí* was meant to be a metacommunist credo articulating an activism cognizant of cosmological rhythms and indeed incited by those rhythms. The exercises accordingly proceed from vision to action, and the conclusion, while attempting to fuse participation with withdrawal, emphasizes the former:

> This highest degree of our training [áskisis] is called silence.
>
> Not because its contents are the acme of despair, annihilation, incurable ignorance. Silence means: every person, after completing his service in all labors, finally reaches the highest summit—the summit of non-effort, beyond every labor, beyond all contents, beyond purpose and certainty. . . .
>
> Yet within the deep silence, may your mind be plunged into ecstasy and your heart into actions by this confession of faith:
>
> I believe in one God, Digenís Akrítas, . . . warrior at the frontiers. . . .
>
> I believe in the innumerable masks assumed by God throughout the ages and I listen with awe to the indestructible unity.
>
> I believe in his ever-vigilant struggle that tames matter and makes it fruitful . . .
>
> I believe in man's heart, that arena of clay where Akrítas wrestles with death day and night.
>
> Lord, you cry "Help" and I hear.
>
> Blessed be all those who hear, because they shall be saved, by fighting.
>
> Blessed be all those who are saved, because they liberate God, by creating.
>
> Blessed be all those who on their shoulders bear the Supreme Responsibility. (Kaz. 1927f:631)

In the revised version, the material on the silence, altered in part, is separated off as a distinct chapter that Kazantzakis characterized as "a bomb that blows up the entire *Askitikí*" (Prev. 1965b:77). In addition, the beatitudes are changed, with the result that the concept of silence receives an extended meaning. The silence is not now just the thirteenth labor of non-effort beyond every labor; it is the degree of áskisis in which we realize that

> Fire will surely come one day to purify the earth. Fire will surely come to obliterate the earth. . . .
>
> Fire is my God's first and last mask. We dance and weep between two enormous pyres.

Suppressed in the revision is the original text's assertion that the highest degree is called the silence not because its contents are the acme of annihilation and incurable ignorance. This paragraph now reads:

> This highest degree of our training is called the silence. Not because its contents are the extreme of ineffable despair or the extreme of ineffable joy and hope . . .

Instead of the exhortation that our minds may be plunged into ecstasy and our hearts into actions, we now find: "Within the deep silence, . . . sing this magic, proud incantation as you hang over the abyss." The "incantation"—the former "confession of faith"—once more invokes God the defender of frontiers, Digenís Akrítas, with his innumerable masks covering an indestructible unity. Once more this God cries "Help" and is heard by man. But instead of the blessings falling on those who proceed to fight, create, and bear the supreme responsibility, the blessings now fall upon

> . . . all those who . . . rush to deliver you, Lord, and who say: "Only you and I exist."
>
> . . . all those who liberate you and become united with you, Lord, and who say: "You and I are one."
>
> And thrice blessed be those who bear on their shoulders, without faltering, the great, splendid, revolting secret: Even this one does not exist!

What does this mean?

In answering this question (or attempting to answer it), we had best be circumspect. Although certain critics have assumed that it means a single thing that they can paraphrase and then question or condemn, I prefer to see it as a complicated, elusive doctrine that needs to be approached tentatively from various directions. I am also ready to consult Kazantzakis's glosses, hoping that they may encourage us to reduce a multiplicity of interpretations to a single "authorized" one, even though I am simultaneously wary of an author's possible distortion of his own work.

Among various directions of approach, three strike me as the most potentially fruitful: (1) Buddhistic nihilism, (2) Buddhistic and Schopenhauerian subjectivism, and (3) Christian mysticism.

That Kazantzakis's revision of *Askitikí* derives from Buddhism, or at least from his understanding of Buddhism, is shown by an anecdote related by Eléni Samíou in her book on Istrati. Apparently Kazantzakis was in the habit of playfully tormenting the pragmatic, antimystical Istrati with a Buddhistic parable relevant to our concern. We hear about this as Samíou describes the life of the two couples—herself and Kazantzakis, Bilili Baud-Bovy and Istrati—as they traveled around the Soviet Union. At this point they were in Erivan, the capital of Armenia, which they reached on 5 November 1928 (Prev. 1965b:100; 1958:224; 1961:136), that is, five months after Kazantzakis had revised *Askitikí*:

> Unforgettable sunsets in the gardens of Erivan. . . . Kazantzakis . . . would fix his small black eyes on the red sun that slowly slipped between the branches. . . .
>
> "Blockhead, say something!" . . . Panaït suddenly exclaimed. . . .
>
> "*You* speak . . . ," Kazantzakis replied. . . .
>
> "Amusing type, this Bagdassarian. Have you noticed the Buddha he wears on his head? I really don't understand anything . . ."
>
> "And why do you need to understand? How often do we have to say it: and such a thing does not exist." . . .
>
> "O! You dog! I'd forgotten. O! 'Such a thing does not exist!' Go to the devil! . . . Say it, say it, you filthy Buddhist! I want to hear one more time. Buddha was once passing through the gardens of the beautiful prostitute Ambali . . . Then?"
>
> ". . . Ambali opened the doors of her palace, kneeled . . . , and touched the great Liberator's knees. 'Master,' she exclaimed, 'condescend to enter my house . . .'
>
> ". . . Buddha sat down. . . . He put out his hand like a beggar: 'Ambali, my sister,' he said, 'give me alms . . .'
>
> " 'Oh, master . . ., when I see my beloved approaching, I say to him: "Only you and I exist! . . ." '
>
> " 'I am not satisfied, my sister. My hand is empty.'
>
> " 'O! master,' continued Ambali, 'when I take my beloved in my arms, I shout: "You and I are but a single being! . . ." ' "
>
> "Yes, yes!" interrupted Panaït . . . "This is what friends should always say: 'You and I are but a single being.' "
>
> "But, have you already forgotten what comes next, Panaït?"
>
> "No, absolutely not. Ambali thought she had reached the summit. But Buddha was still not satisfied. . . ."
>
> "Yes, Buddha asked for more. 'My sister, my sister,' he told her, 'I have reached greater heights in love. Listen, my sister: "And such a thing does not exist!" ' "

> "O! 'And such a thing does not exist!' " exclaimed Panaït. . . . "Go to the devil, Cretan; you're breaking my heart. The amorous sensation of Nada truly does surpass love and friendship." (Eleni Kaz. 1938:128–132)

The Buddhistic background to Kazantzakis's revision is established as well by a section of his notebooks where he transcribed Buddhistic tales under the heading "La sonorité de silence." We should also realize that in Hinduism the fourth ingredient of the mystic syllable AUM is the silence surrounding the previous three—which are waking consciousness (A), dream consciousness (U), and dreamless sleep (M). This silence constitutes the breakthrough into unity that seems equivalent to what Kazantzakis in one of his letters to Papastefánou termed the "exodus from the exodus"—the fourth degree of initiation following the previous exoduses from humanity, earth, and universe (Mitsotakis 1972:94; Kaz. 1979:36).

What Buddhistic doctrine actually means by this nihilistic denial of existence is elucidated by the Zen master Nyogen Senzaki:

> . . . our mind and body are not two different things, but just one substance with two aspects. Moreover, the same relation which obtains between your mind and your body obtains between your body and the whole universe—and between your mind and the minds of all sentient beings. So you see, the worlds of desire, of the material and of the nonmaterial are one. This sameness is absolute and infinite.
>
> *To avoid the possibility of misunderstanding, however, we speak of this sameness negatively, calling it "Nothingness" or "Nirvana."* (Nordstrom 1976:68; italics added)[39]

But Buddhism also teaches that this "ultimate" enlightenment—this exodus from the other exoduses into Nada and silence—is not ultimate in the sense that nothing follows: ". . . in Buddhism there is no last-act curtain. (The Buddhist conception of time is circular, not linear.)" (Nordstrom 1976:76). As the master Rinzai Zenji explains, after I "shut off both subjective and objective worlds, living in nothingness[,] . . . I open up my subjective world and enter freely into the objective world. . . . You are forbidden . . . to linger [in absolute nothingness] too long. You must move on, move on! [After] you see the beautiful interwovenness of thatness and thisness[,] the struggle of your life becomes your paradise, and you enjoy your work, no matter what you are doing" (Nordstrom 1976:82–83).

The second direction of approach that should prove useful is the subjectivist one. For the source of Kazantzakis's doctrine in this regard we can look again to Buddhism directly, and/or to Schopenhauer, who of course was greatly influenced by Buddhism and helped to insert its doctrines into the discourse of Western philosophy, quite aside from being the first to bring Kazantzakis himself into contact with Buddhistic thought (Prev. 1965b:xliv).

In Buddhism, "the center of the universe is a transcendental subjectivity," not a transcendental objectivity as in Christianity and Islam. This means that there is nothing outside of mind: mind being defined as "an endless chain of three processes: craving, acting and suffering." The entire universe is "subsumed under these three processes. . . . Outside [them], there is nothing. . . . If you ask . . . other religions about their conception of this center, they will respond with names only—'God,' 'Allah,' 'Brahma' and the like. . . . But if you ask a Buddhist, the answer will be [that] you yourself are the creator of the world; 'you' and 'the world' are but two names for the same thing, and that thing is Mind" (Nordstrom 1976:75).

As early as 1906, the very first year of his career, Kazantzakis was musing, "Who knows if the entire universe is not one enormous Thought" (Kaz. 1958i:1022). As early as 1910, he was linking Schopenhauer and Buddha as life-deniers. It was Schopenhauer who introduced him to the radical subjectivism that in the definitive beatitudes of the revised *Askitikí* equates the "Lord" with the thinking self, denying any transcendental objectivity.[40] Schopenhauerian pessimism, although much gloomier than Kazantzakis's vision in *Askitikí*, is a useful part of that work's intellectual background not only because of its link with Buddhism but also in its own right chiefly because it opposes Will to Representation and in so doing includes in one dialectical system what Kazantzakis sometimes—despite his avowed monism—expressed in two separate systems, the Bergsonian and the Buddhistic, the first elaborating the creative, evolutionary will to life,[41] the second constituting the "bomb" which blows that up, just as the silence blows up the entire *Askitikí*. What is important is to see these two in an ongoing dialectical relationship rather than in a relationship of implacable opposition according to which the second annihilates the first. As our Buddhist masters remind us, there is no last-act curtain; time is not linear but circular; subjectivity may undermine and uproot the will to life, but, strangely, we do move on, past the nothingness. Or, as Kazantzakis declared in *Symposium*, the highest initiation is not just an ending; it stimulates the beginning of a new cycle of creativity. Compare Lionel Trilling's view that Representation may be life-enhancing:

> Committed to will as we of the West are, we yet on certain occasions seek to qualify and even to negate its authority and to assert the life-affirming power of idea, or, to use the word that has been proposed by the latest translator of Schopenhauer's great work, to

> say that life is best affirmed by *representation*, by will realized and negated. . . . However committed to expressive action and significant utterance the western paradigm of personhood may be, the western person . . . is not wholly without the capability of finding value in what is fixed, moveless, and silent. (Trilling 1976:252)

Trilling is actually discussing the power of art—of tragedy in particular—to transmute into an object of representation "what is intrinsically and ineluctably painful when it is an element of the experience of will." His value for our discussion, aside from the implicit suggestion that Kazantzakis's "bomb" may be just as aesthetic as metabiological, is to remind us that the latter's alleged nihilism may be not only positive in its own manner but also part of our Western heritage and not an outlandish imposition.

This leads to our third tentative direction of approach, Christian mysticism. In my circumspect attempt to discover what is meant by "only you and I exist, you and I are one, even this one does not exist," I am going to accept the hypothesis that *Askitikí*, although repeatedly condemned as anti-Christian, is in some ways rooted in Christian thought—and in a positive sense, not just a negative one. Negatively, we could conclude that the silence terminating *Askitikí* reaches back to the anguished discovery in *Comedy* that the loving Christian Father-God has nothing more to say to mankind; that Kazantzakis—still driven by the Christian world-view—is haunted and frightened, as was Pascal, by the eternal silence of infinite space and is trying desperately to exorcise its horror by making Nothingness the culmination of meaning rather than meaning's abrogation. But the negative approach is insufficient. It may be more fruitful to see in Kazantzakis's "theology" certain positive similarities to the mystical theology of the Eastern Church (and also the Western),[42] similarities that, once discovered, will serve to gloss his meaning.

Kazantzakis's spiritual exercises lead the postulant toward (a) unity, (b) apathy (in the sense of cessation of effort), and (c) ignorance. Regarding the first, a meditation recorded by him in October 1927 may serve as a useful gloss. "All these months," he began, "I have been sensing that . . . my life is acquiring a unity. . . . The inquiries along various paths are beginning to fall into harmony and to lead to one . . . still point. 'God' grant that I may ripen and enrich myself in this way until I die, and that, without denying anything, my entire life may become a 'profuse unity' [μονὰς πλουσία], as the Byzantine mystics say" (Eleni Kaz. 1977:209; 1968a:166). In the mystical tradition of Orthodoxy,[43] God is a threefold unity (monás), three being "the number which transcends all separation" (Lossky 1957:47). Regarding the second similarity, the acquisition of apathy ("Silence means: every person, after completing his service in all labors, finally reaches the highest summit—the summit of non-effort, beyond every labor . . ." [Kaz. 1927f:631; cf. 1962a:93; 1960b:129]), the mystical theology of the Eastern Church teaches that spiritual exercise bestows upon the human soul a "stability in the midst of passions": a "serenity, or apathy which is the beginning of deification" (Lossky 1957: 48). Regarding the third similarity (in the silence, the "apathetic" person merges with the abyss, where "teaching does not exist," and in which "each person . . . escapes . . . his tiny question-filled brain" [Kaz. 1927f:631; 1962a:93–94; 1960b:130]), mystical theology prescribes spiritual exercises that lead to total ignorance. "If in seeing God one can know what one sees, then one has not seen God in Himself but something intelligible, something which is inferior to Him. . . . Proceeding by negations one ascends . . . in order to draw near to the Unknown in the darkness of absolute ignorance" (Lossky 1957:25). In Kazantzakis's system, *knowing* (gnosis)—"You and I are one, Lord"—is necessarily followed by *unknowing* (agnosia): "even this one does not exist." Only such darkness of absolute ignorance can be the highest degree of initiation. In the Christian system, this apophatic theology (theology of negation) "deals with the negative way which leads towards the *silence* of the divine union" (Lossky 1957:29; italics added). Interestingly, the "apophatic way does not lead to an absence, to an utter emptiness" (Lossky 1957:43), but rather, as we saw, to the profuse unity that in the Christian system is called the Trinity.

Given the Buddhistic, Schopenhauerian, and Christian approaches as possible aids to the discovery of an elusive yet rich meaning in Kazantzakis's doctrine of the silence, it is disappointing to encounter narrowly assured interpretations by certain readers, including sophisticated ones—Reverend Papastefánou, for example. Kazantzakis wrote him from Berlin in late 1922 or early 1923 to explain: "I cannot tell you what we say in the third and highest degree. No one can say to another. Silence." (Mitsotakis 1972:76–77; Kaz. 1979a:32). Papastefánou, taking the term at its face value, replied expansively in order to complain:

> In other words, everything [is] vanity, effacement, ashes, nothingness, nullifying. We create hallucinations of God, make ghosts, force our imaginations to fashion poetic daydreams, artificial exultation (opium, more or less); . . . philosophically, religiously and poetically we build profound occult palaces and then—Silence! . . . (Stamatiou 1975:1036)

Poulakidas, with the revised text in front of him, reaches the same conclusion:

> In this Silence or Nirvana, there is one reality: that of the oneness of the I and Brahma. Whether this reality is or is not, is not

> known. Buddha refused to divulge this secret or to discuss it, . . . whereas Kazantzakis commits himself. Bergson cannot be considered a nihilist. Buddha can perhaps be accused of nihilism. Kazantzakis, on the other hand . . . can be accused of nihilism. . . . There is only the unlimited and deathly silent Abyss. (Poulakidas 1975:216–217)

Prevelákis joins this chorus, calling the revised beatitudes "a proclamation of absolute nihilism" and concluding that the new ending "really does blow up the work's philosophic (more precisely, its Bergsonian) basis. If the 'Invisible One' suffuses matter with his breath and releases it from inertia, how can this force be proclaimed devoid of existence? Can the source of life be Nothingness?" (Prev. 1977:30–31; 1981:46).

Vrettákos's reaction is equally categorical: "Humanity listens, has shoulders, the shoulders falter or do not falter, but, despite all that, no Responsibility exists to be carried on humanity's shoulders. Everything is a void. . . . No further discussion is possible. . . . This revision was dictated by a tragic obstinacy for nullification, a sort of psychic condition run amok" (Vrettakos 1960:150).

To these dicta may be added the conclusions of Elli Lambrídi when she studied the metaphysics of the *Odyssey* in 1939. Kazantzakis gives us the entire Bergsonian evolution of inanimate and animate creation, she says, but then all this gets tangled up with solipsistic Buddhism: I close my eyes, and the outside world disappears. "The two world-views employed by Kazantzakis are incompatible, . . . the one refutes the other, . . . it is . . . absolutely impossible even for the most metaphysical mind to consider the first a stage of the second" (Lambridi 1939:11 March).

Frangópoulos, in a more recent study, concurs: "The imperturbability in non-existence . . . which Buddhism desires is nullified by the everlasting effort of humanity to build and move forward, which Kazantzakis desires. . . . I fear that Kazantzakis, instead of reaching a 'synthesis' . . . , arrives at nothing but an incessant hesitation between elements that refute each other" (Frangopoulos 1977:53).

Each of these commentators takes Kazantzakis's silence at face value and can hardly be blamed for doing so.[44] Contrary to his usual practice, Kazantzakis did not publish refutations or elucidations—with one exception, namely "An Open Letter for Mrs. Elli Lambrídi" concerning her critique of the metaphysics of the *Odyssey*. Here, after listing the expected four steps of initiation—"1. good and evil are enemies, 2. good and evil are co-workers, 3. good and evil are one, 4. this one does not exist"—he goes on to confirm the role of Christian as well as Buddhist mysticism in his system: "In the first stage live all men of action; in the second, many men of theory . . . ; the third stage is common to all the mystics of Europe and the East; the fourth, only to those of the East" (Kaz. 1939a:13; 1958f:823).

Although directed at *Odíssia*, this gloss is equally applicable to *Askitikí* in its revised form (since the treatise is the epic's intellectual template). It encourages us to read apophatic theology into Kazantzakis's system and to resist understanding his words logically—something that critics who accept the terms "silence" and "abyss" at face value fail to do. Once we insert *Askitikí*'s ending into its broader context, we will perhaps begin to allow that "apathy" is not necessarily the eternal abrogation of effort, but stability in the midst of passion, and we will understand the need for the "unknowing" of the fourth stage if total ignorance is ever to break the intellect's lordship over the Western personality.

Kazantzakis's one published elucidation is supplemented by *Symposium* (unpublished in his lifetime) and by some private letters that encourage us all the more to resist a simplistically nihilistic interpretation. *Symposium* at least hints that the absolute is not the concluding abyss but rather the entire cycle that brings us from one abyss to another. Regarding the letters, when Papastefánou interpreted *Askitikí*'s ending to mean "vanity, effacement, ashes . . ." Kazantzakis took pains to correct this view in his reply:

> I say "Silence" for the highest degree. Not because I give Silence the content that you do. It is not extreme despair; it is not nullification or incurable ignorance. Silence means: Each person, after he has passed the two degrees[45] and has ended his service in all the labors, finally reaches his self's highest summit, beyond every labor, beyond every content, beyond purpose, certainty, joy, hope. All these contests are labors that went before; he passed them and needs them no longer. Now he does not question, does not struggle, does not differentiate. . . . He has adapted himself at last and has inserted himself into the Abyss—like a male sperm in the innards of a woman. . . .
>
> How can one attain the innards of the Abyss in this way and make it fruitful? This cannot . . . be communicated in words. . . . Each person climbs above his own head, escaping time and place.
>
> Yet we are compelled to speak. Let us struggle with myths, metaphors, allegories, images . . . (Mitsotakis 1972:81–82; Kaz. 1979:33)

This can be comprehended in the Schopenhauerian context as the degree of initiation in which we undo our individuality and egotisms, spurred by the deep understanding of life's vanity, and also as the degree in which the process of uprooting the will to life paradoxically becomes life-affirming. In the Buddhistic context the key word is "differentiate." Kazantzakis's initiate does not differentiate any longer on this highest level of áskisis. He has come to realize—and accept—the absolute sameness between (a) his body and the whole universe, (b) his mind and the minds of all sentient beings. But to avoid compromising this undifferentiatedness by the differentiations implicit in words, we enter the silence, and if we must say anything at all, we say "Nothingness" or "Abyss" in order to affirm the unknowing that is required when we have climbed above our own heads, escaping the differentiations of time and place.

Kazantzakis in his reply to Papastefánou allows that the silence is ignorance (as he must) but adds the following qualification: it is not "incurable ignorance." Does this suggest the possibility of an (unstated) continuation in Kazantzakis's system or is Lambrídi correct when she sees the Buddhistic element totally abrogating the Bergsonian one, that is, halting evolution? My own view is that *Askitikí* offers an implicit dialectic between Bergson and Buddha, will and idea, action and contemplation—a dialectic consistent with Buddhism's position that there is no last-act curtain, time being forever circular. Yet nowhere in *Askitikí* does Kazantzakis show his initiates moving ahead after they experience the beautiful interwovenness of thatness and thisness.

Fortunately, we have two additional letters that treat this question. Although they do so in relation to the *Odyssey*, they apply equally to *Askitikí*. Both were addressed to Emile Hourmoúzios in 1943. Since both say more-or-less the same thing, I shall cite only the more expansive one:

> . . . At certain moments of great intensity or of prolonged crisis, there is a lightning flash . . . ; all forms crack, everything vanishes. Wasn't this true of Pindar, the great admirer and praiser of the youthful male body, of the palpable exploit, of the certainty that life has value? Yet this Pindar must have once been ready to burst, and even he let out his repulsive, nihilistic cry: σκιᾶς ὄναρ / ἄνθρωπος ["The dream of a shadow is man"; Pythia 8.95–96] . . .
>
> The same with Odysséas. Every great soul is sometimes ready to burst because it senses that the highest labor and the highest joy and sorrow and the most daring ideal are all too large for it. Nothing will fit into it except Nothing. It utters a cry. Then it regains its strength and courage, silences the evil spirit inside it, and resumes the ascent.
>
> Odysséas does the same. The nihilistic cry "Even this one does not exist!" is not the climax of his struggle; it is an escape valve that he opens for a moment in order not to burst. He listens intently, *gains courage from the horror*, and resumes his chosen path: the Ascent. (Kaz. 1977a:187, cf. 184)

Prevelákis, whose interpretation of the silence as "absolute nihilism" we have already seen, views this letter as evidence for an "insolvable contradiction" between Kazantzakis's nihilism and "his former conception whereby man obeys 'the cry of his epoch' and, by struggling, 'saves' God"—a contradiction that "caused Kazantzakis some uneasiness later on" (Prev. 1977:31; 1981:46), namely, in 1943 when he wrote to Hourmoúzios. Preveläkis may be right. Yet the two letters to Hourmoúzios, when added to the 1923 letter to Papastefánou correcting the latter's view that the silence is "vanity, effacement, ashes . . ." encourage us to reject the view that Kazantzakis had retreated from the "absolute nihilism" of the revised *Askitikí* by 1943 and had returned to his "former conception" owing to the conditions of the German occupation and everyone's hope for a radically improved Greece in the postoccupation period. We cannot speak of a retreat from absolute nihilism if the silence was never absolute to begin with, but merely a metaphor for a form of psychic renewal consistent with the teachings of both Buddhism and Eastern Christianity.

What the silence conveys is not an insolvable contradiction between nihilism and activism but a creative, ever-adjusting dialectic between the hypostases of a *monás plusía*—a dialectic that allowed Kazantzakis to veer sometimes toward one element, sometimes toward the other, just as Christians may in different moods cleave sometimes to the Father, sometimes to the Son or Holy Ghost, without compromising the Trinity's mystic integrity.

This is just an opinion, although one supported, I trust, by sufficient argumentation. We must admit, however, that the actual text of the revised *Askitikí*, taken at face value without glosses or implied contexts, is radically subjectivist and nihilistic, since it posits a universe defined by our own mental development and erased when we stop thinking about it.

What, then, are we to believe? Should we not trust the text itself and be wary of Kazantzakis's glosses with their protestations of non-nihilistic intention?

As a possible way out of this dilemma I suggest that we interpret *Askitikí* by virtue of what we find in other texts, accepting Kazantzakis's own view that all subsequent works in his oeuvre were representations of this central representation—a position he expressed in 1951, for example, to Max Tau: "[*Askitikí*] is my credo, the core of my *oeuvre*—beyond that, the core of my entire life" (Kaz. 1977b:308). This, too, is a gloss; yet if we allow the oeuvre (not to mention the life) to "comment" on *Askitikí*, we will be encouraged to see in that work not absolute nihilism but rather the aforementioned dialectic between effort and noneffort, substance and abyss, with the balance tipping toward Responsibility. In *Christ Recrucified* and *The Last Temptation* particularly, there is a promised renewal after dissolution: all is erased, yet we do not linger in Nada; we carry on . . . , carry on. There are times when the nihilistic element is more pronounced, as in the play *Buddha*, yet even this is a creation issuing from Kazantzakis's ongoing energy, not from resignation. If *Askitikí*'s true meaning is projected onto the works and the life, then the credo would seem to be not an insolvable contradiction but a synthesis bravely imaging life's manifest and hidden gifts to human beings rather than the betrayal of those gifts by a cosmos ultimately meaningless and void.

THE ROUSSAKOV AFFAIR; BREAK WITH ISTRATI

As prelude to the events that led to the break with Istrati, we might do well to review the chronology of this momentous period in Kazantzakis's life. So far, we have seen him in Athens in January 1928, then in Aegina expecting to be tried for the Alhambra events, then returning to Russia for the fourth and last time in April, staying in Kiev at first, writing scenarios, then rejoining Istrati near Moscow in early June and revising *Askitikí*. Later that month he and Istrati met Victor Serge and Serge's father-in-law, Alexander Roussakov, in Leningrad before they continued north to Murmansk. In August, Samíou arrived from Paris; the two couples set out on a huge tour of southern Russia that lasted until early December.[46] Back in Moscow, Leningrad, and then Moscow again later that month and in January 1929, Kazantzakis and Istrati argued furiously over the Roussakov affair. On 20 January, Kazantzakis departed Leningrad for a colossal journey all the way to Siberia—alone. Istrati remained to fight for Roussakov's vindication; in February he left for Paris, vowing to expose Bolshevism's iniquities.

Although this chronology should be helpful, it may also be deceptive. On the surface it indicates that Kazantzakis and Istrati's joint scheme for activism proceeded on schedule for the remainder of the year until the Roussakov affair caused the Dioscuri to quarrel and part. This is deceptive because it disguises their previous friction, something we have already encountered in Kazantzakis's ultimatum of 17 May 1928. It also disguises another fact that we already know: Kazantzakis's ever-increasing dedication to the *Odyssey*. "Action!" was the recurrent cry in the letters during the first tour with Istrati (November–December 1927) but not during the second tour. "On the new 'pilgrimage,' " writes Prevelákis, "the prevailing theme is the *Odyssey*. . . . The only remaining refuge is poetic creativity: Lenin has given way to Odysseus." Prevelákis then proceeds to quote from letter after letter in which the epic is Kazantzakis's obsessive subject (Prev. 1958:224–225; 1961:136–137). Thus, although the plans for a joint journey resulting in scores of articles, and eventually in a three- or four-volume book, were developed with Kazantzakis's customary enthusiasm, and although he wrote a flowery introduction stressing the cooperative nature of this venture by "two men with hearts ripened by suffering,"[47] the trip was a forced pilgrimage by friends whose relationship had already essentially (though not manifestly) ruptured, with Kazantzakis no longer interested in activism and Istrati increasingly disillusioned by what he saw, even before the Roussakov affair brought everything to a boil.

Having concentrated so far on Kazantzakis, let us now examine what was happening to Istrati, since the latter's indignation against Soviet iniquity serves as a foil to Kazantzakis's Olympian equanimity vis-à-vis the realities of Soviet communism in this period when Stalin was consolidating his power. The different viewpoints of the two friends are a necessary prelude to the Roussakov affair and therefore must be described at some length.

Istrati's eyes were opened by his journey and also by the particular case of Victor Serge, whom he had sought out during the tenth anniversary celebrations, having read some of his writings beforehand (Istrati 1929a: 145). Istrati's trouble (if this is a trouble) was that he could not see the forest for the trees whereas Kazantzakis seems to have been unable to see the trees for the forest. Serge sums him up as follows:

> It is with deep emotion that I recall [Istrati's] memory. . . . He was incapable of theoretical reasoning, and so could not fall into the trap of convenient sophistry. People told him, in my hearing: "Panaït, one can't make an omelette without breaking eggs. Our revolution . . . ," et cetera. He exclaimed, "All right, I can see the broken eggs. Where's this omelette of yours?" We came out of the model penal colony of Bolchevo, where hardened criminals worked in freedom under their own supervision. Istrati's only comment was, "A pity that you can't have all this comfort and such a wonderful system of work unless you've murdered at least three people!"[48] Of the editors of reviews who paid him 100 rubles per article he would inquire curtly, "Is it true that a postman here earns fifty roubles a month?" And he would add: "I'm no theoretician, but I have an entirely different understanding of socialism." At every turn he would burst into fits of violent indignation. . . . (Serge 1951:301–302; 1963:278–279)

Kazantzakis's temperament was entirely different. "They had contrary natures," writes Samíou in her book on Istrati: Kazantzakis was "hermetic, without hope, avoiding easy contact with people, firmly believing that 'such a thing does not exist,' and working with all his strength as if he were convinced of the opposite . . ." (Eleni Kaz. 1938:151). She goes on to recount various incidents that brought the two temperaments into open conflict. In one example Istrati bursts out:

> "Everywhere we've seen those propaganda sheets the soviets distribute . . . : instructions for cultivating the land, fertilizing it sci-

entifically. But look what happens. Those who follow these instructions produce more, acquire greater comfort. The village soviet, enraged, intervenes, talks to the bold 'kulaks,' confiscates their so painfully amassed property and curses them as enemies of the régime. A man from here . . . had planted a vineyard. With the new instructions and with the chemical fertilizers, the vineyard prospered. Everyone should be happy, right? Well, no. He is a kulak. The village soviet . . . wants to confiscate everything. . . . Then what does the poor devil do? He calls his wife, sons, relatives and, during the night, they destroy the vineyard. . . . Saved! 2500 vines pulled out by the roots. He has saved himself. Do you understand? Do you understand?"

Panaït is beside himself. He paces back and forth like a lion in a cage. Kazan, also moved, tries to find a broader explanation. . . .

"Listen to me, Panaït. . . . Your heart surpasses your intellect. . . . Try to see the complete circle. Don't . . . stop with the detail that is alive and warm, but at times partial and limited. . . . The realization of a sublime idea is a mosaic composed of stones that are almost always bloody, ugly, even horrible. . . . Russia is great. The Idea is great: do not let one isolated case . . . divert you. . . ."

"You are heartless . . . , impassive, cold. You don't love people. . . . That is why you never lose your head."

"Perhaps. . . . But I love the . . . flame that consumes [man]. . . . Man perishes, he turns to ashes, but the flame continues its insatiable course through other bodies. I am faithful to that flame, Panaït. . . . That is why I shall unhesitatingly love the reality—so often atrocious—of the U.S.S.R. . . ." (Eleni Kaz. 1938: 115–119)

In the first volume of *Vers l'autre flamme*, the book in which he recorded his disillusionment, Istrati confessed that toward the middle of July he had begun "to have serious doubts about the morality of the revolutionary régime, but they were only doubts, not a certainty" (Istrati 1929a: 151). By the end of September he felt himself a lost soul, unable to mouth what was expected of him regarding the Soviet Union, whereas Kazantzakis was "confident about being able to say things so adroitly that the publication of our book in Moscow [would] still be possible" (Istrati 1929a:181). He follows this with a vitriolic description of the oppression of regional authorities by the central government in Moscow, whose policy is to "crush every slightest show of spiritual independence and true criticism," while the lodging cooperatives rage unchecked with a cruelty that the tsarist security police never dared to display (Istrati 1929a:190)—

the point being that Soviet citizens are harassed in the elementary areas of life: the right to work, and the right to have a roof over their heads.

This is precisely what was confirmed for Istrati by the particular case of Serge's father-in-law. Everything was already ruined between Istrati and Kazantzakis, but at least they endured each other in morose silence as they traveled by train back to Moscow in December: "Our compartment, which had known so many boisterous discussions, so many bursts of laughter, was now no longer anything but a stagnant dormitory. We no longer spoke to each other . . ." (Istrati 1929a:196). What the Roussakov affair did, as I indicated earlier, was to bring this quiescent rancor to a boil.

"Who Is Victor Serge? (And Why Do We Have To Ask)" was the headline of a *Village Voice* Literary Supplement reviewing Serge's *Memoirs of a Revolutionary, Men in Prison, Birth of Our Power, Conquered City, Midnight in the Century, From Lenin to Stalin,* and *The Case of Comrade Tulayev* (Hoberman 1984:12). Peter Sedgwick, in his Introduction to the *Memoirs of a Revolutionary*, answers the first question succinctly: Serge (1890–1947) "was an anarchist, a Bolshevik, a Trotskyist, a revisionist-Marxist, and, on his own confession, a 'personalist.' Belgian by place of birth and upbringing, French by adoption and in literary expression, Russian by parentage and later by citizenship, he eventually became stateless. . . . He was a journalist, a poet, a pamphleteer, a historian, an agitator, and a novelist" (Serge 1963: ix). The second question, "And why do we have to ask?" is perplexing, considering that Serge "may have been the most celebrated political prisoner of his day. In June 1935 [his] case rocked the European intellectual community when it was raised in Paris at the International Writers Congress for the Defense of Culture. 'Immediately,' according to one participant, 'the audience was divided between Trotskyists and Stalinists. Adversaries insulted each other'; the uproar threatened to become violent when 'in a . . . dramatic intervention,' André Malraux 'declared that anyone who mentioned Victor Serge would be expelled from the hall'" (Hoberman 1984:12). However, the uproar was sufficient to make Stalin release Serge from his second Russian imprisonment as a favor to Romain Rolland, deprive him of his Soviet citizenship, and expel him.[49]

All this happened, of course, after Kazantzakis had crossed paths with him in 1928, but it alerts us to the cause of Serge's earlier difficulties. In 1922 he had been sent to Berlin as editor of the Comintern's European press service. When he returned to Russia, Lenin was dead and the struggle for succession in progress. Serge joined Kamenev, Zinoviev, Trotsky, Rakovsky, and others to form a left-wing opposition to Politbureau policies such as favoring Chiang Kai-Shek over Mao Zedong in the Chinese Revolution and advocating a peasant petite bourgeoisie at home (Serge

1963:216–224). The Oppositionists were soon ousted from power—in November 1927 to be exact, precisely when "official" Russia was celebrating (with Kazantzakis's participation) the "triumphant" first decade. "In ten years," says Serge, in a very different evaluation, "the exhausted Revolution had turned full circle against itself" (Serge 1963:225).

However, Serge fared better than most of the others, at least temporarily. Although he was imprisoned, his "arrest . . . caused some commotion in Paris, and so was considered awkward in high circles" (Serge 1963:242). Thus he was released from this first Russian imprisonment owing to foreign pressure, just as he was from the second.[50] The condition was that he refrain from anti-Soviet activities. At the onset of 1928, he was practically "the only known Oppositionist in Leningrad still at liberty" (Serge 1963:244). In June of that year, Kazantzakis had met him for the first time. His analysis of Serge helps explain his own stance six months later vis-à-vis the persecution of Roussakov. Kazantzakis seems to have projected onto Serge a Kazantzakian dilemma: "Serge knows that a man's supreme responsibility, in this critical moment through which Russia is passing, is to hurl himself into action. . . . Serge knows this and tries to act, but . . . comprehends too much; his glance embraces too wide a circle. . . . Serge sees both the pro and the con, he analyzes and 'understands' the enemy. Isn't understanding just one form of justifying? And isn't justifying pardoning?" (Eleni Kaz. 1938:159). When Kazantzakis conveyed this analysis to Istrati, the latter remonstrated: "And what should he do, then? Cross his arms?" Kazantzakis's answer again betrays self-analysis: "Write! Serve with his pen as though it were a sword" (Eleni Kaz. 1938:160).

It is instructive to pursue the Serge-Kazantzakis relationship further because Serge in a sense was everything that Kazantzakis aspired to be: a man capable of action while at the same time glancing widely at the complete circle. Serge was not at all naïve or confused about this polarity in his own life, as we see from an exchange of letters between him and Kazantzakis in the summer of 1929. "You are not 'active,' " he wrote Kazantzakis, ". . . because you believe in the incompatibility of action and contemplation. I am (or want to be) active, because I don't admit that contemplation is separate from action. That 'unity' is life. If we are adversaries it is because you do not pass beyond such antinomies" (Eleni Kaz. 1938:165–166). And Kazantzakis—exasperating as always, agonizingly split despite all protestations to the contrary—wrote to Serge in a letter that we shall have occasion to see again at greater length: "I am not a man of action." Yet in the next paragraph he goes on to contradict himself: "You have viewed me only as a mystic. Or, rather, as a bookworm. I've just written a confession in the form of a novel on the subject of the Soviet Union. The central character is a Negro, Toda-Raba, . . . my true countenance" (Eleni Kaz. 1968b:228; 1977:273). In other words, I am not a mystic but an activist. Perhaps the exposure to Serge is one more factor explaining Kazantzakis's reaction in the Roussakov affair. He wanted Serge to mount to his own—to Kazantzakian—Olympian heights with respect to injustice, and Serge refused. Istrati also refused, but he, incapable of contemplation in the sense that we are discussing (glancing widely, justifying, pardoning), constituted less of a threat to Kazantzakis than did Serge, who effortlessly exhibited the versatility that Kazantzakis desired for himself but could not gracefully attain. When we see someone else achieving a complicated goal that we yearn to achieve but cannot, we are tempted to set ourselves a less complicated goal that we are able to achieve to perfection—competing by refusing to compete on the other person's terms.

At all events, Serge's personality and actions were new factors added to the accumulated previous ones—the disintegrating relationship with Istrati, the disgust after the Alhambra imbroglio, the obsessive concern with the *Odyssey*—in determining Kazantzakis's refusal to join Istrati and Serge in their campaign to set right a particular injustice.

To these factors we can add still two more, the first of which is certain, the second speculative. The certain one is Kazantzakis's metacommunistic view of Bolshevism's role in human development, something that he was to expound again at length in *Toda-Raba*. The application of this view to perversions such as the persecution of Roussakov—which, as we shall see, boiled down to a komsomol's greed for a better apartment—is expressed succinctly in a letter:

> I become increasingly intransigent precisely because such abominations happen in "Mother Russia." Certainly I find communism's . . . materialistic basis odious. Yet it is necessary because, as I have long been convinced, communism is not the start of a new civilization but the termination of an old one, and it consequently intensifies that civilization's efforts—materialism, the machine, Americanism—to the utmost extreme. (Prev. 1965b:179–180)

The speculative factor (not unrelated to the certain one) is Kazantzakis's position in the conflict between Trotskyism and Stalinism. It would seem that Kazantzakis did not share Istrati's and Serge's partisanship for Trotsky, which is strange considering that Trotsky in Kazantzakis's view was the more spiritual and ascending of the two, Stalin the more inert. As he says in *Taksidévondas. Rusía*, "Trotsky is flame, Stalin earth" (Kaz. 1965e:202, cf. 211; 1989:195, cf. 204).[51] In Vienna in 1922, at the start of his leftist phase, Kazantzakis had assumed that Trotsky would inherit Lenin's power and had looked upon this with approval: "Lenin seems to be dying. Trotsky, who will succeed him, will be as fierce as can be; he'll crack skulls open in order to put Salvation inside them" (Kaz. 1958a:26; 1979:49). In Berlin a year later, he reiterated his allegiance: "Even though Lenin recovered, he is still tired and has lost his impetuosity. Perhaps Trotsky—who is ferocious and without scruples, a massive organizer of the masses—will play the role of an intellectual Genghis Khan" (1958a: 148). By the end of 1927, however— that is, by the time (a) he had gained some direct experience of Soviet politics and (b) the factions vying for power after Lenin's death (left, center, and right, led by Trotsky, Stalin, and Bukharin, respectively) had clarified their positions—Kazantzakis had come to appreciate Stalin's slower approach: his conviction that purity would have to be sacrificed at least temporarily if the Soviet Union were to survive. He elaborated on this in his Alhambra speech, explaining that Trotsky wanted to weaken the kulaks and nepmen by converting all peasants into agricultural workers through the enforced industrialization of agriculture, whereas Stalin, "*true to Lenin's teaching*" (Kaz. 1928b:196; my italics), wished to compromise, distinguishing the poor peasants from the rich and eliminating only the latter. In foreign policy, Trotsky was for encouraging immediate revolution throughout the world, Stalin for waiting, as in the case of Mao Zedong versus Chiang Kai-Shek. Kazantzakis's conclusion was that both leaders had the same aim, the victory of communism, but were using different tactics.

These sentiments had already appeared in Kazantzakis's article printed in *Proïa* on the morning of the Alhambra speech under the headline: "Stalin and Trotsky. The Duel Between Lenin's Two Successors. The Crude (σκαιός) Stalin and the Wildcatlike (αἰλουροειδής) Trotsky. . . ." (Kaz. 1928c). The article reappears in *Taksidévondas. Rusía*, integrated into Kazantzakis's account of the tenth anniversary celebrations. Listening to Trotsky address the crowds from an "opposition balcony," Kazantzakis sees him as "the flaming eruption that still had not solidified . . . He cannot tolerate reality, which, congealing, draws together and constricts; he wants to blow up the crust composed of kulaks, merchants, and bureaucrats that solidifies daily and smothers the Revolution's darting, insuppressible flame" (Kaz. 1965e:201; 1989:193). As for Stalin, he "advances slowly . . . toward . . . his goal. He does not shout, . . . does not lose his temper. . . . He has the patience of the peasant and the earth" (1965e:202; 1989:195).[52] Trotsky in Kazantzakis's hearing accused Stalin of pushing Russia toward the right: "from the proletariat toward the bourgeoisie, from ordinary workers to specialized foremen, from the simple communist to the career communist, from the poor peasant to the rich kulak. Stalin is betraying the Idea! . . . Today's régime is hindering the vanguard of the worldwide proletariat . . . betrayal! betrayal!" (1965e:202–203; 1989:195).

"Who is correct in this titanic duel . . . ?" asks Kazantzakis—and refuses to answer. Or, in answering that the two leaders form a higher synthesis spurring reality toward a succeeding power "at once prudent and rash" (1965e:204; 1989:197), does he in effect side with Stalin? We cannot be sure. As I said, this factor is speculative.

Yet we can be sure that he sided against Istrati and Victor Serge. If we ask how he could do this, betraying his allegiance to mobility and flame, one possible answer is his delight at perceiving hidden collaboration in cases where everyone else saw nothing but antagonism, as when he had dared to assert that fascism and Bolshevism were fellow-workers. Another possible answer is the "certain factor" discussed above, namely, Kazantzakis's long-range view in which communism is not the start of a new civilization but the end of an old one. In tolerating Stalin, Kazantzakis was indicating that the Russian experiment had already exhausted its interest for him, had already reached the decline of the inevitable human curve. Istrati objected to Roussakov's persecution so impetuously because he saw the Idea threatened, its purity compromised. His reaction was to fight for its preservation and then, exhausted and embittered, to curse the Stalinist villains and expose them to the world. Kazantzakis refused to react because, viewing the revolution's decline into Stalinist inertness as inevitable, he considered Istrati's concern a squandering of energy on ephemeralities: the hopeless dream of transforming a transitory phenomenon (the Idea's initial purity) into an eternal essence. As he had made amply clear earlier in "Crucified Russia" and elsewhere, he harbored no illusions about the continuation of a revolution's initial élan. His own interests lay in (a) the first descent of the Spirit—the violent event that brings the fire—and, this having passed, in (b) Olympian contemplation of the eternal cycle by which the original idea gives way to stultification. Thus, quite aside from his refusal to side with Trotsky on grounds dictated by a theory of political development, he could not be morally moved by "the rest of it, the way the terrible moment gets channeled into prudent, everyday necessity" (Eleni Kaz. 1977:237; 1968a:189). If he were to be interested at all, it could only be aesthetically. As I have stressed so often already, *politics for Kazantzakis was subordinate to (yet a necessary prerequisite for) a contemplative effort to discover the ultimate meaning of life and death viewed now as a spectacle to be contemplated in equanimity*. His aesthetic and religious impulses always overcame activism.

With all this by way of introduction, we can now speak about "L'Affaire Roussakov" itself. We have accounts by Serge, Istrati, and Samíou regarding what happened.[53] "My father-in-law," says Serge, "had fought in the 1905 revolution at Rostov, . . . and was expelled from France in 1918 for organizing a strike on ships loaded with munitions for the Whites. Now he was a cloth-capped worker, living with his family in a princely couple of rooms in the same communal apartment as ourselves"

(Serge 1963:277). Despite his revolutionary history, Roussakov became a suspect by association because his daughter had married the Trotskyist/Oppositionist Serge. The affair was precipitated by a sordid argument over Serge's apartment. A female komsomol coveted it. According to law, the Serges and Roussakovs were occupying one room too many. The girl, presenting herself as a student, applied to occupy this room and was taken in (Eleni Kaz. 1938:167). Once there, she conspired with a friend named Maria Sviertsieva, a director of the lodging cooperative for that building, to secure the remainder by arranging an "inspection" of Roussakov's own room. Roussakov demanded their warrant, whereupon Sviertsieva replied, "I don't have to show a warrant to speculators and counter-revolutionaries." Roussakov's daughter tried to intervene and was struck by Sviertsieva, whom Serge and Roussakov forcibly evicted from the room (Istrati 1929b:457; 1929a:244). This led to an inflammatory article in *Leningradskaïa Pravda* accusing Roussakov of using the apartment for speculation and of being a bourgeois as well as a kulak and nepman. His arrest and severe punishment were demanded (Istrati 1929b: 445–446).

What happened next was precisely what Istrati had witnessed on his pilgrimage to southern Russia: the power of the lodging cooperatives to harass Soviet citizens concerning the elementary areas of life—the right to a job and a home. Roussakov was expelled from his union and denied his cooperative book, that is, the right to eat. What particularly incensed Istrati, who had traveled to the Soviet Union convinced that for the first time in human history the working man would be insured elementary decency, was that all this was happening to a genuine proletarian. The Roussakov affair undermined his convictions so drastically that he left no stone unturned in his frantic effort to prove his worst fears mistaken. He sent telegrams to newspapers and officials, ran to the editor of *Leningradskaïa Pravda* to set the record straight, visited Kalinin himself, threatened to "act energetically, here and abroad, against such ignominies" (Istrati 1929b:447–449). "Either Roussakov is rehabilitated or I spit in their faces; I will return to Europe and shout my honest testimony. I know how to shout, good god. I will shout until I burst the eardrums of Stalin and his gang!" (Eleni Kaz. 1938:169).[54]

On top of all this, Istrati had to deal with Kazantzakis's refusal to share his concern. Kazantzakis felt that Istrati, in devoting himself so monomaniacally to this single case, was negating what ought to have been his true contribution. He could not agree that a single incident, or even many such incidents, invalidated an entire system (Eleni Kaz. 1969). We know that the two friends quarreled so severely that they parted without shaking hands (Eleni Kaz. 1938:171). Their exact words we do not know; yet we may surmise that they resembled those we saw when the Dioscuri quarreled over the injustices in southern Russia, or—even more likely—those that Kazantzakis assigns to Géranos and Azad in *Toda-Raba*:

> "You are a heartless man, [says Azad]. Russia for you is nothing but an interesting tragedy. . . . Why? Because you have no love in you. Anyone who loves does not watch things; he suffers. . . . I'm not a philosopher like you. . . . I'm a human being! . . . My heart . . . tells the truth!"
>
> "The truth! . . . Truth, justice, happiness! Have you no shame?"
>
> "Then is everything in vain . . . ? Love, friendship, mankind's struggle?"
>
> "I'm not interested in moral problems. . . ."
>
> "So it's the metaphysical problem, is it? . . . You've come . . . here as a spectator . . ."
>
> ". . . I feel that we're going to part company . . ."
>
> "It's the kiss of Judas! . . . Ah, you want to go away all alone? Well, then, go!" (Kaz. 1962c:190–192; 1964f:157–159)

So Kazantzakis went away all alone to Murmansk, then traveled for a month to Vladivostok and back via the trans-Siberian railway, then took a fortnight's tour of Tashkent, Samarkand, and Bukhara—thinking all the while about the *Odyssey*, but also reflecting on what had just happened. His first reaction (20 January 1929) was self-justifying: "My companion lost heart, gave up, degenerated [λιγοψύχησε, κουράστηκε, ξέπεσε], and cannot wait to return to Paris. . . . I've escaped a companion who was good but uneven and somewhat cowardly . . ." (Prev. 1965b:106). At the end of January he fired a Parthian shot at Istrati:

> Je te laisse de moi ce souvenir atroce:
> Que mon âme fut loyale et que ton âme fut fausse.
> (Prev. 1965b:172)
>
> I leave you this dreadful souvenir from me:
> That my soul was loyal and your soul false.

Even a year later, he stood by this appraisal, as when he concluded that Istrati was "uneven, superficial, deceitful, and sentimental" (Prev. 1965b: 172). In the meantime, however, he had also reflected on himself in ways that prepared the ground for the more objective portrayal of his own obduracy in *Toda-Raba*. The following was written on 16 February 1929 in the middle of the night while Kazantzakis awaited his train in a tiny station on the Manchurian border. It authenticates Istrati's criticisms and suggests that the fictional argument in *Toda-Raba* does not differ from the real one:

> I lost many years of my life searching in a multitude of "exits," without any guide, in order to discover my own exit. I loitered more than was proper in intermediate or deceptive stations. I was first detained by scholarship, then by philosophy, then by action, then by art (I still have not escaped that one), "λιλαιόμεναι πόσιν ἔμμεναι" [sic].[55] Now I clearly understand the following: What interests me is not mankind, not the earth, not heaven, but the flame that consumes mankind, earth, and heaven. I must capture this flame and express it in words—only then will I travel beyond all the former stations. I understood this perfectly again in Russia. Russia does not interest me in the least, [nor does] human justice, comfort, or virtue; the only thing that interests me is the flame that burns up humankind with justice, comfort, and virtue, those popular [laïká], humble, ephemeral lures.
>
> This is monstrous, as Istrati screamed at me when he abandoned me. "You don't love humanity, you are a heartless man, you don't care about the fortunes of the masses!" And I had no more to say, because his simplistic, sentimental soul was incapable of understanding this tigress, this bloodhound of "God's" that I am clutching—like the Spartan boy who stole the fox—and that is lacerating my breast. (Prev. 1965b:111–112)

As for Istrati, he dealt his blow by arranging with the newspaper editors in Germany, England, France, Holland, Spain, and Sweden who had agreed to publish "their" articles from Russia, to have these articles suppressed.[56] Of the scores that Kazantzakis had completed, only a few appeared (Prev. 1965b:106). In any case, their contents were too "red" for publication in *Les Nouvelles Littéraires* and too "white" for publication in Russia itself (Prev. 1965b:106). In addition, Istrati now refused to lend his name to the three books on Russia for which Kazantzakis had signed a contract with Rieder, Istrati's Parisian publisher (Prev. 1965b:103, 106), a turn of events that Kazantzakis knew would make publication of his own books extremely difficult, since all doors had been opened to him solely because of his collaboration with the then world-famous "Gorky of the Balkans."

Istrati had vowed, upon leaving the Soviet Union, to write an "enthusiastic and mournful" book in which he would "tell the whole truth" (Serge 1951:302; 1963:279). He arrived in Paris on 15 February (Istrati 1929a:57). The first fulfillment of his vow came a week later in an interview with Frédéric Lefèvre in *Les Nouvelles Littéraires* entitled "An hour with Panaït Istrati back from Russia." In it, Istrati was relatively restrained. While affirming his faith in Trotsky, he refused to condemn the Stalinists as fascists (the term suggested by Lefèvre), reserving his indignation for bureaucratic cliques in the Party and the unions "whose sole aim is to rise in the world and lord it over others" (Lefevre 1929:9).[57]

Despite its restraint, the interview was not appreciated by the Bolsheviks. On 11 March, when Kazantzakis reached Moscow after his return from Siberia, he went immediately to the home of Itka Horowitz, his old acquaintance from Berlin days who, still a fanatical communist, had settled in Russia.[58] Bursting with anger, she told him that Istrati had given a dreadful interview to *Les Nouvelles Littéraires* and that everyone in Moscow was heaping insults on him and saying that they ought to keep a better eye on such "friends" (Eleni Kaz. 1977:257–258; 1968a:208). Kazantzakis himself reacted with equal anger five months later:

> I read Panaït immediately. Horrible! The article is very well written: lively, sensational reportage that makes an impression. But what he says about Russia and the unjust and superficial way he generalizes out of one case—and what if there be thousands?—makes this article revolting and macabre. What Panaït says is definitely true. But it is one side of the truth, out of many. Whoever reaches generalized conclusions about good or evil in this manner is either superficial or dishonest. Panaït is simply superficial—exciting and excitable. The article will do harm in Russia. Generally, I find it disgusting, because Panaït, lost in a single case, forgot whatever good he saw and touched in Russia. (Eleni Kaz. 1977: 274; 1968a:223)[59]

Istrati's vow to write an enthusiastic and mournful book in which he would tell the whole truth resulted in the publication, at fortnightly intervals beginning in November 1929, of three volumes of *Vers l'autre flamme* (Toward the Other Flame): I. *Après seize mois dans l'URSS*; II. *Soviets 1929*; III. *La Russie nue*. Of these, only the first was written by Istrati himself.[60] It is an important book: one of the earliest testimonies of deconversion by a Western writer.[61]

Although uncompromising in its exposure of the Russians, it did not bring Kazantzakis into the arena of its scorn. On the contrary, the chapter that Istrati devotes to his traveling companion preserves the admiration he felt for Kazantzakis from the time of their first meeting, throughout the Alhambra/Sotiría adventures, and during their initial travels in the Soviet Union. About the estrangement there is only one short passage (Istrati 1929a:196); even here, however, Istrati does not reproach Kazantzakis but merely laments the cancellation of their plans to continue together to Siberia. It is clear that he valued Kazantzakis's friendship even after their angry separation. His account of their relationship, although based on "Parmi les gueux de Grèce," which was written shortly after the Alhambra affair, is clearly a revised version. If he had wished to alter his initially favorable view in order to color it with rancor against his friend he could have done so in the revision. Instead, he accuses himself of infidelity, speaks of his time in the Soviet Union as blessing him with one of the most beautiful encounters of his life, then expands on the need for a friendship in which each party gives of his "stock of love" until he is emptied. Is there anything else in life? asks Istrati. No—unless we add the bitterness of separation (Istrati 1929a:110–111). The remainder is a tribute and also one of the rare character-sketches of Kazantzakis that we possess:

> The Cretan was extremely methodical . . . Not a bit of verbosity. . . . Never an elocution, despite all the provocation. Awkward during visits to factories and hospitals. . . . [W]hat he sought most fervently was the human document, the hero. How forcefully he attacked every illusion in order to discover on occasion a splendid reality! I never knew a man with a greater thirst for purity and heroism.
>
> Sprung from a Cretan peasant with an iron fist and a strong-box crammed with pounds-sterling, he steeped himself in the full range of ancient wisdom and modern science, then cut himself off from his father, his class, even from wisdom, in order to adhere to a Bolshevism still making its début and still heroic. . . .
>
> . . . He lives on a bowl of soup, a pound of apples, or a kippered herring. His luggage: ten kilos—to voyage around the world! His apartment: a cot. But his desires: a universe. His companionship: an all-consuming happiness. . . . (Istrati 1929a:114, 116)[62]

For his part, Kazantzakis was eventually just as forgiving as Istrati, despite the bitter criticisms that appear for a time in the letters. In *Toda-Raba* the portrait of Istrati as Azad is sympathetic; Kazantzakis leans more toward self-criticism in his depiction of himself as Géranos. By 1930, although retaining his scorn for minds such as Istrati's (Prev. 1965b:218), he admitted that he would much enjoy seeing his ex-friend again (Prev. 1965b:215). By 1933, he had softened toward him completely. Istrati, now severely ill, had begun to write huge letters, and Kazantzakis admired his undiminished spiritual vitality even when three-quarters of his lungs were ravaged by tuberculosis: "I am writing him in my turn with emotion, erasing all the past" (Prev. 1965b:356). "I love this man exceedingly, despite everything, because he is 'warm.' What importance do all his defects have compared to seething blood? As we have said: all the warm ones to Heaven and the cold ones to Hell!" (Prev. 1965b:361).[63]

When Kazantzakis learned from Eléni Samíou that Istrati was no more, he unwittingly composed an epitaph to their friendship and estrangement: "I received . . . the terrible news that Panaït had died. Life is horrible and we do not realize this and waste it in small talk and wretched acts. Only when someone dies whom we love do we sense that we are walking on the edge of the abyss" (Eleni Kaz. 1977:382; 1968a:317). What Kazantzakis must have realized was that—despite everything—his developing relationship to communism after the beginnings in Berlin and Iráklion, and almost his entire relationship to the Soviet Union, were mediated through Istrati, who served as a whetstone enabling Kazantzakis to sharpen his enthusiasms and hesitations alike. That is why in October 1936 (Prev. 1965b:464–465), a year and a half after his friend's death, he cited Istrati as the "shadow" that he felt next to him, if only faintly, throughout the entire rise and decline of his allegiance to the left.[64]

CHAPTER SIX

Toda-Raba and the waning of Kazantzakis's communism

Sweet to gaze on woes ourselves escape:
Sweet too to watch the great contests of war
Arrayed along the plain, ourselves at ease,
But naught more pleasant than to hold the forts,
The forts serene of calm philosophy
Established by the learning of the wise,
To look down from their heights and others see
Still wandering all abroad, and straying far
To reach the path of life . . .
—Lucretius 2.4–10

Kazantzakis left Moscow on 16 April 1929. He reached Berlin on 20 April and remained there for less than three weeks (Prev. 1965b:122, 125). As always, he was exhilarated by change. Berlin struck him anew as one of the "most interesting cities in the world," especially because of the efforts of intellectuals there to synthesize the bourgeois and communist ideologies (Prev. 1965b:130). But his main energies were devoted to his concern "to acquit himself of his debt to 'crucified Russia' " (Eleni Kaz. 1968a:215). Although he had contracted with the French publisher Rieder six months earlier to submit three books on the Soviet Union by 1 July (Prev. 1965b:103), what he had in mind now was a single volume—a novel. Also, he was eager to find a German publisher in addition to Rieder, convinced as he was that his mentality had "no affinity with the French spirit. . . . My ardent and at the same time independent mode startles them. They're unable to classify me, and their Latin clarity grows impatient" (Prev. 1965b:109). By early May he had located some German firms who were interested (Prev. 1965b:131). Thus he decided to write *Toda-Raba* in French, translate it himself into German, and submit both versions.[1]

Although he found Berlin interesting, he predictably longed to be finished with "all the ephemeral things that are occupying me now" (Prev. 1965b:130) in order to escape to the mountains of Czechoslovakia, finish the "tedious and necessary job" of writing *Toda-Raba* (Prev. 1965b:131), and then turn to the *Odyssey*: that is, to poetry, "the soul's one and only salvation" (Prev. 1965b:135). Fortunately for his finances, he was able to sell some articles to the *Kölnische Zeitung* (Prev. 1965b:161–162; Eleni Kaz. 1977:274; 1968a:224). This and other journalistic income enabled him to prolong his residence in the forests of Gottesgab, the ideal place to write.[2]

A NOVEL OF SELF-REVELATION

Having settled in Gottesgab on 10 May, by the twenty-eighth he was already well along with *Toda-Raba*. Rising at 4 A.M., working until 8, stopping for breakfast, working again until 2, then walking in the forests until evening (Prev. 1965b:133, 139), he was eager to deliver himself from Russia by writing about it—just as in *Víos ke politía tu Aléksi Zorbá* the boss delivers himself from Buddhism by completing his manuscript on Buddha. Afterwards, he vowed, he would "never turn back. *Odíssia*, that and nothing else!" (Prev. 1965b:133).

Yet *Toda-Raba* is not just the discharge of a debt to crucified Russia; it is a novel in which Kazantzakis attempted as well to deliver himself from some of his personal dilemmas by solidifying them in art. In it, as he stated to Prevelákis later, he bared his soul (Prev. 1965b:261). An open hint comes in the epigraph, where we are told that the characters "ne sont que les diverses facettes d'une seul conscience" ("are merely facets of a single consciousness"). "In other words," as Kazantzakis makes clear in a letter, "they are the seven people I have inside me and who saw Russia all together. Géranos and Ananda are somewhat deeper inside me. But all are there . . ." (Prev. 1965b:136, cf. 261).[3]

More importantly, *Toda-Raba* bares Kazantzakis's soul because in it he confesses his failure to succeed in the active life. Zográfou (1960:221) argues this most broadly, claiming that *Toda-Raba* records every one of Kazantzakis's incapacities: with women (Rahel gives herself to the Big-Jawed Man and not to Géranos), with friends (Géranos breaks with Azad), and with the phenomenal world (Russia). On the other hand, she praises Kazantzakis for knowing his weaknesses, removing the mask of the superman or messiah, and revealing to us what she calls the impotent failure beneath, as when Géranos questions his motives for coming to Russia by asking whether he is willing to "intervene,"[4] and his inner voice refuses to answer (Kaz. 1962c:134–135; 1964f:114–115).

The book dwells on this political impotence. At one point Géranos confesses to his "son," Pantéli (– Pandelís Prevelákis, of course), that his duty is "to join the communist cause and begin to work. . . . But I cannot," he continues; ". . . I love the truth, but I cannot serve it" (1962c:225; 1964f:186). At another point, as we saw in the previous chapter, Azad berates Géranos for heartless insensitivity: "Russia, for you, is nothing but an interesting tragedy. . . . Anyone who loves does not watch things; he suffers" (1962c:190; 1964f:157).

In sum, Kazantzakis bares his soul so thoroughly that we are tempted to support Zográfou's view that *Toda-Raba* is a lament for his failure to succeed in the active life. But surely such an interpretation, although partially cogent, is too restrictive. It requires us to believe that Kazantzakis went to Russia solely to suppress his ascetic tendencies, conquer his metaphysical obsessions, and learn to act. Yes, the book would record a failure if this were the case. But it is not the case. As the epigraph forewarns us, the single consciousness that experienced the Soviet Union has many facets. Of these, activism is only one. We should remember that even at the height of his communist enthusiasm in 1922, when he was staking everything on the opportunity to live and work in Russia, Kazantzakis exhibited his other side: "I'm working on the plan to go to Russia and I know what awaits me there and cannot devote myself fully to the joy and *illusion* of the new journey" (Kaz. 1958a:133; 1979a:77; my italics). In addition, we should remember that *Askitikí*, which he hoped to promulgate in Russia, aimed to subsume activism beneath a pessimistic world-view. Moreover, the Alhambra incident had reconfirmed to Kazantzakis that specific action was ephemeral. What mattered for him—even before the Roussakov affair, and doubly so afterwards—was the comprehension of an overall plan of our existence, and that comprehension's mythopoesis in art.

Prompted by these considerations, we should read *Toda-Raba* less restrictively than Zográfou does. When we do, we discover that Géranos does not begin with a single-minded desire to intervene. On the contrary, from the very start he aspires (like Kazantzakis) to comprehend abstractly: "to detach [suffering], placing it above the individuals who were in pain and discovering a metaphysical synthesis for these earthly struggles" (Kaz. 1962c:11; 1964f:15). Although tempted to desert this original goal in favor of intervening, he does not succumb to the temptation. Seen in this way, the novel presents its hero's abiding allegiance to metaphysical vision.

Extending this approach, I would say that a broader interpretation of *Toda-Raba* shows it reworking *Askitikí* and anticipating *Odíssia*. In all three texts the basic conflict is between participation and withdrawal. *Toda-Raba* polarizes the two extremes in Azad and Ananda. The former, ignoring the abyss, wants to intervene; the latter, seeing it, craves impassivity. Both tendencies exist in an uneasy balance in Géranos, who insofar as he desires to act wants to do so within the larger context of the abyss. He does intervene up to a point; yet the purpose of active experience for him is not to keep futility at bay but, on the contrary, to confirm futility as action's end. The heart of this particular novel and also of Kazantzakis's political philosophy in its mature form is the paradox that participation is needed to teach us the futility of participation.

In what way, then, does *Toda-Raba* reflect failure? I hope we may agree that Zográfou's answer is inadequate, based as it is on the false assumption that Géranos yearns single-mindedly to escape his nihilistic constraints. My own answer would be the following: *Toda-Raba* bares Kazantzakis's soul in that Géranos fails to achieve and maintain an assured balance between the conflicting tendencies. Instead, we are exposed to the author's anguished fear that perhaps an equilibrium is impossible.

In this respect, *Toda-Raba* differs from both *Askitikí* and *Odíssia.* All three works explore the same problem, yet the treatise and the epic display an assurance lacking in the novel, in which Géranos accomplishes the synthesis only tentatively at the beginning, is tempted to abandon it, then frantically seeks it again after his communistic dream lapses into materialistic finitude owing to the realities of political life. When measuring *Toda-Raba* against the other two works, one suspects a defect of artistic execution rather than a change in Kazantzakis's perspective. Oddly, this is confirmed by the book's most artistically arresting portion, the epilogue describing Toda-Raba's vision. Here the attempted union of participation and withdrawal is displaced by an ethos of frenzied activism. It is as though Kazantzakis had suddenly collapsed under the burden of maintaining warring opposites in an ever-threatened equilibrium, and had imagined himself an unfettered, unthinking revolutionary burning up the world—exposing in the process his own uneasiness. Whereas he tries to believe that his true self is Toda-Raba and that all the other characters are but masks, in truth Toda-Raba is the most artificial of the masks he dons. His confusion is revealed in the self-justifying letter to Victor Serge that we saw in part in Chapter Five:

> . . . If I am not a Marxist, it is first of all because my metaphysical sense is not sufficiently elementary. I am not satisfied with overly simplistic assertions and denials; it is also because I am not a man of action. . . .
>
> You have viewed me only as a mystic! Or, rather, as a bookworm! I've just written a confession in the form of a novel on the subject of the Soviet Union. The central character is a Negro, Toda-Raba. I hope that you will read this book and will then discover in this Negro my true countenance, my deep self: an enemy of erudition.[5]
>
> All the other masks—the seven persons who function in this book—are simply convenient masks that I don in order to move about in society . . . (Eleni Kaz. 1968b:228–229; 1977:273; 1968a:222–223)

Concentrating as he does on this antimystical enemy of erudition, he conveniently forgets that a revolutionary activist cannot be the true countenance of someone who is not a man of action. Yet Kazantzakis's simplistic identification with Toda-Raba is seen not only in the letter to Serge quoted above but also in his asseveration to Jouvenel, "My mind is western . . . , my flame Asiatic, my heart African." "Should we go back to Toda-Raba?" inquires Jouvenel. "Yes," Kazantzakis replies, "I am he" (Jouvenel 1962:1578).

Given this self-deception, it is curious that the epilogue should turn out to be the book's best part, a foretaste of the apocalyptic prose enlivening portions of *The Last Temptation*, for example. Its intrinsic merits and its importance for the future encourage us to investigate it further in both content and technique. Its content reflects the attitude engendered by Kazantzakis's ill-fated attempt to intervene in Iráklion in 1924. Disillusioned with the workers and peasants he had tried to help, he subsequently recorded in his diary conclusions, quoted in full in Chapter Four, about the unlikelihood that either Russian or European communists would ever create a new culture, seeing that "the positive, creative role has always been taken by the 'barbarians' " (Prev. 1965b:159–160). These initial hesitations were formulated in March 1925. In "Sizítisi m'énan arhigó" (1926), we witness the same attitude:

> I remember a Negro with the jaws of a gorilla who got up to speak at a meeting the other day in Moscow. His gestures were violent, wild; his yellow eyes flashed. He too repeated over and over again the words already uttered a thousand times—"proletariat," "freedom," "justice"—with such passion that he gave them an unimaginably threatening meaning. The white Europeans below him in the hall applauded, believing that these words spoken by the Negro possessed the same content that the Europeans gave them. But when the Negro howled "Justice!" I saw massacres, impalements, feasting, and the desert in his eyes, whereas when the westerners said "Justice!" their eyes filled with well-nourished workers and large cities. (Kaz. 1965e:231–232; 1989:223)

By the time he left the Soviet Union for Berlin in 1929, Kazantzakis had placed his hopes entirely in African blacks as the last remaining seed-bearing barbarians uncontaminated by Western culture. It is this conclusion that the epilogue reflects.

As for the epilogue's technique, this too derives from Kazantzakis's experiences in Russia. The idea occurred to him in 1928 in Kiev while he was planning a film meant to open with a long queue of pilgrims waiting to enter Lenin's tomb.[6] One of them,

> the moment he faces . . . Lenin's shiny skull in the catacomb, becomes aware of a huge, instantaneous vision in his mind.[7] He sees the entire evolution (a) of Lenin, (b) of Russia, (c) of the earth. . . . Then the person in back of him pushes him a little to make him keep moving, and my hero leaves by the other door. His vision lasted one second. Most interesting to me is that the pilgrim who has the vision will be an African Negro. Just think: what apparitions of violence, war, and at the same time what cacti and African masks, and landscapes! (Prev. 1965b:73)

As originally planned, the novel *Toda-Raba*, like the scenario, was meant to be an extended vision entirely African in character. But Kazantzakis feared that the resulting manuscript would never be accepted by a publisher. Thus he compromised by inventing the seven consciousnesses who see Russia from seven different perspectives. From the original visionary plan he retained only the prologue and epilogue, complaining to Prevelákis, "I would have liked to continue the whole book like the prologue. But publication would be impossible. Thus I was limited to merely placing the book between two flames" (Prev. 1965b:134).

These permutations show us Kazantzakis's artistic problem both at this stage in his career and later. It was a situation of heads I win, tails you lose. His goal of one hundred percent flame tended to lead him into overextended sublimities that degenerate into rhetoric; conversely, this same goal encouraged him to churn out "non-flame" material too quickly, convinced as he was that anything without "flame" meant compromise. When both defects are yoked together, as in *Toda-Raba*, the result is doubly disappointing. On the other hand, since the dialectic of expectation and compromise that we see in *Toda-Raba* remained a constant in Kazantzakis's subsequent career, and since he learned to combine the two modes more suitably in later works, *Toda-Raba* remains instructive for anyone concerned with aesthetic analysis—quite aside from its ideological and autobiographical interest.

We know that Kazantzakis recognized its defects: he once confessed that it was a tiny offhand job (Prev. 1965b:146). But he probably did not recognize the degree to which the apocalyptic epilogue is arbitrarily appended to the loosely fictionalized argumentation (relieved by travelogue) that sits between the two flames. The book's case against the Russian experiment is so convincing that the African's vision of Lenin's apotheosis at the end seems to belong to another work.

Additional defects abound. Chief among these is unconvincing characterization. Azad recounts experiences that clash with his personality (Kaz. 1962c:182; 1964f:151–152); moreover, he voices ideas that sound too much like Kazantzakis's own and therefore belong in the mouth of

Géranos (Kaz. 1962c:129–130; 1964f:110). It may be objected that all the characters are facets of one central consciousness; nevertheless, each is meant to be an identifiably separate facet—Kazantzakis is not experimenting here with the deliquescent interpenetration of personalities that we find, for example, in Virginia Woolf's *The Waves*. Another defect is melodramatic plotting. In Chapter 16, Souki dies, Amita is converted and burns his manuscripts, Rahel commits suicide, and Azad beards the communists in their den—all on the great day of the anniversary celebrations!

I dwell on such problems not from the perverse pleasure of damning an easily damnable book, but because of *Toda-Raba*'s interest for anyone concerned with aesthetic analysis. Kazantzakis's problems are faced by all novelists: how to subordinate real events, conversations, and people to artistic needs, and conversely how to make imaginary invention seem real. He improved with time. In *Alexis Zorbás*, he was able to alter his own experiences in the interests of aesthetic form, to characterize consistently, and to neutralize the melodramatic elements of plotting by flavoring the entire book with whimsy.

In sum, *Toda-Raba* deserves our attention because, in technique, it provides a foretaste of some of the most successful aspects of Kazantzakis's future practice while at the same time displaying defects that enable us to discern what was improved—or not improved—in later novels.[8]

But the novel's greatest importance lies in its content, for it presents Kazantzakis's definitive view of Russian communism. There is no need for me to summarize this view; the indefatigable Kazantzakis did so himself in the form of an encyclical letter. This document is so important that I shall translate its main points more-or-less in full.[9]

> After my long trip to Russia, . . . and upon the eve of what is for me a great moment—resumption of work on the *Odyssey*—, I truly feel that I have an obligation to . . . state precisely . . . the point . . . at which I have arrived in my attempt to confront today's world-wide problem. . . .
>
> 1) After experiencing Russia at first hand—experiencing, that is, a dream come true—, I have reached the following conclusion: assault is more important than conquest. . . . [Prev. 1965b:151]. The sublime moment of intoxication cannot be prolonged; inspiration becomes unavoidably constricted and humiliated when it seeks durability in words—all this we know. Yet it is immensely painful to see this terrible law of human incapacity operating today to make Russia's huge inspiration durable. The realization of the ideal has diminished the souls of those who are struggling for the ideal; having achieved an equilibrium that strikes them as convenient, they do not wish to move further ahead. The revolutionaries

have become comfortable. Those who are comfortable quickly end up as conservatives, and little by little the conservatives turn into reactionaries.

I do not wish to disparage this curve, which is necessary and in certain cases useful for the waves of human change. The soul naturally finds continuous exaltation unendurable; it naturally seeks to rest: to live at last without anxiety—forgetting, like a vegetable. The soul is not so very different from matter. It forms dregs easily, becomes immobile, turns into matter. But specifically in Russia we have the following dual problem:

a) This natural evolution of the soul into matter is happening very rapidly.

b) Since the Russian and international proletariats are profoundly united, a premature decline such as this is extremely dangerous and discouraging for those comrades who are still at the preceding stage, the impetuous one of assault. . . . [Prev. 1965b: 152].

2) In order for the masses (and also the elite) to be swept up into an assault that contains so many dangers, an appropriate slogan must be found. To be appropriate, the slogan must contain certain elements: a) it must respond to contemporary needs; b) it must not just respond to these needs but exaggerate and distend them, make them appear tragic, surpassing reality; c) it must be stated in simple terms.

Every era that created a civilization possessed such a slogan, which often took the form of a religion. For our own era, this slogan is unquestionably the communist one. . . . [Prev. 1965b: 153].

Marx discovered the appropriate slogan for our age, one able to marshal the masses, give them an illusion, represent this illusion to them as realizable (indeed as historically determined), and assure them that every incidence of class struggle and war will cease after the proletariat's victory, and that justice will come. In other words, he gave them a faith.

What are the chief characteristics of this faith? They are two: a) materialism, b) worship of the machine. The ideal of Soviet Russia is America. This is entirely natural. Communism is not something wholly new, not a change of fronts in mankind's battle; it is simply the utmost and most logical consequence of bourgeois civilization, which, by developing the mind's critical faculties, broke down every religion and created what we know as science, i.e. the laws by which we can comprehend and subdue natural forces. Communism deifies these fruits of bourgeois effort and merely strives to achieve—and does achieve—a more equitable distribution of material goods [Prev. 1965b:154]. . . .

3) Communism's mission is to undo bourgeois civilization, not to create a new civilization. Communism is not the beginning but the end. It has all the symptoms of the end: unadulterated materialism, exaggerated rationality, lethal analysis of every faith that transcends the five senses, deification of practical goals.

4) What, then, is our duty? In the age in which we have been born, we must be communists if we want our actions to . . . aid mankind's progress, but communists who are aware, i.e. enlightened, relentless, fully knowledgeable about what motivates them, and devoid of superficial, excessive hope. Let us not be like those naïve communists who suppose that happiness and justice will follow communism's triumph. We should feel a) disgusted by simple-minded, superficial optimism of this sort, b) strengthened in our fanaticism and power by this severe, sober conception of communism.

Just as the firefighter who has entered a burning forest must keep advancing at double speed instead of turning back if he is to escape the conflagration, so we who have entered this fearsome age must try our best to stretch all the tendencies of communism to the extreme so that deliverance may come as soon as possible. What deliverance? The destruction of this world and the beginning of the creation of another with different foundations, one in which the cults of machinery, rationality, and practicality will be deemed unworthy. A new slogan [Prev. 1965b:155].

5) If, on the other hand, we are not men of action, we have the right to desire this metacommunistic slogan now if possible [and], divining it, to start living it at once. Communism comes at the end. Yet, like every end, it naturally contains many elements of a subsequent beginning. What elements? Among all the desires, needs, and premonitions surrounding us, which will survive and be of use in the coming civilization? . . .

For today's creative theoretician, this is the anguished concern and great duty.

. . . I believe that the second period of my life commenced after my long trip to Russia. For me right now, Russia is a violent turbulence that is already beginning to find its place in memory . . . [Prev. 1965b:156]. . . .

For the next two or three years, I am assigning my life a single goal: to conceive in the womb of the *Odyssey* the kravyí of future humanity . . .

> This is the duty that I am assigning to my life. Everything else—liberating the proletariat, cultivating the mind, the eye's curiosity to see, the ear's to hear, the heart's to love—must be nothing more for me than a painful march toward this kravyí. . . .

There are eight main points in this statement that I would like to emphasize. Some are explicit, others implicit.

1. Kazantzakis assumes, as does Bergson, that motion is vitally creative whereas stability is deadening.

2. Although he reaffirms his dogma of the transitional age, he surprises us by assigning Soviet communism a new position in our current transition. Previously he had viewed the Bolsheviks as cosmogonic barbarians leading the creative assault; now he places them at the end of the bourgeois era.[10]

3. Kazantzakis refuses to let his disillusion affect him in ways seen in other intellectuals who changed their minds about the Soviet Union. Unlike Istrati (or Solzhenitsyn in a later day), he avoids the no-man's-land in which the politics of both West and East are equally abhorrent; unlike John Dos Passos, he does not rebound to a defense of the Western status quo; nor does he revert to pretechnological agrarianism or medievalism as antidotes to modernity's worship of the machine.[11]

4. Instead, Kazantzakis tries to convert disillusion into the impetus for fashioning a new syncretistic synthesis.[12]

5. In order for this synthesis to evolve properly, it must occur only after communism attains its acme.

6. Thus if we wish to surpass communism we must first be fanatical communists. As Géranos cries out in *Toda-Raba*: "Yes, yes, let us be communists! Let us go on intensifying this cult of the machine and of matter. . . . Let us drive the world to an exaggerated Americanism! There is no other way to liberate ourselves from the machine" (Kaz. 1962c:219; 1964f:181).

7. Kazantzakis himself, however, since he is not a man of action, will concentrate on something else: creating in advance the new slogan or kravyí, the river bed into which reality will flow when it is ready.

8. Kazantzakis is entering a new period in which artistic creation will be the sole means enabling him to produce this kravyí.

These eight points define his position shortly before he began the decisive second draft of the *Odyssey*.[13] Let us dwell on his resolve to concentrate on art rather than politics. He calls this his second period, a claim gainsaid in the letter to Prevelákis dated 12 October 1936 in which he assigns this same advance to 1933, not 1929, naming it his third period, not his second. Whether the new phase was the second or third is not important. Nor is the discrepancy in dates. What is important is Kazantzakis's growing conviction during the final year of his experience in Russia that freedom in his case had to be sought in the imaginative realm of artistic creation rather than in the practical realm of politics. Periodization, whether practiced by critics or authors, is an inexact science. We cannot date the precise end of Kazantzakis's communism; yet it did wane at the turn of the decade.

SORTING OUT KAZANTZAKIS'S POLITICAL ALLEGIANCES AFTER 1929; WHY HE WAS NEVER A COMMUNIST

In February 1930 Kazantzakis was still calling himself an intransigent communist but was careful to repeat qualifications that are already familiar to us: "Certainly I find communism's narrow and assured materialistic basis odious. Yet it is necessary because, as I have long been convinced, communism is not the start of a new civilization but the termination of an old one; consequently, it intensifies that civilization's efforts—materialism, the machine, Americanism—to the utmost extreme" (Prev. 1965b: 179–180).

In December 1930 he joined Galatea Kazantzáki, Dimítrios Glinós, Kóstas Várnalis and other left-wing (and centrist) intellectuals in signing a protest published in the communist newspaper *Rizospástis* against the maltreatment and court-martial of young soldiers in the army prison at Kalpáki, Ipirus (*Dianoúmenon tis Athinas* 1930).

At the turn of the year 1930–1931, faced in all probability with a renewed attempt by the public prosecutor to arraign him for the Alhambra speech and/or for *Askitikí*,[14] Kazantzakis expanded the Confession of Faith that he had prepared in the autumn of 1924 in order to defend his involvement with Iráklion's disgruntled veterans. There is no need for me to reproduce the expanded document since the Greek text is readily available (Prev. 1965b:221–230), as are full translations in both English (Eleni Kaz. 1968a:565–570) and French (Eleni Kaz. 1968b:575–582). The orientation here is still firmly toward the left: Kazantzakis reaffirms his beliefs that the bourgeoisie is destined to be replaced by the working class (Prev. 1965b:223) and that Russia is now the "center of the earth" (Prev. 1965b:225). But he draws back in the peroration in ways that we have come to expect:

> I am neither a narrow-minded detractor nor a superficial apologist. This is because I am not a man of practical action but someone who has assigned his life the aims of trying (a) to think and (b) to formulate his thoughts. . . . If I were a "man of action" . . . I would proclaim rough-hewn dogmas easy to comprehend.
>
> . . . My purpose has been to make as many people who are ca-

> pable of thought confront more profoundly the age in which we live and prepare themselves for a renaissance of their individual and communal lives: a renaissance naturally psychological at first, then intellectual and social, and finally—in due course—economic and political. (Prev. 1965b:229–230)

This refusal to proclaim dogmas was carried one step further at roughly the same time (early 1931) in an essay on populism in the novel. The sole hope for the revival of any art form, Kazantzakis argues there, is "a new faith that will sweep away everything . . . What is this new faith? Communism? I don't know. If I knew, I would not be engaged in literature" (Cossin 1931:601).

In October 1932, while residing in Madrid, Kazantzakis hastily translated Jacinto Benavente's "Oración a Rusía," the exuberantly pro-Soviet prologue to the latter's play *Santa Rusía* (Holy Russia). The play concludes with the young Lenin joining Russian emigré revolutionaries in a park in London in 1903, surrounded by children carrying a banner proclaiming "Workers of the world, unite," whereupon everyone sings the *Internationale* as the curtain falls. Kazantzakis's reaction after he attended a performance is instructive: "Benavente's play is nothing special. Old clichés, tirades, etc." (Prev. 1965b:330). He was still serving the cause, but obviously his heart was no longer in it.[15]

Although 1933 is the year that supposedly terminated Kazantzakis's allegiance to the left, the evidence shows him still ambivalent. Writing about Saint Teresa in Η Καθημερινή on 26 May of that year, he implies that if she had been born in the twentieth century she would have been a communist fighting hunger and oppression, since that is the contemporary form taken by the spirit in its struggle to ascend (Kaz. 1962b:57; 1963c:64). Simultaneously, however, appalled at the political anarchy in Spain, he speaks of "a mindless communism without a program" (Prev. 1965b:356) and confesses that he can no longer work up any interest in "social reforms and similar superficialities" (Prev. 1965b:360). Yet from the nineteenth to the twenty-first of May 1934 he composed the ferociously Bolshevik terzina "Lenin" in which the communist leader appears Christlike as "the son of man"—not a lamb this time but a wolf seeking freedom and promising the fiery destruction of Paris and London, plus hunger marches in New York that will make the skyscrapers shake!—(Kaz. 1960c:51–57, lines 16–18, 104–105, 147–150; dating on p. 181).

After the Italians invaded Abyssinia, Kazantzakis was asked to join with other Greek intellectuals in signing a protest. He refused. In July 1936 he defended his position in a newspaper article entitled Ο φόβος και η πείνα (Fear and Hunger). I shall speak of this in the second volume when examining Kazantzakis's continuing attraction to fascism, but it is also relevant here. He justifies his refusal as follows: War is healthy; pacifism is a camouflage for fear. Every healthy civilization—Italy in this instance—is brutal in its need to expand. The real villains (against whom he would gladly sign a protest) are England and France, the "inhuman satiated capitalists" who "do not permit other peoples, the proletarians, to rise up in revolt" (Kaz. 1936). The rhetoric is familiarly communist. But in other respects Kazantzakis departs from the party line. For example, he stresses the similar role played by Lenin, on the one hand, and by Hitler and Mussolini, on the other. The only thing that matters is the ferocity, purity, and intensity with which leaders respond to the promptings of their endangered peoples. As for him, although he "has linked his fate with the left for many years," he is now striving to view both fascism and communism with respect because he realizes that they are "fighting for the same goal. What goal? That man's soul may be stirred, may remain as vigilant as possible, may tremble a little from fear or may lash out insatiably all around it, spurred by hunger." And he is not afraid of being called a fascist. "Why should I be afraid?" he responds. "Wasn't I also called a communist? I can never be either the one or the other, because I am a free man. And I am free because I am not a man of action who needs dogmas, certainties, and practical considerations in order to participate."

Behind Kazantzakis's Olympian detachment lay a Bergsonian adulation of any and all sources capable of stirring mankind's soul (that is, its aspirations). This is what dealt the finishing blow to his communistic leanings: the essential deviation was his Bergsonian faith that spiritual energy can push evolution forward.[16] I must stress again that he was never a truly political figure but rather one whose philosophical/religious interests brought him willy-nilly into the political arena.

His Olympian stance was confirmed when he traveled to Spain in 1936 to report the Civil War, accredited to Franco's side but endeavoring to escape narrow partisanship; his articles show that he was attracted equally to the far right and the far left, at least insofar as both opposed anemic liberalism and flabby pacifism (Kaz. 1962b:145, 223; 1963c:161–162, 252).

In the remaining years of the 1930s he transferred his hatred of flabbiness from the Spanish context to the Greek one in his articles on the Peloponnesus, and he continued his flirtation with fascism until the invasions of his homeland first by Mussolini and then by Hitler propelled him toward a mellowed nationalism—more precisely, a "nationism" (εθνισμός)—that was to be crucial for the remainder of his career. All these permutations I will discuss in volume two. Here, I wish simply to list some additional data directly relevant to Kazantzakis's waning communism—data that will seem bewilderingly inconsistent.

In 1945, after the Dekemvrianá eruption of civil strife, he re-entered active political life as head of a small socialist group whose aim was to unify all who wished to institute the socialist economic system in Greece by democratic, that is, peaceful, means as opposed to the revolutionary means attempted by the Communist Party of Greece. Thus Kazantzakis was once again persona non grata for the far left. Yet in the same year we find him contradicting his socialist manifestos (e.g. Kaz. 1945a) in an Introduction that he wrote for the Greek translation of Serafima Gopner's *L'Essor de la culture en U.R.S.S.* (The Soaring Rise of Culture in the U.S.S.R.), published in Moscow the previous year. Here he sounds exactly as he did from 1923 to 1928. Peaceful means are forgotten. The Introduction begins with an exhortation to all honorable people to consider as their primary duty the destruction of the rotten, unethical world in which we live. The remainder explains why the Soviet Union should be everyone's model for the ensuing construction of a just society (Kaz. 1945b; Elli Alexiou 1966:242–244).[17]

A similar bellicosity permeates Kazantzakis's speech welcoming Paul Eluard to Athens on 26 May 1946:

> Anemic intellectuals are afraid; they think that freedom can come one lovely morning like the springtime, without violence. Freedom, however, has always been the daughter of war and love. (Kaz. 1946)

This rhetoric does not mean that Kazantzakis had now returned to the communist line. He continued to march to his own drummer, as evidenced by his refusal in 1950 to sign the Soviet-backed Stockholm Petition against the atomic bomb.

In 1954 he was still bellicose, but had discovered a new nation to replace Russia:

> China is the tomorrow of mankind. . . . Whether we like it or not, we are going toward socialism. . . . I don't think we shall get there peacefully. . . . There will have to be a war. . . . That's why I refused to sign the Stockholm Petition. (Yalourakis 1958:159)

Those who know Kazantzakis's consistent advocacy of war must find it ironic that two years later he was offered the Peace Prize by the Soviet bloc. At first he declined because he assumed that the honor was given only to communists. He wrote the committee that he was not a communist nor would ever be one, whereupon "they replied that it is given to whoever uses his writings to fight for freedom and human dignity, that it was awarded to me unanimously, and that I should not decline. So I accepted . . ." (Prev. 1965b:704).[18]

In 1957, the last year of his life, Kazantzakis visited China at the invitation of Zhou Enlai. From his journal, which Mrs. Kazantzakis has published as an epilogue to *Japan China*, we can tell how impressed he was with what he saw and how much he admired Mao Zedong and the heroism of the Chinese communists in their struggle for freedom (Kaz. 1964d:323, 326; 1963a:328–329, 332).[19] At the same time, however, the diary makes clear that Kazantzakis's ostensibly political reactions were still governed by the philosophical-*cum*-religious conviction that vibrancy of faith is the true measure of an individual or a civilization. In Hong Kong, speaking to an interviewer from *Time* magazine about the dilemma of freedom versus slavery in the communist world, he told the journalist that to formulate the dilemma in this way was inadvisable. "Whoever has a faith feels so much freer . . . so much more enslaved to his faith. Remember Saint Augustine: Lord, I am free only when I obey thy will. Hence faithless westerners are wrong to charge the communists with being slaves. Their slavery commences when they cease believing" (Kaz. 1964d:345; 1963a:348–349).

Do these data help us reach a conclusion about Kazantzakis's political allegiance? Was he or was he not a communist? Surely the question has already been answered. Nevertheless, I want to attempt a systematic summary based upon the facts we have encountered. This is needed for two opposite reasons. On the one hand, many people persist in labeling Kazantzakis a communist and therefore either exploit him for leftist propaganda or vilify him, according to their own alignment; on the other hand, many cannot determine how to label Kazantzakis and therefore reproach him for confusion, irresponsible eclecticism, and/or opportunism. Let us consider these two reasons seriatim.

Although supporting the left most of the time, Kazantzakis was never a communist, and could never have been one, owing to the following six considerations, most of which apply just as well to the ardent beginnings of his allegedly communist period as they do to the cooler years of his disillusionment.

1. He never accepted the promise of a future in which strife would cease and society would become classless. On the contrary, he assumed that the revolutionary proletariat would develop in its own turn into a flabby, selfish, reactionary bourgeoisie and would consequently incite a new revolutionary movement and renewed strife (Eleni Kaz. 1977:31; 1968a:27–28). Strife, for him, was cosmogonic; even if peace were possible, it would not be preferable. Lenin gave recipes for overcoming anxiety, Kazantzakis for overcoming tranquility.

2. Believing as he did that ontogeny recapitulates phylogeny, he could never view his own attraction to communism as permanent. It, too, like the rule of the proletariat itself, would be merely one phase in a larger development, one of many sirens to which he listened with ears un-

plugged, body not tied to the mast, yet soul untouched (Prev. 1965b:141; Kaz. 1962c:112; 1964f:95; cf. 1962a:82–83; 1960b:117).

3. Wary of Marxism's materialistic emphasis, he insisted that economic factors are not the primary motivation of human activity. A sardonically playful dialogue in *Taksidévontas. Rusía* says it all:

> The young professor of sociology at the Communist University in Moscow, analyzing all the economic factors of ancient Greek times with assurance and clarity, proves that the smiles of the caryatids on the Athenian acropolis are due to economic causes.
>
> His audience, orthodox Marxists, unhesitatingly accepts the learned explanation and bursts into applause.
>
> I smile. The young professor turns, annoyed.
>
> "Why are you smiling?"
>
> I answer: "I assure you, comrade professor, that my smile is not due to economic causes!" (Kaz. 1965e:216–217; 1989:209)

Kazantzakis suggested at least three basic motivations for human activity, all of them nonmaterialistic: (a) "the appearance of a great personality" (Kaz. 1965e:222; 1989:214), (b) the driving force of an idea, ideology, or faith (Eleni Kaz. 1977:262; 1968a:212), and (c) passion (Kaz. 1962b:145; 1963c:161).

4. Kazantzakis never honored the rationalism that is so basic to Marxist thought. The ostinato of his career was a fundamental antirationalism underpinning variations in political allegiance. Bolshevism was merely one of those variations, one that could last only so long as Kazantzakis saw no incompatibility between communism and antirationalism. Note how he describes his allegiance in the first flush of enthusiasm, early in 1923, comparing himself to Demosthenes Daniilídis:

> His intelligence is clear and he codifies it with splendid European lucidity. . . .
>
> He's a socialist, i.e. he wants a just distribution of wealth without violent communist upheavals. We always differ on this: I'm a Bolshevik extremist even if our momentum may not be perfectly logical and just. . . .
>
> He's a European; he admires European organization, progress, reason, tightness. I'm an oriental. . . . There is something else beyond logic, something deep and ardent that directs my innermost desire. (Kaz. 1958a:152–153)

As soon as he convinced himself that the Bolsheviks had lost their original irrational élan and were extending the Western emphasis on reason, machines, and sociology, he transferred his interest, as we have seen, to African primitives.

5. Philosophically, Kazantzakis assigned himself to the category of those who impose upon existence "a form that is *consciously* transitory but that helps us advance." This form must be a fiction, not a hypothesis, because a hypothesis aspires to be proved correct—that is, to correspond to truth—whereas a fiction "makes no such naïve claim" (Kaz. 1926a). Consistent with this philosophical position, Kazantzakis, insofar as he accepted communism, did so because he found it a fiction temporarily useful for human progress in our age. Knowing full well that for this and other reasons he stood outside the pale of communist orthodoxy, he named his heretical faith metacommunism (Kaz. 1965e:259; 1989:251).

6. Artistically, Kazantzakis held that the mentality of sociologists emasculates the creative imagination. Hence his refusal to write in the mode of socialist realism.

These six considerations should help convince us that communists have no right to claim Kazantzakis any more than conservatives have a right to vilify him as a left-wing extremist. Both responses convert him into something that he was not.

Turning now to those who accuse him of confusion, eclecticism, and/or opportunism: it is true that he resists easy placement. As he himself realized at least as early as 1928 (Prev. 1965b:100), his work was too revolutionary for the bourgeois West, too mystical for the Marxist East. "Apparently there is no régime that can tolerate me," he complained in 1941, but then added: "and rightly so, since there is no régime that I can tolerate" (Prev. 1965b:498; Eleni Kaz. 1968a:401). Where does this leave him? In 1947, he wrote from France: "Here the two camps are organizing themselves, extreme right and extreme left. The middle road, the correct one, has been lost" (Eleni Kaz. 1977:549; 1968a:472). This is a tempting answer but not a good one for Kazantzakis's career as a whole, since he generally abhorred the compromise and prudence that middle roads imply. He was a synthesizer, not a compromiser. Thus he saw himself as the forerunner of a third force that would direct the lost souls of both the right and left toward a spiritualized future that he could never satisfactorily define. This crying in the wilderness, although vague, should not be dismissed as confusion, irresponsible eclecticism, or opportunism. Whatever we may think of Kazantzakis's illusions, he was systematic, consistent, and disinterested in their pursuit.

THE ATTITUDE OF GREEK COMMUNISTS AND OTHERS TOWARD KAZANTZAKIS

These factors separate Kazantzakis from the ideology that so many people have attributed to him, without knowing the facts. Because confusion persists even today, it might be useful to remember as well that in

Kazantzakis's lifetime the Greek communists were united in considering him a heretic.

We have already seen the controversy that followed his 1926 article "Discussion with a Leader." The Marxists who responded then—Kordátos (1926; 1926b), Karoúzos (1926), and Lagákos (1927)—found Kazantzakis well-meaning, perhaps, but at odds with their principles. Two years later, Kóstas Várnalis expanded on the ideological gulf between Kazantzakis and communism. The pretext was a review of Kazantzakis's play *Hristós*.

> Thus Mr. Kazantzakis, in remaining within the Christian tradition, . . . hymning faith in miracles, in supernatural powers, in divine and human eternity (in survival and recompense after death), is writing not just religious poetry but (these things are inseparable) reactionary poetry. No liberated heart or advanced mind can accept this poetry without becoming upset or angry. And a reactionary result of this kind (whether the author wishes it or not) not only denies the profoundest reality of our day but also sharply contradicts Mr. Kazantzakis's own intellectual assumptions, at least their main line, historical materialism,[20] whose essence is the complete denial of mysticism as an explanation of the world and of history. Moreover, this work contradicts even the selfsame author's latest revolutionary appearance [*Askitikí*]. That work is so additionally reactionary (read: repulsive) that it attempts to unite Christian self-abandonment with Buddhist nihilism, i.e. is doubly blind. (Varnalis 1928:498–499)

Leftists continued to attack Kazantzakis well beyond the 1920s. Their complaints fall into three predictable categories: his divorce from "real life," his neglect of socialist realism, and his Olympian refusal to take sides.

Among the numerous reactions following the *Odyssey*'s publication in 1938, none is so antagonistic as Márkos Avyéris's. Kazantzakis's trouble, asserts this Marxist who had become Galatea Kazantzáki's second husband, is that he makes a virtue out of losing touch with life. Because of his philosophical nihilism, Kazantzakis concludes that existence lacks justification. Feeling no pity for man's plight, he exults at the thought that the human species will be annihilated. Then he "struggles to obliterate this humiliating feeling and to present it as heroic insouciance . . ." (Avyeris 1939:1346).

We should note that this attack was published in September 1939, precisely when Hitler invaded Poland. The deteriorating international situation prompted not only leftists but also a centrist liberal like Yórgos Theotokás to object publicly to the view (of which Kazantzakis was the chief proponent in Greece) that since opposing forces collaborate to produce a new synthesis, all sides in every conflict are historically necessary. Theotokás argued that the logical conclusion of such a view is that all sides are right, a conclusion that he found ethically unacceptable in light of the current crisis in Western Europe (Theotokas 1939:1–2; 1961:369–370).

During the civil war Theotokás's objections were expanded in a vitriolic mode by Fríxos Lambrídis, writing under the pseudonym L. Tasolámbros. In a booklet that Kazantzakis at first angrily called a libel (Prev. 1965b:577) but then, with his customary Olympianism, dismissed as full of "comic quarrels, coarse provincialisms—how can anyone possibly be interested?" (Prev. 1965b:578), Lambrídis accused Kazantzakis of believing in everything and consequently in nothing; of refusing to see art as necessarily dealing with the real world and having sociopolitical impact; of insisting falsely that writers should care about the future, as if those who cared about the present were cheap propagandists; of having recourse to miracles instead of honoring science; and of advancing naïve politicoeconomic ideas as for example in the prologue to *England*, where he claims that the class struggle between rich and poor is what causes the human spirit to advance, whereas we all know that class struggle is not a cause but a consequence, in this case of a faulty system of production and distribution (Lambridis 1947:18ff., 25ff.).

Theotokás's article should serve to remind us that Kazantzakis could be repugnant to liberals as well as to people at the extremes of the political spectrum; Tasolámbros's shows that he continued to be attacked by the left throughout the civil war, at the same time that he was vilified as a communist by the right. Nor did the leftist attacks stop at the civil war's conclusion. In 1957, for example, Galatea Kazantzáki published a novel called Ἄνθρωποι και υπεράνθρωποι (Men and Supermen), sending it to her ex-husband a few months before his death.[21] She had been a major factor, we should remember, in pushing Kazantzakis toward communism in the period 1917–1925; his letters to her, the Επιστολές προς τη Γαλάτεια (Kaz. 1958a) are always cited by those whose aim is to "prove" that Kazantzakis was indeed an adherent. Yet Galatea's final verdict in her thinly veiled account of her relationship with Kazantzakis is that he was never a communist.[22]

Since Kazantzakis's death, many more books have been written about him in Greece, some good, some bad. One of the best is Nikifóros Vrettákos's Νίκος Καζαντζάκης, η αγωνία του και το έργο του (Nikos Kazantzakis, His Anguish and His Oeuvre), which argues that Kazantzakis, far from agreeing with communism, displays the very traits of bourgeois decadence that communism despises. Vrettákos cites Kazantzakis's dualism, denigration of reason, scorn of the real world, obsession with death and "no exit," yearning for a metaphysic to assuage his emptiness—staples encountered in Kafka, Camus, the early T.S. Eliot, Gide, Papini, and others whom Kazantzakis imagined to be very different from himself (Vrettakos 1960:563–567).

Lilí Zográfou reminds us of Kazantzakis's statement "I felt that I was saved: I did not change the world—I was unable to do that—but I changed the sight which views the world." She concludes, "It is therefore a joke to consider Kazantzakis a communist" (Zografou 1960:185). In 1908 when he was repulsed by French socialism, in 1922 when he admired Leninism not because he believed in communist ideology but because he wished to ride the wave of history and be carried along with it to immortality, in 1923 when Mussolini attracted him, in 1927–1928 when he was unable to sense the Russians' need to enhance their productive capacities and could only call them materialists, in 1936 when he found Franco's charisma so exciting, in 1940 when he refused to sign a petition against war, in the 1950s when his self-laceration vented itself in the figures of Jesus and Saint Francis—at every stage in the career, claims Zográfou, Kazantzakis demonstrated conclusively that he was never, and never could have been, a communist (172–180, 201–202, 293–299). "Many have considered Kazantzakis a communist or have condemned him as such. This is the greatest possible error with regard to his reputation" (168).

Yánnis Kordátos subjects Kazantzakis to a devastating critique in his *History of Modern Greek Literature.* Here are some excerpts:

> . . . apart from Nietzschianism and mysticism, [Kazantzakis] also embraced Bergsonism. [Bergson] was the philosopher whom a large portion of the French bourgeoisie admired because his philosophy was the *ne plus ultra* of reactionary idealism. . . . Every time that new philosophical pronouncements were put forward in Europe, [Kazantzakis] was among the first of the Greek intellectuals who heeded . . . them. Only dialectical materialism failed to attract him. He was at bottom a mystic [Kordatos 1983:II, 561]. . . . From his youth onward he presented himself as a pioneer. He was not, however. . . . He admired the Russian Revolution as the overthrow of a vicious and tyrannical regime. On the other hand, he mocked dialectical materialism and fought against the Marxist world-view. . . . Kazantzakis often . . . invokes big names: "Christ, Buddha, Lenin . . ." Among these three there is a theoretical gulf. These declarations by Kazantzakis testify to his adoption of ideas from here and there, but he was unable to assimilate these ideas because the contradictions between idealism and dialectical materialism are unbridgeable [568]. . . . Sometime in 1928 he declared that he was an "orthodox Marxist." With his ego-

> ism . . . he meant that he alone was a genuine Marxist—not, naturally, as a follower of Marx but as someone who would revise and supplement Marxism. . . . His ideas bear no relation—none whatsoever—to the scientific socialism of Marx-Engels. I emphasize this because many leftists, out of ignorance, deem that Kazantzakis belongs to their ranks. . . . Kazantzakis does not belong to the ranks of intellectuals who mobilized their thoughts and their pens in order to enlighten . . . the proletariat according to the . . . method imposed by the basic canons of communism. That is the truth, the only truth [573–574].

Finally, we have the conclusions reached by Elli Alexíou in 1966. The accusations are familiar.[23] Kazantzakis may have been called a communist by various people, she maintains, "but he was never called a communist by any communist" (Elli Alexiou 1966:283).

ARISTOTELIANISM VERSUS EXISTENTIALISM; THE MIDDLE GROUND

I have paraded these testimonies in order to show the degree to which Kazantzakis was persona non grata for Greek communists. Again and again he is accused of the very bourgeois decadence that he assumed he was battling. This is the "bottom line" of Avyéris's charge of philosophic nihilism, Vrettákos's equation of Kazantzakis with Kafka, and Kordátos's censure of Kazantzakis's reactionary idealism. Perhaps the Greek Marxists' case against Kazantzakis is summed up most systematically in a short essay that Kóstas Várnalis published in the communist newspaper *Rizospástis* in 1947. Entitled "Existentialism: the Philosophy and Literature of Reaction," the essay first expounds Várnalis's own position and then specifically cites Kazantzakis's nihilism along with Sikelianós's mysticism, Tsátsos's mythologism, and the surrealism of the Clique[24] as forms of existentialism and accordingly manifestations of reaction (Varnalis 1984:186).

In existentialism, says Várnalis, we are dealing with a philosophy that is "nihilistic, anarchic, antidialectic, suicidal, anti-social" (1984:185). Furthermore, this philosophy preaches that the pure biological being (man as animal) is the true existential being: "the less a person thinks, the more truly does he exist." All this tends to isolate the individual from the community, halting "the deliberate effort by peoples to accelerate change" because it devalues science and evolution. By using the ruse of metaphysical freedom, the existentialists wish to divert the attention of the oppressed to one or the other of existentialism's two termini: fideism or death. Várnalis of course rejects these values along with Nietzsche's superman and Sartre's subman. What he extols is "the complete man," that is, the one who combines experience, knowledge, and action, struggling continually; "the person who deliberately . . . transforms the world, the optimist who loves life . . . , who conquers nature and his enemies" (186).

The charges advanced here against Kazantzakis and the other "reactionary" purveyors of existentialism in Greece are, once again, subjectivism, the cult of death, philosophical pessimism, revulsion against life, antirationalism, dualistic sequestering of the subjective "I," the claim that man in his essence is an ahistorical being as opposed to a being affected by history and society, and the cult of metaphysical as opposed to practical freedom.

On the other hand, when Várnalis speaks of the "complete [read: Marxist] man" as the person who combines experience, knowledge, and action, struggles continually, and loves life, we detect Kazantzakis just as much as we do when Várnalis catalogues the symptoms of bourgeois decadence.

Várnalis, Alexíou, Zográfou, Vrettákos, Lambrídis, Galatea Kazantzáki, Theotokás, and the others make us realize how difficult it is to categorize Kazantzakis—precisely because their formulations are so categorical. Surely he cannot be placed with the communists. But does he belong with the bourgeoisie? I have said before and I repeat now that his real position lies in a no-man's land between the two camps: his work is too revolutionary for the Western establishment while at the same time it is too mystical for the leftists. A figure whom no régime could tolerate, he may be valuable precisely because he fits nowhere.

Before we judge, we ought to consider his entire career, for it is paradoxically in the later stages, when he had renounced his communist leanings, that his work begins to satisfy certain Marxist criteria, whereas what he wrote during his supposedly communist years often aligns him with a bourgeois *Weltanschauung*. But such dichotomizations are misleading in Kazantzakis's case. An unbiased examination of his works will show in most instances the extent to which, at any stage, he had one foot in each of the camps yet his head and heart in the middle, striving—not always successfully—for a synthesis.

This view can be better argued with the help of a less pugnacious exposition of Várnalis's point that the political rivalry between West and East reflects an ideological contest between dialectical materialism and existentialism. Fortunately, Georg Lukács's small volume *The Meaning of Contemporary Realism* offers a more disinterested exposition of these philosophical differences.

The "fundamental reality of the modern age," says Lukács, is "the struggle between socialism and capitalism" (Lukács 1962:13). In the sense of *Weltanschauung*, this translates into the struggle between Aristotelianism and existentialism, two fundamentally different concepts of the nature of being. Existentialism rules that man "is by nature solitary, asocial, unable to enter into relationships with other human beings" (20). This implies a static view of the world (19) in which man is "an ahistorical being" burdened with a human condition that is constant at all times and in all places because it "is identified with reality itself" (24). Aristotelianism, contrariwise, rules that man is a social animal, a *zoon politikon*. This implies a developmental view of the world in which men and women's individual existence "cannot be distinguished from their social and historical environment" (19).

These distinctions explain, among other things, why characterization is so static in modernist (that is, existentialist) novels as opposed to the novels of nineteenth-century realism. The negation of history "takes two different forms in modernist literature. First, the hero is strictly confined within the limits of his own experience. There is not for him . . . any pre-existent reality beyond his own self, acting upon him or being acted on by him. Second, the hero . . . does not develop through contact with the world. . . . The only 'development' in this literature is the gradual revelation of the human condition. Man is now what he has always been and will always be. The narrator, the examining subject, is in motion; the examined reality is static" (21).

Let us remember that Lukács's quarrel with such characterization is ideological, not aesthetic. His objection is to the failure by modernist authors to understand that the alienated solitariness with which they invest their characters is not the immutable human condition but a historically determined impasse arising from a given time and place.

With this in mind, we may proceed to some of his other complaints about modernist characterization. I shall confine myself to three strictures bearing an obvious relation to Kazantzakis:

1. Subjectivism. Since modernism finds the objective world so inexplicable, it takes refuge in subjective experience and then proceeds to invest that subjective experience with meaning by identifying it with reality.

2. Neuroticism and primitivism. Prevented by ideological dogma from creating characters who develop in response to objective conditions of time and place, modernism flees not only to subjectivism but also to psychopathology, escaping into neurosis "as a protest against the evils of society" (31). Neurosis becomes another version of an immutable human condition, as does its cousin, the primitivism that "is presented as a triumphant return to nature, as the liberation of impulse from the slavery of convention" (32). Thus both primitivism and neuroticism are paradoxically offered as "healthy" responses to the tedious meaninglessness of contemporary life. Lukács's comment is sardonic. "Life under capital-

ism," he says, "is . . . presented as a distortion (a petrification or paralysis) of the human substance. But to present psychopathology as a way of escape from this distortion is itself a distortion. We are invited to measure one type of distortion against another and arrive, necessarily, at universal distortion" (33).

3. A false view of time. For Bergson, "subjective time . . . became identical with real time; the rift between this time and that of the objective world was complete" (37). Accordingly, in Proust, for example, meaning is restored only when experience is mediated by memory, that is, when objectivity is subsumed under subjective time. " 'A lived event is finite. . . . But a remembered event is infinite, a possible key to everything that preceded it and to everything that will follow it' " (38). This false view identifying subjective time with real time is one more way by which dynamic characterization has been undermined in modernism.

Returning now to the communists' case against Kazantzakis, we should be able to add a Lukácian critique to the animadversions loaded upon him by Kordátos, Várnalis, and the other Greek leftists. It is clear that he subscribes in some sense to the existentialist ontology with its dogmas of ahistoricism, subjectivism, and Bergsonian duration—dogmas that make each human being equatable with all other embodiments of an ineluctable *condition humaine*. The result is that a technique of correspondences operates in most of Kazantzakis's works, making the characters belong (so the argument goes) not to a given historical situation but to a universal one. Beyond this, Kazantzakis leans toward primitivism in characters like Zorbás and toward neuroticism in self-lacerating protagonists like Saint Francis and Nikifóros Fokás.

These tendencies align him with the bourgeois ideology he pretended to despise, confirming the duplicity for which the Greek communists censured him.

But surely it is too simple to assign Kazantzakis wholly to the bourgeois *Weltanschauung*. Too slippery to be held in the grips of a single world-view, he exhibits traits that align him just as much with the Aristotelians as with the existentialists. It may be that he is caught squarely in the middle of the conflict between socialism and capitalism, with the individualism, isolation, and political impotence of his characters being one side of the coin while his society-builders are the other. The *Odyssey* presents the fullest spectrum. Its protagonist begins as a typical existentialist rebel from society's drabness, then goes through an Aristotelian phase in which—to cite Lukács's desideratum for socialist realism—"isolation gives way to an increasing involvement with the new social forces; a new and higher type of personality emerges" (Lukács 1962:113). At the end, however, he returns to isolation, mediating experience by memory.

This mélange encourages us to place Kazantzakis neither with the bourgeois decadents nor with the social realists but rather with the "critical realists," who, in Lukács's formulation, present "the problems of our time . . . wholly within a bourgeois framework. . . . Thomas Mann," Lukács adds, "is the great exponent of this method" (Lukács 1962:99), whereupon he quotes Mann in the latter's *Paris Diary*: "I am a bourgeois, certainly . . . [Y]et to understand the condition of the bourgeoisie today does imply a detachment from it, an awareness of the new forces" (Lukács 1962:104).

Let us pursue the problem of Kazantzakis's placement further by posing three principal questions, each of which leads to subsidiary questions:

1. Is Kazantzakis as ahistorical as he at first appears? Although he may transform subjective terror into the reality of human existence, calling that reality the abyss, does he not also struggle against his own existentialist impulses insofar as he attempts to see the abyss "as a horrific interlude in the continuity of human life" (Lukács 1962:59), that is, as the product of historical forces called the transitional age?

2. Is Kazantzakis's concept of freedom as exclusively existentialist as it first appears? Although it purports to liberate us from "objective forces of society" into subjectivism and aestheticism, does it not at the same time partake of freedom as understood in socialist society, namely, freedom "as conscious acceptance of historical necessity" (Lukács 1962:112)?

3. Is not the bulk of Kazantzakis's work an attempt to find a rationale for social action within the larger context of death's inevitability? Does this not translate into an attempt to place the Aristotelian world-view within the larger context of the existentialist? Kazantzakis's shorthand for this is the assertion that we are God's saviors, which means that humanity's historical struggle in society is the prerequisite for transcending both history and society. Is it not true, then, that Aristotle's *zoon politikon* becomes, for Kazantzakis, the prerequisite for ahistorical consciousness—that our objective environment, although in one sense a threat to subjective development, is for him the means by which we mature into subjectivity?

These questions could of course be answered either negatively or positively. They are offered not to prove anything but merely to make us wary of affixing labels to Kazantzakis. If it is wrong to call him a communist, it is probably just as wrong to dismiss him as a decadent bourgeois. My own hope is that we will place him somewhere between these extremes, acknowledging that he attempted to confront the fundamental reality of the modern age by recognizing the partial truth of the existentialist *Weltanschauung* without turning his back on the partial truth of the Aristotelian.

Earlier, I used Lukácian formulations to strengthen the views of Várnalis and his fellow leftists in Greece. Opposing views can also be strengthened by Lukácian analysis.

Consider narrative detail. Kazantzakis's novels provide an abundance of realistic observation offered neither as a projection of psychological trauma nor as the evolving record of a character's subjectivity but rather as a means of *placing* the action historically and geographically, consistent with Lukács's prescriptions.

Returning to characterization, we can say that Kazantzakis's practice sometimes meets the Lukácian criterion of integral figures defined by their clash with the surrounding environment. Whether these figures meet Lukács's additional criterion of typicality is another matter. They do insofar as "the determining factors of a particular historical phase are found in them in concentrated form," making them different from the average, the crudely illustrative, or the merely eccentric (Lukács 1962: 122). Perhaps Kapetán Mihális, the Boss, Fótis, Manoliós, and others can be called typical in this Lukácian sense of the term. But I hesitate to carry this too far because we know that Kazantzakis, never satisfied with objective forces at work in society, required that his characters reflect something beneath or above the flux of quotidian reality. For him the great artist "sees eternal, unchanging symbols. Behind the spasmodic, frequently inconsistent activities of living men, he plainly distinguishes the great currents that sweep away the human soul. He takes ephemeral events and relocates them in an undying atmosphere"—the "symbolic atmosphere of myth" (Kaz. 1964a:208; 1965c:173).

This seems to bring us back to the ahistorical Kazantzakis condemned by Greek communists. In arguing for the middle ground, I would reply first that Lukács's typicality is an insufficient notion to explain great art. Is King Lear merely typical? Are Ahab, Antigone, Heathcliff, Falstaff, Tom Jones? Each is integral in the Lukácian sense, and each displays in concentrated form the determining factors of a particular historical phase. Yet each, escaping history, enters the symbolic atmosphere of myth. What matters is not the transcendence itself, but whether it is achieved gratuitously or organically, that is, whether through arbitrary imposition driven by a particular world-view or through natural extrapolation from objective data. In arguing still more for the middle ground, I would reply that the static human condition posited by the existentialists is fully as much a realistic part of human experience as is our existence as Aristotelian social animals able to shape our destiny.

Kazantzakis occupies the middle ground between these positions not because he is a traitor to either or because he cannot make up his mind but because human life is truly, "realistically," a dialectic between the essences that we have been labeling existentialist and Aristotelian. To his credit, he acknowledges both.

But does he convince us that the two are complementary? Does he make his bivouac between the two camps in a way that comfortably links them or does he frantically retreat to the existentialist side after experiencing defeat on the Aristotelian? These questions can be answered only after his entire career is surveyed. The best we can do now is suggest as a provisional conclusion that Kazantzakis does retreat to subjectivism. The paradigm appears to be: temporary participation as a *zoon politikon* followed by compulsive withdrawal into private salvation. In the last analysis, the apparently political works are not driven by societal concerns. I call the conclusion provisional because we shall discover later that the retreat to subjectivism is paradoxically intended by Kazantzakis to enhance one's contact with external reality.

Let us therefore reserve judgment. Depending on the evidence we choose and our own bias, we could arrive at any number of conflicting interpretations. Consider, for example, *Alexis Zorbás*. The central character, even though a *primitif*, satisfies many of Lukács's Aristotelian criteria. He exists in significant relation to outside reality and is defined by that relation; he fulfills himself by affecting others and the natural environment; his innermost being is determined by objective forces at work in society—which makes him typical rather than allegorical. On the other hand, if we emphasize Zorbás's aboriginal elements, we align him with the existentialist faction condemned by Lukács. As for the Boss, his final allegiance is to art, not history; everything, including Zorbás's Aristotelian personality, is aestheticized by virtue of the novel's ultimate value system. The same discrepancies occur to an exhaustive (and exhausting) degree in the *Odyssey*. Nonetheless, perhaps the epic establishes a creative dialectic between the opposing world-views in that it presents a hero who, in order to arrive at isolation, subjectivism, and aestheticism, must journey through and beyond their opposites in a way that does not negate them.

Similarly, we can say that Kazantzakis's metacommunism does not negate his communism but passes beyond it as a consequence of having passed through it. This "transcendentalism" is what turned the Greek communists against him, but perhaps we can be more tolerant. Let us think of the two orientations as old age and youth. In youth we assume that the world truly exists and we believe that we can change it; in old age we see death as omnipotent, accomplishment as evanescent, the individual as alone with his subjectivity. Since age grows *naturally* out of youth, it does not negate the latter's beauty or vitality even though it passes beyond those qualities.

In order to experience life's riches we must inhabit more than one of its mansions. Just as each individual combines youth and age, so each is both a part of society and apart from society, objective and subjective, able to affect the world and helplessly crushed by the world. Existentialism focuses too exclusively on one side of our lives, Aristotelianism too exclusively on the other. Kazantzakis asks us to overcome these partialities in order to become whole. The Greek communists refused to listen.

CHAPTER SEVEN

Aesthetic freedom

Ξέρω τώρα· δεν ελπίζω τίποτα, δε φοβούμαι τίποτα, λυτρώθηκα από το νου κι από την καρδιά, ανέβηκα πιο πάνω, είμαι λεύτερος. Αυτό θέλω. Δε θέλω τίποτα άλλο. Ζητούσα ελευτερία.

—*Askitikí*[1]

The term freedom as used by Kazantzakis is a pomegranate showering us with innumerable seeds when we split it open. Most basically, freedom is the condition of a creative soul expressing itself. But to understand this concept more fully we must also consider the seeds that it throws out. This means reviewing Kazantzakis's notions of the transitional age, the kravyí, and the lógos.

THE TRANSITIONAL AGE

We know Kazantzakis's partiality to his doctrine of the transitional age. This doctrine maintains that we are living between myths, having lost one faith without having acquired another. Specifically, we find ourselves in an age of decadent rationalism and we yearn for a second religiousness.

Since the transitional age frustrates the creative soul, we must find ways to counteract that frustration. What ways? Kazantzakis recommends several. When he views the problem psychologically, he suggests action as an antidote to despair. When he views the problem existentially, considering the transitional age to be a constant factor in the human condition, not just a temporary historical situation, he invokes another favorite doctrine, that of heroic pessimism, which teaches us how to reconcile action with an assurance of universal vanity. Since in either case the transitional age guarantees that the ultimate result will be frustration (whether historical or existential), action must be self-justifying. Hence the hero acts out of a need to struggle as opposed to a need to succeed. To be heroic means to act without being sure. Whoever does this is truly free.

THE *KRAVYÍ*

But these formulas do not exhaust Kazantzakis's responses to the transitional age. If we think back to *Ksimerónei*, we will remember suicide as another one—in this case suicide by a "broken soul" who does not even attempt to fight the inevitable. The same play introduces an additional element: the conviction that in a transitional age right ideas may be possible even though right actions are not. Yet these, too, are inadequate; Kazantzakis insists that thought per se is not enough. Right ideas must be mixed with passion and uttered by a voice crying in the wilderness, heralding future salvation. They must be a kravyí.

Future salvation? How can this optimistic note be introduced when frustration is guaranteed? Kazantzakis provides an answer: The great challenge is to die well, which means to die not as life's passive victim but as the active master of one's fate, willing of one's own accord what is imposed by our existential condition. In character after character in his works, self-consciousness and suicidal volition constitute, respectively, the thought and passion that combine to produce the character's kravyí in and through death. This form of salvation is the best that one can manage, given the impasse of a (permanently) transitional age.

But Kazantzakis did not always have the strength of his convictions about the permanence of transition. We noted in Chapter Two his opinion that even Nietzsche required some chimerical hope (Kaz. 1964a:391–392, 406; 1965c:327, 339). Kazantzakis's own chimera is the belief that the transitional age will give way to an age in which the creative person may flourish. Given this hope, to leave a kravyí behind by dying well is not enough. That cry must linger after the mouth that utters it has ceased to exist. The best analogy is Kazantzakis's image in *Askitikí* of the light we continue to perceive after the star that produced it has exploded (Kaz. 1962a:73; 1960b:109).[2] Indeed, this analogy encapsulates the entire process we have been discussing, for Kazantzakis views man as a lump of matter infused with vital energy, a being who lives vibrantly, plunders life's offerings, and in so doing burns up his material substance, transforming it to flame. In the paroxysm of death the flame is extinguished but its light remains. As Kazantzakis says in the same passage of *Askitikí*, the light "proceeds and labors eternally." Thus in the early play *Hristós*, Christ cries out in anguish:

> Archangels, help me to strip myself of my body;
> I want to remain a cry without a larynx.
> (Kaz. 1956c:114)

This is Kazantzakis's chimera because the undying light/cry presupposes a viewer/hearer in some hypothetical nontransitional age succeeding the transitional one. Moreover, the kravyí helps to bring this future age about. In hero after hero in Kazantzakis's oeuvre, we accordingly see salvation attained not only through a good death that fulfills rather than negates life's struggle, but also through an assurance that one's spirituality will shine on in perpetuity.

THE *LÓGOS*

With the help of this review of the concepts of the transitional age and the kravyí, we can begin to understand why freedom, for Kazantzakis, is the condition of a creative soul expressing itself. But one more seed thrown out by this term still remains, namely Kazantzakis's notion of the lógos.

A kravyí is incomplete by its very nature. Suspended between one age and another like a fragile bridge, it needs to be fulfilled by a person or culture that eventually heeds it. A John the Baptist requires a Christ.[3] But a lógos possesses its own integrity. Kazantzakis's concept becomes clearer in a little note he wrote to himself at the start of his outline for the projected epic "Akrítas": Να περιμένω ωσότου η Κραυγή μέσα μου να γίνει Λόγος (I must wait until the cry inside me becomes a lógos; Prev. 1965b:485). In short, the lógos is art.

Here now is his definitive answer to the problem of how to act in the permanently transitional period that frustrates the creative soul. The kravyí—that combination of thought and passion remaining as light from the heat of a freely willed death—is not enough. Its inchoate understanding of the human predicament must be made coherent. Paradoxically, then, *freedom consists in the coherently expressed understanding that we are not free.* In the summer of 1925, Kazantzakis had written in a letter: "I have understood everything. I am free. For me, freedom has always been the fruit of the highest use of the human understanding" (Eleni Kaz. 1968a: 125). It took him another decade to begin to narrow "the highest use of the human understanding" to the creation of artistic works concerned with our understanding that we cannot be free.

What happened in the period roughly between 1920 and 1935 is that Kazantzakis's concept of freedom underwent a transubstantiation from the material (and largely political) level to the immaterial (and largely aesthetic) one. Earlier, he had spoken of Lenin as harboring an Idea around which a new society would develop (Kaz. 1965e:208; 1989:202). In other words, illusions can clothe themselves in flesh, producing the very material they need in order to redeem themselves from immateriality.[4] But this concept of the word becoming flesh was then immaterialized by Kazantzakis so that the flesh that the word became was an imaginary flesh, the forerunner's cry in the wilderness producing not a real-life messiah but instead a vision bodied forth in the letters of the alphabet: a work of art created out of the mind's subjective freedom within the objective prison of an inimical universe.

THE FOREGOING discussion of Kazantzakis's concepts of the transitional age, the cry, and the lógos should help us fathom what he means when he speaks of his final period as freedom. Freedom can now be conceived only as the condition of a creative soul expressing itself in art. When Kazantzakis wrote in 1936 that he was entering the third stage, which he named freedom, his key sentence was: "I know that ideas are lower than a creative soul" (Prev. 1965b:465). Although he then went on to speak of deliverance from the hope of reward and the fear of punishment, the sentence that pierces to his true conception of his new position is the one just quoted. Despite his tendency to avoid admitting to himself that he was an artist, he was sufficiently forthright at this and subsequent moments (although not without backsliding) to acknowledge the particular form of total freedom to which he was "condemned," as Sartre would say. What he really wished to declare here was what he did declare in another letter six months afterwards: "The creator is the only man who is free" (Kaz. 1937:323).

HEROIC ACTION TRANSUBSTANTIATED

This "new" concept of freedom may appear to be a regression to the earlier stage in Kazantzakis's development in which right thought is possible but right action is not. Or, the new concept may appear to hark back to *Toda-Raba*, where refuge is taken in an Olympian detachment that prevents a person from "intervening." In sum, the new concept of freedom may appear to obviate heroic action.

For Kazantzakis, however, a creative person expressing himself in art does not retreat from heroic action; instead, he transubstantiates it. Like the mystics of the Orthodox Church (see Lossky 1957:203), Kazantzakis resolves the conflict between the active and contemplative life by deeming contemplation the highest form of action. The artist is a spiritualized Napoleon, a good line of verse a spiritualized brave deed (Eleni Kaz. 1977: 192; 1968a:152). By opening a river bed into which reality may flow, art performs an action in the present that connects with the real world of the future.

Similarly, art connects with the real world of the past since, in order to overcome the limitations of phenomenal reality, the artist must employ that reality as a ladder on whose rungs he climbs into spirituality. Just as starlight emanates from a material body that subsequently burns itself out, so subjective freedom emanates from material struggles for objective freedom. Since the final stage must derive from the earlier ones, it does not negate them.

I emphasize these connections lest we erroneously conclude that Kazantzakis in his final period renounced political engagement in order to devote himself to art for art's sake. His aestheticism was not a divorce from life but one partner in a marriage; in order to vitalize the noumenal half of this marriage, he had to sink deeper roots into the phenomenal half, which he did both in his own life and in his books, especially the novels. So we find in Kazantzakis's concept of freedom not a Buddhistic withdrawal but a marriage in which life exists in order to be transubstantiated into art and in which art exists as complete in itself, to be sure, yet nonetheless *available* to enrich real life in unpredictable ways. To say this in philosophical language, "There would be no freedom if appearances were the very things-in-themselves, if the noumenal exhausted itself in . . . phenomena. Nor would there be any freedom if there were absolutely no activity of the noumenal in phenomena. . . . The one world can invade the other and act creatively within it. . . . What is important [in freedom] is . . . creative energy" (Berdyaev 1952:155–156).

THROUGHOUT this study I have emphasized the continuity of Kazantzakis's thought. Seeds for his "new" concept of freedom were planted early in his career by Dragoúmis—for example, "I am free because I create everything" (Dragoumis 1926:53–54)—and of course by Bergson. Dragoúmis's philosophy allows for fulfillment in the real world of materiality whereas Bergson's confines fulfillment to consciousness,[5] implying a shift from the outer to the inner self as a precondition of freedom.[6] To arrive at his own position, Kazantzakis had to evolve through Dragoúmis and Bergson, transubstantiating the former's teaching to make it compatible with the latter's. The continuity is everywhere evident. For example, whereas Kazantzakis had originally followed Dragoúmis in considering despair to be the stimulus to action in the real world and action the antidote to despair,[7] now he considered despair to be the stimulus to action (read: artistic creativity) in the imaginary world, viewing this form of action as an even more effective antidote to despair. Whereas in his nationalist period he had followed Dragoúmis in considering a man to be free insofar as he was able to change the world, making it over in the way he wanted it like Napoleon juggling the boundaries of Europe, now he considered a man to be free insofar as he did the same thing on the aesthetic/subjective plane, fulfilling himself by imposing his will not on recalcitrant matter but on words.

Thus Kazantzakis's concept of aesthetic freedom evolves in a continuous line out of previous concepts that are transformed without being rejected.[8] As Berdyaev says, "Creativeness . . . is a victory over the world" while at the same time it "presupposes the material which the world supplies" (Berdyaev 1952:173).

This line of development did not suddenly cease in 1936. If we look ahead, we will see that the Kazantzakian concept of freedom, having evolved from a political to an aesthetic level, continued on to a religious one. This is not the place to examine what in the second volume I shall be calling Kazantzakis's eschatological mentality; nevertheless, it might be useful to note here that he had begun to think eschatologically even while the aesthetic concept of freedom was ripening. The eschatological vision is articulated in the following manner by Berdyaev:

> Creative power anticipates the transfiguration of the world. This is the meaning of art. . . . And creative power . . . is an end of this world and a beginning of the new world. . . . The world must be turned into an image of beauty. . . .
>
> This then is the eschatology of creative energy. The failure of the creative act consists in this, that it does not achieve its purpose of bringing this world to an end, of overcoming its objectivity. Its success, on the other hand, lies in the preparation it makes for the transformation of the world. (Berdyaev 1952:174, 188)

Compare Kazantzakis in 1933, groping toward a similar vision: ". . . a perfect work of art liberates us. . . . We . . . transcend death because . . . we feel that everything—man and beast, past and future, life and death—is unified" (Kaz. 1962b:92; 1963c:101). His definitive articulation appears in the maxim that became one of his favorites: "Our kingdom is not of this world" (Prev. 1965b:342–343).

I TRUST that the many ingredients of Kazantzakis's concept of freedom are now clear. Like every other culmination in his development, this one synthesized seemingly antithetical elements—in this case activism and philosophical pessimism. It also released huge amounts of energy, fueling his most sustained attempt to understand the futility of our efforts within a permanently transitional age, and to transform the resulting understanding first into a kravyí and then into a lógos meant to help life transcend its own being. I am referring, of course, to his *Odíssia*, whose 33,333 verses unify Kazantzakis's development up to the point of their composition, tracing an evolution from action on the lower plane of reality to contemplation on the upper plane of imagination, an evolution that is eschatological since its culminating synthesis announces a world transformed (see Kaz. 1954:1636). More personally, the *Odyssey* attests to Kazantzakis's recovered possession of an inner self. For all these reasons, its overriding theme is freedom.

CHAPTER EIGHT

Odyssey

the dream of a shadow / [is] man
—Pindar

. . . all things happen by strife and necessity
—Heraclitus

I have already said many of the important things I wish to say about Kazantzakis's *Odíssia.* I have done this deliberately throughout the preceding chapters in order to prepare the reader gradually, orienting him or her in advance by means of scattered references, because the *Odyssey* is too huge to be confronted all at once. Now that we are finally ready to discuss it in a concentrated fashion, I intend to recapitulate the earlier points and to add new ones systematically, treating the problems of successive drafts and of the allegedly nihilistic world-view before turning to the aids that Kazantzakis offers for a holistic reading, then to the epic's specifically political content, to Odysséas's development through aesthetic, ethical, and religious stages, and lastly to a summary of how the *Odíssia* reflects Kazantzakis's political convictions.

SUCCESSIVE DRAFTS

The published epic is the result of seven drafts that occupied Kazantzakis off and on from the winter of 1925 until 1 December 1938. In the second draft (October 1930–March 1931) the plot received its definitive elaboration (Prev. 1977:27) and the verse was radically revised (Prev. 1965b:163–164, 167; 1958:235; 1961:142). We should remember that intervening between the first and second drafts were crucial experiences both external and internal: the bitterness at the poor reception accorded *Askitikí*, the Alhambra embroglio, the revision of *Askitikí*'s ending, the break with Istrati, and the composition of *Toda-Raba*—a succession of disappointments involving Kazantzakis's writing, his active involvement in affairs, and his political beliefs, all of which presumably strengthened the *Odyssey*'s allegedly nihilistic side.

Yet from the sources available we have no way of knowing precisely what Kazantzakis changed or added to the *Odyssey* in its successive revisions.[1] The most responsible conclusion remains the one I advanced previously: that the epic's essential scheme—certainly of the first half in detail, and also of the second half at least in broad outline—resided in Kazantzakis's head in the winter of 1924–1925 during his involvement with Iráklion's disaffected reservists, and consequently is reflected in the initial draft (1925, 1927). The evidence for this conclusion was presented earlier and need not be repeated here. What should be emphasized now, even if repetitiously, is the importance of resisting (a) Kazantzakis's claim that he "never knew anything in advance" (Kaz. 1977a:186), improvising the plot as he went along,[2] and (b) the claim of various critics that a nihilistic element resulting from disillusionments in the Soviet Union in 1928–1929 invaded the second draft. Regarding (b), both the theoretical and practical bases for the epic's alleged nihilism were already operative in 1925 when Kazantzakis first set to work. Philosophically, the *Odyssey* rests on *Askitikí*, which underwent in its 1928 revision not an essential change but merely one of emphasis; practically, the epic reflects Kazantzakis's inability to fulfill himself as a man of action, a problem clear enough after the Iráklion incident and merely confirmed by the failure of subsequent attempts in Athens and Russia between the first and second drafts. I continue to feel, in sum, that the major incentives for the *Odyssey* remain the metacommunism developed by Kazantzakis in Berlin in 1922 and the repeatedly frustrated activism that ensued.

WORLD-VIEW

Are we to join Vrettákos, then, in stating that the *Odyssey* is a "work generated out of [Kazantzakis's] despair" (Vrettakos 1977:40)? Prevelákis was one of the first to take this position; it led him to harp on the "absolute nihilism" (Prev. 1985:12) of Kazantzakis's world-view before the supposedly decisive change in the novels. The same view was strengthened by Vrettákos, as we have seen, and by Prevelákis's disciple, Basil Laoúrdas.[3]

These are formidable critics. Their disparagement (they all view nihilism as an artistic defect as well as a philosophical embarrassment) is easily supported by Kazantzakis's depiction of himself in *Toda-Raba* and by his general alienation from humanity during the time of composition. As for the epic itself, it is pugnaciously subjectivist, announcing this position boldly in the prologue:

> ψευτόνειρό 'ναι τα γεράματα και φαντασιά 'ναι ο χάρος·
> όλα 'ναι της ψυχής καμώματα και του μυαλού παιχνίδια
> (Od. 1.65–66)
>
> old age is a false dream and death is fantasy,
> all are the soul's doings and playthings of the brain
> (Od. Prologue 65–66)[4]

Operative here is an "inhuman" aestheticism that, instead of sharing mankind's misery, contemplates that misery as a spectacle. Finally, the epic is energized by a Spenglerian assurance that Western civilization is doomed.

This evidence—and more—supports those who disparage the *Odyssey* as generated out of despair and as governed by a nihilistic world-view. Yet I will dare to disagree on both counts. Despair leads to paralysis, not to energetic productivity. In spiritual biographies, the despairing individual is rescued not by his or her own endeavors (those have led nowhere) but by God's grace; restoration comes only through passive receptivity. Kazantzakis's case is entirely different. Far from succumbing to paralysis, sensing the absence of personal worth, or yearning for external inspiration, Kazantzakis while composing the *Odyssey* displayed abundant amounts of self-confidence, autonomy, and self-generated energy. He was driven not by despair but by hope and vision—hope for, and vision of, a completed work that would possess (a) the aesthetic force to redeem life's fragmentation by means of a unified re-presentation and (b) the ethical force to carry its readers beyond the present "decline of the West" to a new world-view capable, in Kazantzakis's opinion, of regenerating civilization—all of which means that the *Odyssey* is not nihilistic.

Nihilism denies value; the *Odyssey* asserts value. More precisely, the epic denies old values in order to assert new ones. It is neither a nihilistic nor a Buddhistic work but a Bergsonian one. Once we understand this, we should be able to appreciate the degree to which Kazantzakis was energized by hope rather than despair.

When I say that the *Odyssey* is a Bergsonian work, I mean the following: The epic attempts to portray the entire cosmic situation as the life force's evolutionary journey through matter in a creative process that unmakes itself, transubstantiating matter into spirit. This journey begins and ends nonmaterially. What happens in the interim is life, the luminous interval between two dark abysses. Since consciousness is nonmaterial in the Bergsonian system, in Kazantzakis's Bergsonian epic the mind of Odysséas can equal the life force and take a similar journey through matter in a creative process that gradually "coagulates" ideas into action (civilization) but then proceeds to dissolve those coagulations. Thus the epic moves from brutishness to refinement, instinct to deliberation, sexuality to intellectuality, sensation to morality, morality to religion, martial exploits to political ones, political to artistic—proceeding finally to an entirely subjective self-consciousness that reveals the events during the previous struggle to have been nothing but creations of Odysséas's mind. Nevertheless, it is wrong to conclude that all is therefore vanity in Kazantzakis's *Odyssey*, for consciousness in the Bergsonian system is not the real world's negation but its presupposition and fulfillment, the creative force that, eternally renewed thanks to its release from matter, continues to evolve in the only way it can, through a process that repeatedly makes and unmakes material congealments. Although the epic appears to lead in linear fashion to negation and vanity, it is actually circular, poetizing a world-view whose "god" is an ever-vital creativity operating in cycles of formation and deformation.

Of course the *Odyssey*'s Bergsonian element has been recognized by those who accuse the work of nihilism. Let us cite just the most important commentator, Prevelákis. In a speech on the one hundredth anniversary of Kazantzakis's birth, he states that although the "circle opened by Homer is truly closed by Kazantzakis," our spirits in this case are not assuaged by a geometrical figure connoting perfection, since Kazantzakis's circle "means nothingness" (Prev. 1985:217–218). He then goes on to cite as the "other leg of Kazantzakis's thought" Bergson's *élan vital*, "which Kazantzakis deified in his *Askitikí*. This "creates and destroys unremittingly," continues Prevelákis; ". . . 'God's nature is to make something out of nothing. Consequently, God cannot make anything from whoever has not yet become nothing' " (Prev. 1985:217–218, citing Luther). Although Prevelákis displays here an awareness of the periodicity implicit in the *Odyssey*'s Bergsonian leg, he fails to proceed to the logical conclusion that when the epic ends in nothingness the expectation is that creativity will resume. Similarly, in his book on the *Odyssey*, although he acknowledges the creative side of Bergson's system and its role in the *Odyssey* (e.g. Prev. 1958:294, citing Kaz. 1912:328), he then returns to his nihilistic bias by declaring the epic's Bergsonism to be merely one element locked in conflict with its antithesis, Buddhistic nihilism. In this he is supported by Elli Lambrídi, whose conclusion I cited earlier but must now repeat. Speaking of the epic's Bergsonism on the one hand and on the other of its solipsistic Buddhism, in which all is a dance of shadows created by the mind, she holds that the "two world-views employed by Kazantzakis are incompatible, . . . the one refutes the other, . . . it is . . . absolutely impossible even for the most metaphysical mind to consider the first a stage of the second" (Lambridi 1939, 11 March). This dualistic analysis tempts even kindly disposed critics to view the work as energized by a dialectic between opposites such as activism and contemplation, politics and art, will and idea, phenomena and noumena, weak pessimism and strong pessimism.

If we accept this analysis we are likely to join Lambrídi and Prevelákis in assuming that the opposites involve an "insolvable contradiction" (Prev. 1977:31; 1981:46). My hope, however, is that we shall conclude in this case as in the case of *Askitikí* that the incompatible opposites are actually the hypostases of a *monás plusía* involved in an ever-adjusting dialectic in which "one world can invade the other and act creatively within it" (Berdyaev 1952:156). But I want to go further, hoping that our interpretative capacity will enable us to comprehend the epic's Bergsonism and Buddhism as no longer contending in opposition or even merely collaborating in mutually fructifying interpenetration. What I hope we shall see is the epic's Buddhism subsumed under its Bergsonism. Understood in this way, the circle allegedly closed by Kazantzakis does not mean nothingness, for the subjective and apparently nihilistic cry "Even this one does not exist" is not the denial of value but a necessary, temporary rest in the life force's evolution toward ever-increasing value, a freedom from materiality that insures the renewal of the creative energy necessary for further evolution through materiality.

All this is very mystical, of course. I trust that it does not sound merely rhetorical, as Kazantzakis's own formulations so often do. It would be simpler to remain on the dualistic level, taking his subjectivism at face value. However, in an effort to go further, I shall offer four approaches meant to show that the work's Buddhism is not an equal partner in irresolvable conflict with its Bergsonism.

The first approach is via Kazantzakis's doctrine of the transitional age. From the start of his career he always assumed that degenerative periods are merely middle ages that will be followed by a renaissance. There is no reason to believe that he abandoned this view while composing the *Odyssey*; on the contrary, every external indication shows him consciously employing his epic to depict not the omnipotence of nothingness but instead the periodicity by which dematerialization precedes a renewal of creative energy. Answering Laoúrdas's accusations of nihilism in 1943, for example, he replied:

> In transitional ages, an intellectual effort can either look backward, justifying and judging the old civilization that is crumbling, or look ahead, struggling to prophesy and formulate the new one. Odysséas struggles, looking ahead. (Kaz. 1943:1028–1029; cited in Prev. 1958:314; 1961:183)

Equally indicative is a statement composed in Siberia on 22 February 1929 as Kazantzakis was obsessively thinking about the *Odyssey*'s second draft. This is the text that prompted Prevelákis, in his speech on the centenary of Kazantzakis's birth, to state that the circle opened by Homer is truly closed by Kazantzakis:

> The *Odyssey* . . . continues the huge epic of the white race—Homer. It closes a circle that so many centuries have left open. And it closes it precisely in an age astonishingly similar to the state of the world in the twelfth century B.C., shortly after the

> Achaeans' invasion, shortly before the invasion of the Dorians *and the creation—following a middle age—of a new civilization.* (Prev. 1965b:114; italics added; cited in Prev. 1958:109; 1961:63)

These statements, albeit unequivocal, are merely external indications. As primary evidence we must consider what the poem itself tells us. Actually, the concluding cantos do not seem to make Odysséas look ahead to a renaissance. Indeed, the epilogue closes the circle precisely as Prevelákis says it does—in nothingness, the "great hollow silence" in which "the earth vanished, the sea dimmed, flesh dissolved" (Od. 24.1410, 1412–1413; Od. Epilogue 14, 16). Buddhistic vanity does seem to overwhelm Bergsonian periodicity despite Kazantzakis's statements about the transitional age.

The only way we can appreciate the deceptiveness of this conclusion is to review what we already know about the meaning of silence in Kazantzakis's thought. Let this be our second approach to the problem of Bergsonism versus Buddhism in the *Odyssey*.

The doctrine of silence may be understood in two different ways that are seemingly contradictory. The first takes silence at its face value as the end of all endeavor while the second takes it as the prerequisite for renewed endeavor. Most literally, silence signifies the absence of any answer from a world beyond—the abandonment portrayed so clearly in Kazantzakis's early play *Comedy*. Thus the end of Odysséas's endeavor is neither reward nor punishment, but extinction. Prevelákis cites a relevant gloss from one of Kazantzakis's unpublished notebooks: "Odysséas's religion . . . was based on emptiness: neither God nor hope nor fear nor eternity" (Prev. 1958:309). But the question remains whether this is as nihilistic as it sounds. The answer is that it is not; on the contrary, silence is precisely what makes possible a new kind of value. We see this in the continuation of Kazantzakis's gloss on Odysséas's religion: "Every moment = immortality, and he has no need of any other immortality. He lived every moment intensely, qualitatively." This existentialist reply assuages our spirits even if we accept the closed circle as meaning nothingness, for the nothing beyond the circle does not now vitiate the something within it. But this is still not enough. We must also see the silence as a necessary link in periodicity—a view that we have encountered already in Buddhism's teaching that there is no last-act curtain, since time is circular, not linear. Kazantzakis expresses this difficult concept in the crucial letter to Emile Hourmoúzios cited in Chapter Five during my discussion of *Askitikí*'s revision: "The nihilistic cry 'Even this one does not exist!' is not the climax of [Odysséas's] struggle; it is an escape valve. . . . He listens intently, *gains courage from the horror*, and resumes . . . the Ascent" (Kaz. 1977a:187). The letters to Papastefánou, although glossing

Askitikí, not the *Odyssey*, are equally illuminating: "Silence is not extreme despair; it is not nullification. . . . Silence means: Each person . . . now . . . does not question, does not . . . differentiate. . . . He has adapted himself at last and has inserted himself into the Abyss . . . [to] make it fruitful . . ." (Mitsotakis 1972:82; Kaz. 1979:33).

Seen in yet another way, silence is the freedom achieved through transcendence of antinomies—that is, through organic synthesis, synthesis in Kazantzakis's system always being a beginning as well as an end.[5]

Some of these formulations are metaphorical and difficult. What should emerge from them clearly enough, however, is that silence is (a) wholeness overcoming differentiation, (b) the sperm and womb of rebirth.

To continue: These two characteristics are necessarily related, since creative power in Kazantzakis's Bergsonian system presupposes undifferentiated wholeness. Regarding such wholeness, Samuel Beckett demonstrates brilliantly in *L'Innommable* that only silence can abrogate the differentiation implicit in words (which is why for Quakers it governs a mystical ritual meant to tease into consciousness the wholeness called God). Only the dark abyss abrogates the differentiation all too explicit in the manifold shapes of the luminous interval that we call the phenomenal world. Odysséas's "ascent," as we shall emphasize in the third approach, is toward ever-increasing unification. That is why it must end in silence and the abyss, which may now be understood as the fulfillment of his life rather than its negation. Because of the necessary relationship between wholeness and creativity, this fulfillment pertains to the future as well as to the past, for the undifferentiated wholeness is none other than the *élan vital*, the inexhaustible reservoir of new cycles of differentiation.

To achieve his vision of undifferentiated wholeness, Odysséas withdraws into the contemplative life and may therefore seem to be going in the direction of Buddhism. Let us examine this as our third approach to the problem of whether or not the epic's Buddhism is subsumed beneath its Bergsonism. It is true that what happens in Canto 16 and beyond may be considered the replacement of material struggle by contemplation of the futility of material struggle—the replacement, in other words, of activism by nihilistic subjectivism. In this view, the best we can say is that the epic holds the dualistic opposites in a satisfying equilibrium that, restoring the precarious balance abandoned in *Toda-Raba*, expresses Kazantzakis's hope, articulated shortly before he began the first draft, that he might "experience the vanity of all endeavor and simultaneously the eternity of every moment" (Eleni Kaz. 1977:145; 1968a:117). The worst we can say is that the Bergsonism of the Telemachia (cantos 1–2) and of the Odyssey proper (cantos 3–15), on the one side, and the Buddhism of the Nostos (cantos 16–24), on the other, are yoked together by violence.

What I hope, however, is that we may escape the trap of these dualistic interpretations and realize that the *Odyssey* is monistic. Material evolution in Kazantzakis's system *produces* contemplative self-consciousness. Contemplation is not the abrogation of what preceded but its natural continuation. Contemplation discovers that there is no essential division between action and self-consciousness because the manifold forms that provide the context for action are nothing more than coagulations of the undifferentiated creative energy that evolves toward self-consciousness.

The key word is always "differentiate." Odysséas's ever-increasing ability to differentiate in the world of action leads paradoxically to his ever-increasing yearning, in the world of contemplation, for the undifferentiatedness that originally produced the differentiation. Or, as Kazantzakis says in an unpublished letter kindly furnished me by Professor Apóstolos Sachínis, Odysséas's Herculean labors bring him finally to an "organic synthesis (. . . synthesis, not obliteration) of all antinomies" (Kaz. 1950). Whether or not in Kazantzakis's personal life (a) his activism ultimately subtended from his subjectivism and thus may be deemed false, as suggested by his opponents in the *Anayénnisi* debate, or (b) his art in general and the *Odyssey* in particular became his only recourse for the resolution of contradictions irresolvable through interaction with other human beings, is not here the question. We are concerned with a literary text, not with the psychology of literary composition. Seen dualistically, this text seems to divide into two parts at Canto 16 when the previously active hero withdraws into contemplation. Buddhism seems to replace Bergsonism, not to mention Leninism. Seen monistically, however, the Buddhistic/subjectivist/aesthetic/nihilistic Nostos is subsumed under an overall Bergsonian schema in which, as noted earlier, a creative process unmakes itself by means of differentiations that lead to the ability to overcome differentiation.

This monistic view brings us to the fourth approach by which we may avoid the nihilistic trap that Kazantzakis feels constrained to set for us because of his forthrightness in creating a fictional universe in which all familiar gods, both Christian and pagan, are dead. We have spoken of the transitional age, the meaning of silence and the abyss, and the progress toward undifferentiation. Now, no longer obstructed by linearity or dualism, we may proceed more easily to examine precisely which new god governs the *Odyssey* (here and elsewhere I use lower-case "g" for Kazantzakis's concept—despite his own capitalization in his playful doxology Δόξα τῷ μὴ ὑπάρχοντι Θεῷ [Veï 1963:1689]—reserving capital "G" for the specific deity of Judeo-Christianity). Of course, if we heeded Kazantzakis's formulations in previous works—especially *Askitikí* and *Sympósion*, but also *Taksidévondas. Eyiptos* and *Toda-Raba*—we already know. God is shorthand for that which subjects the disordered vision of life to an ordered hierarchy. Kazantzakis accepts this traditional view. At the same time, however, he rejects the traditional Christian linearity by which we encounter God at the end of a quest. We see this in Odysséas's debate in Canto 21 with the fisher-lad (the type of Christ), who understands God as pure spirit and defines humanity's struggle as the effort to escape the flesh in order to merge with the Almighty. Odysséas, contrariwise, knows that god is not encountered at the end of life's journey but is with us at all stages of that journey—indeed *is* the journey. As in *Sympósion*, so here, the absolute is not the concluding abyss but the entire cycle bringing us repeatedly from one dark abyss to another across the luminous interval called life; it is, as always, the *élan vital.* As I said in Chapter Two when discussing Kazantzakis's Bergsonism, god is the entire evolutionary process, the primordial essence that first wills its own congealment into life and then wills the unmaking of that creative action. This is why the *Odyssey* defines god in so many different places and ways. God is constantly changing form, its essence being the undifferentiated wholeness behind all of these differentiations.[6] The ordered hierarchy governing the seemingly disordered vision of life presented in the *Odyssey* is the entire Bergsonian system of a creative process that *repeatedly* unmakes itself as transition replaces transition, differentiation yields yet again to the undifferentiations of silence and the abyss, and the active life overcomes its antinomies by progressing to contemplative self-consciousness.

I trust that these four approaches will raise the argument above the dualistic level of interpretation. Once this happens, Kazantzakis's apparent subjectivism, aestheticism, disgust, and autonomy will no longer be accepted at face value; instead, the epic will be seen as his attempt to overcome nihilism by thinking rationally about experience.[7] Far from denying value, the *Odyssey* in its unified totality strives to demonstrate that every manifestation of life fits into a meaningful pattern.

AIDS TO A HOLISTIC READING

An obvious consequence of the previous discussion is the importance of seeing Kazantzakis's huge canvas as an organic synthesis in which every part has meaning not in isolation but in relation to what precedes and follows. We must avoid a merely linear approach; instead, once a first reading familiarizes us with the whole we must attempt on subsequent readings to register the work organically, ranging backwards and forwards over the text in order to see each movement as part of an overall composition. In this respect Kazantzakis's work makes the same demands upon its readers as do Joyce's *Ulysses*, Mann's *Der Zauberberg*, and Proust's *A la recherche du temps perdu*, although in other respects it surely does not vie with those twentieth-century classics as a model of modernist technique. Joyce was forced to reveal his organizational chart in order to aid a bewildered public; Proust explained his scheme in the final volume. Kazantzakis, too, comes to our rescue with various aids, and in both the Joycean and Proustian ways—that is, both outside the text and within it. But we must not expect consistency. As always, he challenges us to find what is undifferentiated behind apparent differentiations.

Let me first exhibit these aids one by one. Afterwards, we will worry about whether or not they coalesce.

Two have already been mentioned. According to an external gloss that I adduced in relation to *Askitikí* (even though Kazantzakis formulated it in relation to the *Odyssey*), Odysséas's journey is divided into four stages: (1) good and evil are enemies—identified with men of action; (2) good and evil are co-workers—identified with many men of theory; (3) good and evil are one—identified with the mystics of Europe and the East; (4) this one does not exist—identified with Eastern mystics only (Kaz. 1939a: 13; 1958f:823). Although these stages are presented as linearly sequential in the gloss, we must resist this linearity when we apply them to the poem, realizing that this aid, like the others, ought to encourage us to move to and fro across the text, understanding the value of early stages in relation to later ones and vice versa, until little by little we intuit that the poem's supreme value is not the "nihilistic" fourth stage but rather all four stages in organic synthesis.

The second aid has been anticipated in a footnote. It is the seven-headed ivory totem that Odysséas obtains from a peddler in Crete. As I noted earlier, here Kazantzakis helps us comprehend the epic's totality not only by showing god's multiform—yet unified—nature but also by having the seven heads diagram the ever-increasing dematerialization that characterizes creative evolution. Thus the first head, all flesh and no spirit, is the coarsest and most bestial (5.598). Then we advance to two heads representing martial bravery and sexual pleasure, respectively. These ought to be in reverse order and indeed are in Odysséas's life,[8] since sexual pleasure, as depicted, is still very bestial, with goatlike lips (5.607), while martial bravery is motivated by ethical principle: although it trembles when confronted by death, its pride makes it ashamed to run away (5.603–604). Fourth in this progressive refinement of matter comes intellect, a head that makes one feel as though "οι ρίζες γίνηκαν ανθός και νους αγνός το κρέας" ("roots had turned to flower and flesh to pure mind"; 5.610).

Before proceeding, I must add a numerological observation (surely legitimate in a poem consisting of 33,333 verses). Seven denotes completion. It is traditionally divided into triads of 1 to 3 and 5 to 7, with 4 serving to link the two triads. Thus the seven deadly sins consist of carnal faults (1–3) and spiritual ones (5–7) linked by sloth (4), which may be either carnal or spiritual. In Kazantzakis's system, heads 1–3 involve carnal refinement, heads 5–7 spiritual refinement, and head 4—intellect—serves as the link because intellect may be applied equally to practical affairs in the world of objects (warfare, city planning, and the like) and to spiritual ones (art, theology, and so forth).

Considering now the second triad, we find that sorrow (5) comes first because grief and suffering, although primarily mental, still involve the body; consequently, the face depicted on this head "bites its thin lips in desperation to keep from screaming" (5.614). Next comes serenity (6). Transcending all antinomies, this head has reached a height of understanding in which "όλα του φαίνουνταν ονείρατα και παρδαλή κατάχνια" ("all seemed dreams and parti-colored haze to him"; 5.621). We have reached the stage of initiation common to the mystics of Europe and the East. But one step remains: complete dematerialization. Accordingly, the seventh and final face is blank: "without ears and eyes, / nostrils, mouth, forehead . . . ; / all its flesh had turned to spirit and all the spirit to air!" (5.627–629). Especially noteworthy at this point is Kazantzakis's reminder to us that we have *not* reached the termination of a linear progression whose end is the supreme value, the prior steps being merely bridges along the way. It is true that the final blankness is an unmoving flame that leaps up and away; yet, at the same time it resembles a red thread stringing all the previous heads together like a row of beads (5.625–626). The immaterial force liberated at the end of the progression, the force whose total otherness requires us to exclaim "And even this one does not exist!" is nevertheless *present throughout the progression*. Once again we see that the god or absolute governing the epic's development is encountered not just at the end but everywhere, since the entire process of materialization and subsequent dematerialization is what Kazantzakis deifies in his Bergsonian theology.

There is nothing cryptic about the centrality to Odysséas's journey of this seven-faceted schema, seeing that Kazantzakis makes his hero exclaim:

> Αχ, νά 'ταν, Θέ μου, και ν' ανέβαινε κι η σκοτινή ψυχή μου
> σκαλί σκαλί τα εφτά πατώματα και να χαθεί σα φλόγα!
> (5.632–633)
>
> Ah, my god, if only my dark soul could mount
> the seven storeys step by step and vanish like flame!

Later, when he reaches stage 4 (intellect), he is called the "eftápsihos" (the "seven-souled one"; 14.273) and is made to recall first his caveman origins (14.260ff.) and then his development from sexuality to military service, now in that order (14.219–242). The final triad—of suffering, serenity, and liberated flame—will come in cantos 16–24, the Nostos.

Let us proceed to aids not mentioned previously. I will restrict myself to three. The first occurs in Canto 14, which presents Odysséas's meditation on the mountain, a meditation that lasts the magical number of seven days. The scheme offered here is based on *Askitikí*, but on the first draft, since the meditation takes place before Odysséas has evolved to the mystical consciousness of Eastern sages. Thus the seventh day (14.1247ff.) is altered so that it stresses, as did *Askitikí*'s original ending, not the silence but "the soul's ultimate exploit, action" (14.1327).[9] However, the preceding days reinforce what we saw in the seven-headed totem of Canto 5. Thus Odysséas concentrates at first on his affinity with wild beasts and hails the caveman as his "former body" (14.104). On the third day (14.162ff.), he first reviews his growth through sexuality and martial prowess, as we saw a moment ago, then begins to advance beyond the limits of his ego to his relation with physical and spiritual ancestors. The fourth day (14.444ff.) sees him expand his awareness to the future (14.489) until the vision of the most immediate evolutionary process of which he is a part, namely his family's "eternal tree" (14.509), liberates him sufficiently from his ego so that his mind may henceforth view the circumambient world with "all the eyes of his people" (14.511).[10] Next, he proceeds beyond both family and race to an awareness of his kinship with all races, "όλοι τής μάνας γης οι γιοί, ξανθοί, λασπουδεροί, αραπάδες" ("all sons of mother earth, the blond, muddy-brown, black"; 14.611), after which he knows that he must proceed beyond mankind (14.650) to embrace trees and animals (14.622)—all of nature, including the earth itself (14.693–695, 728–730). Why? Because all of nature partakes, as he does, in the evolutionary movement toward dematerialization (14.697). The fifth day (14.738ff.) is devoted to a hymn of identification with his true ancestors the beetle, ape, weasel, hedgehog, wasp, cricket, flea, fly, and ant. It culminates in Odysséas's awareness that all dividing walls have broken down (14.894). He has passed beyond differentiation. It is therefore appropriate that on this version's sixth day (the seventh being reserved for action, we must remember) he should meditate on organic synthesis itself, that is, on god in all his/her/its contradictory yet unified guises (14.951ff.). This day ends with a recapitulation of the "march" from ego to race, mankind, nature, and god (14.1098–1117), god being summarized, predictably, as sex, death, and flame (14.1119–1125): the progress of Bergsonian evolution.

Still another aid may be found in Canto 11. This one divides the hero's journey into five stages. While in prison in Egypt Odysséas recalls going with Rala, his fellow revolutionary, to recruit Egyptian embalmers to their cause (11.1079). After watching bodies being prepared for burial, they notice a crew of slaves adorning a tomb with carvings in five ascending bands that represent the same evolutionary development that we saw earlier, this time adjusted so that the iconographic symbolism applies to

Egypt. Band 1, the lowest (11.1098–1101), represents nature in its potentiality, ready to be transubstantiated upward by mankind's efforts.[11] Bands 2 and 3 represent mankind's ascent, initially via agriculture and sex, subsequently via leisure and the arts (11.1102–1112). Next, on Band 4, we see immortal gods, the disembodied soul standing before them like a "naked worm" (11.1117). Finally Odysséas watches as the fifth and highest band, blank at first, is adorned with flame by an artisan (11.1130–1131). In case all this is not sufficiently clear, the narrator remarks that as Odysséas observed the successive bands he "climbed life step by step, . . . his heavy body continually / growing lighter and breathing purer air" (11.1113–1115).

Canto 17 introduces an aid that is less comprehensive because it dwells only on the human arc of the evolutionary circle.[12] Kazantzakis has adjusted his scheme here to reflect its location along Odysséas's road to enlightenment, just as in Canto 14 he utilized *Askitikí*'s unrevised form since Odysséas had not yet attained the degree of initiation in which "even this one does not exist." In Canto 17 we have entered the Nostos. What may be omitted now is the opposite end of the evolutionary spectrum; hence we hear nothing this time about earth, rivers, or beetles, but instead commence straightaway with human development, analyzed according to the celebrated Kierkegaardian paradigm of aesthetic, ethical, and religious stages, which Odysséas summarizes as the pursuit, respectively, of beauty, virtue, and truth (17.74). But on closer scrutiny the scheme turns out to be fourfold since Odysséas proceeds to the realization that the aesthetic, ethical, and religious stages were decoys diverting him from, but at the same time leading him to, complete freedom (17.75–85). Odysséas's journey may now be understood as an evolution from sensual experience to political involvement, from political involvement to ascetic contemplation, and finally from ascetic contemplation to transcendence even of the self-consciousness attained in ascetic contemplation. The passage in question supplies few details. It does, however, cite Helen and beauty in connection with the aesthetic phase (17.59); more importantly, it confirms that "aesthetic" here does not mean devotion to art but rather the attempt to gain happiness through sensual gratification (17.62). The ethical stage is associated with Odysséas's awareness of injustice (17.63) and with his efforts to help goodness prevail, the religious with his attempt to construct a head (that is, a mind, a theology) in which god may find shelter (17.71).

These minimal suggestions are glossed by Prevelákis in a helpful passage that is worth quoting at length:

> In the early cantos, Odysséas experiences the world aesthetically; he is driven to action by the spectacle of phenomena. . . . Even when he performs works of world-wide historical significance,

> such as the burning of the palace at Knossos, our hero is not committed—his soul remains in a state of availability. His actions have the disinterestedness (and the immunity) peculiar to youth. But from the moment he sets foot on the soil of Egypt,[13] human suffering touches his heart. He still remains uncommitted, but he lets the will of history direct him. The specter of hunger becomes his guide. . . . The aesthetic attitude has exhausted itself. . . . The *ethical* attitude is outlined: Odysséas is concerned about relationships among phenomena. . . . He is drawn toward a constructive project: to build a city-state. . . . But his city-state is swallowed up by the earth. . . . Odysséas plunges into despair, . . . cutting himself off from humanity. We shall call his present attitude *metaphysical*: he is interested in nothing but essences. These three positions—which according to Kierkegaard are the only ones possible for mankind—finally bring Odysséas to *absolute freedom*. (Prev. 1958:126–128; 1961: 75–76)[14]

Kazantzakis's reliance on Kierkegaard is extremely important, especially in light of our previous discussion of the epic's alleged nihilism. It confirms his determination to escape nihilism rather than embrace it, since the whole point of Kierkegaard's analysis is to expose insufficient values in order to replace them with better ones.[15]

I HAVE exhibited a total of five aids, four from the text itself and one from a gloss. All of them ought to help in reading the epic holistically and organically rather than linearly. They may seem bewilderingly multiple. The steps vary from seven to three or four. Some of the aids encompass the history of the earth, others of the species, others merely of an individual (the point being, of course, that earth, species, and individual evolve in parallel ways). Despite the differences, however, the various schemata do coalesce. The six days of meditation in Canto 14, for example, recapitulate the steps seen in the seven-headed totem of Canto 5. In both, the movement is from flesh to spirit, differentiation to nondifferentiation, bestiality to a flame that, while surpassing previous stages, includes them. The other aids also conform. Collectively, they chart the epic's movement toward ever-increasing dematerialization while at the same time they remind us of its organic presuppositions. All this may be summarized in a diagram that I have fashioned so that it resembles Joyce's plan for *Ulysses*. In it, I retain the Homeric and Joycean divisions of the epic into the Telemachia, Odyssey proper, and Nostos. To the five aids provided by Kazantzakis I add a sixth meant to direct attention to the prologue and epilogue between which Kazantzakis encloses his gigantic can-

CANTO	SCENE	Canto 5 7-HEADED TOTEM	Canto 11 TOMB CARVING	Canto 14 ODYSSEAS'S MEDITATION	Canto 17 KIERKEGAARD	KAZANTZAKIS'S GLOSS	FRAME
Prologue							abyss; sunrise
I. Telemachia							
Α 1 Β 2	Ithaca	bestiality; sexuality	nature's potential	caveman; ego		men of action; good & evil are enemies	luminous interval
II. Odyssey proper							↓
Γ 3 Δ 4	Sparta		agriculture	sexuality	aesthetic		↓
Ε 5 Ζ 6 Η 7 Θ 8	Crete	martial bravery		martial bravery	Helen; beauty (first stirrings of the ethical)		↓
Ι 9 Κ 10 Λ 11	Egypt		leisure & the arts	beyond ego; race	ethical; hunger; virtue		↓
Μ 12	Desert			beyond race; mankind			↓
Ν 13	Jungle; Nile source			beyond mankind; nature			↓
Ξ 14	Mountain	intellect		beyond differentiation; god		men of theory; good & evil are co-workers	↓
Ο 15	City			reversion to action		reversion to action	↓
III. Nostos							↓
Π 16 Ρ 17	Rim of abyss	sorrow; serenity	gods		religious; truth	all mystics; good & evil are one	↓
Σ 18 Τ 19 Υ 20	Journey toward southern tip of Africa						↓
Φ 21	Southern ocean						↓
Χ 22	Sailing; ice floe						↓
Ψ 23 Ω 24	Iceberg	flame	flame		freedom	Eastern mystics	↓
Epilogue						this one doesn't exist	sunset; abyss

vas, since this frame-construction strengthens the periodic interpretation I have been advocating.[16]

POLITICAL CONTENT

Prepared now with a sense of the whole, and properly warned against linear and dualistic interpretations, we are presumably ready to examine the individual cantos in more detail in the hope that we shall emerge with a fairer appreciation of the poem than, say, Yánnis Kordátos did when he concluded: "Even the most well-disposed reader cannot find the thread of [Kazantzakis's] thoughts" (Kordatos 1983:II,566). Since our interest is politics, and since Odysséas's political phase ends abruptly at the beginning of Canto 16 with the destruction of his ideal city-state, our examination will concentrate initially on the Telemachia and Odyssey proper. Later, however, in deference to the Nostos, which occupies almost forty percent of the whole, I shall analyze Odysséas's doctrine of mind in Canto 17, since this is the heart of the religious stage that emanates from the political-*cum*-ethical activity that preceded.

To begin our examination of the *Odyssey*'s political content, let us look at Kazantzakis's own plot-summary, written most likely late in 1938 to serve as a blurb for the forthcoming publication.[17]

> The new *Odyssey* begins where Homer's *Odyssey* ends. Consisting of 33,333 seventeen-syllable lines,[18] it has justifiably been called "the largest epic of the white race."[19]
>
> Having killed the suitors, Odysséas on his tiny island is ready to burst; his wife, son, former gods, and homeland are too constricting now, and he decides to leave Ithaca again and to undertake his final journey, the journey of no return.
>
> So he chooses some companions according to his own liking—brave, free souls, healthy bodies—puts together a new boat, marries off his son to Nausicaa so that they can produce a grandchild for him and keep his family from perishing, and one morning he sets off and sails out into the offing.
>
> The great, final journey commences. He anchors first of all in the harbor serving Sparta; goes up to the celebrated city-state; rescues his former comrade-at-arms Menelaos from a popular revolt; eats, drinks, and converses with him; abducts Helen, who is ready to burst in her own right in a new daily life without significance; and departs with her.
>
> Now he anchors in Crete, whose great civilization is in decline. Barbarians and slaves, armed now with the new weapon, iron,

conspire to overthrow the aged king, Idomenéas, and Odysséas becomes their leader.

One night during a huge royal banquet, Odysséas gives the signal and the conspirators rush to the attack: the king and the degenerate lords and ladies are killed, the palace of Knossos is burned, Helen becomes the lover of a blond barbarian, and Odysséas and his companions go back in their ship and set sail again toward the south.

He anchors in Egypt. Great agitation here too; the starving slaves have joined with the blond barbarians from the north and want to overthrow the overly well-fed rulers. Odysséas hesitates for a moment but finally makes his decision and goes in the lead with the slaves. But their army is defeated; the rulers capture him and throw him in jail. There he becomes friends with the fierce new comrades, and in the midst of his hunger, anguish, and the slavery of the prison he carves out of a piece of wood the face of his new god: a terrifying, merciless mask full of wounds and blood, resembling war.

Managing to escape prison by means of a ruse, he once again selects from among the warriors the fiercest comrades—slaves and barbarians—and sets off toward the desert with them. Acting as guide out in front is the mask of the new god.

Having fought against savage tribes, he reaches the source of the Nile: the heart of Africa. Then he builds his new city, fortifies it, and engraves his god's proud new commandments on the fortress, legislating new, equitable laws. He is happy that he is going to create a free society of fearless people.

But the very day on which he inaugurates the city, . . . an earthquake occurs, the ground opens up and swallows the city. It is totally engulfed.

At the lip of the abyss that has formed, Odysséas—now completely alone, without companions or hope—concentrates his powers in ascetic contemplation and struggles to conquer fate. Slowly, after a terrible internal struggle, his mind is illumined, his soul conquers, he stands up and resumes the march.

He marches continually southward . . . (Prev. 1965b:476–479)

The blurb continues for six additional paragraphs. But since we are already well into the Nostos, which for the moment does not concern us, I shall stop here.[20]

Kazantzakis's summary identifies the highest peaks of this complicated epic. The first is Odysséas's resolve to abandon Ithaca. The second is the threefold political activity in, successively, Sparta, Crete, and Egypt. The third is the carving of a new, fierce god resembling war. The fourth is the exodus to the heart of Africa, the construction there of Odysséas's ideal city, and the immediate destruction of that city in an earthquake. The fifth is Odysséas's reaction to this, via ascetic contemplation.

Interpreting these peaks, I would say that Kazantzakis's political (more precisely, metapolitical) teaching in the first is that if we are to accomplish anything worthwhile we must begin by renouncing our inherited assumptions. The poem's geographical symbolism leads Odysséas away from the values of Greece (read: European civilization) to the barbarian vitality of Africa. Note his glee when he and his motley crew finally push off from Crete:

> Πάει το λουρί, παιδιά, το κόβουμε, γλιτώνουμε απ' τη μάνα (8.1006)
>
> The cord is gone, lads, we're cutting it, we're escaping our mother

The teaching connected with the second peak is that after renouncing our inherited principles (which we do only gradually), we attempt to find new values and to apply these to existing conditions, but this process is haphazard, imperfectly prepared, doomed to various degrees of failure because the opposing forces are still too great. The third peak tells us that we proceed henceforth with adequate forethought, the fourth that our subsequent actions involve the gathering of a saving remnant and the construction of our own utopia outside of established polities. Finally, the fifth teaches that when this is destroyed, as it inevitably will be, we nevertheless continue in our inner, private lives to adhere to these principles and if possible to leave behind some form of nonpolitical witness that may affect political development in the future.

All this is political, of course, but also theological. If European civilization is to be overcome, then the two major components of its value system, the Hellenic and the Christian, must be scrapped. Thus Odysséas ostentatiously disposes of the twelve Olympian deities who stand for Europe's Hellenic inheritance. First he despises the Olympians as either "bugbears" (4.1268) or—worse—mere bibelots in the homes of Crete's overfed aristocracy (5.311). The Zeus of friendship given him by Menelaos he unceremoniously sells (5.439–447). Later, he cruelly mocks the Olympians by fashioning them as grotesque marionettes with lopped ears and crossed eyes who whine "I'm hungry!" when he pulls the string (11.714–719). Finally, as though the point were not already clear, he slays six cocks and six hens representing the twelve gods whom once "he had worshipped with fear and exultation to the complete shame of his mind," and buries them in the foundations of his new city (15.467–470), which of course is dedicated to very different gods.

Odysséas is unable to mock Christianity so straightforwardly if only because Christianity has still not been invented. However, Kazantzakis makes his iconoclastic hero despise two of Christ's central teachings: the "stupid hope" that the dead will rise again (8.818; cf. 9.510–539) and the refusal to do evil, seen in the pacifistic Pharoah Ikhnaton, who declares, "I am good and proclaim love to the world, / and hold not a sword . . ." (10.760–761).[21]

Having disposed of European civilization's Hellenic and Christian heritages, Odysséas enthrones his own pantheon, the war-god being just one among at least seven faces or heads of a multiform deity resembling Creative Evolution rather than either Zeus or Christ. What this means, I think, is that Kazantzakis rejects as acceptable foundations for political theory the ancient Greek concept of circular recurrence and the Christian concept of linear progress toward an eternal City of God. These he replaces with a cosmology that combines both insofar as it places linear ascent inside the repeated, nonmechanistic flux and reflux of the *élan vital* by virtue of materialization, dematerialization, and rematerialization. On the other hand, his cosmology also rejects both insofar as it avoids Hellenism's steady state as well as Christianity's teleology.

Let us dwell on this new god, Creative Evolution. Since Odysséas himself is governed by this deity, he cannot begin with a ready-made theology but instead must discover one "creatively," that is, haphazardly, as his experience unfolds. All we get at the beginning, therefore, are hints. When Odysséas invokes his pirate grandfather with testicles and brains just before leaving Ithaca (2.1493), he is unwittingly honoring the twin channels of Bergsonian evolution: sex and self-consciousness. The sexual mode is then emphasized by Orpheus's song about reproduction conquering death (3.181), the mental by Odysséas's repeated obeisance to man's mind in place of the discredited gods (e.g. 4.1270). These disparate hints come together in the seven-headed evolutionary totem of Canto 5 and again in the five tiered painting of Canto 11. By the time we reach Canto 14, Odysséas has gained the intellectual sophistication he needs to understand his new theology in properly Bergsonian terms. Thus we find him aware that

> life is a martial assault, and the luminous forces,
> struggling to ascend, fight to rend the darkness,
> obstinately seeking freedom and immortality on earth.
> Two omnipotent and contrary winds, male
> and female, clashed on the threshing floors of earth and mind;
> they balanced for a moment, and this world was born.
> (14.1337–1342)

Since man imitates god, his evolutionary duty is also worked out on the threshing floors of both mind and earth. The mind's evolutionary goal is to discover and enjoy the style or course (ρυθμός) that God displays as he walks gasping on the ground (14.1345–1346), that is, to formulate a theology for this new god who is coextensive with the process of his own development. The earthly aspect of man's evolutionary duty is first to mobilize sexuality in a martial assault against death (the "lawless god" [14.570] – Bergson's downward stream) and then to mobilize technology against other forms of material entropy, improving earthly and human nature by creating a higher civilization. Thus Odysséas's goal must be to build a city.

All this is clearly understood by our evolving hero at the end of the exodus. Creative Evolution has utilized the human mind as the vehicle through which evolution becomes self-conscious of its own course.

The foregoing interpretation of Odysséas's resolve to abandon Ithaca and of his subsequent resolve to construct a utopia based on the new god he discovers after deposing old gods should convince us that his journey starts negatively and then turns positive. What must always be re-emphasized is (a) that the positive phase is a consequence of the negative one, not its antithesis, and (b) that as a logical next step in his mental evolution Odysséas reaches the understanding that destruction and construction, evil and good, can be co-workers, or even identical. This realization enters his consciousness briefly during the exodus (12.1271–1272) and then more extensively during his meditations in Canto 14, in which he develops the precise theory (resembling that of *Askitikí*) that will be incarnated in the city:

> Ανέβηκες ψιλά, κι ο πόλεμος ακέριος πλοκαμίστη,
> νεκροί και ζωντανοί κι αγέννητοι, ξόμπλια αλαφριά διαβήκαν
> το μαγληνό κρουστάλλι το αδειανό του αϊτόλαμνου ματιού σου·
> κι είδες και το καλό και το κακό, κι οχτροί και φίλοι αντάμα,
> όλοι μαζί συντρόφοι στο στρατό του ρουφουλοθεού σου.
> (14.1269–1273)

> You mounted high, war spread its massive tentacles,
> dead, living, and the unborn, delicate ornaments, passed through
> the smooth and empty crystal of your eagle-swift glance
> and you saw good and evil, friends and foes alike,
> all comrades in the army of your devouring god.

Odysséas transcends contradiction because he now sees the opposites in a larger, positive context that subsumes and integrates them. Once we, too, appreciate Kazantzakis's employment of negation and destruction as parts of a larger, positive scheme, we shall be less likely to honor charges of nihilism against him, less willing to agree that, believing in nothing, he creates as his hero a desperado who destroys indiscriminately and gratuitously. On the contrary, for Kazantzakis as for Nietzsche, destruction is motivated positively since it is the necessary prelude to the replacement of inferior values by ones considered superior. In addition, negation must exist in Kazantzakis's system precisely so that his hero may advance to the mystic awareness that contraries may be secret collaborators. However, perhaps the most important point to emphasize yet again, before proceeding, is that everything in the *Odyssey* is part of a developmental process and consequently understandable only in terms of what precedes and follows. No episode in Odysséas's story can be accurately interpreted if it is discussed in isolation; each stage must be treated organically, in relation to everything else.

We have taken an initial look at the process that begins negatively and then becomes positive, concentrating on Odysséas's gods and on the theological meaning of his city. Let us look at the same material again now, focusing more on cultural and political factors, and also on Odysséas's personal development as he moves through the sensual and ethical experiences that culminate in his inspiration for the city.

The first victim of Kazantzakis's negative assault is Homer himself. It is not just that the Olympian gods are mocked and discarded. Kazantzakis said it best when he declared in an interview much later, "Actually, my *Odyssey* has nothing to do with Homer's poem" (Sadoul 1955:5). Certain areas of divergence should be obvious: Homer restores the family and its hierarchical relationships; Kazantzakis breaks down the family and frowns on the traditional subservience of son to father; Homer's epic is centripetal, Kazantzakis's centrifugal; Homer values rationality, Kazantzakis intuition. Less obvious perhaps is Kazantzakis's internalization of Homer. As Vrettákos has observed, "we know that epics relate external events. . . . What characterizes the Homeric Odysseus's adventures is his battle against nature and the gods. This same battle characterizes Kazantzakis as well. The former fought outside in open space, the latter fights in his inner space" (Vrettakos 1983:200). Open space in Kazantzakis's epic is often primarily metaphorical, as when Odysséas defines the Nile as the soul and his journey up-river as a journey up-soul (9.1317), or when he declares that the more he penetrates the desert the more he enters himself (12.1192). What we find in Kazantzakis's epic, in short, is not a Homeric voyage but instead a Cavafian one, especially during the Kierkegaardian aesthetic stage—a voyage of individual development in which external events are but pretexts, the battle against external nature becoming an excuse for enriching one's inner nature. Despite his scorn for the cult of experience fashionable among European intellectuals, Kazantzakis does seem, here, to share André Gide's doctrine of *disponibilité* (availability)[22] and/or the existentialist position carried to an extreme by Georges Bataille in his *Expérience intérieure*:

> I call experience a voyage to the end of human possibility. Each person can neglect to take this voyage but, if he does take it, that implies denying those authorities and operative values that limit what is possible. From the fact that it is the negation of other values and authorities, experience that has a positive existence becomes expressly in its own right the value *and the authority*.

> Inner experience . . . can have no concern or purpose other than itself. In opening my mind to inner experience, I thereby establish value, authority. Henceforth I cannot have any other value or authority. (Bataille 1983:19, 18)

The difference between Gide or Bataille, on the one hand, and Kazantzakis on the other, is that Odysséas's *disponibilité* is part of a cosmological scheme of evolution that makes even interior experience undo what it itself has striven to achieve, overcoming itself. Kazantzakis's anti-Homeric internalization borrows, to be sure, from a strain in French existentialism but cannot be explained by that philosophy alone. Ultimately, it rejects Gidean immoralism and self-centeredness.

Having noted this cultural negation established at the epic's start, we may proceed to more specifically political forms of negativity, always remembering that they, too, will open the way to positive action and thought, especially when Odysséas builds his city. One of the more interesting aspects of the hero's initial negativity is the way in which he gradually turns against his own class. In Ithaca he still defends aristocratic values despite his disgust with wife and son. During the peasant revolt in Sparta he supports King Menelaos even though he despises him;[23] soon afterward, however, he not only favors the bastards over both nobles and workers in the games that Menelaos has arranged (4.789–793) but rejects the concept of inherited sovereignty in favor of the principle that "the strongest spirit in the flock" should rule (4.822). Even before he reaches Crete, he has been sensitized in a way that enables him to respond immediately to the stark contrast he witnesses there between the suffering of the masses and the conspicuous consumption of the rulers. His destructive actions at Knossos, although still part of his negativism, nevertheless already contain a degree of positive motivation since he is aiding the oppressed to gain reasonable sustenance and treatment. In Egypt this same dynamic is repeated but there is an important new factor, namely, Odysséas's growing realization that his political activities fall within the broader context of a search for new gods.

Parallel to the negative process by which Odysséas frees himself from the values of his own class is the process by which he systematically undermines the chief sociopolitical manifestations of those values, namely the family and the state, the former in Ithaca and Sparta, the latter in

Crete. But the end of this negative process is once again positive, as he determines to reconstitute both family and state according to new values in the city.

By the time that Odysséas reaches the source of the Nile, he has deposed old gods and discovered new ones, turned against his own class, risen against the established structure of family and state, and, perhaps most importantly, internalized his experience. The city will reflect all this. Unable to inaugurate a new polity externally, in Egypt, he inaugurates another polity that is largely an internal triumph. This is his utopia.[24] Odysséas's city-state is not an achievement by enlightened masses. On the contrary, the chosen people whom Moses-Odysséas leads out of Egypt to populate the promised land are entirely unfit. Squabbling over trifles, preferring well-fed slavery to abstemious freedom, they are prepared to worship any god who fills their bellies (12.367–370). So inadequate are they that when Odysséas descends his mountain resolved to turn theory into action, he bites his lip and swears that he will *make* these people benefit from his ideal society willy-nilly (15.284–286). Although the city is the positive consequence of Odysséas's political negativism in Ithaca, Sparta, Crete, and Egypt, it does not arise from any solidarity on its founder's part with the people it is meant to serve. Instead it is imposed from on high in conformity with the great-man theory of history that Kazantzakis generally favored despite certain statements to the contrary. We should be wary, therefore, of calling it revolutionary, at least if we agree with Yánnis Kordátos that "revolutions are the results of class struggle and not of individual A or B, or of whatsoever Christ or hero" (Kordatos 1983:II, 572).

What sort of utopia does Kazantzakis offer? Certainly not a communist one, except by Kazantzakis's own imprecise definition of the communist as a person "who cannot fit within today's ethical, intellectual, and social frameworks and seeks to smash them and to create wider ones; seeks, that is to say, a new justification for life: to find a new reason for existence and to base his life on that reason" (Darakis 1935)—a definition tartly sabotaged in the epic itself when Kazantzakis makes "Lenin" say to Odysséas: "You hold air in your hands and we a fistful of earth" (Od. 11.1345). In any case, Kazantzakis's utopia is incompatible with his own definition of socialism as a system that "starts with class war and sets as its goal the triumph of the proletariat" (*Eleftheros Tipos*, 11 February 1927).[25] Can we call his political vision anarchist? The rigidity of the system elaborated in Canto 15 would undoubtedly be repugnant to those who preach "that everyone has the right to develop without any limitation and to possess happiness and freedom as a right" (Kaz. 1959c:87). Yet certain elements might be compatible, for example, rebellion for pure freedom rather than revolution for a specific end.[26] I fear, however, that if a single label needs to be attached to Kazantzakis's polity, it will have to be "fascist." The state apparatus serves to produce a biologically superior people aspiring to ever-greater physical and intellectual strength. This is "the city of the son who surpasses his father . . . ," Odysséas the master builder reminds his apprentices (15.564). Such an ideal requires euthanasia; Odysséas would like to have all old men lined up along the edge of a cliff and kicked over (15.558–560, 609–610). But compassion for the weak is not the only bourgeois prejudice that is overcome. Private property is abolished (15.1096–1097). Boys are housed, raised, and educated communally, away from the heavy shadows of their parents (15.561–562). (A similar provision does not seem to exist for girls. But no matter, for their only purpose is to bear children—preferably male [15.704].) Marriage and the family are further broken down by an orgiastic festival each spring: "whoever wants to have sex with a girl," Odysséas counsels, "let him seize her" (15.555). Finally, there is a rigidly authoritarian class system, with Odysséas assigning all men (women being excluded as always) to their proper rank in the hierarchy as manual laborers, fighters, or intellectuals (15.538–544). Let us recall his own definition of fascism in the concluding article of his series in *Eléftheros Típos* on Primo de Rivera's Spain, quoted previously in a footnote in Chapter Five: "Fascism is a system of accountable answers to all the problems of mankind's political and social life in community. It abrogates the citizens' small liberties because it believes that only in this way will it save the large liberties of the whole." This was published on 7 January 1927, six months before he began creating the utopian polity of Canto 15 (Prev. 1965b:30).

Whatever label we attach to this polity, we will presumably agree that it is imposed from above and is drawn out of its founder's internal development rather than out of any real grappling with external sociopolitical problems. This in turn tells us something important about Kazantzakis's mentality. Despite all the external vicissitudes he endured, and the diverse contacts he enjoyed with people engaged in political action, the city he created in the *Odyssey* is essentially bookish. Some elements undoubtedly did come from experience, but most seem to derive not only from reading but from reading that was meaningful to him at an earlier stage of his career, before the watersheds of the Asia Minor disaster and his sojourns in Vienna and Berlin. Thus we see reflected here not so much Marx, Lenin, Shestov, or Sorel as Plato, Nietzsche, and—inevitably—Bergson.

For Plato, as for Kazantzakis, "politics is not the art of winning or maintaining power, but a . . . vision of the Good *beyond mankind*" (Pouliopoulos 1972:232; italics added). In addition, Kazantzakis shares Plato's preference for an elite class of guardians who rule according to a system of laws meant to subordinate the individual to the whole. Plato's two lower classes—commoners and soldiers—are adopted by Kazantzakis, as are the former's provisions for communal living and the abrogation of private property.[27]

Nietzsche's influence on Canto 15 seems to have come via Kazantzakis's dissertation, written in Paris in 1908 and early 1909, as we know. Pandelís Prevelákis rightly observes that in this document we encounter tenets that entered Kazantzakis's system of belief at this early stage and remained "remarkably firm" throughout the succeeding decades that encompass *Askitikí* and *Odíssia* (Prev. 1958:20; cf. p. 286, fn. 10; 1961:15–16).[28] I discussed the dissertation at length in Chapter Two. We should remember that it concentrates on Nietzsche's negative positions and pays relatively little attention to his positive ones; also, that Kazantzakis disagreed with some of the latter. Nonetheless, certain elements in the *Odyssey*'s utopia, whether negative or positive, correspond to points in the dissertation. The regulations curtailing family life, for example, presumably derive in part from Nietzsche's assertion that domesticity hampers the male's strength by tying him to the hearth. The preference for euthanasia would seem to be founded on Nietzsche's view that the morality of compassion transgresses the law of selection, which rules that the sick and aged should be eliminated in the interests of racial vibrancy. And although the dissertation questions the criteria of selection used by Nietzsche to divide society into servants and lords, the *Odyssey*'s utopia, reflecting Nietzsche's scorn for social equality and democracy, maintains an inflexible hierarchy of workers, fighters, and the creative elite.[29]

Bergson is probably the most important of the bookish influences. Creative evolution in its double aspect, sexual and intellectual, is the *Odyssey*'s governing principle. In Canto 15 this principle is applied in various ways. Odysséas's advocacy of euthanasia (15.578–610), for example, quite aside from its relation to Nietzsche, is based on the cruel realities of carnal reproduction as evidenced by the behavior of termites. (Bergson's arguments drawn from insect behavior are well known.) But carnal reproduction in the Bergsonian system is a mechanism meant not just to maintain the species but to enable it to evolve into the freedom of self-consciousness. Thus the city rests on the principle of self-overcoming; it is designed to be a "περανθρώπινο . . . κάστρο" (15.576)—a "superman city" or, in Kimon Friar's periphrastic rendering, "a town that strained beyond man's reach." This Nietzschian precept is placed within the larger Bergsonian context that makes the city consist of storeys, the lowest anchored in the rock and clay of biological reproduction, the middle controlled by laws, the highest consisting of an invisible kravyí (15.1243–1246).[30] Like its expression the pear tree, which Odysséas adopts as an appropriate symbol, the city takes soil, water, and stone and turns them into weightless flowers (15.322–323). Describing his utopia as the embodiment of Odysséas's thought (15.1242),[31] Kazantzakis hints that the world itself, by analogy, is the embodiment of the *élan vital*. But he also tells us indirectly that this utopian city in the *Odyssey* is the embodiment of *his* thought: a bookish invention emanating from his reading of Plato, Nietzsche, and Bergson.

In sum, we have in Kazantzakis's utopia a hodgepodge of fascist, anarchist, existentialist, Bergsonian, Platonic, and Nietzschian elements that coalesce to form the positive culmination of Odysséas's interior journey "up-soul" that started so negatively by overturning Homer, established gods, the bourgeois family, and the decadent state. But all the diverse ingredients that form this bookish conception are made to serve creative evolution, which quite appropriately has the last word.

Bergson's rule, as we know, is that every creative action must unmake itself; otherwise the movement toward freedom that such an action has fostered through material evolution will become irreparably "coagulated" and turn against itself, abetting the downward, dark powers of inertia rather than the luminous élan of ascending motion. Odysséas begins in a transitional age, welcoming it as an opportunity: "Βλογώ την ώρα που γεννήθηκα στα μεσοβασιλίκια!" ("I bless the hour in which I was born between two reigns!" 3.742). His energies are devoted—at first unconsciously, then consciously—to hastening the end of this transition by means of right thought transformed into right action. Paradoxically, however, no sooner does he seem to succeed than this very success turns into a threat. If evolution is to advance, what is needed is a continuing transition, but on a higher level. Odysséas must accordingly be robbed of his achievement lest he succumb to the "last temptation": happiness, the guarantee of stagnation. Through failure and the ensuing anguish—spiritual equivalents of the hunger that spurred the slaves in Crete and Egypt—he must be challenged to continue his movement toward freedom. Thus creative evolution's last word regarding the city is that the city must crumble even before it is officially inaugurated, avoiding the reflux to materialism that Kazantzakis so lamented in postrevolutionary Russia, and liberating Odysséas to evolve mentally in accord with Bergsonian precept. We come to the fifth peak identified by Kazantzakis in his summary of the epic: "At the lip of the abyss that has formed, Odysséas—now completely alone, without companions or hope—concentrates his powers in ascetic contemplation and struggles to conquer fate" (Prev. 1965b:478).

Biological evolution must of course continue as well; Odysséas invoked his grandfather via testicles in addition to brains. Accordingly, Hálikas encourages the survivors in the midst of the city's charred ruins by reminding them that a single couple will suffice to fill the earth again with sons and daughters, whereupon he leads a fresh remnant northward, incited by the vision of "a new sowing ahead and a new human family"

(16.299). Kazantzakis, however, is no longer interested in this arm of evolution and says nothing more about it.[32] What interests him exclusively now is our *mental* resistance to fate, that is, to death. True, we resist death by sexual reproduction, as Orpheus proclaimed in his song in Canto 3 and as Hálikas and his followers will continue to do now in practice. But this is not enough. Assuming as it does that life and death are enemies, it is a proper stance only for men of action. Odysséas, a man of theory as well as action, has already been initiated into the understanding that life and death (good and evil) may be collaborators. Henceforth, renouncing action completely, he will attain the still higher levels of initiation vouchsafed to mystical ascetics. In this way he will surpass human limits, if only for an instant, by attempting to imitate god, the god who employs materiality to pass beyond materiality. The city's demise ushers Odysséas into religious consciousness.

THE KIERKEGAARDIAN PARADIGM: AESTHETIC, ETHICAL, RELIGIOUS

With this in mind, we can review his odyssey[33] yet again, interpreted now according to the Kierkegaardian paradigm whereby life's way leads to the religious stage via the aesthetic and ethical.

I maintained earlier that the whole point of Kierkegaard's analysis is to expose insufficient values in order to replace them with better ones. This is done in the context of how human beings may best confront the reality of death—"come l'uom s'eterna"—which naturally has everything to do with how they relate to time.

For Kierkegaard, the aesthetic man is bound to be the least successful in this endeavor. The word "aesthetic" as used here has nothing to do with art or artists, at least not necessarily. The aesthetic man is one who seeks to have moments of such strong feeling that he is lifted out of the threatening world of ambiguity into some other realm akin to eternal bliss. Time is his greatest enemy because it makes feelings grow stale and, for those whose feelings are occasioned by love, because it ages the beloved and ultimately removes her, not to mention one's own capacity to feel. What the aesthetic man does to counteract this enemy is to fragment time into discrete units, each of which possesses the capacity to make him eternally happy only because it has been separated in his mind from past and future. The aesthetic man tries to be happy by transforming time's ineluctable flow into a series of snapshots. If his intense feeling comes through love, then he will have a succession of girlfriends, each one a snapshot, so to speak, who is then discarded so that another snapshot may succeed her.

The ethical man is more successful, although he too will ultimately fail in his quest for happiness. Just as the word "aesthetic" as used by Kierkegaard has nothing necessarily to do with artistry, so the word "ethical" has nothing necessarily to do with goodness. The ethical man is one who seeks eternal happiness in an ambiguous world by means of commitment to a code. This involves a very different relation to time from that of the aesthetic man. Instead of fragmenting the flow of time into a series of independent moments, the ethical man lives in the flow of time, indeed is obsessed by the past in relation to the present and also by both past and present in relation to the future. His happiness comes not from discontinuous moments of heightened feeling but from the satisfaction of knowing that he has remained true to his commitment and will continue to do so despite all the vicissitudes that arrive with the flow of time. Whereas the aesthetic man relates to others through idealization of the person who arouses his intense feelings, the ethical man relates through judgment and choice. He selects this person over that one or this mode of action over a competing mode, judging the selected entity as superior. Whereas the aesthetic man relates to himself through self-love, expecting others to love him for what he is, the ethical man relates to himself judgmentally: he is willing, indeed eager, to improve himself or sacrifice himself in order to keep his commitment alive. He controls his own life to a much greater degree than does the aesthetic man. His reality as a person—his selfhood—is not defined so much by others as by himself through rational choice.[34] He attains reality as a person because he establishes a meaningful relation not with another, as does the aesthetic man, and not with the Absolute, as does the religious man, but with himself. In sum, the ethical man attempts to find eternal happiness in the world as given as opposed to the world as idealized. He does this by thinking and acting within a framework of law and allegiance that he has chosen by an act of his own will.

Kierkegaard maintains that the ethical man, like the aesthetic one, is bound to fail. The aesthetic man is doomed because time is ineluctably continuous despite his efforts to convert it into discrete moments of perfection. The ethical man is doomed because he, too, in a futile effort to escape not continuity but ambiguity, is attempting to separate out what cannot be separated. What he fails to realize at first is that the very judgments he makes in order to overcome ambiguity are themselves ambiguous. Eventually, however, he does realize this, after which his life is subverted by guilt and despair.

The despair at the end of ethical endeavor may be either unconscious or conscious. If conscious it may become the impetus driving a person to take the leap into the religious mode, the only one in which eternal happiness is obtainable. The word "religious" as used here has nothing to do with church membership or adherence to a particular creed. Rather, it describes a life-style through which we confront the temporality and ambiguity of our existence. The aesthetic man's chief weapon in this confrontation is feeling; the ethical man's is commitment. The religious man's chief weapon is love—more precisely, caring and forgiving. This love is very different from the love practiced by the aesthetic and ethical types. In the former, love is disguised self-love and depends on a love-object that is idealized; in the latter, love is a mode of commitment and has as its object someone chosen specifically because he or she purportedly deserves to be chosen. Religious love, on the other hand, neither idealizes the love-object nor chooses it. This form of love does not even vow a commitment. Casual and spontaneous, it simply cares for others in their ambiguity and temporality, as givens. Religious love is acceptance of love-objects that do not deserve to be accepted, indeed that cannot—by the very nature of the world's ambiguity—be acceptable.

It is this love, Kierkegaard insists, that brings us closest to eternal happiness. To understand why, we must review some of the religious man's other characteristics. We know that each of the modes involves a certain relationship to time. In the religious mode, time is neither the enemy of happiness, as in the aesthetic mode, nor the medium of happiness, as in the ethical mode. The religious man dances in and out of time. Like the aesthetic man, he appears to be an opportunist since he loves with full intensity whenever the chance arises. The moment of caring is sufficient unto itself; it does not require a continuing commitment to a particular love-object. But although he appears to be like the aesthetic man in this regard, he is very different because his existence is not defined—his selfhood not established—by discontinuous moments of intense relationship with others any more than it is defined by all moments taken together, as in the case of the committed ethical man. Instead, his existence is defined by his relationship to the Absolute, which is a relationship of someone in time to something altogether outside of time. This explains why the religious man can be eternally happy in the real world of temporality and ambiguity. *He does not need it.* He can be eternally happy because insufficient values have been replaced in his life by an infinitely greater value. His happiness no longer depends on that which is bound to fail him. Yet his reliance on an absolute outside of time does not lead him to renounce the real world of temporality and ambiguity. On the contrary, since he is essentially free from all finite things he can affirm such things for what they are worth without either fearing or idealizing them. He can accept them casually, good-humoredly, with infinite patience. Lastly, because his selfhood is not something that he developed for himself or received as a reward on account of his goodness, but is instead something that he discovered in his despair, the religious man exhibits a humility unknown to the aesthetic or ethical man. He expresses this humility through gratitude for the gifts of life and happiness: the condition of being accepted although he is unacceptable.

Kazantzakis adapts all this to his own needs, adding a Tillichian touch to Kierkegaard in the sense that Odysséas, having found god, must proceed one step further to "the God above God"—to the "content of absolute faith" (Tillich 1952:182), which in his case is silence: the refusal to try any longer to define god, thereby limiting him.

Odysséas begins "aesthetically" in the sense that his major motivation is sensual gratification. He craves experience and is appalled by dullness: how can he bear to live with the likes of Telemachus and Penelope? At first his sensual gratification is sexual. Then (although this may seem strange) it becomes political. The two forms run concurrently until this stage ends (more or less) when Odysséas lands in Egypt.

Within each form there is an interesting development. Odysséas already enjoys a deserved reputation for womanizing—witness the scores of bastards he sired before sailing to Troy (Od. 2.1057ff.). Immediately after leaving Ithaca on the voyage of no return, he lives up to his reputation by presenting himself as a sea-god to a peasant girl and seducing her (3.500–518), whereupon he nonchalantly slaughters the calf she is watering, assuring her that the son she will soon bear will be ample recompense (3.545–547). It is the only humorous moment in all 33,333 lines. This is not the last time he copulates, but it is the first and last time he does so with the uncomplicated carnality of an adolescent. When he decides to visit Helen his motives are not at all lascivious; indeed, the Spartan queen draws him upward from carnality to "desire's summit," the *idea* of beauty (3.670–672). Kazantzakis then synthesizes the antitheses. When a lascivious orgy is about to occur in Crete, puritanical Karterós wants to avoid the filth but Odysséas determines to sleep with Díktenna because he knows that he is strong enough to transubstantiate the carnal experience upward in the "brain's laboratory" (6.720–721). Although this may sound like an ascent from sensuality to mentality, it is merely aestheticism in a more refined form, since Odysséas's assurance of personal meaning and worth, that is, his pleasure, still derives from a relationship to his own bodily life as opposed to an allegiance to moral law. That he is still governed by a craving for experience is indicated soon afterward:

> δεν καταδέχουντα ούτε μια πικρή σταλαματιά φαρμάκι
> στα χώματα να πέσει να χυθεί, να μην το πιεί η καρδιά του
> (6.751–752)
>
> he disdained to let even a drop of bitter poison
> fall to the ground and spill, unless his heart drank it up

In the final manifestations of the sexual theme, he refuses to fornicate in act or thought as he glimpses luscious girls as firm as "fuzzy fruit" (8.505–

515). Yet he still cultivates "earth's sweetness" (8.955–960) and even allows himself two more copulations with Díktenna (8.1126–1131, 1333). In his soul, however, he is beyond all this now; thus when his ship beaches at the mouth of the Nile and Pétrakas proposes that Díktenna be left behind (8.1312–1316), Odysséas readily agrees: "there's no room for a woman any more" (8.1325). Here endeth the aesthetic stage. The next woman we meet is Rala, the impassioned revolutionary and epitome of ethical dedication.

Even in this narrowly sexual form, the aesthetic exhibits an evolution that eases the way to the next stage. The political form that joins the sexual after a time and then runs concurrently with it, continues and extends this same development since it prepares a very clear bridge to the ethical. But we must not assume that political activity is by definition ethical. Indeed the whole point of Odysséas's initial involvements is that they are still largely aesthetic—a more advanced aestheticism than his womanizing, assuredly, but not essentially different. It is true that exposure to unjust suffering awakens an ethical consciousness in him, making him feel that he is personally to blame for human misery and alone able to comfort the afflicted (6.432–433). Yet a craving for experience as opposed to adherence to moral principle continues to be his primary motivation as he engages in revolutionary activity, especially in Sparta and Crete. Witness his inability to plan in advance on the basis of allegiance. We see this on his way to Menelaos's kingdom (3.576–577); his departure thence (5.137–142); his arrival on Crete (5.685–689); even as late as his decision to join the revolt in Egypt: "I don't ask if it's just or right, truth does not concern me" (10.558).

The division between aesthetic and ethical is fuzzy, not precise. Nevertheless, the political part of the aesthetic stage exhibits a development that allows Odysséas to move toward the ethical as he matures out of his "adolescence" into the responsibilities of maturity. We have already specified Egypt as being clearly in the ethical stage even though a trace of aestheticism remains. By the time of the exodus, Odysséas's sense of personal meaning and worth is determined exclusively by his adherence to moral principle, the aesthetic having been fully overcome.

Before proceeding to examine Odysséas's ethical activity in more detail, I must take issue with Prevelákis's interpretation of our hero's behavior during the aesthetic stage. Mention was made earlier of André Gide's fashionable doctrine of *disponibilité*. It is true that Odysséas makes himself available to every experience that comes his way; but Prevelákis carries this several steps further, invoking the Gidian term "immoralist" and insisting that Odysséas at this stage (and even later) is capable of nothing but "irresponsible actions born of momentary whim" (Prev. 1958:167; 1961:102). Finally he calls him a "desperado." He takes this last term from

Stefan Zweig's comparison of Nietzsche with sixteenth-century Spanish pirates (Prev. 1958:102, 303–305; 1961:58). A desperado is defined by Kazantzakis himself as "he who knows well that he has nothing to hold on to, who believes in nothing, and, not believing, is overcome by rage" (Kaz. 1962b:156; 1963c:174; Prev. 1958:305; 1961:178). The definition is amplified by Zweig when he argues that the desperado "does not conquer anything either for himself, for anyone after him, or for God, king, or faith; he struggles for the joy of struggling, because he does not want to possess anything, to acquire anything, to gain anything" (Zweig 1925: 264).

Preveläkis calls Odysséas an immoralist and desperado in order to support his view that the *Odyssey* is a nihilistic work, a view that I oppose, arguing that the epic does not deny value but rather overturns an old table of values in order to promulgate a new one. If we keep the epic's totality in mind we shall appreciate the fundamental difference between the immoralist/desperado and Odysséas. Of course a surface similarity does exist since both the immoralist and the desperado are aesthetic figures in the Kierkegaardian sense. But they differ from Odysséas because they are the end-products of a tired civilization whereas Kazantzakis's hero is a reborn child who, if he believes in nothing at the start (in nothing, that is, beyond the joy of experiencing everything), does so not so much out of cynical disgust at the status quo as out of the openness to life's infinite variety of every intellectually and physically lively child and adolescent. Furthermore, to describe Odysséas as an immoralist or desperado is to overlook the evolutionary basis of Kazantzakis's characterization. Without presuming to suggest that Kazantzakis's epic is artistically equal to Homer's *Odyssey*, Sophocles' *Ajax* or *Philoctetes*, or Joyce's *Ulysses*, I do wish however to note that Odysséas's characterization in all of these treatments is nondevelopmental; in each we are presented at the start with a fully formed personality that is maintained throughout.[35] This is not the case in Kazantzakis's treatment. Consistent with the epic's Bergsonian presuppositions, his Odysséas cannot enter the work with a personality that remains unchanged until the end, but must develop new traits and values experimentally, haphazardly, via creative evolution. When we see Odysséas's immoralism in light of this evolutionary totality we realize that it serves as prelude to subsequent stages in which value is acquired.

We can return now to Odysséas's ethical activity. As I said earlier, it is impossible to specify precisely when such activity begins, since creative evolution is a continuum, not a succession of mutually exclusive moments. Nevertheless, we may venture that at the end of his stay in Crete, Odysséas starts to act out of a truly political consciousness (instead of using politics to satisfy his aesthetic craving for experience). This consciousness will govern him increasingly in Egypt, during the exodus, and finally in the creation of his ideal city-state. A clear sign already noted is his decision at the end of Canto 8 to abandon Díktenna. Earlier, while still in Crete, he tells Karterós how to revive the polity they have just put to the torch: ". . . pen in justice and injustice with laws, / . . . place fences around desire, / and carve out untraveled roads . . . so that deeds may begin to move" (8.736–738). Following this, he lectures him on the qualities that define the good governor (8.855–866). Something new has been added to the personality supposedly capable of naught but irresponsible actions expressing momentary whim. Analyzing this "something," we find at least three factors. Odysséas is motivated now by the suffering he sees around him—a development that began in Crete and that reaches its acme during the exodus (12.492–496); he is aware of the values he espouses; and he believes that action should be guided by principles consciously understood. All three spell the end of the aesthetic man's whimsical, unpremeditated activity for experience's sake.

A particularly felicitous sign of this maturation is the scene near the start of the Egyptian section in which Odysséas and his crew, having become tomb robbers, discover an archeological treasure of incalculable value—amber, gold, rubies (9.890–891)—whereupon Odysséas stolidly throws everything overboard. The Cavafian voyage is finished. The incident serves as a memorable parable illustrating the deceptive temptation of aesthetic gratification while asserting the primacy of ethical behavior: "We spin great works in our minds, with toil mount / the muddy body and reach the divine peak, and suddenly / a momentary prosperity turns us into pigs again" (9.935–937).[36] The bankruptcy of the aesthetic solution has already been suggested. Just before they land in Egypt, Odysséas's companions are challenged by Hálikas's advocacy of suicide.[37] Their only response is adulation of intoxication, gluttony, and—in Díktenna's case—sex (8.1199–1211). By contrast, Odysséas is beyond bodily needs; as he adjures his mind when resisting the orgiastic rites of the primitive blacks in darkest Africa, "take the sperm from the loins / and bring it now to the head" (12.993–994), which in Bergsonian and Kierkegaardian language means, respectively: proceed from the biological to the mental, proceed from the aesthetic to the ethical. Accordingly, when he hears the obscene giggling and groaning of the copulating couples, he keeps "his body untouched for other expeditions" (12.1052).

Increasingly throughout the epic's ethical portion (cantos 9–15) Kazantzakis makes Odysséas's activity not only derive from ethical motivation but take a political form. A good example occurs when our hero imagines himself standing up to death by virtue of a principle to which he tenaciously adheres (11.145–147) and then resolving to apply this same principle in the political arena by instructing the fair-haired herds of barbarians who "lack the great shepherd, mind" and hence do not understand what motivates their revolutionary actions (11.239–242). That Odysséas's principle in this case is partially religious—"I've always fought to purify the wild flame into light" (11.146)—should not disturb us. What is important is that he displays an ethical attachment to this religious principle: his sense of self-worth depends on his adherence to a specific code of belief. He still has not developed the nonchalance that characterizes Kierkegaard's religious stage. This paradox, and the one we saw earlier whereby Odysséas can display an aesthetic approach to ethical behavior, attests to the skill with which Kazantzakis, in true Bergsonian fashion, has made his hero's development a divisionless continuum in which both the past and the future interpenetrate the present instead of being divided into independent units.

At the same time, this paradox opens a road toward the religious consciousness that will follow. Odysséas's ethical stage, like his earlier aesthetic one, is developmental. Even before the example just cited, his supposedly political principles are already sufficiently religious to bring him into conflict with "Lenin," who correctly concludes that Odysséas will "continue to hunt after gods" whereas the true revolutionaries, "bent over the earth, / will keep fighting to bring some bread and justice to the world / and as much liberty as we can to the enslaved masses" (10.570–572). His religious vision brings him into conflict as well with Rala and the members of her cell-group, whom he chides for being motivated by the hope of victory (10.899–900). All this bothers Prevelákis. In Egypt, too, he insists, "Odysséas once again meddles in politics in an irresponsible manner"; he acts politically only during the exodus (Prev. 1958:168, 169; 1961:103, 104).

What is happening in this ethical phase, of course, is that Odysséas, even before he can function as a man of political action, convinced that good and evil are enemies and that right is able to triumph over wrong, has become a man of theory, specifically, someone who realizes that good and evil may be co-workers and that all so-called triumphs of the good contain within them the seeds of their own negation. This, and not a continuing aesthetic stance, I repeat, accounts for his refusal to become fully engaged in Egypt. Insofar as, during the exodus and city-building, he does act politically in a manner acceptable to Prevelákis, he reverts, with a part of his being, to the belief that good and evil are enemies.

Yet the religious answer is now increasingly the dominating one for Odysséas. By this I mean an all-encompassing vision of "god" as an ever-renewed and ever-refined creative energy manifested in a process by which the vital force employs materiality in order to pass beyond materiality. This vision is fully articulated in Canto 14, where Odysséas, pursuing truth now instead of either beauty or virtue, builds a head—a theology—in which god may take refuge (17.71). He then reverts to the ethical stage, or so it seems, in order to construct the city.

However, the city itself, although the culmination of its builder's ethical development, is the incarnation of a truth that necessarily includes the aesthetic and religious in addition to the ethical, since, as we saw when we considered it earlier, it is governed by the entire process of creative evolution. It includes the aesthetic insofar as it enhances sensuality, even though it accomplishes this "ethically" since it does not esteem sensual or other types of bodily experience as self-justifying ends. It includes the ethical because all its regulations are based on a commitment to enhance creative evolution, a commitment that stretches across past, present, and future. Finally, it includes the religious because, as explained earlier, it is largely an internal triumph. Corresponding less to social forces, class struggle, or the enlightenment of the masses than to Odysséas's own mental development, it therefore includes potent seeds of its own destruction such as (a) the principle that biological evolution achieves its fulfillment in better minds, not better bodies, and ultimately in nonmaterial self-consciousness, and (b) the principle that ideas are vitiated as soon as they become institutionalized. The culmination of Odysséas's ethical activity includes the wisdom that both the ethical and the aesthetic responses to fate and death are inadequate. Present in the constitution of the city is the awareness, however latent, that the city is not needed, an awareness that emerges later in its builder's religious consciousness.

The ethical as we have seen it develop in cantos 9 through 15 is, like life itself, a process that unmakes itself. There is nothing left now but the religious response.

The city's destruction indicates this in perfect Kierkegaardian fashion. All of man's adherence to law, all of his institutionalizations of principles specifying the proper relation of person to person in family and society, are powerless before fate. Human fulfillment has to rest on something less vulnerable than either sexual reproduction or institutionalized duty. It is true that Kazantzakis sends a few survivors northward to replenish the race, but his precaution will simply set the aesthetic and ethical wheels turning again. Above and beyond the maintenance of previous accomplishments, evolution must also be allowed to move forward to the contemplation of its own processes.

For Kazantzakis, this advance to the religious state involves a total concentration on mind. To emphasize this, I want to quote once again from his article Το κοινωνικόν πρόβλημα (The Social Problem), published in Iráklion in February 1925: "Dark waves full of gore undulate rhythmically across the centuries. The only light that foams, white and ephemeral, at the crest of these heavy seas is the mind" (Kaz. 1925c; Mitsotakis 1972:128–129).

After a brief rage against the darkness as the final flicker of his ethical consciousness (Od. 16.143–146), Odysséas enters the contemplative state. This does not make him despise the body or the earth; on the contrary, he realizes that biological evolution, strife, hunger, and tragedy are the necessary precursors of his present position. Yet he escapes the rhythmic rise and fall of the dark waves because he has now transubstantiated the body and the earth into thoughts of the body and the earth (16.1289–1292). Transcending ethical hope as well, he acquires religious serenity (16.1191–1193). It is no surprise that immediately afterward (16.1255–1256) he remembers the seven-headed totem of Canto 5, for he has now reached, via suffering, the "last head but one, / beyond all joy or grief" (5.615–616).

What does all this really mean? Should we interpret it as subjective idealism, saying as Prevelákis does that after the city's destruction Odysséas's "last consolation is to declare the ungovernable world to be a transient fantasy of the human mind" (Prev. 1958:176; 1961:108)? Seeming evidence for this interpretation abounds, starting with the lines from the prologue that I quoted earlier:

> old age is a false dream and death is fantasy,
> all are the soul's doings and playthings of the brain
> (Od. Prologue 65–66)

Later, Odysséas dispels a subjective tempter by declaring: "My mind has climbed earth's highest peak and knows— / 'I am the savior, and there's no salvation for the world!' " (18.504–505). Accordingly, when his mind is extinguished in the epilogue, "the earth vanished, the sea dimmed, flesh dissolved" (24.1410; Epilogue 14). These and many other passages strengthen Prevelákis's interpretation. Nevertheless, I believe it misleading to conclude that Kazantzakis's last consolation is the refuge of subjective idealism. The key passages for a proper understanding of Kazantzakis's idealism are Odysséas's lengthy hymn to the mind and his ensuing meditation (17.1175–1272, 1293–1351). Kimon Friar's summaries are helpful:

> [Odysseus] addresses the Mind as the creator of all that lies fallow and shouts to be born, and to which the Mind gives form on the shores of insanity, which is life. There the Mind sits and plays the game of life, creates and destroys. Some have called Mind Spirit and declared that it begat the flesh; some have called it Flesh and declared that it begat the Spirit; but it is something beyond both, and it plays in the abyss of the Universe. Man, with the free play of his mind, locks and unlocks the chambers of life, though he hopes for nothing; he does not complain under life's blows, but

> strides through the nonexistent palace of his desires as though it were real, holding the keys of Nothingness, for he knows that at bottom all is a dark abyss and an oblivion.
>
> . . . Odysseus . . . sees that through his mind and senses now all creative impulse flows and plunges, laughing, down the abyss: an image of a deathless flowing stream. Within him War (the ceaseless strife of evolutionary creativity) and Mind (that which gives the stream direction, order, body, shape) embrace in a creative strife. (Kaz. 1958f:802)

The hymn and meditation summarized above are difficult texts. We must bend over them, and also over Friar's gloss, like rabbis over the Torah, attempting to extract some meaning.

The mind contains within it the potential for earthly evolution (17.1179ff.), an evolution that necessarily begins sexually, producing teeming creatures, lawless desires, and the battle between reproduction and death that Odysséas later calls "war" (17.1305) and that Friar glosses as "the ceaseless strife of evolutionary creativity." But this same evolution also produces mind, which comes as a savior (17.1202ff.) because it discovers principles governing the apparent anarchy of creation, the most basic of these principles being that the discouraging chaos called life proceeds from a τελετάρχης, a "master of ceremonies" who is "the father of time" (Od. 17.1175), that is, someone/something *outside of time* that manages the whole temporal show called earthly creation. On one level, this "something" discovered by mind is of course mind itself—sanity—"that which," as Friar says, "gives the stream direction, order, body, shape" as it sits on the shores of insanity and creates. Since flesh emanates from mind while at the same time the self-consciousness that understands all this is the flower produced by fleshly evolution, the master of ceremonies may be called both spirit and flesh (17.1220–1221). In any case, the stream to which he/she/it gives direction evolves through ever-renewed bodies and also through ever-renewed thoughts: evolution is both biological and mental (17.1224–1235). Whole civilizations rise and fall but once again huge leafed-out oaks snuggle into tiny acorns (17.1253): the potential for renewal continues.

Odysséas ends his hymn by invoking the mind once more as the "δαιμόνιο στερνογέννητο" (the "last-born spirit"), that is, as the noncorporeal end product of fleshly creation and at the same time, paradoxically, as what contains in potential form, like a Trojan horse, all the teeming multiplicity of fleshly creation: "O mind . . . , head pregnant / like the ample mare the citadel-wreckers set up before the city" (17.1263–1264). This is the light described in Kazantzakis's 1925 newspaper article as foaming at the crest of the stormy, dark waves of life's tragedy. Now it is described as "clear"—that is, logical, sane—in relation to the "mindless night" of the flesh that it illumines (17.1265–1266). Odysséas concludes by thanking mind for teaching him how to confront life's tragedy through the knowledge that the desires and fleshly manifestations that cause so much pain are nothing (17.1272). Lacking an independent existence and hence an independent meaning, they are but playthings of the master of ceremonies who employs flesh to produce a mind capable of understanding the futility of fleshly endeavor.

In the short meditation that follows, Odysséas is seized by an "ineffable sweetness" because he has now transcended all antinomies between flesh and spirit, that is, between war and mind, as they are now called (17.1304–1305). By means of an overall religious vision that offers a metaphysical explanation *for the entire process of fleshly creation* (as opposed to declaring the ungovernable world to be merely a fantasy produced by the human mind), Odysséas achieves what eluded him in the aesthetic and ethical stages of his life's way, and what we all desire: happiness.

Kierkegaard teaches us why. The aesthetic answer to death is insufficient; intoxication, gluttony, even sex, are no match for temporality's destructive chaos. The ethical answer is better, but still insufficient; our efforts to impose justice and rationality upon creation's ambiguous material are too vulnerable. We sail nonchalantly above tragedy's dark waves only when, beyond not merely the senses but also the social nexus that ethical behavior presupposes—beyond, in sum, any need for this world—we embrace in solitude an all-encompassing, all-explaining truth, taking a leap of faith to do so. Odysséas cannot attain the religious vision until (a) repletion in aesthetic endeavor and (b) suffering and failure in ethical endeavor have ripened him beyond the pleasures of sensual gratification or fulfillment of duty, casting him out of society's nexus and leaving him face to face with universal mystery.

Yet, although he no longer needs the world, all this is accomplished in the world. This is why Odysséas bows low at the end of the meditation and reverently kisses Mother Earth as though it were bread (17.1312)—kisses the materiality that idealists say does not exist—whereupon he dreams of Earth and her two sons, War and Mind, the fleshly and intellectual fruits of creative evolution. The point is that Mind, the younger of the two, is dearer: it is evolution's flower. But Odysséas's religiosity enables him to deal with both on equal terms. As Kazantzakis stated in an interview given at a time when the *Odyssey* was very much in his thoughts, "the free man is he who, while not hoping for anything, struggles . . . to see life's spectacle as intensely as possible; and not only to see but also to hear, taste, smell, and feel" (Darakis 1935). For the religious man, fleshly life is no longer a threat.

I have analyzed the hymn to the mind and the ensuing meditation at such length in the hope that these key passages will help us see Odysséas's existential idealism as very different from a denial that reality exists. His position at this stage is anything but nihilistic, despite what critics say.[38]

In arguing against the charge of nihilism earlier, I emphasized the need to transcend a dualistic reading in which Buddhism clashes with Bergsonism and hoped that the work might be understood monistically and organically. I also discussed the doctrines of silence and the transitional age. Now I wish to supplement those earlier arguments with two others based, respectively, on the nature of art and on Martin Heidegger's phenomenological ontology. The two are intimately connected.

We are still interested in what Odysséas's new life as an ascetic really means. When the bereaved leader sits on the lip of the abyss after the destruction of his city, he does not read holy scripture, pray, or follow a regimen of spiritual exercises, as we would expect an ascetic contemplator to do; nor does he empty his mind of images in an attempt to experience the godhead's unified effulgence. Such manifestations of traditional asceticism, well known to Kazantzakis from his experiences at Mount Athos and from his extensive acquaintance with mystical literature, are deliberately rejected. Instead, Odysséas becomes a poet in various genres, the hymn to the mind analyzed above being preceded, for example, by a lengthy play (Od. 17.336–1165).[39] In practice, the religious stage looks more like an artistic one. Throughout the Nostos, Odysséas makes a virtue of inventing and then extinguishing multitudes of characters, reminding us of Kazantzakis's delight at the Buddhistic possibilities of the cinema (Prev. 1965b:73). He does appear to be retreating to a consoling subjectivism that declares reality a transient fantasy of the human mind, as though to confirm the view that Kazantzakis's religiosity is a barely disguised aestheticism. I spoke earlier of the inhuman autonomy from which Kazantzakis likes to view the *spectacle* of life's capitulation to death: the declining human curve that only through art can be transformed into an ascending arrow. Perhaps we can say that art, for Kazantzakis as for Nietzsche,

> is a kind of playing with the world; it consists in seeing it—in part or *in toto*—as *in* a play, making a picture or spectacle of it. So far as we follow this impulse we disembarrass ourselves of ourselves and the world as immediate experience, and view everything as outside us, detached from us—we *contemplate* rather than experience, even the terrible we can look upon undisturbed. That is, the burden of actual life is momentarily lifted, and we may even enjoy

> rather than suffer. (Salter 1917:39; drawing on *The Birth of Tragedy*, sections 22, 24, and 25)

Indeed the *Odyssey* announces in its prologue:

> Κοράσια με τ' αγριοπερίστερα στο δροσερό σας κόρφο,
> λεβέντες με το μαυρομάνικο το λάζο στο ζωνάρι,
> ξερό δεντρό 'ναι η γης χωρίς ανθούς, όσο κι αν πολεμάτε
> εγώ, μωρέ, με το τραγούδι μου θα την ανθοβολήσω!
> (1.49–52)
>
> Girls with wild doves in your refreshing breasts,
> brave lads with the black-handled dagger in your belt
> earth's a dead tree without flowers, no matter how you battle;
> I, my friend, shall make it blossom with my poem.
> (Prologue 49–52)

This proclaims that both the sensual life (the girls) and the ethical life (the boys) are bankrupt unless redeemed by art. Yes, it is tempting to conclude that Kazantzakis's religiosity is aestheticism: overt, not even disguised.

To argue against such a conclusion our first evidence will be once again the epic in its totality. Let us recall that the Absolute depicted by means of Kazantzakis's characters and plot is the entire metabiological system formulated by Bergson, a system in which both politics and art serve as steps in the progressive transubstantiation of matter. For Kazantzakis, this system is not itself merely another dramatic poem created by the mind; it is reality, truth, dogma, gospel. It redeems the sensual life, the ethical life, and even the artistic life (each of which exercises its own degree of redemptive power) because it places all three in an organic synthesis that confers ultimate meaning, giving each a purpose beyond itself. This is why art is not a self-justifying absolute for Kazantzakis: because it serves a higher purpose. He explains this in a letter to Professor Sachinis dated 2 March 1955:

> . . . I'm . . . a pen-pusher (γραφιάς) and I mobilize the 24 little soldiers of the alphabet and undertake . . . to catch the Invisible. Like the savages who paint in caves the beast they desire to capture, so that the beast will see its outline and enter, I too set words as traps, not to catch beauty, as do easily satisfied quill-drivers (καλαμαράδες), but to catch "God."
>
> From this you'll understand that I have no relation to so-called literary men, to so-called literature. Of course I use the same means—words—but for an entirely different end; and beauty, too, is a means for me and not an end, because I know that the Invisible

is seduced much more surely by beauty than by ugliness. (Sachinis 1967:33–34)

Art for Kazantzakis, far from being a self-justifying absolute, is meant to constitute a dry river bed that will provide direction for humanity in the future. The *Odyssey* in particular, he once declared, represents this effort to "prophesy future humanity" (Yalourakis 1958:159). All this brings us full circle back to politics via art and religion, but back to what I like to call eschatological politics since the future fulfillment is indefinitely postponed.

The question remains: By what right does Kazantzakis assume that his artistic metamorphoses of reality may bear some relation to reality in the near, distant, or unspecified future? To answer this—or attempt to answer it—we have to continue our rebuttal of the charge that Kazantzakis's religiosity is aestheticism in disguise. Let us do this by examining the deeper similarity between the religious and the aesthetic visions.

Both art and religion, far from being escapes from life, bring us into a more meaningful contact with reality than we achieve via quotidian experience. This is especially true of tragic art, which teaches us to understand suffering and death; but it is also true of comedy, which celebrates human foolishness. To the degree to which art, whether tragic or comic, escapes subservience to everyday reality, to that same degree will it succeed in returning us more meaningfully to that same reality, because it will have concerned itself *with the meaning of being rather than of things*. Far from avoiding a confrontation with the problem of value, it will have placed itself in a position where value can truly be discovered and formulated. In other words, it will have refuted nihilism. The very "playing with the world" commonly scorned as irresponsible aestheticism is precisely what strengthens our capacity to act in the world instead of merely making a picture or spectacle of it, because it teaches us to live in the truth. We should remember Kazantzakis's assertion to Hourmoúzios (Kaz. 1977a:187) that the Silence neither paralyzes Odysséas nor is the climax of his struggle; instead, it enables him to re-engage with life. If the occasion had presented itself, Kazantzakis would have said the same about Odysséas's artistic reveries at the lip of the abyss.

That Odysséas's artistic/religious phase is meant to honor life's gifts rather than escape them is shown by a fortuitous encounter between Kazantzakis and Martin Heidegger's phenomenological ontology. Reading an article on this subject in January 1949, a decade after the *Odyssey*'s publication, Kazantzakis was astonished to encounter "precisely one of the central pillars of the *Odyssey* and all my work" (Kaz. 1972:302; Dimakis 1975:21). Here is a digest of what he read:

> *Catastrophic Heroism*. . . . A superficial scrutiny would assume that anguish, confronting us with nothingness, would lead us to paralysis of every disposition toward practical action. The truth is that, on the contrary, the confrontation with nothingness has a . . . practical influence that is energizing. Nihilism propels us to the discovery of true existential meaning, . . . inviting the individual to develop all his courage and capacity for action. With all this, a person's practical-ethical activity is elevated to a metaphysical degree. . . . The resoluteness of active behavior becomes evident if we remember that the measure for assessing planned possibilities is death. In other words, only those decisions that the individual makes without retreating before the fear of death are worth being characterized as genuine. . . . The supreme achievement of a person or a people, says Heidegger, is to assume the weight of his/their fate. As a consequence . . . , it has been said by many that philosophy's moral ideal attains its summit in a tragic and catastrophic heroism . . . (Yeorgoulis 1948:976)[40]

This passage, although not applied specifically to art, explains art's power to reveal the truth by concerning itself with the meaning of being ("true existential meaning") rather than with the meaning of things, and its concomitant power to return us with increased resolve to the practical world of action. No wonder that Kazantzakis read it with astonishment, for it articulates why he placed Odysséas on the lip of the abyss and then turned him into an artist. The specific applicability to art of Heidegger's existential ontology, especially to tragic art, is examined in a study by Professor Michael Gelven. "Both Heidegger and the tragedians," Gelven begins, "struggle with a similar problem: how to focus our attention on *being* rather than things; how to understand the meaning of existence and not merely our actions and their consequences" (Gelven 1976:556). The precondition for this ontological understanding is precisely what we have seen in Kazantzakis's *Odyssey*, namely the transcendence of ethical activity, since such activity derives from our sensitivity to human need and is predicated on our hope that we will successfully alleviate that need (559). What Heidegger teaches and tragedy demonstrates is that we do not begin to focus our attention on being rather than on things—on Heidegger's "Frage nach dem Sinn vom Sein" ("the question of what it means to be"; 568)—until we realize our "fundamental . . . capacity to fail at existing." (Kazantzakis would say: until we achieve freedom from hope.) This failure, whether demonstrated by the collapse of Othello's marriage or of Odysséas's utopia, whether caused primarily by inner weakness or outer fate, becomes "the basis by which one's existence can be *thought* about" (561). Said in another way: failure (ultimately, death) provides the basis by which we may inquire into the meaning of life (which includes the meaning of death). This inquiry, in turn, enables us "to affirm, to accept, indeed to *celebrate* [our] being precisely in the light of this capacity to fail" (561).

Such is the teaching of Heideggerian philosophy and the witness of both tragic and comic art. "The artist's skill . . . forces our attention solely to the realization of the worth of our *existence*" (Gelven 1976:560). And although this affirmation required as its presupposition the crumbling of our value system and its replacement by the realization of our capacity to fail, "both Heidegger's thinking and the tragedian's art are affirmative . . .—they both refute nihilism." The nihilist claims that "there is no way . . . in which my existence can be rationally thought about. Both Heidegger and the tragedian show the nihilist's position to be untenable. Heidegger does so by . . . developing . . . a thematic analysis of the ways in which we exist and grounding them in the reality of our being. The tragedian confounds the nihilist by showing our affirmation of the nobility of being, even when all *other* sources of affirmation, such as pleasure, well-being, ability, and even moral approval, are violated" (561–562).

Applying this to Odysséas, we can say that when he sits at the lip of the abyss and becomes an artist after failing at other sources of affirmation, sensual and ethical, he focuses his attention on the "Frage nach dem Sinn vom Sein." His confrontation with nothingness, far from paralyzing him, propels him to the revelation of the meaning of being rather than of things. Taking the weight of his fate upon himself, transmuting it into the basis by which his existence may now be thought about, he affirms, accepts, indeed celebrates his being precisely in the light of his capacity to fail. In sum, he confounds nihilism.

But what about future action? In what sense, if any, does Odysséas's confrontation with nothingness influence him to engage in political activity? By dwelling at such length on Odysséas's religious stage we seem to have come a long way from politics. Yet all we have done is to confirm what we already know about Kazantzakian engagement, namely, that it is subordinate to, and indispensable for, religious inquiry, the futility of politics being the precondition for the religious vision that shows political activity to be not so futile, after all, in the grand scheme of creative evolution. We have encountered this teaching in *Askitikí* and will encounter it again in the postwar novels treated in volume two. But *Odíssia* is Kazantzakis's fullest expression of the complete system. In it, he strives for a monistic solution to the traditional materialist-mental dualism of the West by attempting to convince us that matter is basically nothing but the way in which mental reality manifests itself.[41] But this does not mean that he loses interest in matter. On the contrary. It is no accident that Odysséas's head fills with memories of *things* as he nears death (Od. 23.518–614) even though all things are held in suspension, as it were, in his mind; nor that he blesses the elements that constitute his body—earth, water, fire, air, and also mind (23.772–1068). As I have emphasized so often, Kazantzakis's system, although idealist and subjective in appearance, is not meant to lead us away from care for this world to some other world (there is none) but rather to show us a meaning of being that provides for periodic renewal through repeated participation in material struggle and development. This is why Kazantzakis insisted that his *Odyssey* was the "kravyí of future humanity" (Prev. 1965b:157), by which he meant that he hoped the epic would provide a new understanding into which reality would flow, as into a waiting river bed, when the proper moment arrived.

Addressing the question of how Odysséas's confrontation with nothingness influences him to engage in political activity, we can say, therefore, that the *Odyssey* employs politics in order to reach a point at which political activity is abandoned only to be resumed in some indefinable future on a higher level of universal evolution. The time for resumption cannot be specified. It may never come at all. Yet we must continue to act *as if* its coming were certain.

KAZANTZAKIS'S *Odíssia* is not a great work of art, although it might have been had its author possessed superb poetic gifts as well as the strength to reduce his monstrous creation to manageable size. As it stands, it is verbose, digressive, repetitive, deficient in characterization, bloated with hyperbolic emotions. But the *Odyssey* is strangely very important, certainly in relation to Kazantzakis's career if not more broadly. It proved that he could produce something extraordinary, even if only an extraordinary failure. His career up to 1938 reveals promising beginnings in drama, the novel, and lyrical philosophy, but no sustained artistic growth. In quantity, it reveals a meager production for someone who was then fifty-five years old. But Kazantzakis never lacked ambition; the contrast between what he expected from himself and what he had actually accomplished galled him. As in the case of his Odysséas, it was the awareness of failure that launched his inquiry into the question of what it means to be. He needed to make up for lost time in every possible way; thus in the *Odyssey* he forced together into a single work materials that other writers would have spread over many works. Among those materials are the varied political experiences he underwent in Vienna, Berlin, Iráklion, Athens, and the Soviet Union. On the level of "things" he had failed in each instance: his metacommunism, ignored or scorned, never produced the slightest effect. But what an opportunity these failures offered him to demonstrate that things are but manifestations of mental reality while at the same time infinitely important in themselves!

SUMMARY: HOW THE *ODYSSEY* REFLECTS KAZANTZAKIS'S POLITICAL CONVICTIONS

It is time now to summarize the ways in which Kazantzakis's political convictions are reflected in the *Odyssey*. Central to everything is the belief that we are in a transitional age. Earlier I quoted Odysséas's "I bless the hour when I was born between two reigns!" (Od. 3.742). He exclaims this in reference to the blond invaders, the Dorians, who are going to overwhelm both the Mycenaean and Minoan civilizations, "pouring new salty blood into shrunken veins" (3.729). The epic foresees the presumed end of this transitional period in a new Hellenic race resulting from the marriage of rude Dorian energy and cultivated Mycenaean sophistication, a race that will lead, after a dark age, to the golden years of classical Greece. This is why Kazantzakis has Helen impregnated by a barbarian invader: their son, Hellene, will balance "the intoxicated barbarous heart and the upright, / sober mind" (8.914–915).[42] More generally, the Homeric world appealed to Kazantzakis owing to its link with our own situation because both involve transitional ages. I have already cited the relevant passage of his letter of 22 February 1929 to Prevelákis in which he characterizes the twentieth century as "astonishingly similar to the state of [Homer's] world in the twelfth century B.C." (Prev. 1965b:114). The *Odyssey* reworks materials first presented in *Ksimerónei*, "Spasménes psihés," and *O protomástoras* regarding our efforts in a transitional age to transform right thought into right action. Odysséas succeeds up to a point; in this sense he is another *protomástoras*—the term is actually applied to him during the city's construction (Od. 15.549). Beyond that point, however, he fails; but of course he is not another broken soul ripe for suicide. On the contrary! In the *Odyssey*, Kazantzakis amalgamates his previous approaches to the doctrine of the transitional age and reworks them within the larger context of tragic heroism.

The second political conviction reflected in the *Odyssey* is Kazantzakis's belief that twentieth-century European bourgeois civilization is moribund. This is why the cultures opposed in varying degrees by Odysséas—Sparta, Crete, and Egypt—are all sick. The murals in Menelaos's palace deliberately suggest those of decadent Pompeii (Od. 3.1106–1108), which in Kazantzakis's mind evoked contemporary London and Paris (Kaz. 1958a:245–246; 1926c). The King of Crete is sexually impotent and his attempted remedies pathetic. As for the Egyptian Pharaoh, his pacifism is a trait that Kazantzakis despised as indicative of the twentieth century's sapped vitality.[43]

All this reflects the European decline that Kazantzakis had confirmed through his own experience. In Vienna and Berlin he witnessed an economic system that had ceased to function, as well as a political system unable to deal with inequities between rich and poor. But his quarrel with Europe had begun earlier, during his nationalistic days. At first he hoped that Greece might be exempt from the European "sickness of the century," exhibiting instead a proud, youthful egotism worthy of Nietzsche and Dragoúmis. But the Asia Minor disaster showed him otherwise, and when he returned to Crete in 1924 he was dismayed by the social prejudices, morality, and religion of his family and friends. His awareness of a new vitality in the disaffected masses of Berlin, and of Iráklion itself, is reflected of course in the downtrodden revolutionaries whom Odysséas encounters in Crete. But Kazantzakis shared Spengler's pessimism to such a degree that he ultimately shows even the disaffected to be incapable of creativity or grandeur.

Regeneration, in his view, must come through an injection of additional vitality from outside. This is the third major political conviction that is mirrored in the *Odyssey*, where the decadent societies of Crete and Egypt are threatened by external invaders as well as by native dissenters, and where the remedy for Idomenéas's sexual impotence is demonstrated by the African blacks who regularly slay impotent kings so that a "lusty head-ram may enter the human flocks" (Od. 13.106).

The fourth political conviction that we see in the *Odyssey* declares that the regeneration of contemporary civilization can be accomplished only through violence. Kazantzakis never minced words about this in his public utterances; the Iráklion debate and the 1927 speech in Moscow are examples. The first significant god fashioned by Odysséas to replace the ones he has discarded is a ferocious god of war.[44]

Kazantzakis expected at first that the postrevolutionary Russians would continue to play the regenerative role. But we know that after his firsthand experience in the Soviet Union he concluded that the Russians were not a healthy young race outside the European stream but, on the contrary, the end product of European materialism and decadent rationalism (Prev. 1965b:154–155). In Iráklion in 1925, before his disillusioning sojourn in the Soviet Union, he could still hope that the Russians might play the role of "Asiatic barbarians" capable of bringing a new seed, even though he had already convinced himself that proletarian communists had little to offer beyond superficial ameliorations (Prev. 1965b:159–160). But the disillusionment recorded in *Toda-Raba* four years later shows the end of this limited hope as well. This mixed view of the Russians is the fifth major political element that is reflected in the *Odyssey*. Appropriately, it is reflected in a mixed way. On the one hand, Russian-like Dorians stimulate revolutionary movements, and a cell-group led by "Lenin," "Trotsky," and "Stalin" directs operations in Egypt.[45] On the other hand, (a) "Lenin" and Odysséas fail to see eye to eye, the former being unable to appreciate the latter's metacommunism,[46] and (b) the city-state that represents regenerated society is associated not with Dorians but with primitive blacks since it is built in the heart of Africa after Odysséas has experienced the barbaric vitality of Negro ritual.[47] Kazantzakis's definitive view of the Russians honors them as forerunners only, not as saviors.

Yet his general position even after his disillusionment with the Soviet Union was that all "strugglers" must support the communists. The reason—which we can list as the sixth general political principle reflected in the *Odyssey*—is this: by strengthening the materialistic forces of communism we will help to exacerbate the disease of materialism until it becomes so bad that a true regeneration, that is, a spiritual one, will take place. These "homeopathic politics" tend to make Odysséas hold back with part of his being. Even when he gives himself to the revolutionary cause in Egypt—his most genuine political involvement before the exodus—he does so not because he believes notionally in the cause but because his emotions tell him that he ought to support it (Od. 10.522–560). Earlier, in Crete, when he incites the enslaved workers with a metacommunistic message (tailored to their simplicity) and is rebutted by a man who exclaims, "The only god is food, wine, and women," he bitterly realizes what "proletarians" want and what they will be like as soon as they emerge victorious; yet, seeing them as part of a larger metacommunist plan that will bring a spiritual revolution after the materialist one is accomplished, he joins them in this "holy moment that aims at destruction," in full awareness that "he thought one thing to himself, and the slaves something else" (Od. 7.955–995).

A seventh general principle is Kazantzakis's belief that a revolution will betray its own principles as soon as it succeeds. Lest this happen, Odysséas's city-state is destroyed even before its official inauguration.

The eighth general political principle reflected in the *Odyssey* pertains more to the epic's overall conception than to specific passages. It is that revolutionary activity, simply because it upsets the inertia of the status quo, hastens universal progress toward the spirit. Kazantzakis shows this in personal terms rather than political ones. What I mean is that he does not make Odysséas envision an even better utopia than the first one. Instead, the political activity of the first fifteen cantos, which in a sense adds up to nothing, produces the new element of inwardness that Spengler predicted would follow the demise of the decadent West. Perhaps it was cowardly of Kazantzakis to avoid, in the Nostos, a new visionary community that would be the imaginary application of Odysséas's increased personal inwardness. But I think that this avoidance is consistent with his feeling, based on the teachings of creative evolution, that the future will have to be worked out in ways that the present generation cannot even begin to imagine. What he wanted as a result of political activity was a heightened inwardness *in individuals* that would provide a vague, nonspecific potential for a higher level of communal realization in an unspecified future. That is precisely what governs the epic's overall conception whereby extensive political actions lead to a higher level of *personal* development. I hope, by the way, that this will justify my neglect of cantos 18–24 in this study that is meant to concentrate on Kazantzakis's politics. The political significance of these cantos needs no further gloss beyond the one already given.[48]

The ninth and final "political" principle I wish to include concerns Kazantzakis himself. His own life had begun to assume the same rhythms that his theories told him governed universal evolution: involvement in materiality followed by heightened spirituality leading to a new involvement in materiality, ad infinitum. The cycles are clear. After his crusade for demoticism and nationalistic awakening in the period preceding and during the Balkan Wars, he retired to Mount Athos, felt a compelling affinity with Tolstoy, and adopted "come l'uom s'eterna" as his motto (Prev. 1965b:9). Next, political involvements in the Caucasus and Berlin were followed by the heightened spiritual awareness expressed in *Askitikí*. This in turn led to the Iráklion incident, which provided the impetus for the *Odyssey*'s first draft. Additional political engagement in Athens and the Soviet Union prodded Kazantzakis to launch the *Odyssey*'s second draft in October 1929. If a "political" principle can be abstracted from this pattern, it is that Kazantzakis's role was more as a manipulator of words than of people, but that in order to fashion a refined lógos out of a raw kravyí he needed to begin each time—and fail each time—as a manipulator of people, involving himself in materiality as a prerequisite for heightened spirituality. This is reflected in the epic insofar as Odysséas, too, starts as a manipulator of people and ends as a manipulator of words, thoughts, and images.

HAVING WRITTEN 33,333 lines of the *Odyssey*, Kazantzakis proved to himself that he could produce something worthy of his ambition. Whether the poem would prove the same to its readers remained to be seen. That was one problem. The other was this: Once a writer has poured all his practical and intellectual experience into an immense synoptic conception realized in epic (the supreme literary genre), what can he possibly do next? In hindsight we can say, of course, that the basic rhythms of Kazantzakis's life were bound to continue, and to provide the necessary openings. New involvements in materiality would stimulate new ways to manipulate words. But neither Kazantzakis nor anyone else could have predicted in 1938 what forms his renewed contacts with political reality were destined to take first in 1940–1941 and subsequently in 1944–1946. Nor could either he or anyone else have predicted in 1938 the turn to prose fiction that began with *Víos ke politía tu Aléksi Zorbá* in late August 1941.

In 1938, with the *Odyssey* about to appear, Kazantzakis was understandably apprehensive. On the other hand, although he could not foreknow that a decisively different stage in his career lay ahead, he was certain about the need to keep going and also about the impulse that would enable him to do so:

> I will have done nothing, my life will go to waste, if the *Odyssey*, which is now in press, is no good. But even if it is good, again my life will go to waste—that is its nature and its supreme nobility, and that is why I love it so passionately.
>
> We know this and are not afraid, and we work as if we were immortal. . . . (Kaz. 1972:245; Dimakis 1975:16–17)

Notes

CHAPTER ONE

1. The one exception is the ambitious four-act play Έως πότε; written no later than the summer of 1907 (Aposkitou-Alexiou 1978:137), never produced, and not printed until twenty years after the author's death. A historical drama about the abortive insurrection led in 1570 by Yeórgios Kandanoléos under provocation of the Venetians' demand for 14,000 Cretans to man their galleys, it bears some relation in addition to Venizélos's Thérisos revolt of March 1905 and to the internal dissension among Cretans at this time. Thus one of the play's themes is the need for concord (Kaz. 1977e:214)—a theme that was to reappear in many of Kazantzakis's subsequent works, notably in *Kapodístrias*. For discussion of the play see Gounelas 1977:166–167, 175–177; 1984:262, 264–266; Papahatzaki-Katsaraki 1985:24–27. For Kazantzakis's reactions to the contention between Venizélos and Prince George ca. 1903–1905, concerning Crete's *énosis* with Greece, and the contention between Venizélos and Andónis Mihelidákis, who favored Prince George, see Kazantzakis's letters to Harílaos Stefanídis, helpfully annotated by Martha Aposkítou-Alexíou (Aposkitou-Alexiou 1978:118, 123, 126–130, 160, 163). These letters support my view that Kazantzakis was only marginally interested in politics at this time, i.e., during his years as a university student in Athens.

2. Reviews were divided. Pétros Vlastós objected to its puristic language and the similarity to D'Annunzio. I. Kondilákis was revolted by the novella's "sick voluptuousness." But the great Palamás hailed the author as "talented" and the work as a prose poem that mixes mystical ecstasy with priapism. He hoped that future works from the same pen might be healthy as well as beautiful. These and other comments are reprinted in Katsimbalis 1958d. Although Kazantzakis had repudiated the novella, Mrs. Kazantzakis was obliged to reissue it in 1974 after forcing the withdrawal of a pirated edition with an introduction by Elli Alexíou (reprinted in Alexiou and Stefanakis 1977: 65–72). Regarding Mrs. Kazantzakis's difficulties, see Friar 1977b:311; Eleni Kaz. 1983. For opinions occasioned by the reissue and the 1980 translation, see Friar 1977b and Mackridge 1980, respectively.

3. Similar ideas are found in "Nostalgía" (Kaz. 1958k), in which both paganism and Christianity are declared inaccessible dreams, and romantic melancholy is condemned. Cf. "Hristuyenniátiko" (Kaz. 1958l), written later (1908) in Paris.

4. On the relation of *Ofis ke kríno* to the affair with Galatea, see Zografou 1960:67, 92–104; Alexiou and Stefanakis 1977:67. Zográfou maintains that the only way Kazantzakis could respond to Galatea's affections—owing to his sexual indifference and/or incapacity—was by composing erotic fantasies. The question of Kazantzakis's alleged sexual incapacity continues to be raised by critics such as Yánnis Goudélis and offered as a supposed key to his writings (see Goudelis 1987:419, 434, 462–463). For a brief refutation see Friar 1977b:313.

5. The indebtedness to Ibsen is indirectly acknowledged by Kazantzakis in an article (Kaz. 1958m) defending his play and especially its feministic aspects after

it was criticized in *Estía*. See Katsimbalis 1958e for full documentation on the dramatic competition plus some reactions in the press. Aside from some brief excerpts printed in *Pinakothíki*, August 1907, p. 98, and reprinted in *Néa Estía* 63:746–749 (15 May 1958), the play remained only in manuscript form until it was finally printed in full along with Kazantzakis's other unpublished dramas written during this period (Kaz. 1977d). For discussion of *Ksimerónei* see Gounelas 1977:166–167, 171, 174–175; 1984:262–264; Bien 1972a:95–100, 123–124, 151, 153–156, 168, 170; Papahatzaki-Katsaraki 1985:12–24.

6. That the doctor's views are indeed Kazantzakis's own is confirmed in an extensive and most helpful gloss in the form of a letter by the author to the editor of *Pinakothíki* dated 22 August 1906 (Markakis 1959b:32).

7. Kazantzakis's studies in Paris extended from October 1907 until the end of February 1909, a total of seventeen months, but he was away on vacation for five months during the summer and autumn of 1908.

8. For discussion of Jaurès and Kazantzakis see Pouliopoulos 1972:81–82; 1975:50.

9. Kazantzakis's opinion of Barrès was contradictory. He applauded his nationalism (Kaz. 1958c:1284) but was aghast at hearing him defend the Church (Kaz. 1958q:1211–1212). On balance, however, he considered Barrès's pagan-Christian eclecticism a useful tonic for the "enfeebled blood of today's France" (Kaz. 1958q:1286).

10. See Augustinos 1977 for a study of the nationalist movement ca. 1897–1914, concentrating on Kostís Palamás, Pericles Yannópoulos, and Ion Dragoúmis.

11. Dragoúmis developed his position in the course of an active political life beginning in 1897, when as a youth of nineteen he served in the disastrous war against the Turks, and ending with his assassination in 1920. Of his major political books the most systematic is *Ellinikós politismós* (Greek Civilization), published in 1913. Here, Dragoúmis takes the demoticists' admiration for the spoken language and widens it until he makes the demotic tradition the source of Greece's creative life from the first centuries A.D. to the present, hence the one and only basis for the craved neohellenic cultural revival (see Dragoumis 1913:20; L. Palamas 1921:106; Sherrard 1959:190). But his basic ideas can also be seen in the books he published between 1907 and 1911, precisely when Kazantzakis was most susceptible to his influence. In *Samothráki* (1909), for example, he presents a catalogue of Nietzschean doctrine: heroic pessimism; the strong have a particular right to live; liberal ideals of equality and compassion are symptoms of weakness; democracy, socialism, and cosmopolitanism are forms of degeneracy; voluntarism is superior to rationalism; truth is made rather than discovered; egoism is superior to altruism; egoism is in the best interests of the state; nationalism is an irrational, mystical bond to *volk* and land. All this is employed to exhort the Samothrakians to fulfill their duty to themselves and their nation instead of remaining content to languish under Turkish rule. He urges them to exult in the beauty of the body, recalling their Hellenic heritage. But they should not imitate ancient Greek rationalism; rather, they should be voluntarists. To try to find truth is tiresome; we

ought to *make* it. How? Not with theories but with war—whereupon he hymns strength and expands on the weakness of democracy (Dragoumis 1926).

12. Kazantzakis's activism in his nationalist period was intimately connected with the fortunes of Venizélos. Even as early as 1909, it was the public outcry against the Solomos Society for the National Language, in which Venizélos was involved in Hanyá, that determined Kazantzakis to form a similar society in Iráklion (Bien 1972a:160–161; Kaz. 1913?b). For the relationship between Venizélos and educational demoticism during Venizélos's first premiership (1910–1915) see Bien 1972a:176–183; the favorable climate channeled Kazantzakis's energies into the Educational Association and the composition of school textbooks in demotic. All this changed when Venizélos was forced to resign early in 1915 because the General Staff and King Constantine, who favored Germany, opposed the prime minister's desire to have Greece aid the Triple Entente in its efforts to capture the Dardanelles—Venizélos being motivated, of course, by his dream of reconstituting a Megáli Elláda with Constantinople as its capital. On 26 February 1915 (Old Style), Kazantzakis wrote to his sister: "Things have taken a very bad turn and Venizélos has fallen. You cannot imagine my sorrow. With him have fallen all the people who held power and were my friends. Now all are unknown to me and enemies. But that is nothing. I feel sorry for Greece, because only Venizélos was worthy of governing her . . ." (Dimos Irakliu 1961:plate following p. 32; Alexiou and Stefanakis 1977:53–54 and 1983:135–136, misdated 15–2–1915 in both cases). This explains Kazantzakis's abrupt turn, in 1915, from activism to withdrawal in order (most likely) to write a book on Mount Athos, as well as the plays *Herakles*, *Christ*, *Odysséas*, and *Nikifóros Fokás*. This is also the time when he declared "come l'uom s'eterna" to be his motto (Prev. 1965b:9). When King Constantine was forced to abdicate in June 1917 under pressure from the French, enabling Venizélos to return to Athens as prime minister, Kazantzakis did not at once resume an active involvement in political life. (In 1917 he was mining lignite with George Zorbás, perhaps to escape conscription [Anapliotis 1960:31–32]; in 1918 he was in Switzerland dreaming of founding a secular monastery for select spiritual souls [Prev. 1965b:10].) But when Venizélos appointed him to the Ministry of Welfare in May 1919 he accepted and in July of that year set out on his mission to the Caucasus, acting now as a servant of beleaguered Hellenism. In August he was in Versailles to report the results to Venizélos (Prev. 1965b:11). In the following months he supervised the refugees' resettlement in Thrace and Macedonia. In 1920, when Venizélos suffered defeat at the polls on 14 November, Kazantzakis resigned from the Ministry and on 4 December boarded a train for Paris and his first brief period of self-exile. For his fortunes after Venizélos resumed power in 1928, see Bien 1972a:194–195. Pouliopoulos 1975:38–41, 45, offers a summary of Venizélos's importance ca. 1905–1920 and of Kazantzakis's involvement with the premier. Documentation for that involvement is conveniently assembled in Stefanakis 1973.

13. Lambrídis is citing *Néoi Protopóroi*, February 1935. The material in the remainder of this paragraph and part of the next is paraphrased from Theotokas 1958.

14. This table is in the Venizélos Archive of the Benáki Museum in Athens.

15. The bibliography on the Megáli Idéa in Greek is of course immense. Some sources in English and French are Bryer 1965, 1975; Douglas 1919; Megas 1953; Nicolopoulos 1985; Theotokas 1955:103; Voyatzidis 1953. Bryer 1975 reminds us that the Great Idea predates 1453: When the exiled emperor Michael VIII Palaiologos "heard in 1261 that Constantinople had at last been retaken from the Latins . . . , [he] made a speech at the Nymphaion in which modern Greek scholars find the germ of the baleful 'Great Idea', the dream of a Byzantium restored in Constantinople. He implied that the principle of God-given autocracy required the God-given City."

16. His involvements in demoticism and educational reform are discussed at length in Bien 1972a and briefly in Bien 1972c. It is important to realize how intimately connected these linguistic and educational activities were with Kazantzakis's political vision during his nationalistic decade. For Kazantzakis and his fellow demoticists, the demotic language and tradition were the chief proof of the young nation's imaginative and intellectual vitality. Behind their emphasis on language was an assumption that as soon as the nation learned to respect its demotic tradition the directly political corollaries would follow.

17. Gounelás, disagreeing with my interpretation, has contended that the play's message is that the true leader of a society is not a single strong individual but the people collectively (Gounelas 1984:270–273, 285). The message perceived by Athenian producers, however, must have been much more threatening, since no one was brave enough to mount a production of Kazantzakis's drama even though the text had been awarded a prize. Furthermore, whereas *Ksimerónei* had been debated in the press, *O protomástoras* was more or less buried in silence, even though a full account of the play had been publicly given at the prize ceremony on 16 May 1910 and the text published a month later in the periodical *Panathínaia*, which also distributed offprints in pamphlet form. (Katsimbalis 1958a:41–42 shows us that there was a flurry of scandalized horror because the prize had been awarded to such a play. But no one discussed the play itself or as much as read it—except perhaps Palamás [Palamas 1911] and E. Voutierídis, who accused Kazantzakis of plagiarizing his own play on the same theme [Voutieridis 1911].) Kazantzakis responded furiously in an article entitled "I Ragiádes" (The Rayahs). The rayahs were now of course the critics—more broadly, the entire intellectual establishment: precisely the group that Kazantzakis had hoped would disengage itself from the sheepish herd. "The true man, " he bitterly reminded them, "likes to throw stones into stagnant water"; the rayah "crosses his arms, compromises, is afraid of noise and light" (Kaz. 1910d; excerpts from Kazantzakis's diatribe are reprinted in Papahatzaki-Katsaraki 1985:39–40). He had expected at least controversy if not praise or understanding; instead, he received indifference. Later in his career Kazantzakis was to suffer from too much vituperation; in this early episode he suffered from too little. The effect is indicated in the headnote he affixed to *Nikifóros Fokás* (whose first draft probably dates from 1915) when it was published in 1927: "This work was not written at all for the theater" (Kaz. 1927g:6; Katsimbalis 1958a:6).

18. The words of the first passage cited are placed in the mouth of Yánnis Stavridákis, but the sentiments are Kazantzakis's own. For a strong criticism of

the Dragoumian-Kazantzakian subjectivism see Lefteris Alexiou 1926, reacting to an article by Kazantzakis occasioned by the sixth anniversary of Dragoúmis's assassination (Kaz. 1926d). Alexíou complains that both Kazantzakis and Dragoúmis only pretend to work for humanity. In both cases " 'I shall save Greece' [means] 'I shall save myself.' " "Woe to the hero, " Alexíou concludes, "who rushes into heroic action not because he is filled with the belief that it is his duty to accomplish that action but in order to become a hero, to profit psychologically, to be saved."

A case in point is Kazantzakis's hero Nikifóros Fokás in the eponymous play, the first draft of which may date from 1915 but which was subsequently reworked in the 1920s and afterwards. Because of its Christian theme this play will be treated in the subsequent volume in connection with *The Last Temptation*. Here, however, we should note that Fokás begins as a kind of master builder, vibrant and assured in his service to Megáli Elláda. Yet, he is more complicated than he seems; infected by heroic pessimism, he is really a spiritual struggler more interested in personal salvation than in national progress. In the end his "activism" becomes totally internalized, taking the form of how he may die with dignity instead of running away to Mount Athos. Caught in a transitional age, he finds an exit that has personal but not political significance. If the versions of this play that we possess (Kaz. 1927g; a second edition in 1939 [Athens: Pirsos]; and the definitive version [Kaz. 1956c:323–477]) bear any relation to what Kazantzakis composed in the first draft in 1915 or thereabouts, then we can say that of all the works written during Kazantzakis's nationalistic period *Nikifóros Fokás* is the most complete in projecting the author's metapolitical politicism.

19. In 1926, as mentioned in the previous footnote, Kazantzakis wrote a tribute on the sixth anniversary of his friend's death (Kaz. 1926d; Vrettakos 1960:748). In the 1930s Dragoúmis seemed to be continually in his mind; thus we find him extolling him in 1935 as "a brilliant man full of contradictory forces and lofty anxieties" (Kaz. 1963a:166); in 1937 as the man whom Greeks should admire if they wished to create a truly neohellenic civilization (Kaz. 1965b:9, 172). In early 1940 he spoke of Dragoúmis (along with Pétros Vlastós) as one of "the two people I have most respected and loved in my life" (Kaz. 1964c:106; 1965a:107–108). Finally, in October 1940, just a few weeks before the Italian invasion, Kazantzakis dedicated a poem to Dragoúmis in which he invoked him as an Akrítas guarding the Greek race in its present danger (Kaz. 1941). We shall hear more about this poem when, in the second volume, we consider the political context of *Víos ke politía tu Aléksi Zorbá*.

20. *Komodía* (Kaz. 1958t) was published in 1909; Kimon Friar holds that it was written in 1908 (Friar 1977c:27). I shall treat this play in volume two when we consider the religious background to *The Last Temptation*.

CHAPTER TWO

1. His interest in James may have been roused by a series of lectures he followed at the Sorbonne in 1908. Given by René Berthelot, these treated Nietzsche as one of the leading forerunners of pragmatism (Kaz. 1958h:1374). It seems that Kazan-

tzakis wrote a treatise called "Pragmatism," in French, presumably in the same year, and at some point tore it up (Prev. 1965b:722; 1958:286). In December 1910 he announced tentative plans to complete an essay on James for a periodical to be brought out in Athens by the publisher Yeórgios Féxis (Yalourakis 1983:2601). The essay never materialized; yet the first text among the many that he translated for Féxis was the section called "Instinct" from James's *Principles of Psychology* (James 1890); this appeared in 1911 under the title Ἡ θεωρία τῆς συγκινήσεως (The Theory of Emotion; James 1911).

2. Kazantzakis's "quotation" is a free rendering of James's testimony in *A Pluralistic Universe*: "I have now to confess . . . that I should not now be emancipated, not now subordinate logic with so very light a heart, or throw it out of the deeper regions of philosophy to take its rightful and respectable place in the world of simple human practice, if I had not been influenced by a comparatively young and very original french [*sic*] writer, Professor Henri Bergson. Reading his works is what has made me bold. If I had not read Bergson, I should probably still be blackening endless pages of paper . . . , trying to discover some mode of conceiving the behavior of reality which should leave no discrepancy between it and the accepted laws of the logic of identity" (James 1909:214–215). James then proceeds to devote an entire chapter to "Bergson and His Critique of Intellectualism" (1909:225–273). Kazantzakis presumably read *A Pluralistic Universe* in its French translation under the title *Philosophie de l'expérience*, published in 1910. For an examination of the relation of James to Bergson see Kallen 1914.

3. The contrast between discovery and invention is used as well to form the climax of Kazantzakis's argument in the Προεισαγωγικό σημείωμα (Kaz. 1926a:137).

4. For example, in the numerous articles he sent back to Greek newspapers while he was in Paris (e.g. Kaz. 1958c; 1958q) his attitude toward French culture is shaped by what he was reading in Nietzsche; Bergson is overlooked. (Katsimbalis 1958c:1208 complains that Nietzsche's "corrosive influence" completely distorted Kazantzakis's impressions of French life and culture at the time.) Similarly, the chapter on Paris in *Report to Greco* is devoted almost exclusively to Nietzsche, with Bergson scarcely mentioned. In addition we have a newspaper article (Kaz. 1926f) that forms the basis for most of the Paris chapter in *Report to Greco* and also for the long section in *England* (Kaz. 1965a:185–198; 1965a:186–199), written at the beginning of World War II, that ends with Kazantzakis making Nietzsche approve of Hitler. Nor should we forget that Kazantzakis translated *Die Geburt der Tragödie* and *Also Sprach Zarathustra*; his versions were published by Féxis in 1912 and 1913, respectively. There are also some important remarks in the letters to Galatea Kazantzáki (Kaz. 1958a:70, 210), Eléni Samíou, Pandelís Prevelákis, and others; a terzina on Nietzsche (Kaz. 1938); and various articles (e.g. Kaz. 1958d; 1910a) and interviews (e.g. Jouvenel 1958) that are relevant. Nietzsche is invoked as well in "I epistími ehreokópise?" (Kaz. 1958h:1377) in connection with the aesthetic as opposed to ethical approach to life, and is quoted at length in Kazantzakis's piece on Flaubert (Kaz. 1913a), again in connection with the aesthetic approach being the only salvation that enables us to bear life's horror. Furthermore, there are numerous indirect references, in particular to the famous Ap-

ollonian-Dionysian duality that Nietzsche expounds in *The Birth of Tragedy*. For example, in 1910, criticizing Jean Moréas's romanticism, Kazantzakis defined the problem as the need "to express our Dionysianism classically" (Kaz. 1910b:360), a position he had already taken in 1909 with regard to Greek poets like Skípis (Kaz. 1909c). In 1925 he was happy that Mihális Kalimerákis's poems evoked a Greece that was "neither Dionysus nor Apollo, but something deeper . . ." (Kaz. 1925d). The concept took a political form as well, as when Kazantzakis claimed that Greece's mission was "na kánume lógo tin anatolítiki kravyí" ("to make reason of the oriental cry"; Kaz. 1965d:329; 1965b:171). On Kazantzakis's use of the Apollo-Dionysus terminology, see Oikonomidou 1985:124–130.

5. The question of Kazantzakis's involvement with the legal profession is examined in "O Kazantzákis nomikós" in Papathanasopoulos 1985:19–32.

6. Kazantzakis's sense of a personal affinity with Nietzsche haunted him. Among other things, he kept Nietzsche's death mask pinned to the lintel of his Athenian "cell" at Ermoú 59, relinquishing it only at the end of December 1927, wrapped in a red cloth, as a symbolic way of proclaiming that Nietzsche had been replaced by Lenin (Prev. 1958:29, 216–217; 1965b:63). Recalling a visit to the master's birthplace in Naumburg in 1923, he commented to his first wife, Galatea, that he was shaken by "the tragic face of that man who bears such an affinity to my spiritual and corporeal constitution" (Kaz. 1958a:210). In the same period, one of great loneliness and psychological struggle for Kazantzakis, he confessed more boldly still: "I fear I am of Nietzsche's quality. We'll see. Let us hope that I do not share his maladies" (1958a:70). We should not be surprised if we find the portrait of Nietzsche painted by Kazantzakis in his dissertation to be a psychological double of himself. Indeed, one of the dissertation's assets is the unintentional revelation it provides of its author's personality. (For an expansion of this view see Bien 1972d:247–252.) I should add here that Kazantzakis's first wife claims in her fictionalized biography that he read Nietzsche initially in high school (Galatea Kazantzaki 1957:22). Nietzsche's thought was well known in Greece in those years (1899–1902) and was already exerting an influence on Greek intellectuals. For Nietzsche's general influence in Greece see: George Thomson's introduction in Palamas 1969:2–12; Mousopoulos 1972:3–14; Gounelas 1977:173; 1982:46, 56 et passim; 1984:77–79 et passim; Karandonis 1958b:134; Paraschos 1956; Tziovas 1986:332–335; Hourmouzios 1948. Vrettakos 1960:41 says interestingly that Nietzsche was admired philologically rather than philosophically, an attitude confirmed in Ioánnis Zervós's review of Kazantzakis's dissertation on Nietzsche in which Zervós claims that Nietzsche is a poet and has influenced literature but that he cannot influence philosophy because he has no philosophical system (Zervos 1909).

7. The material in this and the next three paragraphs is summarized from Kaz. 1909b:5–7, 24–26.

8. Nietzsche's influence is evident throughout Kazantzakis's corpus in both style and content, the clearest example being *Askitikí*. In the *Odyssey* the entire first half is governed by Nietzsche's homeopathic negativism as the epic hero sweeps away decadent kingdoms and gods in preparation for a new table of values. The second half reflects one of Nietzsche's most important positive teach-

ings, the exaltation of art as the free play of a mind no longer constrained by fixed conceptions about the world—aptly glossed by Nehemas 1985:90–91: "Nietzsche's model for the world, for objects, and for people turns out to be the literary text and its components; his model for our relation to the world turns out to be interpretation. . . . Like an artwork, the world requires reading and interpretation, 'good philology,' in order to be mastered, understood, and made livable. The 'death of God,' both as hero and as author, allows Nietzsche to deny that the world is subject to a single overarching interpretation, corresponding to God's role or intention. And its self-creation introduces the most paradoxical view yet, the fact that the readers of this text are some of its own parts, some of its own characters, who in reading it further its self-creation." The Nietzschian element in *Víos ke politía tu Aléksi Zorbá* has been the subject of considerable comment. For example: "Zorba's actions are direct reflections of Nietzsche's ideas. . . . He is the natural born Overman who knows that 'there is . . . no true, rational, orderly, permanent, or benign universe for us' " (Merrill 1975:104). Also see McDonough 1978; Bien 1965.

9. Kazantzakis's changing attitude toward science is articulated in an interview. At first, he says, "I considered science capable of satisfying the problematism that existed in my soul." He then found, however, that it could not answer the great, eternal questions. Nor could philosophy. But in art "I discovered what I was seeking . . . because it is the only 'human method' that can . . . suddenly reveal life's mystery to human eyes" (Darakis 1935). During and after World War II, Kazantzakis worried a great deal about the deleterious effects of science. For an interesting survey of the subject of "science as deliverance" in relation to Kazantzakis, see Lea 1979:72–83. I should add that Kazantzakis's momentary attraction to scientific rationalism while he was in Paris, followed by his movement toward faith and intuition upon his return to Greece, is mirrored in the autobiographical character Kosmás in *Kapetán Mihális*.

10. Brunetière (1849–1906) was a literary critic who believed that evolution is applicable to literary genres as well as to biological species. See Wellek 1968:21.

11. On 8 December 1914, at Mount Athos, Kazantzakis noted in his diary: "Tonight I was deeply moved by Tolstoy. His tragic flight—confession of defeat . . ." (Eleni Kaz. 1977:70; 1968a:56). On 19 March 1915, at another monastery: "A young man . . . told me tonight that my face resembles Tolstoy's. This moves me, because the essence of Tolstoy's effort is my own work" (Eleni Kaz. 1977:73; 1968a:58; Prev. 1965b:7). Kazantzakis's interest in Tolstoy goes back at least to 1907, when he published an appreciation stressing Tolstoy's continuous anxiety, his inability to find a definitive explanation for the human condition, the "tragic grandeur" of his life (Kaz. 1907). In December 1910 he announced plans to write an essay on Tolstoy (Yalourakis 1970:40; 1983:730), but there is no evidence that this was accomplished. In 1917 he took a large number of Tolstoy's works with him to the Mani to study while Zorbás was mining lignite (Anapliotis 1960:30, 80). In 1923 he was reading *Anna Karenina* in the original as a way of improving his Russian (Kaz. 1958a:163)—he considered this work to be the world's most beautiful novel (Eleni Kaz. 1977:468). His thoughts on Tolstoy finally appeared

in his *Istoría tis rosikís logotehnías* (Kaz. 1930) and were incorporated in *Taksidévondas. Rusía* (Kaz. 1965e:144–150; 1989:136–141).

12. Nor does it help that the three brief references to Bergson in Kazantzakis's autobiography are contradictory. The first asserts that Kazantzakis's calmness "always returned when [he] went to hear Bergson's magical voice" after Nietzsche had upset him. Bergson's "words were a bewitching spell that opened a small door in the bowels of necessity and allowed light to pour in" (Kaz. 1964a:394; 1965c:330). Yet he found himself yearning for more anguish, which is why he says in the second reference that "Bergson's mystic salves could not heal" the wounds opened by Nietzsche (1964a:399; 1965c:333). Nevertheless, in the third reference he lists Bergson along with Homer, Buddha, Nietzsche, and Zorbás as one of his life's greatest benefactors, because he "relieved me of various unsolved philosophical problems that tormented me in my youth" (1964a:535; 1965c:445).

13. There are numerous other places where Kazantzakis invokes Bergsonism indirectly in non-Bergsonian language. One example is *Sympósion*, where "god" is hymned in effect as the *élan vital* (Kaz. 1971b:17–18; 1974:23–24); another is the passage in *Taksidévondas. Ispanía* on the role of spirit in history (Kaz. 1962b:55–56; 1963c:63). His Bergsonism is expressed in scientific language in only three instances that I know of, aside from the 1913 lecture. None of these mentions Bergson. The first is "Sizítisi m' énan arhigó" (Kaz. 1926b), where Kazantzakis argues scientifically because he is contending with a Russian positivist. The second and third are "Prosisagoyikó simíoma" (Kaz. 1926a) and "Déftero simíoma" (Kaz. 1926e), in both of which he is addressing Greek Marxists in the "scholarly manner" required by Dimítrios Glinós for the *Anayénnisi* debate. All three are in many ways rehashes of the 1913 lecture on Bergson.

14. My source for this date is Karapanayiotis 1913; cf. Katsimbalis 1958a:42, no. 812. The printed version of Kazantzakis's talk bears the date 22–1–13; this is presumably when Kazantzakis completed his manuscript. The dating is further complicated by the fact that the printed version appears in the October *1912* issue of the Educational Association's *Bulletin*. I assume that this issue was delayed and was not actually published until the winter or spring of 1913. All dates are of course Old Style.

15. See Karapanayiotis 1913. Although Bergson exerted some influence on Greek writers active ca. 1900–1910 (Paraschos 1956), his major role came after the Asia Minor disaster in connection with novelists of the 1930s like Theotokás and Xefloúdas (Mackridge 1985:4; Vitti 1977:115–120), and in the ongoing debate between Marxism and idealism (Theotokas 1958). An example of this debate is the *Anayénnisi* controversy (1926–1927), in which Kazantzakis's Bergsonism is attacked by one participant (Karouzos 1926) and defended by another (his friend Elli Lambrídi [Lambridi 1927]). We will examine these documents at the proper time. For a general discussion of Kazantzakis's Bergsonism, see Oikonomidou 1985:59–92.

16. All of his characters strive for freedom, which of course can be interpreted politically in many cases but which in all cases should be interpreted à la Bergson if we wish to understand the concept most deeply. When Aziz Izzet quite rightly states, for example, that the novel *Víos ke politía tu Aléksi Zorbá* is Kazantzakis's

"homage to his teacher Henri Bergson" (Izzet 1964:353), what he has primarily in mind is Zorbás's exhibition of the Bergsonian notion of freedom.

17. "Toute l'histoire de la vie, jusque-là, avait été celle d'un effort de la conscience pour soulever la matière . . ." (Bergson 1907:286). Note that Kazantzakis substitutes *élan vital* for Bergson's *conscience* (consciousness)—which is fine, for they are the same! Bergson's statement is of course the source of Kazantzakis's favorite dogma, the transubstantiation of matter into spirit.

18. Kazantzakis does not do justice to Bergson's famous comparison (Bergson 1911:260–261; 1907:268–269), which I reproduce here in full: "Let us imagine a vessel full of steam at a high pressure, and here and there in its sides a crack through which the steam is escaping in a jet. The steam thrown into the air is nearly all condensed into little drops which fall back, and this condensation and this fall represent simply the loss of something, an interruption, a deficit. But a small part of the jet of steam subsists, uncondensed, for some seconds; it is making an effort to raise the drops which are falling; it succeeds at most in retarding their fall. So, from an immense reservoir of life jets must be gushing out unceasingly, of which each, falling back, is a world. The evolution of living species within this world represents what subsists of the primitive direction of the original jet, and of an impulsion which continues itself in a direction the inverse of materiality."

19. Bergson says this more clearly: "Instinct is sympathy. If this sympathy could extend its object and also reflect upon itself, it would give us the key to vital operations. . . . Intelligence and instinct are turned in opposite directions, the former towards inert matter, the latter towards life. . . . [I]t is to the very inwardness of life that *intuition* leads us, —by intuition I mean instinct that has become disinterested, self-conscious, capable of reflecting upon its object . . ." (Bergson 1911:186; 1907:191–192).

20. Again, Bergson says this more clearly. As Ian Alexander writes, "Bergson has himself explained at length the function of the image in his work. As he sees it, the aim of the intuitive philosopher is to excite at each stage in his reflection corresponding intuitions in the mind of the reader. . . . '. . . No image will replace the intuition of duration, but many different images . . . will be able . . . to direct the consciousness to the precise point where there is a certain intuition to seize on' [Bergson 1946:195]. Each image, in itself revealed inadequate to the object, calls up another, initiating a continuous advance of mind towards a final term where imagination is transcended in intuition. . . . Far then from being merely decorative, Bergson's use of imagery is part of a veritable maieutic or dialectical method of communication" (Alexander 1957:17–18).

21. Homeomerous: characterized by division into equal parts.

22. Sorel, who attended Bergson's lectures, as did Kazantzakis, repeatedly invokes Bergson and considers his own methods of investigation to be Bergsonian (Sorel 1941:4, 28–29). In 1927 Kazantzakis wrote an article on Sorel and Mussolini (Kaz. 1927h). Kazantzakis's relation to Lev Shestov I will discuss when we reach the Berlin period. Shestov's antirationalist assumptions and methods are Bergsonian (e.g. his argument against the law of sequence as a crutch deluding us into the belief that we can predict the future—*savior pour prévoir* [Shestov 1920:16]).

He formed a link for Kazantzakis between Bergsonism and existentialism. Regarding Schopenhauer, Kazantzakis adds a footnote to his Bergson lecture (1912:326; 1958b:24) warning his readers not to confuse Bergson's *élan vital* with Schopenhauer's will. His summary of Schopenhauer's philosophy is available in the article he wrote for the Eleftheroudákis Encyclopedia (Kaz. 1931), and his evaluation of Nietzsche's debt to Schopenhauer is in *Taksidévondas. Anglía* (Kaz. 1964c:187–188; 1965a:189). The relation between Bergson and Schopenhauer is discussed by Baillot, who says that Bergson was one of the first to understand Schopenhauer's work (Baillot 1928:513), and that Schopenhauer's "will to life" becomes Bergson's "instinct" (1928:517). Marx and Bergson are incompatible if only because the former encourages mankind to hasten history's march along a predictable course whereas the latter considers evolution to be creative, i.e. unpredictable in the particulars of its development. We will consider Kazantzakis's complicated relationship to Marxism in due course. For a treatment of this relationship in the larger context of Bergsonism see Georgopoulos 1979.

23. Izzet 1965:107–108; Jesus "is the symbol of incessantly creative creation . . . , the purest manifestation of the 'incessantly gushing reality' of eternal creation."

24. Ayer's influential *Language, Truth and Logic* holds that metaphysical assertions are nonsensical because they fall outside the domain of verifiability. Verifiable propositions are limited to the analytic and the empirically verifiable. In the first category fall logic and mathematics, whose propositions are without factual content; in the second fall all those scientific assertions that lend themselves to empirical tests. It should be added that recent discussion tends to question the cogency of Ayer's arguments for excluding metaphysical assertions. See Macdonald and Wright 1986.

25. "There is cosmic time, there is historical time and there is existential time. . . . Existential time is not susceptible of mathematical calculation, its flow depends on intensity of experience. . . . In existential time, which is akin to eternity, there is no distinction between the future and the past, between the end and the beginning. In it the eternal accomplishment of the mystery of the spirit takes place" (Berdyaev 1952:206–207; cf. 231–232).

26. See Bidal-Baudier 1974:229–243 for an extensive comparison of Teilhard and Kazantzakis, with Bergson of course as the common denominator. She quite rightly emphasizes in her conclusion (239) "la qualité essentiellement optimiste de leur philosophie—qualité frappante après l'existentialisme. . . . [L]a mort n'est plus pour eux qu'un passage inévitable pour parvenir à l'achèvement total. . . ." For a discussion of Teilhard's animistic vitalism and how it differs from Bergson's metaphysical vitalism, see Monod 1971:31–32.

27. The central texts in Shaw's case are *Man and Superman* (1903) and *Back to Methuselah: A Metabiological Pentateuch* (1922). In the "Epistle Dedicatory" to the former, Shaw writes, for example, that "the true joy in life" is "the being used for a purpose recognized by yourself as a mighty one; the being thoroughly worn out before you are thrown on the scrap heap; the being a force of Nature instead of a feverish selfish little clod of ailments and grievances complaining that the world will not devote itself to making you happy" (Penguin edition, p. 32). Also

see Shaw's lecture reprinted as "Modern Religion II" in Smith 1963, especially pp. 74–80 on Darwin, Samuel Butler, and Bergson. Lawrence's theoretical position is encountered most easily in *Apocalypse* (Lawrence 1966:87, 199–200 for example). Woolf's *Mrs. Dalloway*, which favors intuition over intellection, is based on Bergson's opposition between duration and mathematical time.

CHAPTER THREE

1. George Seferis helps us understand why some Greeks found the murder of Dragoúmis and the fall of Venizélos to be a foretaste of the total disaster that was to come later. Arguing that Cavafy's Ὑπὲρ τῆς Ἀχαϊκῆς Συμπολιτείας πολεμήσαντες is about the Asia Minor disaster even though it was written a year before that event, Seferis says that Cavafy was among those who felt that "the real disaster . . . was the domestic collapse of 1920" (Seferis 1983:195).

2. The feelings of the Greek man-in-the-street may be indicated by none other than Yeórgis Zorbás, who wrote to Kazantzakis in unpunctuated Greek shortly before the Six were executed:

> the king is the instrument of Interests and every evil instrument You must destroy guns, canons, sharp knives and what good are they. . . .
>
> And the people . . . haven't taken care to obtain a greek-loving prime minister to see the Interests of greece that is that the people get reconciled and Delivered from Slaughter . . . (Eleni Kaz. 1977:117–118; 1968a:94–95)

3. This was not just a snap judgment made in the heat of the event. Kazantzakis repeated it several months later (1958a:128–129; 1979a:76), reaffirming his long-range faith that the massive shift in population caused by the Asia Minor disaster would enable Greece once again to "put forth artistic and intellectual blossoms." In retrospect, we know that he was right.

4. The ease with which Kazantzakis changed costume is indicated by the language he chose. An example is the nationalist slogan ὅσοι ζωντανοί, previously employed by Dragoúmis as the title of one of his most influential books and reused by Kazantzakis as a password for Greeks who understood the need for a revolutionary turnabout in their country (Kaz. 1958a:86). Quite aside from this linguistic carry-over from nationalism to communism, he conceived of the journal that "ósi zondaní" aspired to publish (1958a:71) as a revival of the *Lógios Ermís* published in Vienna in order to prepare the national uprising of 1821 (1958a:33; 1979a:51).

5. Kazantzakis held Walther Rathenau in great esteem at this time. He took pains to have one of Rathenau's books translated into Greek, and upon hearing of his assassination in June 1922 wrote to Galatea of his "love and admiration for this greatest of contemporary German writers" (Kaz. 1958a:38; 1979a:52). Although Rathenau was opposed to socialism, Kazantzakis was attracted by his attempt to achieve better relations with the Soviet Union, his antimaterialistic world-view, his analysis of the effects of mechanization on contemporary society, and his combination of an unworldly devotion to the kingdom of the spirit with advocacy of

a hardheaded reformation of capitalism that "would give the ruling elite the power to enforce its puritanical and ascetic values on the masses" (Joll 1978:942). But perhaps it was Rathenau's Bergsonism that Kazantzakis found most compelling. "Rathenau had been accused so often of plagiarizing Bergson that he felt it necessary to deny any affinity with the philosopher who, by origin and attitudes, was indeed related to him" (Pachter 1978:18).

6. Simultaneously, he attempted to place his unpublished plays *Nikifóros Fokás*, *Odysséas*, *Promethéas*, and *Hristós*, works that failed to interest him any longer owing to his "new perception." *Odysséas* eventually brought him ten British pounds, which yielded 2,500,000 Austrian crowns, easing his financial stress for a time (Kaz. 1958a:51, 53, 54, 60, 68). During this period Kazantzakis was on a retainer of 500 drachmas a month from the Athenian publisher Dimitrákos, for whom he wrote history textbooks meant for elementary school, cribbing from German texts (1958a:20, 45, 47, 68). Also, he watched the Athens stock exchange and profited from the sale of appreciated securities (1958a:36, 44).

7. These feelings return, of course, in *Alexis Zorbás*, with the significant difference that the antidote to detached intellection is now a full-fledged heroic pessimism energized by joyful Bergsonian irrationality, and is no longer a political system that from the start was at odds with Kazantzakis's deepest convictions. But very much had to intervene between 1922 and 1941 to produce the conditions enabling Kazantzakis to write such a book.

8. The English version of *Spain* translates Kazantzakis's "Felaholaoí" strangely as "debtor-races" and thus obscures the Spenglerian allusion. For parallels between Spengler and Kazantzakis, see Leontaritou 1981:29, 109–110, 144–145, 229.

9. A third thinker, Georges Sorel, must also be mentioned even though his influence is not connected primarily with Kazantzakis's sojourn in Berlin. In 1927 Kazantzakis presented Prevelákis with an edition of Sorel's *Réflexions sur la violence* (Prev. 1965b:26) soon after writing an article on Sorel's accurate prophecy regarding Mussolini and Italian fascism (Kaz. 1927a). Earlier, around 1920–1922, it was this seminal book, according to Prevelákis, that "supplied Kazantzakis with the theory which made him pass . . . from aristocratic nationalism to totalitarian socialism." Kazantzakis was attracted, Prevelákis continues, by "Sorel's utopian spirit and fanatical anti-intellectualism. . . . Let it be added that [Kazantzakis's] aversion to the counterfeit idealism of bourgeois democracy had been strengthened by the explosive argumentation of the French sociologist" (Prev. 1958:210; 1961:129). Kazantzakis also followed Sorel in his advocacy of violence as the unavoidable means for social struggle and as a salvation from bourgeois effeminacy (see Sorel 1941:90, 205–206), attitudes already familiar to Kazantzakis because they had been advocated by Dragoúmis with reference to a different struggle. More generally Sorel and Kazantzakis shared an appreciation of life as struggle, not pleasure (Sorel 1941:240–247, 272); a hatred of liberalism; a discipleship to Bergson, whose lectures in Paris both had attended; and a belief in the efficacy of sublimity, faith, and myth in motivating mass action. (When we come to "Discussion with a Leader" in Chapter Five we will see Kazantzakis invoking the Sorelian term "myth" after his assertion to a positivistic Russian communist that the masses need "a divine folly, a faith" [Kaz. 1965e:226; 1989:217].)

10. "I'm going to write it completely militantly, without any sentimental phraseology, poetry, or constraint," he added, noting that he hoped it would thus be worthy of Galatea (Kaz. 1958a:195). In the event, he changed both the contents and the style, broadening the former and opening the latter to his customary lyricism and imaginative extravagance. The revised outline for the contents became: "Half of the book, the first part, is: 'What is the course of human history; at what historical point do we find ourselves today; what is our nation's duty; what is our individual duty in the contemporary struggle?' The second part is the application of all this to the schools" (1958a:203; 1979a:97). Insofar as we know the manuscript—some excerpts did appear in installments in the Athenian periodical *O Noumás*—it seems to be a mixture of *Symposium* (both are in dialogue form) and the "Confession of Faith" prepared during Kazantzakis's activist involvement in Iráklion after he left Berlin. Note also that the pseudonymous author, Γερανός, turns up again as the main character of *Toda-Raba*. At the end of the first installment, which concerns the transition in Greece from nationalism to the need for a new ideology, Kazantzakis's mouthpiece concludes, "What is our greatest duty? To cry out, to cry out in the wilderness!" (Kaz. 1923:406). This is what Kazantzakis was doing in Berlin—precisely, since no one was listening!

11. Rosa Luxemburg became one of Kazantzakis's most admired personalities, on a level with Gorki and Lenin (Kaz. 1958a:33; 1979a:51). In Berlin he bought all of her books and planned to have many of them translated into Greek (1958a:83–84). In a 1927 tribute to her (1958e) he says that she exhibited every virtue: she had a sensitive heart and a clear theoretical mind, plus the ability to act. He especially admired her capability for transforming abstract thoughts into concrete deeds (1958e:171).

12. In *Toda-Raba*, Géranos announces: "Like Loyola . . . I, too, have my spiritual exercises. 'First degree: contemplate the entire circle, the human waves rising and falling. Second degree: concentrate all the luminous beams on the precise point of my own era. Third degree: burn it up' " (Kaz. 1962c:148; 1964f:124). In one of Kazantzakis's unpublished notebooks there is a heading: "New Askitikí. Loyola. Exercises."

13. It helps to remember that in Greek the term "abyss" (α-βυσσος) literally means "without a bottom"; the "byssos" is the floor of the sea. The word was employed in the Book of Revelation (e.g. 17:8) and subsequently came to mean the opposite of heaven, that is, the bottomless pit, hell. In *Comedy* the main theme is that heaven does not exist. For Kazantzakis, the abyss is not hell in an ethical sense, but the extinction that is our guaranteed end once we no longer believe in Christianity's afterlife of eternal bliss.

14. Kazantzakis's understanding of Schopenhauer is conveniently summarized in *Taksidévondas. Anglía* (Kaz. 1964c:187–188; 1965a:189).

15. We should not be entirely swayed by the "anti-Buddha" disclaimer affixed to *Askitikí* when it reappeared in *Le Jardin des rochers* (Kaz. 1959b:223; 1963b:186). *Askitikí* does contain Buddhistic elements (see Poulakidas 1975) even though, as I note later, it believes in matter. For Kazantzakis's understanding of Buddhism, consult his lengthy article in the Eleftheroudákis Encyclopedia (Kaz. 1928a), most

likely written in late September or early October 1927 (Prev. 1965b:43; Eleni Kaz. 1977:207; 1968a:165 [where the letter is misdated—it should be 20 September]).

16. This was no surprise to Kazantzakis, at least not by December 1926, when, speaking about the exposition of his metacommunism in "Crucified Russia," he acknowledged that it was "a big rupture with communism—not in a backward direction, of course, but terrifyingly forward. All my communist friends will be furious; those who agree will misinterpret again . . ." (Eleni Kaz. 1977:196; 1968a:155).

17. This statement clearly applies to the 1922 version. It may seem not to apply to the definitive version, which incorporates the revision that Kazantzakis made in 1928. My own view, however (as I shall argue in Chapter Five), is that the revision is still "activist" rather than nihilist.

18. Buddhist: ". . . many have proclaimed: The goal of life is death." Christian: ". . . many have proclaimed: The goal of ephemeral life is immortality." Bergsonian: "In temporarily living bodies, . . . two streams wrestle: (a) the inclination toward composition, toward life, toward immortality; (b) the inclination toward decomposition, toward matter, toward death" (Kaz. 1927f: 599; 1962a:9; 1960b:43).

19. The gamut of reactions is evident from early reviews. Vassílis Rótas scorned Kazantzakis's subjectivism, doubted that *Askitikí* preached anything but doubt, wondered why those who lose faith in God become ecstatic and hysterical, and concluded cruelly: "This Credo is nothing but lyricism. If you want to, you can sing it . . ." (Rotas 1927:175). Prevelákis compared Kazantzakis to Zarathustra descending from the mountain. He correctly identified the book's dilemma as the impossible choice between stagnant materialism and saccharine idealism, but politely refrained from judgment (Prev. 1927:177). G. N. Polítis, identifying the impossible choice once more as materialism versus idealism, went on to praise Kazantzakis for bravely attempting a synthesis. He summarized how Kazantzakis remedied the materialistic narrowness of Marxist thought, then how he avoided the nostalgia of the idealists, concluding with harsh words against the torpor that prevented such a work from stirring up the minds of Greek intellectuals (G. N. Politis 1927:440–443). Fótos Polítis was equally favorable, demonstrating that a small coterie did notice and appreciate Kazantzakis's efforts. He too lamented the general sterility of Greek intellectual life at the time (one year before Karyotákis's suicide, we should remember). He agreed with Kazantzakis's conclusions that the bourgeois are decadent, the communists ideologically narrow, and he correctly identified Kazantzakis's solution as close to Shestov's while asserting that Kazantzakis denied all forms of philosophical idealism (Fotos Politis 1927). Kléon Paráschos joined the chorus of praise, viewing the work as anticommunist and as offering vitalism to replace the cul-de-sac of idealism, especially of Pascal. He was also impressed by Kazantzakis's sincerity and by his genuine lyricism (Paraschos 1927).

20. In 1930 Grigórios Xenópoulos, then editor of *Néa Estía*, was asked to support Kazantzakis and Dimítrios Glinós when they were threatened with legal proceedings for publishing *Askitikí*, which allegedly derided the Orthodox Church. He defended them in an amusing way, writing that perhaps journalists ought to

be held responsible for deriding the Church but not a poet-philosopher like Kazantzakis, whose *Askitikí* "did not have a single repercussion on the man in the street. Those who read and understand an essay such as this are people who read, in many languages, other essays . . . and much worse!" (Glinos 1930:490).

21. When I concentrate on the *Odyssey* in Chapter Eight I shall endeavor to show that it was *not* generated out of despair.

CHAPTER FOUR

1. On his birthday, 18 February 1924, he visited Pompeii, writing to Galatea about the decadence of its inhabitants in A.D. 79 and continuing: "I felt deeply . . . that today we are living in exactly the same era at the feet of a colossal Vesuvius. I repeated over and over: God grant that I may walk in this same way through the deserted streets of Paris and London, speaking Russian to the comrades!" (Kaz. 1958a:245–246). This experience gave rise two years later to his essay "The New Pompeii" (Kaz. 1926c), in which, characteristically, he transfers the subversive wish about London and Paris to someone else, a stranger whispering in his ear. Pompeii also helped him visualize the destruction of Odysséas's ideal city in Canto 16 of the *Odyssey* (Prev. 1965b:31–32). At the same time that he dreamed of communists in control of Paris and London, he was fascinated by fascism. On first impression he found it "a great social (not just political) current," speculated that Mussolini was "much greater than what we have been accustomed to think up to now," and concluded that "Bolshevism and Fascism are the two poles around which today's Europe revolves" (Kaz. 1958a:236).

2. Mrs. Kazantzakis extends the imprisonment to "a few weeks." Page 2 of *Néa Efimerís* for 15 February 1925, however, states that Kazantzakis was detained by the police for only twenty-four hours. Perhaps he was imprisoned on two different occasions. In any case, Mrs. Kazantzakis describes the prison as "far too comfortable for his exaltation, a place where his friends came to keep him company and the guards brought him succulent dishes prepared for him by his mother" (Kaz. 1962c:ii; 1964f:205).

3. When I treat *Christ Recrucified* in the second volume I shall discuss its affinity with the Iráklion incident. Most obvious is the conflict between homeless refugees and civil authorities over access to land. Less obvious is the role of the Church—its defense of establishment values against revolutionary Bolshevism. The most direct tie with *Alexis Zorbás* is the fascinating Greek who hates the Greeks in that novel, a character whose original—a certain Ayisílaos S. Karabásis living in Tanga, East Africa—entered Kazantzakis's life because of the Iráklion incident. The antithesis of Yánnis Stavridákis, he strengthens the political interpretation of *Alexis Zorbás* that I shall be offering in volume two. For the relevant material, see Karabasis 1925.

4. *O asimvívastos* prints "Chekhov" instead of "Shestov," but Shestov seems to be right; confirmation comes in Kazantzakis's diary as reported by Prevelákis (Prev. 1965b:15). Unfortunately, Mrs. Kazantzakis cannot locate the holograph of this letter. Kazantzakis probably spelled "Shestov" as "Chestov" in the French style, making the confusion with Chekhov in transcription that much easier.

5. At Tríkkala, for example, the army had fired in order to disperse communist demonstrators, killing five workers and farmers. (*Nea Efimeris*, 4 Feb. 1925:3).

6. The problems of dating this expanded defense are discussed at length by Prevelákis (Prev. 1965b:230–231), who believes that it was prepared for the Alhambra trial sometime between 22 October 1930 and 20 June 1931, when Kazantzakis was resident in Greece. For concurrence see Pouliopoulos 1975:76. Mrs. Kazantzakis strengthens this conjecture by indicating that Kazantzakis reworked the "Confession of Faith" in June 1931 just before leaving for Paris to view the Colonial Exposition there, but she cites the impending *Askitikí* trial as the occasion (Eleni Kaz. 1977:293; 1968a:240). Dimítrios Glinós's letter to Grigórios Xenópoulos (Glinos 1930:490) proves that the *Askitikí* case was still alive in the spring of 1930, at least.

7. See Eleni Kaz. 1977:37, 141, 146; 1968a:32, 116, 117. The letter conjecturally dated September 1924 (Eleni Kaz. 1977:140; 1968a:115) should be dated no earlier than the ninth or tenth of October, since it indicates that Kazantzakis was already occupying the house in Poros, which he still had not occupied by 7 October.

8. Prevelákis reminds us (Prev. 1977:25; 1981:40) that the full body of the epic was not fleshed out until the second draft (Oct. 1929–March 1930), that is, until after Kazantzakis's traumatic experiences in the Soviet Union, his break with Istrati, and the composition of *Toda-Raba*. Charts giving the precise dates for all seven drafts appear in Prev. 1965b:724; 1958:302; 1961:177. In Chapter Eight I will discuss the problem of successive drafts in some detail.

9. As evidence we have a letter written in the autumn of 1924: Odysséas "visits Crete, Africa, the Mediterranean, encounters the ideas, women, exploits he craved, and *surpasses human limits and keeps on going, creating God with the prow of his ship*" (Eleni Kaz. 1977:146; 1968a:117; italics added). The words that I have italicized describe the epic's third part, the Nostos (cantos 16–24). Regarding the second part, the Odyssey proper (cantos 3–15), we have already seen Kazantzakis's statement that Odysséas "goes down the Nile and reaches as far as the black heart of Africa" (7 Oct. 1924). Testimonies like these, made at the moment of composition, should override testimonies after the fact such as the following from 1943 in which Kazantzakis—*who always worked from plans, notes, and research*—invents the kind of writer he would have liked to be but was not: ". . . when I created [Odysséas] . . . it wasn't the head that worked . . . but the entire . . . complex—body, mind, soul—of which I am composed. . . . I never said, 'This is what Odysséas will do or say today and he'll provide such-and-such a solution for such-and-such a personal, social, or universal problem.' Odysséas kept emerging from inside me . . . without intellectual direction . . . , almost unconsciously. I myself—i.e. my conscious self—was curious . . . to see what he would do each day and how he would behave in Ithaca, Sparta, Crete, Egypt, in the 'Exodus out of the land of Egypt,' in his new city, toward the great leaders of world-views when he found himself in front of them, and later when he faced death. For instance, would he side with vapid Menelaos whom he loved or with the coarse masses whom he felt rising and creating for life a new form and essence still unknown to him? I never knew anything in advance . . ." (Kaz. 1977a:185–

186). Such a statement tells us more about Kazantzakis's mythomania than about his working habits.

CHAPTER FIVE

1. Second sojourn: October 1925–January 1926. Third sojourn: October–December 1927. The first trip was of course the one in 1919 to the Caucasus.

2. The evidence for dating *Sympósion* is inconclusive. Mrs. Kazantzakis at first assigned the work to 1918–1920 (Eleni Kaz. 1968a:61), then revised the date to 1922, affirming that it was composed in Berlin parallel to *Askitikí* (Eleni Kaz. 1977:76–77). Prevelákis favors 1924–1925, during Kazantzakis's sojourn in Iráklion (Prev. 1965b:liii). We have a statement by Kazantzakis himself in a letter to Papastefánou from Berlin dated 5 September 1922: "I plan to finish the 'Symposium,' a book I'm writing—a commentary on our religion" (Mitsotakis 1972:55). But then he adds: "We (you, Leftéris [Alexíou], Sfakianós, Sikelianós, and two women) talk about God." So this was not the *Symposium* that he eventually wrote. Reference in *Symposium* to the house by the seashore and inclusion of Míros, whom Kazantzakis saw while he was in Crete in 1924–1925, make us lean toward Prevelákis's view. Yet the similarity of the material on Dragoúmis in *Symposium* to Kazantzakis's 1926 tribute to his former guru (Kaz. 1926d) is perhaps an indication of later revisions, as is the passage in which Arpagós recalls an experience when he was three years old and comments, "Even now, forty years later . . ." (Kaz. 1971b:49; 1974:50)—3 + 40 years from 1883, Kazantzakis's birthyear, gives 1926.

3. This identification is disputed by Elli Alexíou (Alexiou and Stefanakis 1983:170–171).

4. The full course of the Kazantzakis-Sikelianós relationship is described most authoritatively in Prevelákis's chronicle of their friendship (Prev. 1983). What interests us here is only the rupture that Kazantzakis felt after his exposure in Vienna and Berlin to the European ideological crisis. This rupture is revealed in his letters to Galatea: "Huge ferment here; soon we'll have disaster and resurrection . . . [Then about Sikelianós and his circle:] they're . . . still living an idyll, chewing as cud the eternal sweets of blossoming meadows. . . . Good god, they should come here to see the . . . true . . . springtime" (Kaz. 1958a:38–39; 1979:52). ". . . I wrote Sikelianós that our paths have now altered; we can no longer travel together. His life strikes me as false, out of keeping with the times" (Kaz. 1958a:176; 1979:88; cf. Eleni Kaz. 1977:113; 1968a:91; Prev. 1983:11). "His gods, Apollo . . . [and] Christ, do not interest me at all" (Kaz. 1958a:247).

5. Angelos Terzákis, in a lengthy review of *Sympósion* (Terzakis 1972), suggests that Míros—who complains, "I cried out at night, roamed the whole world knocking on God's door and screaming: 'Open up. I am a human being! Not an ant for you to trample!' . . . But no one answered" (Kaz. 1971b:13–14; 1974:18–19)—should be compared to the (unnamed, Karyotákis-like) Greek poet who wrote: "I knocked once on death's door, / I knocked twice on life's door, / On both the upper and lower doors, / But in no door did anyone hear me." What this suggestion makes us recall is that Kazantzakis was not alone in Greece, or else-

where, in registering a metaphysical vacuum. Compare for example the declaration of Thomas Mann's narrator in *The Magic Mountain* (published in 1924): ". . . if the life about [a man] . . . seem . . . hopeless, viewless, helpless, opposing only a hollow silence to all the questions man puts, consciously or unconsciously, . . . as to the final, absolute, and abstract meaning of all his efforts and activities; then, in such a case, a certain laming of the personality is bound to occur . . ." (Mann 1963:32).

6. In Eleni Kaz. 1968a:128 the letter in misdated as 16 October 1925. It should be 10 October. Kazantzakis left on the thirteenth. The following letter should be dated 16 October, not 25 October. Information on the planned trip to Africa is available in a series of letters Kazantzakis wrote to Andónis Anemoyánnis in Athens asking him to expedite the arrangements. In its final stage of planning, the itinerary included Cyprus and Palestine as well as Egypt and Sinai, whereupon Kazantzakis made a last-minute request for Tanga, East Africa—perhaps to visit the Greek-who-hated-the Greeks! (Dimakis 1979:65–68).

7. Kazantzakis's opportunity came through the good offices of Kóstas Ouránis, editor-in-chief and publisher of the newspaper *Eléftheros Lógos,* who personally negotiated with the Soviet Embassy in Athens to get permission for Kazantzakis to go. Ouránis (the penname of Kóstas Néarchos) lived from 1880 to 1953. He traveled extensively in Europe and published travel articles in *Eléftheros Típos* from 1919 to 1923, and in *Eléftheron Víma* in 1928ff. Some books came out later, for example, one on Sinai in 1944 and another on Greece in 1949. The posthumously collected edition of his works includes five volumes of *Taksídia*. The literature of travel, a genre unknown in Greece until inaugurated by Ouránis, was in effect created for Greek letters by Kazantzakis, building on Ouránis's initiative (Markakis 1959a:40). We should remember that until *Víos ke politía tu Aléksi Zorbá* appeared in Greece in 1946, Kazantzakis was appreciated in his own country almost exclusively as a travel writer, having published by then Taksidévondas for Spain, Italy, Egypt, Sinai, Russia, Japan, China, and England. *Askitikí, Odíssia,* and the available plays were known only to the smallest of coteries.

8. Some examples: "In Moscow's Snow-Covered Streets," "Bolshevism in Theory and Practice," "The Dictatorship of the Proletariat," "Communist Propaganda Having Failed in Europe Has Turned Toward Asia," "Russian Communism and English Imperialism in the Boundless and Primitive Asian Expanses," "The Role of the Jews in the Communist Revolution," "The Bolsheviks' 'New Economic Political Line,' " "How Commerce Operates in Bolshevik Russia," "The Ownership of Real Estate Under the Bolshevik Régime," "Communism and Women," "Communism and the Family," "How the Ministry of Health Works in Moscow," "Schooling of the Bolsheviks—We Want Fighters, Not Scholars," "The Christian Religion's Heart-Rending Anguish," "Bolshevik Propaganda Against Religion," "The Red Army" (Katsimbalis 1958a:18–19).

9. *Anayénnisi* commented, for example, that Kazantzakis's impressions were "written in a very lively and descriptive manner in the demotic language and have the advantage of being objective and unprejudiced" (*Anayennisi* A:116).

10. I cite the original version published in the September 1926 issue of *Anayénnisi,* because this is what Greece's communist intellectuals read and rebutted.

The version reprinted in *Taksidévondas. Rusía* includes expansions and also verbal revisions, making a comparison of it with the original text a good exercise for anyone interested in Kazantzakis's working methods. In the part discussed so far, for instance, there is in the reprinted version a substantive addition in which Kazantzakis bolsters his objection to the Russians by invoking the Kantian critique of pure reason before using the Bergsonian analysis of time. In addition, in the paragraph devoted to Bergsonism there are revisions that clarify the argument by adjusting the syntax and adding a key word or two.

11. We should note that although Kazantzakis did not allow others to posit absolute laws governing "vital phenomena," he posited his own! Ch. Karoúzos, to his credit, mentions this (along with much else that hurts) in the rebuttal that we shall consider shortly: "Kazantzakis himself attempts to formulate . . . a law for when economic causes prevail and when other 'deeper impulses' do, a law totally false and arbitrary, of course—which nevertheless shows him unconsciously believing in the uniformity of social phenomena" (Karouzos 1926:139). Cf. E. Lagákos, who observes that Kazantzakis abrogates his own argument against laws governing social phenomena "since the denier himself. . . establishes a sovereign law that in every historical period can bring about a transition in the higher forms of society's communal life," namely the law decreeing that only blood, misfortune, and hunger can engender the saving Word (Lagakos 1927:552).

12. He could keep calling himself a communist for a pair of reasons that enabled him to have things both ways. On the one hand he saw himself serving the comrades' deepest interests by urging them away from narrowly conceived materialism, while on the other he acknowledged the efficacy of narrowness in the struggle's initial stages, going so far as to end his "Discussion with a Leader" by admitting that it is correct for these fanatical Russians to carry out their "cruel duty as forerunners . . . without a clear view of the complete circle" because the only way the "saving Word" will be born is via blood, misfortune, and hunger (Kaz. 1926b:24).

13. "The New Pompeii" begins with Kazantzakis's wish that decadent London and Paris will one day suffer the same fate as Pompeii—a thought that he places in the mouth of a fictional companion (Kaz. 1926c:76). This leads to a meditation on the inevitability of the undertrodden rising against the overfed. Next, Kazantzakis counters the argument of "dreamers" that we should return to a former simplicity. This is romanticism. Life never turns back. Today's alienated worker can never become a medieval artisan. He has no outlet: Christianity's promise of an afterlife is nonsense. So, gradually, the proletarian masses develop new values, a new decalogue that no longer honors hearth, marriage, country, family (Kaz. 1926c:79). Their only hope is in solidarity with others who are similarly oppressed. As for satisfied peasants who are still attached to country and property, they must be obliterated. Our duty must be uncompromising war against the bourgeoisie. We must collaborate with the dark, dirty proletariat even though they will commit injustices like the others, once they achieve power. Yet it is in them that the *kravyí* of the Invisible resides today, although they themselves are incapable of knowing this, and call it happiness, justice, equality, peace. "But the

invisible Struggler, allowing these decoys to entice and encourage the masses, is cruel and pitiless in his battle to surpass this flesh in order to create out of all the contemporary cries of hunger and wrath a Word [lógos] of freedom" (Kaz. 1926c:80).

14. The "Prosisagoyikó simíoma" (Kaz. 1926a) also constitutes a perfect gloss for the *Odyssey* and for *Buddha*, since in both of these works the entire substance so meticulously crafted is revealed to be a fiction spun out by a mind which, when it expires, erases everything it has created.

15. It is important to keep stressing how much of Kazantzakis's thought is pure Bergsonism. The "Second Note" is virtually a précis of Section 1 of his 1913 lecture. As for Section 2 of the lecture, it provides the argumentation about cause and effect that Kazantzakis applied to social phenomena in "Discussion with a Leader." For example, "For the physicist, the same cause always yields the same effect; for the impartial psychologist, however, a deep internal cause gives rise to its effect once only, and never again . . . ," etc. (Kaz. 1912:320). As for Karoúzos, he was given an opportunity to rebut both of Kazantzakis's notes. He objected to the notion of fiction in the "Introductory Note," correctly identifying this notion with the "fashionable philosophy . . . of 'as if' " and with Sorel's "myth" (Karouzos 1927:267–268). (Note: When Kazantzakis revised his "Discussion with a Leader" for *Taksidévondas. Rusía*, he introduced the Sorelian term at the end, after his assertions that the masses need "a divine folly, a faith," and that the Russian's theories are incapable of affecting human history. "What do they lack?" the Russian asks. "Myth" [Kaz. 1965e:226; 1989:217]. This is only one example of the way in which Kazantzakis employed key words that must be related to the source that brought them into his vocabulary if we are to understand them fully.) Continuing with Karoúzos, he used the same occasion to respond to the criticisms of Elli Lambrídi, who had protested against "the unfounded dogmatism in Mr. Karoúzos's polemical study, which may mislead the unprepared reader of *Anayénnisi* into accepting certain implied propositions found therein . . ." (Lambridi 1927:265). Among these is the absolute faith in science, whereas "the most productive scientists in all fields are those who recognize science's limits and know that its furthest roots are always hypotheses that are unsupported yet useful" (Lambridi 1927:266). To this, Karoúzos replied that the trouble with idealists is that "they never deign to examine the relation between their pronouncements and the historical moment of the society from which they emerged" (Karouzos 1927:269). Mrs. Lambrídi's problem is "her belief in the Bergsonian division of time into quantitative and qualitative" and, based on this, her denial of the similarity between phenomena of the inorganic world (physical) and the biological, which she says includes the social, whereas the "scientifically proved truth is that quality is never something independent of quantity . . ." but is causally linked to it (270). Finally, the indefatigable Karoúzos felt obliged to reply to K. Yeorgoúlis, who wrote in from Kalamata that Karoúzos came close to "elevating historical law into a wonder-working being. . . . His understanding . . . is totally mechanistic . . . and he dreams of the kingdom of some social mechanism whose equations will solve sociological problems" (Yeorgoulis 1927:267). To this, Karoúzos replied that to talk about future kingdoms of social mechanism is to indulge in

metaphysical games. "A basic principle of every discussion is that we should not play with words" (Karouzos 1927:271).

16. For example, in November 1926, *To Víma* refused to employ him as a correspondent "because I'm a communist" (Eleni Kaz. 1977:194; 1968a:154).

17. "If we think of . . . the fall of Fascism, an unsuccessful war . . . , [and] if we consider the hatred that will break out between the former Fascists and the new class that wants to gain power, then we can assert that Mussolini is truly the best carrier of communism" (Eleni Kaz. 1977:190).

18. What interested him in fascism is further clarified in his conclusions about Primo de Rivera's dictatorship in Spain, where he had been just prior to his sojourn in Italy: "I was looking for Fascism in Spain but I did not find it. I found militarism. Fascism is a system of accountable answers to all the problems of mankind's political and social life in community. It abrogates the citizens' small liberties because it believes that only in this way will it save the large liberties of the whole. Militarism is the abrupt intervention of unaccountable and uninformed soldiers who abhor liberty, small and large, because they abhor the spirit" (*Eleftheros Tipos*, 7 Jan. 1927).

19. Of the fifteen articles, Kazantzakis kept for *Taksidévondas. Italía* only the last three: the one of 22 February describing the seven hundredth anniversary of Saint Francis's death as celebrated by the Black Shirts, the one of 25 February recounting his interview with Mussolini, and some portions from the concluding article (28 February), combined now with the interview. The other twelve appeared under the following headings: "A higher rhythm—something deeper than discipline issuing from the central idea of a strong man—rules Italy today and has governed it successfully for some years." "A 1912 prophecy by Sorel concerning Mussolini. Fascism the fruit of Italy's internal needs and not a haphazard eruption of violence or megalomania." "The adventurous story of Benito Mussolini. A tempestuous life full of difficult struggle and action." "The 52 people forming the initial core of Fascism. A supremely vigorous spirit instead of another program. Actions first and program later." "Essence of Fascism is a religion of fatherland. The state's all-powerful imposition." "Differences between Fascism and nationalism. Internal reorganization the basis. Even religion a national force." "Fascism and liberal democracy. The conflicting principles of the French Revolution." "Fascism the embodiment of all tendencies. The concept of the individual and the state. War against former theories." "Fascism and class war. Harmonization of capital and labor. Neither the right to strike, nor lock-out." "Italy too small to contain the Italians. Mussolini's foreign policy. How can an excessively vital organism be restrained?" "Results of Fascism. Discipline without military rule." "What Mussolini's opponents say. They accuse him of being violent and medieval. What they acknowledge in him and what they dispute" (Katsimbalis 1958a:22).

20. In addition, the interview inaugurates the leitmotif of Mussolini's "huge primitive jaw" (Kaz. 1965d:22; 1975:17; cf. 1965d:16; 1975:10). We should remember this when we come to the Big-Jawed Man in *Toda-Raba*—clearly Mussolini in part (cf. Prev. 1965b:136). More importantly, the antithesis between everything Francis of Assisi represents and everything represented by Mussolini's

Black Shirts enters the novel Ο φτωχούλης του Θεού in that Brother Elias, the saint's antithesis, is also distinguished by a huge lower jaw (Kaz. 1956d:235; 1962d:240).

21. "When the first nucleus met in Milan to draw up a programme it proposed vast and almost subversive reforms: workers' participation in the management of industry, partial expropriation of wealth by means of special taxes, confiscation of goods belonging to religious congregations, and almost total seizure of the profits of war" (Vita-Finzi 1968:228–229). One reason is that the origins of fascism included syndicalism and, indeed, Marxism (see Gregor 1979).

22. Stravinsky performed willingly under Mussolini's patronage and was proud to have been granted forty-five minutes of the dictator's valuable time. "I told him that I felt like a fascist myself. Today, fascists are everywhere in Europe" (quoted in Craft 1978).

23. Prevelákis, in one of the very few errors in his chronology, specifies the end of December 1926 (Prev. 1965b:19). But the letters (Eleni Kaz. 1977:198–199; 1968a:156–158) clearly show Kazantzakis still trying to arrange the journey in mid-January 1927, and departing on the twenty-third of that month.

24. For example, when writing to Eléni Samíou about the sandstorm that he encountered on his return from Mount Sinai, Kazantzakis commented, "The camel stumbled this way and that; the sand beat on my face and hands, wounding them. And I loved it, because Odysséas should experience this sensation" (Eleni Kaz. 1968a:161–162). Probably the largest benefits reaped by the epic from the Egyptian trip resulted from (a) Kazantzakis's research concerning the age-old mystery of the source of the Nile (Kaz. 1965d:37–38; 1975:31–32) and (b) his tour of the tombs of the Pharaohs in Upper Egypt, where he was enchanted by the sickly, effeminate King Ikhnaton and his queen, Nefretete, the subjects of his article of 8 April (Kaz. 1965d:59–60; 1975:55–56). These are the rulers whom Odysséas and others attempt to overthrow in cantos 10 and 11 of the *Odyssey*.

25. The identification is made in Elli Alexiou 1966:315. We have already encountered Mrs. Lambrídi in the *Anayénnisi* controversy. She was on Kazantzakis's mind throughout this period. His article called "Mudíta and I"—evoking her interests in Russia, educational reform, and feminism—appeared in *Eléftheros Típos* on 4 July 1926; his play *Nikifóros Fokás*, published in 1927, is dedicated to her; she translated *Askitikí* into English in the same year (Eleni Kaz. 1977:207; 1968a:165). In 1939 there was destined to be an important exchange between her and Kazantzakis on the "Metaphysics of the *Odyssey*." She and Kazantzakis had had a brief affair in 1918 (Prev. 1965b:10; Eleni Kaz. 1977:86–88; 1968a:69–70). In Kazantzakis's play *Buddha*, Mudíta is the woman who stands next to Buddha and cools him with a fan (Kaz. 1956e:538; 1983:51). In one of his notebooks containing sketches for a film scenario on Buddha, there is a planned scene of love between Mudíta and Buddha. Lambrídi was a professional philosopher. Her publications include *Die Erkenntnisprinzipien bei Aristoteles* (Leipzig, 1919; Theory of Knowledge in Aristotle); *O Bergson ke i filosofía tu* (Athens, 1929; Bergson and His Philosophy); *La Poésie grecques des cinquante dernières années* (Belgrade, 1937; Greek Poetry of the Last Fifty Years); *Filosofía ke logotehnía* (Athens, n.d.; Philosophy and Literature).

26. He requested Mussolini and fascism as well, but did not get them (Prev. 1965b:43). All in all, he published 174 articles in the Encyclopedia (Katsimbalis 1958a:31–37), but Preveláκis says that he wrote still others that remained unpublished or appeared anonymously (Prev. 1965b:43). Many were cribbed from the Encyclopedia Britannica (Prev. 1965b:50–51), yet Kazantzakis aspired to add something of his own to subjects that interested him. Witness his comments on one of the articles that never got published. He is reacting to certain anticommunist measures recently imposed by the Greek government (Prev. 1965b:53): "I've written half of the article on Lenin, but unfortunately it's going to be entirely filled with biography and events. I'll be able only minimally—and will I be allowed?—to insert my own views about his central attributes" (Prev. 1965b:53).

27. Seven of these ten articles were eventually printed (Katsimbalis 1958a:23–24), each preceded by an editorial disclaimer announcing that *Proïa* did not share its correspondent's views and emphasizing in boldface type that "the Soviet régime is the repudiation of all individual liberty and the enslavement of 140 million by 300,000 communists" (*Proïa* 1928).

28. In Cyprus, Kazantzakis spoke for two hours to a meeting of the Labor Center of Limassol, describing "with enthusiasm . . . the life of the working class [in Russia], the happiness that is beginning to enter poor homes, the brotherhood and justice that exists there." He arrived on 28 May 1926 and departed on 3 June. The effect of his presence in encouraging the city's laborers is described in Haravyi 1980.

29. Could Kazantzakis have known Lenin's almost identical sentiments, written on Armistice Day, 11 November 1918, and published in the Swiss journal *Sotsial Demokrat*? "War," wrote Lenin, "is no accident and no 'sin' as the Christian reverends think. . . . War is an inevitable part of capitalism. . . . It is simply insane to talk about abolishing capitalism without a frightful civil war and without a succession of such wars. . . . The only duty of Socialists, when an imperial war breaks out between the bourgeois classes of different nations, is to transform this war between nations into a war between classes. Down with the sentimental hypocritical slogan 'Peace at any price.' Long live the civil war" (Field 1975:50, citing D. Shub, *Lenin* [New York, 1951], 136).

30. We also have Istrati's account of the same meeting. Kazantzakis entered the room, "a tall man, bony, . . . took off his coat. . . . I asked him to sit on my bed, since we were already intimate. Then I noticed that this man had a head like a bird of prey's, . . . the eyes of a great horned owl, perfectly round, but black, . . . a mouth blending sensuality and renunciation. . . . There was no touch of docility in this man. He must have known this, because sometimes his speech . . . becomes unctuous, insinuating, while he leans over you like a tree-trunk and pries into you with a fiercely intelligent look. . . . He speaks an unconstrained French without affectation and almost faultless; more correct in any case than mine. He steers our conversation to his own liking. . . . At the end of this first encounter, according to a habit I discovered in him later, he takes aim at me with his forefinger at the same time that his eyes, laughing, lean over mine and his lips spell out: 'Tell me what you love the most!' Then I fling at him from the depths of my being, 'I love to believe everything.' He snaps up my answer, accepts it, and com-

pletes it with his own thought: 'Yes, to believe everything. But without counting on anything—don't ever forget that; otherwise we're lost!' " (Istrati 1928b).

31. All this time Istrati was in an advanced stage of tuberculosis. He died of the disease in 1935. See Raydon 1968. For a recent retrospective appreciation, see Geblesco, Talex et al. in *L'Arc* (Paris), numbers 86–87 (1983). Nemoianu 1984 gives a sensitive analysis of his career, work, and reputation. His eccentricities are amusingly conveyed by Mrs. Kazantzakis (Eleni Kaz. 1977:247–248; 1968a:198–199).

32. Upon leaving Odessa for Greece, the two friends drafted a statement:

> Goodbye, U.S.S.R.!
>
> The moment we are embarking in Odessa . . . we send filial greetings to thee, Union of free peoples!
>
> We say "we" because we are two—two men, two friends, two combatants, converted into . . . the Dioscuri of creative love for a new life.
>
> Thou, Russia, hast realized this miracle. We were alone. We hardly knew of each other before meeting a month ago in this ardent land. . . . And from that day onward—illumined by the splendor of thy face, new Russia—we swore to serve thee. Such will be our *raison d'être* in the future.
>
> Nothing will stop us. . . . We shall do as thou didst, two invincible units of the force that thou hast unleashed in the world. We are sure that the future will be thine because thou art already the future. . . .
>
> We shall be covered with injuries. This is what has always happened since the beginning of the world. But our Biblical poverty and the violence of our faith will shield us.
>
> We already know that many doors will be closed to our passage. So much the better, for then we shall speak in the streets. And if the prisons open their gates to receive us, there too shall we cry out:
>
> "Long live the Union of free peoples!" (Eleni Kaz. 1938:27–29; Prev. 1958:322–323 [in part]).

As they were departing, the Dioscuri also sent a letter to Stalin by registered mail. He did not answer. According to Istrati's memory, it ran: "Behold two men who are burning their bridges behind them (as for me, I never had any to burn). We wish to devote ourselves to the proletarian cause. . . . We have the wherewithal to live and ask nothing from you. But we want your legitimate cooperation, so that all doors will be opened to us and so that we can see everything. . . . To demonstrate our sincerity to you, we are now on our way to Greece to cry out our enthusiasm for what we have seen in the U.S.S.R. Then we shall return to live, learn, and struggle" (Istrati 1929a:120).

33. Istrati's fame had reached Athens after Romain Rolland had called him the Gorki of the Balkans. Emile Hourmoúzios's translation of *Kyra Kyralina* came out in 1925, followed by Galatea Kazantzáki's of *Oncle Anghel* in 1928. The celebrated vagabond was flooded with invitations to aristocratic salons, where he charmed the matrons by appearing in high hunting boots and tight pistaccio-colored breeches; even bourgeois newspapers opened their columns to him (Vrettakos 1960:139–140, 752; Eleni Kaz. 1977:222–223; 1968b:177; Prev. 1958:322; Istrati 1929a:124).

34. Characteristically, he added that these two advocates of seemingly antithetical policies are unknowing collaborators on a deeper level. "Stalin, without Trotsky's violent lashing, would perhaps give in more to the vigorous pressure of the kulaks and nepmen. Trotsky, if he had power, would be dangerous because of the impetuosity of his style. Together—the one as action, the other as counteraction—they create a . . . daring compound" (Kaz. 1928b:196–197). He seemed unaware that Trotsky had been expelled from the Central Committee on 16 November 1927, from the Party soon afterward, and exiled in January 1928. However, he was definitely aware of Trotsky's difficulties as an opposition leader, since he had heard him booed as he tried to speak against Stalinist policies during the tenth-anniversary celebrations (Kaz. 1965e:203; 1989:195).

35. At the preliminary hearing, which took place on 16 January, the police produced one witness to identify Glinós as the organizer, a second to certify that according to information at his disposal Messrs. Kazantzakis and Istrati were Russian spies, and a third (Alexander Embiríkos-Koumoundoúros, M.P., a poet who wrote ditties in French [*Anayennisi* B:453]) to testify that Istrati's writings had no literary merit and that they constituted vulgar insults against the Greek and Rumanian peoples (*Anayennisi* B:380). The accused requested a forty-eight-hour respite, which was granted, during which time, they declared, they would indite lengthy defenses and submit them to the public prosecutor (*Proïa*, 17 Jan. 1928:6)—Kazantzakis of course already possessed as a basis for his defense the document he had prepared for the trial in Iráklion. The following day the police chief renewed his request for Istrati's deportation, demanding punishment as well for the Greek Consul who had granted him a visa (*Proïa*, 18 Jan. 1925:6). But the Ministry of the Interior preferred to let the trial take place first and then decide (*Proïa*, 21 Jan. 1928:6). On 8 March Kazantzakis wrote to Eléni Samíou that the trial had been set for 3 April. "There are two tendencies: the judges want to give the trial lots of oomph for publicity's sake and to find us guilty; the politicians want a quick and noiseless end to a case that is not in their best interests. Which of these two tendencies will win out we shall see. We're ready for both. We are not going to give provocation of any kind, but if we are provoked we shall voice our convictions with firmness" (Eleni Kaz. 1977:225; 1968a:179).

36. As background, it is important to know that six weeks earlier there had been clashes between communists and the police, who broke up communist assemblies outside of Parliament. This led to the effort to expel all communist deputies from Parliament. A huge protest was scheduled for 18 December 1927 in Sýntagma Square despite the government's warning that it would call out the army. The assembly took place and was dispersed by the police (Bastias 1927:72). Here is a summary of the debate on Istrati as reported in *Proïa* (31 Jan. 1928:5):

"Merkoúris: The question of Istrati is very serious since it involves the general government policy against communism." How come the government "leaves the doors of the country open to every tramp!" How come a minister accompanied Istrati to Lávrion?

Papanastasíou denies that Istrati accompanied him.

"Merkoúris: Yet you invited him to tea in your home."

"Papanastasíou: That is true."

Merkoúris delivers a long speech on the communist menace, ending, "Beneath the eyes of the authorities . . . there is the so-called Leninist school."

"Máximos: Do you know if there is also a Fascist school?"

"Merkoúris: No, and I'll be happy if there is; it will protect the bourgeois class. . . ."

"Papanastasíou: Both schools use the same means and methods."

"Merkoúris: Don't try to confuse royalism and communism."

"Papanastasíou: They're first cousins."

Merkoúris continues to complain that while one minister is striving to combat communism another invites communists to tea.

Papanastasíou explains that his invitation was a gesture of "respect for the endurance of the human spirit, because this man manages . . . to preserve moral law undiminished." (Shouts from the Right: No! No!) Papanastasíou says he will cite a critic as proof. Shouts: What critic? Papanastasíou: Romain Rolland. General uproar. Papanastasíou: Be quiet. He reads Rolland's praise, and continues, "We must learn to honor men of ethical worth in our land even if they are our opponents. [Applause from the Center.] . . . Do not imagine that we shall put down communism by means of imprisonment and decrees of banishment to the islands. We ought to enlighten the workers concerning the consequences of communism from the workers' point of view, not just from the bourgeois point of view . . ."

"Tsaldáris: The workers, too, are bourgeois. . . . The Minister of Agriculture invited Mr. Istrati in order to admire his spiritual strength and on its account served him a luxurious tea."

"Papanastasíou: I object! It was not luxurious! . . ."

37. For example, Mrs. Kazantzakis says that the Alhambra trial was eventually canceled (Eleni Kaz. 1977:226).

38. Istrati answered obligingly: "Dear traveling companion: For the first time I've received words from you that I expected a long time ago, words that reflect your soul. . . . To write and express yourself with such force, with such precision, is to defeat death and to triumph in life. I want to be able to embrace you this instant. Come quickly" (Eleni Kaz. 1938:121).

39. Poulakidas 1975:209–210 cites Coomaraswamy 1916:354–355: "*Nibbana* (*nirvana*): ethically, the dying out of lust, resentment, and illusion; psychologically, release from individuality. The Recognition of Truth. A state of salvation to be realized here and now. . . . *Nibbana* is one of many names for the *summum bonum*; it may be best translated as Abyss, Stillness, Void, or Nothing (not-thing-ness). . . ." Cf. Poulakidas 1975:216, citing Coomaraswamy 1916:117: "The literal meaning of the word Nibbana is 'Dying out,' or 'extinction,' as of a fire. . . . The salvation of the . . . saint, then, is the dying down—Nibbana—of the flames of lust, hate, and glamour, and of the will to life. Nibbana is just this, and no more and no less."

40. Kazantzakis's attention to Schopenhauer's *Die Welt als Wille und Vorstellung* was intense in Paris while he was studying Nietzsche and Bergson. He returned to the German pessimist near the time of *Askitiki*'s revision because he had to write the relevant article for the Eleftheroudákis Encyclopedia—we have notebook entries showing him reading secondary sources. In his encyclopedia article

he explains that for Schopenhauer the world is an Idea or Representation (*Vorstellung*) "that includes both subjective and objective." We cannot go beyond this Representation to any other center or essence. "The deep understanding of life's vanity . . . unites us and identifies us with all beings; we must undo our individuality and egotism. Thus the unconscious will, . . . evolves into consciousness for the first time in the human being, apprehends life's suffering and turns . . . to annihilation, uprooting the will to life" (Kaz. 1931:618–619).

41. Although Kazantzakis took pains in his essay on Bergson to differentiate the *élan vital* from Schopenhauer's Will (Kaz. 1912:326), Bergson clearly "fait du 'vital' et du 'voulu' des termes synonymes, et le principe vital n'est pas autre chose que le 'pur vouloir' " (Baillot 1928:516).

42. Especially compatible is Meister Eckhart's effort to perceive a positive and nontragic concept of nothingness. What is achieved by it is a saintly peace, as seen in Eckhart's sermon "In all things I have sought peace." The final experience of nothingness occurs when Eckhart prays that God (= nothingness) may quit him of God. Also relevant are *The Cloud of Unknowning*, by an unknown English mystic, and the writings of Saint John of the Cross. For a (somewhat elementary) survey of Western mysticism see Evelyn Underhill's *The Mystics of the Church* (New York: Schocken, 1964). Although we tend to think of Western theology as kataphatic, the apophatic approach is also represented in the Western tradition.

43. Kazantzakis was entirely at home in this tradition. His notebooks show him reading Symeon the New Theologian, for example, as well as his favorite, Nikólaos Kavásilas (Nicholas Cabasilas), a "well-beloved figure" whose "marvelous book" *The Life in Christ* he had pored over one night in his cell in a monastery on Mount Athos (Kaz. 1965d:211; 1965b:31).

44. So far as I am aware, only one commentator, Aziz Izzet, suspected that Kazantzakis's ending might need further interpretation, and he is tantalizingly brief. What is meant by "Even this one does not exist"? he wonders. It is that "this ONE is neither God nor the conception that we have of him, but rather man's heart in its 'minuscule area of freedom' " (Izzet 1965:104). If Izzet had been reading apophatic theology or Zen masters, he might have elaborated. Another commentator does invoke apophatic theology when he comes to the silence in his running account of *Askitikí*, but merely to suggest, without expanding, that only an enlightened heart employing such a theology could possibly solve the perplexities that Kazantzakis creates (Tsiropoulos 1977:177).

45. Kazantzakis preferred to divide his system into four degrees of initiation, as in "An Open Letter for Mrs. Elli Lambrídi," just cited, and in the formulation ending with "(4) exodus from exodus" (Mitsotakis 1972:94; Kaz. 1979a:36). However, in the letter that had provoked Papastefánou's remonstrance, Kazantzakis had specified only three degrees: "In the first degree of initiation we say: We shall win. The good shall win. In the second degree we say: Winning and losing, good and evil, above and below, beginning and end, matter and spirit, are simplistic differentiations imposed by the intellect." He had then gone on to conclude: "I cannot tell you what we say in the third and highest degree . . ." (Mitsotakis 1972:76–77; Kaz. 1979:32).

46. The precise itinerary is given in Prevelakis 1958:223–224; 1961:136. The trip with its ensuing crisis is described at length in Eleni Kaz. 1938.

47. For the plans in various stages see Eleni Kaz. 1977:240; 1968a:192; Prev. 1965b:84, 89. Kazantzakis's introduction, meant for *Les Nouvelles Littéraires*, is reproduced in its entirety in *Toda-Raba*, attributed to Géranos (Kaz. 1962c:137–143; 1964f:116–120), and in Eleni Kaz. 1938:98–104. Despite its hyperbolic tone, it is one more excellent summary of his political position in general and of his relationship to Bolshevism in particular. In *Toda-Raba*, written of course after the break with Istrati, Kazantzakis adds: "A few months later when Géranos re-read the manifesto, he smiled sadly. How pure man's intentions could be! How superhuman the first upsurge [le premier élan] could be, as if materiality—cowardice, laziness, habit—did not exist!" (Kaz. 1962c:144; 1964f:121).

48. In an interview given shortly after his return to Paris, Istrati treats this same prison in a completely positive way. The system, he says, proves how "par des moyens civilisés, on peut réintroduire sans danger dans la société les bandits les plus authentiques" (Lefevre 1929:9).

49. Serge's father, who had been implicated in the assassination of Tsar Alexander II in 1881, escaped to the West and managed to exist in a Brussels slum, where Victor Lvovich Kibalchich was born. (The pen name Serge came later.) Victor grew up among emigrés and anarchists, moved to Paris, edited the newspaper *L'Anarchie*, was arrested in 1914, released in 1917, went to Barcelona amidst its revolutionary ferment, and then to Petrograd in 1919 to fight those attempting to destroy the Revolution. He joined the Party and helped to set up the Comintern publishing house, all the while retaining his contacts with anarchist circles and belonging to the "last free thought society," the one led by the novelist Andrei Bely. After his expulsion by Stalin, Serge went on to become "the leading Trotskyist publicist in France" but then alienated the Trotskyists by his criticism of their sectarian feuding (Hoberman 1984:15). He ended as *persona non grata* for everyone since he was not only anti-Stalinist and anti-Trotskyist but also anti-rightist: he never betrayed the communist cause despite all that had happened. Fleeing Paris just ahead of the Germans in World War II, he managed to reach Mexico, where he died at the age of fifty-seven.

50. Istrati claimed major credit for effecting Serge's release from his first Russian imprisonment: "A cette heure-ci, j'ai une confiance absolue dans la moralité des Soviets. . . . [J]e cours au Guépéou. . . . On m'écoute . . . et quelques jours après, Victor est libre. Je jubile. Vous voyez? Ce n'est pas ce que vous pensez. Des sourires douloureux m'épargnent une réponse que les événements devaient me donner plus tard, . . . car c'est moi qui étais l'imbécile" (Istrati 1929a:147–148). Serge acknowledges in his memoirs, "It is partly owing to [Istrati] that I am still alive" (Serge 1951:302; 1963:279).

51. They are treated similarly in the *Odyssey*, where Yérakas, Búrbulas, and Neílos (Trotsky, Stalin, and Lenin) plot to overthrow King Ikhnaton, the decadent Pharaoh. The first is ferociously idealistic, the second circumspect, tight-lipped, suspicious; indeed, he chides Yérakas/Trotsky for "blabbing" about flame, love, hunger, and revenge (Od. 10.481–482).

52. Despite statements like this, Kazantzakis was more open-eyed about Stalin

than were many leftist intellectuals who traveled to the Soviet Union in the early days. Compare, for example, Henri Barbusse, also in the Soviet Union in 1928, who flattered Stalin in his book of impressions, *Russie* (1930), maintaining that the lies perpetrated by the capitalist press against Bolshevism justified lies by communist sympathizers in defense of the régime (Field 1975:73). The record of credulity and/or willing deception is available in Hollander 1981.

53. Also, the affair enjoyed a moment of general notoriety in the international community, being mentioned for example by André Breton in his second manifesto of surrealism (Breton 1972:156–157).

54. The combined efforts of Istrati and Serge did produce results following Istrati's departure for Paris. Roussakov was acquitted after an initial trial. But the communist cells protested and a new trial was ordered before a "suitable magistrate." Whereas Serge says that this resulted "in a verdict of censure only," Istrati claims that Roussakov was sentenced to three months' hard labor. Roussakov was reinstated in the union after a separate investigation. In any case, for the full year that the affair lasted, Roussakov, his wife, and his daughter were denied bread cards as "ex-capitalists" (Serge 1963:278; Istrati 1929b:474).

55. Kazantzakis slightly misquotes *Odyssey* 1.15, λιλαιομένη πόσιν εἶναι, "longing for him to be her husband."

56. Mrs. Kazantzakis suggests that Istrati contacted the editors before the definitive estrangement in Leningrad, that is, after the falling out that had occurred during the journey to southern Russia (Eleni Kaz. 1938:158). The articles were actually written by Kazantzakis alone (Prev. 1965b:89).

57. In addition, Istrati emphasized that Soviet writers were not free to express themselves as they pleased, that spontaneous gaiety was lacking in Russia, and that one encountered types of ugliness and cruelty there that were absent in the West. On balance, however, he concluded that "Soviet life is more moving to my revolutionary eyes than this old bourgeois life, pleasant yet banal, that I abandoned without regret and am now finding again in spite of myself." Asked if he still considered himself a communist, Istrati replied that he aligned himself with the workers who made the Revolution; hoped that Russia would eventually enjoy a truly proletarian régime; yearned for the day when the terms "communist" and "Bolshevik" would be more hateful to the proletariat than even the term "social democrat" (Lefevre 1929:9).

58. She was destined to be liquidated in the Stalinist purges.

59. Kazantzakis's letter is dated conjecturally as "August 1929." If this is correct, he would seem to be referring to Istrati's "Une page autobiographique. Immortalité," which came out in *Les Nouvelles Littéraires* on 6 July 1929. However, this article has nothing to do with Russia or even politics; it is an inconsequential piece describing Istrati's brief visit around 1911 to Athens, where he met some eccentric "characters." Kazantzakis's anger makes one suspect that he had just read Istrati's "L'Affaire Roussakov" (Istrati 1929b) and that the letter should therefore be dated October 1929, not August.

60. Nemoianu says that the emigré Trotskyist Boris Souvarine wrote either volume II or volume III (Nemoianu 1984). Mrs. Kazantzakis remembers Victor Serge informing her that he wrote both (Eleni Kaz. 1969). All that Istrati himself

tells us is: "Les trois livres qui paraissent sous ce titre: *Vers l'autre Flamme*, sont écrits en collaboration, mais bien distinctement. Si je les publie sous mon seul nom, ce n'est, d'abord, que temporairement; c'est aussi parce que je les signe des deux mains, non pour m'approprier leurs idées, mais pour assurer leur diffusion" (Istrati 1929a:9).

61. Istrati's testimony against Stalin and his gang is well summarized in a review that appeared in December: Lenin was continually active. His successors, contrariwise, are essentially immobile bureaucrats. That is why Trotsky wrote *The Revolution Betrayed*—to argue that revolution must be continuous. Istrati's desire was to learn if the bureaucrats had gotten the better of the initial purity and perfection. He was scandalized by what he saw, by the injustices perpetrated by bureaucrats who do as they please. He found everything enfeebled, faded, made bourgeois; thus his anger. In effect, he gives us a second edition of Trotsky's betrayed and distorted revolution, this time proclaiming the revolution dead. That is why we must proceed "vers l'autre flamme" (Dominique 1929:7). "Coming as it did from a darling of the radical literary establishment, [Istrati's book] . . . provoked a wave of indignation. Rolland had already closeted himself with his protégé and pleaded for days against its publication" (Nemoianu 1984, drawing from Geblesco 1983:71; the evidence is in the Istrati-Rolland correspondence, largely unpublished, housed in Nice in the Istrati archives of the Bibliothèque Universitaire [Geblesco 1983:72]).

62. No wonder that Kazantzakis, when a chance finally arose to have *Toda-Raba* appear and the prospective publisher requested biographical information, thought of this chapter in Istrati's book (Prev. 1965b:314). There was very little else published about him or his work at this time, outside of Greece. The only notices seem to have been two by Philéas Lebesgue writing under the pseudonym "Démétrius Astériotis"—one concerning *Nikifóros Fokás* (Lebesgue 1928) and the other concerning *Hristós* and *Odysséas* (Lebesgue 1930). Kazantzakis had a low opinion of Lebesgue's critical talents, concluding, "He doesn't understand anything" (Prev. 1965b:202; cf. 180, 196).

63. The entire correspondence, which ran from 1933 until Istrati's death in 1935, has now been published (Istrati 1983); it shows Kazantzakis at his best: warm, supportive, and unvindictive. The correspondence began when Istrati discovered that P. Martinescu, a university student, had translated *Toda-Raba* into Rumanian. He greeted Martinescu by exclaiming, "Kazantzakis is the greatest man I ever met!" (Martinescu 1958:9). Some of Kazantzakis's letters are in Eleni Kaz. 1938:177–179; 1968a:271–273, 303; 1968b:279–281, 312–313; 1977:329–332, 365–366. Cf. Talex 1983a.

64. Although long forgotten, Istrati is now in vogue again, thanks mostly to the association of "Friends of Panaït Istrati" founded in 1968. His novels are back in print in France (as well as in Rumania, where they had been banned for fifteen years), and are translated in all the European nations, Latin America, Egypt, Syria, Japan. Archives have been established in Nice and Paris. There is a Rue Panaït Istrati in Nice, where he slit his throat in despair, and a plaque on his apartment building in Paris: 24, rue de Colisée. Although insulted politically by Henri Barbusse in 1935 (*Monde*, 22 February), he was rehabilitated in 1975 by the French

left, which repudiated Barbusse's accusations and acknowledged that "il faut reconnaitre à Panaït Istrati le role glorieux, mais ingrat, de pionnier" (*L'Humanité*, 21 April). In 1980 an international symposium was devoted to him at the Sorbonne. *Vers l'autre flamme* was reissued in the same year (Talex 1983b:177–179).

CHAPTER SIX

1. In the event, neither version of *Toda-Raba* was published in 1929. Rieder, obligated by contract to bring out two additional volumes submitted by Istrati beyond the ones that they had expected, panicked at the prospect of so many books on Russia on their list (Prev. 1965b:146–147); as for the Germans, they were afraid to publish it because it was "too red" (Prev. 1965b:187, 216–217; Eleni Kaz. 1977:274; 1968a:224). The vicissitudes of this novel's eventual publication are too complicated to recount here. Briefly, the French original appeared first (with cuts) in Renaud de Jouvenel's periodical *Le Revue des Vivants* in 1931 and then (complete) in 1934 as a special issue of the same publisher's short-lived new periodical *Le Cahier Bleu.* The first normal publication of the French text in book form did not occur until 1962. Previously, a Greek translation by Yánnis Manglís had appeared (1956). The English translation by Amy Mims is from this and not from the French original. Jouvenel has given us a full account of his involvement (Jouvenel 1958:86–92; 1962:1570–1574). See also Prev. 1965b:208, 240, 245, 264–265, 275, 290–291, 297, 303, 307, 311, 316, 319, 320–323, 426–427, and Eleni Kaz. 1968a:234, 246, 255, 302.

2. How Kazantzakis found this "gift of God" is charmingly related by Mrs. Kazantzakis (Eleni Kaz. 1977:266–268; 1968a:216–217). In 1983, a group of Soviet-bloc neohellenists held a symposium on Kazantzakis in Gottesgab itself, making a pilgrimage to the site of the farmhouse (now demolished) where Kazantzakis and Eléni had boarded (Dostálová 1985:36–37).

3. These same characters are also partially based on external sources. Azad portrays Istrati; Rahel owes something to Rahel Lipstein and also to Rosa Luxemburg, whom Kazantzakis greatly admired (Kaz. 1958a:33, 83; 1979:51; 1958d); the Big-Jawed Man figures Mussolini; Itka recalls Itka Horowitz, whom Kazantzakis had known in Berlin and had met again in the Soviet Union in 1927 (Eleni Kaz. 1968a:171). Nevertheless, more blatantly here than elsewhere in his oeuvre, Kazantzakis projects one part of himself through his main character and certain other parts through secondary characters. There is no use agonizing over the intentional fallacy when criticizing a book like *Toda-Raba.* This novel was not designed to adhere to artistic canons that may override the author's self-conscious conception of his project; it was meant to be little more than a fictionalized essay projecting the author's opinions and anatomizing his soul. Throughout his life, Kazantzakis used art as a means, not an end. His closest counterpart in English literature in this respect is probably George Orwell, whose protagonist George Bowling in *Coming Up For Air* (to cite just one example) is an unmistakable mouthpiece for his author's opinions.

4. I retain the force of the French original: *tu interviens* (you are intervening, interfering, taking sides). The Greek translation renders this correctly in the first

instance as μπερδεύεσαι but then weakens the term's force by employing ενδιαφέρεσαι (Kaz. 1956b:125) when Kazantzakis repeats "tu interviens." The English translation unfortunately picks up only "endiaféresai," rendering Kazantzakis's "tu interviens" weakly in every instance as "you're getting involved." This is what can happen when works are translated from a previous translation and not from the original.

5. I take "enemy of erudition" (the opposite of "bookworm") to be the meaning of Kazantzakis's French coinage "alexandrinophage." Elsewhere, he clearly defines what he means by "alexandrin": "Toute notre littérature, comme notre âme, est alexandrine. . . . nous sommes des raffinés, chargés de science, de livres, d'artifice; nous avons les main pleines de parchemins, et nous attendons les barbares" (Cossin 1931:600).

6. Note how the first few sentences of the epilogue are still in scenario style. "La Place Rouge. Murailles du Kremlin. Le soleil est un boulet rouge suspendu sur l'Occident. Des constellations étranges montent à l'horizon: des faucilles, des marteaux et des Lénine en flamme. Il pleut" (Kaz. 1962c:237). The English translation obscures this flavor by converting half of the present tenses to past tenses (Kaz. 1964f:196).

7. The idea of the instantaneous vision receives its most memorable application in the final chapters of *The Last Temptation.*

8. But it would be a shame to value *Toda-Raba* solely as a foil to the more successful novels that followed, or to obscure certain virtues by dwelling excessively on obvious faults. This tiny offhand job displays Kazantzakis's skill at polemical debate in passages whose vigor, urgency, and lucidity make them models of expository prose. A special felicity derives from similes or parables introduced to render abstract notions concrete, as when a bee dusting its wings with pollen while it fills its belly illustrates the paradox of altruistic egotism (Kaz. 1962c:140–141; 1964f:119), or when a Greek fisherman's fanciful version of Jesus gathering his disciples enlivens the assertion that the masses can be lured only by material benefits, not by ideals or ideas (Kaz. 1962c:195–196; 1964f:162–163). On the other hand, in *Kazantzakis and the Linguistic Revolution in Greek Literature* (Bien 1972a:251–258), I use this passage to illustrate how the folksy flavor enlivening Kazantzakis's later novels depends on demotic Greek as its linguistic vehicle. Kazantzakis's French in *Toda-Raba* is unable to evoke the speech of Greek peasants with comparable force.

9. The Greek text is printed by Prevelákis as Letter 92 in the *Tetrakósia grámmata* (Prev. 1965b:150–157). Mrs. Kazantzakis gives only excerpts in *O asimvívastos* (Eleni Kaz. 1977:269–270; 1968a:218–220). Complete translations appear in Kazantzakis 1989 (English) and in Janiaud-Lust 1970:573–577 (French). The encyclical is addressed to Mihális Anastasíou, an Iráklion high school teacher who had been associated with Kazantzakis's radical activities in that city in 1924 (Pouliopoulos 1972:29).

10. In his argumentation, Kazantzakis adduces the same characteristics that Spengler assigns to the "winter" of a particular civilization: "Materialistic world-outlook. Cult of science, utility, and prosperity. . . . Extinction of spiritual crea-

tive force. . . . Ethical-practical tendencies of an irreligious and unmetaphysical cosmopolitanism" (Spengler 1980:I, Table I; I, 424).

11. Kazantzakis was not immune to the Western cult of pretechnological primitivism; nonetheless, his basic orientation was toward the future, not the past. A clear statement may be found in *Taksidévondas. Rusía*: "To simplify our lives, to turn back to the Middle Ages, to the love of the early Christians, or even further back to savages' tribal land-rights are all dreams of the impotent. Life does not turn back; it moves forward, crushing whoever cannot follow" (Kaz. 1965e:262; 1989:254).

12. Again, Spengler's vision is similar. He prophesies that "a new element of inwardness will arise to overthrow the will-to-victory of science" (Spengler 1980:I, 424). Calling this next phase the Second Religiousness, he explains that it "starts with Rationalism's fading out in helplessness, then the forms of the Springtime become visible, and finally the whole world of the primitive religion, which had receded before the grand forms of the early faith, returns to the foreground, powerful, in the guise of the popular syncretism that is to be found in every Culture at this phase" (Spengler 1980:II, 310–311). Although the next phase as envisioned by Kazantzakis in his doctrine of metacommunism does not conform to Spenglerism in its details, it shares with Spengler's prophecy the primary emphasis on faith: the transubstantiation of a materialistic civilization into a spiritual one. We should also remember—especially when considering the second half of the *Odyssey*—that Spengler cites Buddhism as the example of this Second Religiousness in Indian civilization (Spengler 1980:II, 312–313; cf. I, Table I). If we recall this, we will be able to allow that the Buddhistic elements in Kazantzakis's plan for future civilization might be not just a reversion to an earlier religiosity but also an advance to the next logical step.

13. The encyclical is dated 28 August 1929, two months after the completion of *Toda-Raba*. By 12 July, Kazantzakis had turned to *Kapétan Élia* (Aposkitou-Alexiou 1978:149), which was finished by 20 August (Prev. 1965b:146). Although he was already rewriting some verses of the *Odyssey* in this same month, he set 1 October as his starting date for complete concentration on the epic's second draft (Prev. 1965b:145).

14. Prevelákis (1965b:230–231) conjectures that the Alhambra incident was the cause; he places the expanded text between the end of October 1930 and 20 June 1931, during which time Kazantzakis was resident in Greece. Pouliópoulos agrees (Pouliopoulos 1975:76). Mrs. Kazantzakis, on the other hand, is certain that the publication of the *Askitikí* was the cause (Eleni Kaz. 1977:293; 1968a:240). As for dating, she persists in considering this text merely a "touched up" Confession of Faith, and thus confusedly dates it 1925 although she assigns the revisions to early 1931, when Dimítrios Glinós, co-defendant in the *Askitikí* trial, alerted Kazantzakis about the need to prepare a defense. That both trials were still pending, at least in the spring of 1930, is proved by an editorial concerning the Alhambra incident in *Athinaïká Néa*, 19 April 1930 (cited by Prevelákis [1965b:231]), and by a letter from Glinós announcing that he and Kazantzakis had been summoned to appear on 10 June 1930 on account of *Askitikí* (Glinos 1930).

15. Benavente, the 1922 Nobel laureate for literature, had traveled in the Soviet

Union for several months in 1929. Basically conservative, he nonetheless lived in the Republican zone during the Spanish disturbances and probably wrote *Santa Rusía* "to get into the good graces of the Republic" (Pezñuelas 1968:136). Kazantzakis's translation was published in *O Kíklos*, vol. 1 (1932), p. 193, preceded by a letter about Benavente. The Spanish text is in Jacinto Benavente, *Obras Completas*, vol. 5 (Madrid: Aquilar, 1962), pp. 881–883.

16. The following week *I Kathimeriní* printed a long letter predictably accusing Kazantzakis of abandoning the artist's true role, which is to contribute "to overall social progress," because of his failure to realize that "the economic factor is the chief contributor to life" and that wartime leaders do not draw their strength "from the nonexistent mystical and metaphysical worlds of every writer's imagination" (Zambelis 1936). This was rebutted two days later in *I Ethnikí* by none other than Strátis Myrivílis, who defended Kazantzakis by arguing that no genuine artist allows himself to produce propaganda or even to address his writings to the masses (Myrivilis 1936).

17. Alexiou misdates both the book and the Introduction to 1946 instead of 1945.

18. Mrs. Kazantzakis gives a slightly different version: that Kazantzakis urged the committee to award the prize to a genuine communist who had suffered for peace, recommending Várnalis or Kornáros (Eleni Kaz. 1977:629; 1968a:543). Elli Alexíou, who served on the committee's Greek branch, says that the first choice had been Elías Venézis and that Kazantzakis was selected only after Venézis failed to indicate whether or not he would accept (Elli Alexiou 1966:269–270).

19. Interestingly, p. 331 of the American translation omits the following from p. 326 of the Greek in reference to Mao: "[W]hat suffering, what machinations by the Americans to smother communism, and what sacrifice, what heroism of [the Chinese] for liberty chi è si cara [which is so dear]."

20. Várnalis was evidently deluded about the "main line" of Kazantzakis's intellectual assumptions!

21. He refused to read it (Eleni Kaz. 1977:641; 1968a:553).

22. To support this verdict, she argues that God, not economics, plays the chief role in his books; that he refused to write about contemporary problems in contemporary terms; that in his art he was never truly inspired by the common people despite his protestations to the contrary; that in fact he scorned the common people, treating them as the "dungheap upon which blossom the brilliant figures of superhuman, cruel, dark, aristocratic souls"; and that he made the typical bourgeois errors of (a) dualism, separating flesh from spirit, the material from the animate, and (b) subjectivism, claiming that the sun itself rises and sets between man's two temples (Galatea Kazantzaki 1957:84, 116, 136, 139–140, 264–265).

23. Among Alexíou's charges: Kazantzakis's refusal to write about contemporary problems in contemporary terms, his inability to sacrifice himself for anything except art, his mockery of socialism as democratic and leveling, his failure to oppose the Metaxás dictatorship, his resistance to taking sides in current issues because of his Olympian obsession with eternity, his frantic need for an ideology—even Marxism—to provide him with some kind of chimera. (Elli Alexiou 1966:262–263, 286, 297, 302, 308).

24. By the Clique he means the group connected with Andréas Karandónis and his periodical *Néa Grámmata*, including Embiríkos, Elýtis, Engonópoulos, and Seferis.

CHAPTER SEVEN

1. "I know now. I do not hope for anything, I do not fear anything, I have been delivered from the mind and the heart, I have mounted higher, I am free. This is what I want. I do not want anything else. I have been seeking freedom" (Kaz. 1962a:25; 1960b:59).

2. Kazantzakis may have picked up this image from Nietzsche's famous passage "The Madman" in *The Gay Science* (section 125), where the death of God is first announced: ". . . the light of the stars needs time, deeds need time, even after they are done, to be seen and heard" (Nietzsche 1910:169).

3. On the other hand, this Christ begins (so to speak) as merely an illusion invented by whoever voices the kravyí. "Every forerunner must contain within him the messiah, i.e. the non-existent, the chimera. Otherwise, the messiah does not come" (Kaz. 1958a:196).

4. The clearest statement is probably the one in Chapter 6 of the travelogue on Jerusalem: "Such is reality's secret preparation. The heart suffocates, calls out, seeks an escape; it becomes a kravyí . . . , finds other hearts, sets minds and hands in motion. . . . Only thus does the word become flesh and set foot on earth. What is needed for it to become incarnate? Only this: for the kravyí to remain in the air for many years" (Kaz. 1965d:173; 1975:174–175). Compare another statement, cited in Mános Háris (1961:59): "A voice never goes to waste. The voice existed before the ear, and it called out; the voice called out, the ear was born."

5. Bergson declares that the enterprise of consciousness is "to create with matter, which is necessity itself, an instrument of freedom" (Bergson 1907:286; 1911:278). Other formulations are equally relevant. We should remember from Chapter Two, for example, his characterization of creative reality as "productive of effects in which it expands and transcends its own being" (1907:56; 1911:55). So consciousness, although it derives from matter and must work its way upward through matter, in the last analysis is "distinct from the organism it animates, although it must undergo its vicissitudes. . . . Consciousness is essentially free; it is freedom itself" (1907:293; 1911:284–285).

6. Here, too, Kazantzakis's position is rooted in Bergson's—in his teaching that there are "two different selves, one of which is, as it were, the external projection of the other. . . . We reach the former by deep introspection. . . . But the moments at which we thus grasp ourselves are rare, and that is just why we are rarely free. . . . To act freely is to recover possession of oneself . . ." (Bergson 1959:151; 1960:231–232). Kazantzakis's awareness of this teaching is demonstrated in his 1913 lecture on Bergson, in which we read a paraphrase of the above: "Hence free will is not absolute, since the states of consciousness are rarely so intense that they express the whole of our internal self (υπόσταση). . . . Sometimes, however, . . . our innermost self (εγώ) springs up to the surface . . . and

the action then becomes free, that is to say a faithful and complete expression of our true self" (Kaz. 1912:322–323; 1958b:21–22).

7. For a survey of the view, held in Greece by Dragoúmis and others, that action is not out of keeping with philosophic pessimism and despair, see Paraschos 1956.

8. A systematic coverage of the theme of freedom in Kazantzakis may be found in Grammatas 1983, which employs a primarily psychological approach. Stamatiou 1971 is also useful for its wealth of citations. For a philosophical approach see Koumákis's chapter "Morfés eleftherías ston Kazantzáki" (1985:16–30), which the author summarizes as follows: "A basic point in his philosophy is the problem of freedom in the double sense of the term: metaphysical and political. Metaphysical freedom is presented in his works under four different forms. They are: 1) Freedom as absence of fear and hope, 2) freedom as the transformation of necessity into will, 3) freedom as self-sufficiency, 4) freedom as the deliverance from freedom. Political freedom is the freedom which everybody can enjoy in a democratic society" (Koumakis 1985:107).

CHAPTER EIGHT

1. The best we can do is examine linguistic alterations in individual lines; all else is conjectural. We might suppose for example that the additions in the fifth draft concentrated on defining and developing the essential evolution that occurs in Odysséas in Canto 16 and beyond, conferring on him the freedom to transcend antinomies, since Kazantzakis's declaration of a similar freedom in his own life occurs in the letter of 12 October 1936—that is, between the fifth and sixth drafts. But this remains a dubious supposition. Aside from a few datable embellishments—for example, the use, in Canto 13 of draft three, of Leo Frobenius's findings about tribal customs in Africa (Prev. 1965b:183, 209; 1958:240; 1961:145), or the application, in Canto 22 of draft two, of Kazantzakis's July 1928 experience of Russia's frozen north ("All this: harbors, Laps, sunlit nights, frozen oceans, reindeer, will enter and be yoked to verse" [Prev. 1965b:85])—we can say very little about the poem's substantive growth over the thirteen years of its gestation. Yet the linguistic alterations are extremely interesting for anyone concerned about Kazantzakis's demoticism. For a discussion see Bien 1972a:208–210 and passim. The published excerpts from early versions are catalogued in Katsimbalis 1958a:11, items 66–69, 71–72, 77, 83, 85. Valuable excerpts may also be found in Vrettakos 1960:242–243 and in Prev. 1965b:145, 165, 182, 248–249, 360, where Kazantzakis comments on the rationale for his revisions. Let me add that the third draft (1931) was apparently devoted to improvements in the "dramatic and epic element" (Prev. 1965b:253; 1958:242; 1961:146). The fifth (1935) seems to have swelled the work from the approximately 35,000 lines of the fourth (1933) to the 42,500 that needed to be reduced to 33,333 in the sixth (1937; see Prev. 1965b:423; 1958:268; 1961:161; citing Kaz. 1943:1029). The seventh (1938) was not substantive.

2. Kazantzakis's work habits, despite his claims to the contrary, were extremely systematic. See for example his detailed outline for a proposed second

epic, "Akritas" (Prev. 1965b:487–489; Janiaud-Lust 1970:581–582). Interestingly, Kazantzakis himself (admittedly long after the fact) contradicts his own claims when in *Report to Greco* he describes the process of composing the *Odyssey*'s first draft as a crystallization and harmonization of his diverse experiences into "a single precious journey that knew where it was setting out from and why it was setting out and where it was going; and each stop was not a meaningless whim of chance but the application of destiny's plan" (Kaz. 1964a:567; 1965c:471). On the other hand, an undated notebook entry (which I conjecturally place in the summer of 1924, that is, soon after his return to Iráklion) shows him weaving variations on the basic theme of Odysséas's second departure: the hero goes to Sparta, he sails out into the Atlantic, he visits the gods on the peak of Olympus, he personally travels again to Phaeacia to bring Nausicaa back for Telemachus (Kaz. 1971a:1260–1261). At this point, the exact nature of Odysséas's itinerary was still undecided.

3. The extent to which Laoúrdas was influenced by Prevelákis to alter his initially positive view of the *Odyssey* is fully indicated in Prevelákis 1985:244–248.

4. Wherever possible I retain Kimon Friar's translation, but adjust it if necessary to come closer to the literal meaning. Greek and English references here and henceforth are to Kaz. 1957a and Kaz. 1958f, respectively. In cantos 2 through 23 the line numbers are generally the same. When I give only one reference, it is always to the Greek text, since the English reference will be identical or, at most, one or two lines away. In cantos 1 and 24, however, Friar separated out the prologue and epilogue, respectively, giving them separate numbers, whereas in the Greek text they are part of the cantos in question. In these cases I give the Greek reference first and the English reference second.

5. As he says in a letter to Yánnis Hatzínis, "My entire struggle is this: to convert immediately each and every synthesis I reach into a thesis; this thesis . . . engenders the antithesis and, from their clash and reconciliation, the new synthesis. And once again this new synthesis, the moment it is born, descends again to the level of a thesis and the struggle begins once more" (Petritakis and Hatzini 1984:204). That the synthesis obtained at the "end" via silence is not just an end but also a new beginning should also be apparent from the epic's expressive form, its 33,333 verses. The numerology is clear, thanks to several glosses published by Kazantzakis in response to criticisms of the *Odyssey*. In one, he speaks of classicism versus romanticism. Classicism craves equilibrium; romanticism strives to break every equilibrium in order to form a higher one. Our age, he continues, is romantic. Then he illustrates this with numbers. Even numbers are stable, odd ones unstable. He prefers the odd, and especially the number 3, which "exerts a magical fascination over me" (Kaz. 1939b:1572). In a second gloss, he writes: "The number 3 is holy for me simply because it is the arithmetical expression of the mind's dialectical journey from thesis to antithesis, and from there to the climax of every effort in synthesis" (Kaz. 1943:1029).

6. We see this synoptically in Canto 5 in a figure that I shall discuss in more detail shortly, when we consider various holistic résumés encountered in the text. I am referring to the "god of old ivory / a tower with seven heads one after the other" (Od. 5.588–589) that Odysséas obtains from a peddler in Crete. Here,

Kazantzakis helps us not only by showing god's multiform nature but also by making the seven heads summarize the major steps in man's and god's mutual evolution.

7. Near the end of this chapter I shall offer an additional rebuttal of the charges of nihilism. Based on Martin Heidegger's phenomenological ontology, this stresses that the mere ability to think rationally about experience confers meaning on experience and thus overcomes nihilism.

8. The order is reversed not just in Canto 14, as we shall see shortly, but also in the three-stage dream in Canto 7 (Od. 7.48–109), where only after having completed love's road (7.82) does Odysséas envision himself experiencing the joy of battle (7.84–85). The link between battle and ethical principle is reinforced here since waging war and building cities are treated as a single category (7.85). The order is reversed as well in a notebook entry in which Kazantzakis meditates on mankind's development from elementary needs (warmth, fire, food) to sex, and thence to war (Kaz. 1971a:1258). This particular text shows that Kazantzakis's understanding in all the above-mentioned cases was based on anthropological conclusions regarding human development.

9. *Askitikí*'s revised ending receives its due, of course, in the Nostos. It is worth adding here that Kazantzakis repeatedly insisted that *Odíssia* was basically an expansion of *Askitikí*. Note his reply to Kimon Friar when the latter asked him what he wanted to formulate in the *Odyssey*: "The only answer is: what I formulated in *Askitikí*, my 'Credo' " (Friar 1977a:6).

10. I use the term "people" here rather than Kimon Friar's "race" (which appears in 14.509 as well) because Kazantzakis's words γενιά (509) and σόι (511), given the context, would seem to refer primarily to family, even though γενιά elsewhere (14.632, 650, 691, 698) is closer to "race" or even to "mankind." "People" is nicely ambiguous: it can mean either "race" in the Greek sense, i.e. the collectivity of Greeks, or "relatives," i.e. family.

11. That human beings improve nature is one of Kazantzakis's basic beliefs. Today, of course, many would dispute this belief.

12. I employ the term "circle" rather than Kazantzakis's obsessive "ascent" in order to remind us that the evolutionary progression is periodic, not linear.

13. This happens at the end of Canto 8. The termination of the aesthetic stage is marked by Odysséas's decision that "there's no room for a woman any more" (8.1325) as they contemplate sailing down the Nile, whereupon they abandon Díktenna at the river's mouth—but not before Odysséas holds "the refreshing body of woman" in his arms for one last time (Od. 8.1333; see Prev. 1958:145).

14. The characteristics of the aesthetic stage may be seen in the diary of Johannes the Seducer in *Either/Or* (Kierkegaard 1951:36–80) and in Kierkegaard 1951:21–36, 80–88. The ethical stage's characteristics appear in the story of Judge William in *Stages on Life's Way* (Kierkegaard 1951:172–189), and are given discursively in *Either/Or* (Kierkegaard 1951:88–108). The religious stage is treated in *Fear and Trembling* through the story of Abraham, the Knight of Faith (Kierkegaard 1951:116–134), and in the *Concluding Unscientific Postscript to the "Philosophical Fragments"* (Kierkegaard 1951:207–258).

15. Unfortunately, we have no direct evidence that Kazantzakis knew Kierke-

gaard's work while he was composing the *Odyssey*. A fair conjecture, however, is that he had encountered Kierkegaard's theories at least indirectly during his sojourn in Berlin, via Shestov, whose interest in the Danish theologian eventually resulted in a study called *Kierkegaard et la philosophie existentielle* (Paris: Les Amis de Léon Chestov, 1936), translated as *Kierkegaard and the Existentialist Philosophy* (Athens, Ohio: Ohio University Press, 1969). We can be certain, however, that Kazantzakis did have some acquaintance with Kierkegaard at some point after he had completed the *Odyssey*, since in one of his unpublished notebooks there are reading notes from Enzo Paci's *Esistenzialismo* (Padova, 1943), including the following: "Per Kirkegaard [*sic*] l'istante ha un' importanza decisiva: nell' istante l'eterno che non esisteva esiste si trasmuta nell' essere." In another notebook he copied out one of Kierkegaard's maxims. Finally, in the Sipriot interview (1957), he cited Kierkegaard with familiarity (Izzet 1965:101). But our best evidence remains Prevelákis, who was always privy to Kazantzakis's ideas and reading. That Prevelákis had thought about Kierkegaard and the *Odyssey* long before he wrote about this connection in 1958 may be surmised from the statement by his disciple Laoúrdas, in 1943, that Odysséas "travels from the aesthetic world to the ethical and then to the metaphysical" (Laourdas 1943:1337).

16. In the prologue's first line the sun is the "great oriental." Rising out of the black abyss, it is about to inaugurate the luminous interval called life. In the epilogue, this same sun has descended to its mother's wave-cellar, the sea, and has turned black. (The English version renders μαύρος ήλιος [24.1407] as "black son" [Epilogue 11] instead of "black sun.") The world is dark, the luminous interval obliterated. Odysséas, although he no longer returns to Ithaca in Kazantzakis's centrifugal version of Homer's centripetal voyage (see Stanford 1963:223), does return to the sun that inaugurated the journey; indeed, in becoming flame at the end he identifies completely with the sun, as forecasted in the prologue (1.29–30; Prologue 29–30). The nostos is accomplished. Odysséas (mankind) is ready to rise again in order to resume the ever-repeated process of fleshing and unfleshing.

17. Fortunately, Prevelákis includes this document in the *Tetrakósia grámmata*. There is a French rendering in Janiaud-Lust 1970:588–589. The much more extensive summary by Kimon Friar is inappropriate for reproduction here since it occupies thirty-six pages (Kaz. 1958f:777–813). A medium-length summary may be found in Prev. 1958:111–123; 1961:65–73.

18. The 1938 edition lacked three lines. The deficiency was discovered by Emmanuel Kásdaglis as he was preparing the second edition. Kazantzakis playfully advised Kásdaglis to write three lines himself and insert them (Kasdaglis 1987). Prevelákis tells us, however, that the missing verses were ascertained from the manuscript in his possession and duly restored (Prev. 1965b:733–734).

19. Actually, this dubious distinction may belong to James Bailey's *Festus* (1889), which consists of over 40,000 lines of excruciatingly mediocre verse, for example: "I saw the tears start in her eye, / And trickle down her cheek; / Like falling stars across the sky / Escaping from their Maker's eye: / I saw, but spared to speak." It may or may not be useful to know that Homer's *Odyssey* has 12,110 lines and his *Iliad* 15,693, totaling 27,803, still 5,530 short of Kazantzakis's 33,333. Nonnos's *Dionysiaca*, which dates from the late fifth century A.D., comes closest

to Kazantzakis's bulk, for it consists of 21,286 Greek hexameters. Here are some other figures: *Aeneid*, 9,896; *Divine Comedy*, 14,207; *Paradise Lost*, 10,565. Kazantzakis's monstrous work contains about 300,000 words. Joyce's *Ulysses* has 264,448 "graphic units." Thomas Mann's *Der Zauberberg* contains approximately 311,000 words. But perhaps the closest parallel to Kazantzakis's *Odyssey* in aims and bulk, if not in technique, is James Merrill's *The Changing Light at Sandover* (1982), which, like the *Odyssey*, attempts to create a new cosmological myth for our times. It occupies 560 pages. Kazantzakis is not the only one to have completed an extremely long poem in the twentieth century. Nevertheless, general opinion would seem to agree with C. M. Bowra when he writes: "Long poems are out of fashion, and there is a tacit agreement that Edgar Allan Poe was right when he said that they could not exist. It is true that illiterate Tartars in the Tienshan mountains still compose enormous epics and recite them to wondering audiences of nomads, but in Europe the epic, which was once regarded as the crown of poetry, is out" (Bowra 1959). That Kazantzakis was interested in this question is shown by the following quotation that he copied into his notebook on 18 August 1946 during his sojourn in Cambridge: "Can Epic be written again in these days or has it rarefied itself away into a lost art? . . . I decline the speculation . . ." (Quiller-Couch 1922:157). For an interesting discussion of this question, see Tziovas 1989, which attributes Palamás's and Kazantzakis's defenses of the long narrative poem to the "residual orality and belated textuality" of Greek culture.

20. The remainder of the blurb is translated in the final footnote to this chapter.

21. That Kazantzakis had Christianity in mind is confirmed much later when the contemplative Odysséas encounters a black fisher-lad representing Christ who argues that our earthly life is merely the path to heaven, our true home (Od. 21.1146), and that evil will be conquered not by the sword but by love (21.1158–1160).

22. Gide's doctrine of availability was influential in Greece in the late 1920s. See Mackridge 1985:3–4.

23. A student of mine once wrote an interesting paper comparing the situation in Menelaos's Sparta, as described by Kazantzakis, to the situation in tsarist Russia in 1905: "Like the farming Russian peasants, the peasants of Menelaos's kingdom have risen up against their landlord . . . ; just as the Russian peasants raided their landlords' storehouses for their grain, so the Spartan peasants demand their rightfully earned grain from Menelaos. So, too, do the Russian famines compare with the pronounced hunger of the Spartan serfs, and of course the desire to own land is the key force in bringing both groups to revolt" (Knox 1977:6). What this helps us realize is that for his Spartan, Cretan, and Egyptian sections Kazantzakis undoubtedly took certain elements of political detail from the actual politics of the twentieth century and from Russian politics in particular. But to identify each section with a specific historical event seems to me a Procrustean exercise that should be avoided.

24. It should be noted that the term "utopia" is Kazantzakis's own, as seen in his letter of 7 July 1927 to Prevelákis: "I am working well, I got past the difficulty; in a few days I'll start 15, Utopia" (Prev. 1965b:30). The word I use for Kazantzakis's utopian polity is "city" because the word that Kazantzakis himself em-

ploys repeatedly in Canto 15 is "kástro," which literally means "fortress" but which serves as a synonym for "city" throughout the poem. Cf. Kazantzakis's gloss on Od. 7.1319 in a letter to Kimon Friar: "εδώ κάστρο είναι πολιτεία" (Friar 1977a:17). "Kástro" is the normal way Kazantzakis, like other "Kastrianí," refers to his home town, Iráklion, otherwise known as "Megálo Kástro" ("Great Fortress"). For a helpful explanation of the various names by which Iráklion/Kástro/Megálo Kástro/Candia has been known since it was built by the Arabs in 824 on the site of the ancient Herakleion, see Dimakis 1975:38–39. Greek critics tend to use the word "politía" ("state"; more precisely, "government of a state," "administration," "polity") when discussing Odysséas's utopia because of that utopia's roots in Plato's *Politeia* ("The Republic") and also in Nietzsche's theory of the state. But "city" seems closer to what Kazantzakis desired, and has the advantage of reverberating sympathetically, for English-speaking readers, with the Biblical "City of God," as in Psalm 48 or especially Revelation 3.12. (However, the Greek word in both these cases, in the Septuagint and the New Testament respectively, is "pólis.")

25. It could be ventured that Kazantzakis's utopia is Maoist because of its compatibility with the principle of perpetual revolution (Prev. 1975). One could also try to make a case for Kazantzakis as leaning toward Trotskyism rather than Leninism. I doubt that either position could be argued very effectively.

26. Cf. Herbert Read on Albert Camus's thesis in *L'Homme revolté*: "Camus then turns to the history of revolt in the political sense, his main object being to draw a clear distinction between rebellion and revolution. Here, . . . Camus's ideas come close to anarchism, for he recognizes that revolution always implies the establishment of a new government, whereas rebellion is action without planned issue—it is spontaneous protestation" (Camus 1956:viii).

27. Nikos Pouliópoulos, in his examination of Kazantzakis's indebtedness to ancient Greek political theory, concludes surprisingly that Aristotle is more compatible with Kazantzakis's thinking than is Plato. Both Aristotle and Kazantzakis, he argues, stress the need for an educated citizenry, both assume that man is a political animal, and both work from the hard facts of historical necessity (Pouliopoulos 1972:234–236). I find this unconvincing in relation to the *Odyssey*; indeed, Pouliópoulos is forced to draw his proof-text not from the epic but from Kazantzakis's "Apology," the expanded version of the 1925 "Confession of Faith" (Kaz. 1925a), in which Kazantzakis put his political ideas to a very different use than he did when he set to work on Canto 15 of the *Odyssey* in July 1927. In the epic those ideas are enclosed in a much larger context determined not by the Aristotelian *zoon politikon* but instead by what Kazantzakis later termed the *zoon metaphysikon* (". . . l'homme n'est pas un animal politique, mais essentiellement un animal métaphysique. Le seul vrai problème existant est celui de la recherche du sens de l'homme" [Sadoul 1955]). His basic affinity remains, I believe, with Plato.

28. Specifically, Prevelákis suggests that Odysséas's engraving of the city's basic commandments on slabs of stone (Od. 15.1161–1176), aside from the analogy with Moses at Sinai, derives from Nietzsche's engraving of an excerpt from *Thus Spoke Zarathustra* on a stone in Sils-Maria, where Kazantzakis traveled on pil-

grimage in 1918 (Prev. 1958:311); furthermore, that the idea of a city-state based on the rule that the son should surpass the father comes directly from Zarathustra's prologue, section 3, "On the Afterworldly," and from Part 2, section 12, "On Self-Overcoming" (Prev. 1958:310).

29. "Nietzsche divides society into two classes, strictly separated," says Kazantzakis in his dissertation. His lower class includes not only workers but merchants, farmers, industrialists, and also "scientists and scholars who restrict themselves to some narrow specialty. . . ." The ruling class is that of the fighters, creators, and lords "who supervise the protection of the laws and of social order" (Kaz. 1959c:82–83). From this summary it is clear that Kazantzakis's hierarchy differs from Nietzsche's in its details. But its governing spirit is similar.

30. Note the congruence of these storeys with Kierkegaard's aesthetic, ethical, and religious stages.

31. Unfortunately, "kormí tu logismú," ("thought's body") is inverted to "body's thought" in the English translation.

32. Even earlier, he disposed of this problem rather summarily, first by marrying Telemachus off to Nausicaa and then by coupling Helen with the Dorian gardener—in both cases in order to produce a son.

33. In *Askitikí*, Kazantzakis uses the word *odíssia* to mean the overall evolution of the biosphere, implying that each individual recapitulates in his or her microcosmic odyssey the cosmos's gigantic Odyssey (Kaz. 1962a:44; 1960b:79).

34. Cf. Milton, *Paradise Lost* 3.108: "Reason also is choice."

35. Joyce and Sophocles concentrate their powers of developmental characterization on Telemachus and Neoptolemus, respectively. Homer in the *Odyssey* (the *Iliad* being of course a triumph of developmental characterization) resembles Kazantzakis in denying development to all his characters, primary and secondary. Cedric Whitman feels that only two of the Homeric *Odyssey*'s secondary characters, Elpenor and Eurylochus, "emerge as people. . . . The rest are vapor" (Whitman 1965:292). I would say that all of Kazantzakis's secondary characters are vapor. Yet, like Homer's, they are meant to be "types of something in human experience and never . . . typical simply of humanity" (Whitman 1965:292), as is Odysséas in both epics.

36. The English translation confuses the homonyms χοῖρος, "pig," with χῆρος, "widower." It also freely renders καλοπέραση as "pleasure" instead of "affluence," "prosperity," or "material comfort."

37. It is of course precisely to this challenge that all three Kierkegaardian types, the ethical and religious as well as the aesthetic, must respond.

38. At least one critic, Minás Dimákis, understood this, although still employing "nihilism" as a label: "But Kazantzakis's nihilism does not lead to a negative pessimism. . . . It becomes an active force: it preaches participation in life" (Dimakis 1975:100–101).

39. In the Greek text, this section utilizes the typography found in editions of Greek plays. Unfortunately, the English translation does not employ an equivalent typography.

40. Although Kazantzakis does not mention the next three paragraphs of this same article on Heidegger's ontology, they are equally close to his own philoso-

phy. We will remember that he describes Odysséas's progression from the aesthetic stage to the ethical and religious as a progression from beauty to virtue and lastly to truth (Od. 17.74). This next section of the article on Heidegger bears the subtitle "The Meaning of Truth." It tells us that truth, for Heidegger, is the state in which being is no longer hidden but revealed (Yeorgoulis 1948:977). But since the revelation of being occurs only when we are propelled to it by the confrontation with nothingness, we can say that nihilism is paradoxically the presupposition of its own refutation. This refutation occurs because to focus on being rather than on things demonstrates that existence can be thought about in a rational manner, that is, can be meaningful.

41. For a survey of the materialist-mental problem, see Hardy 1966.

42. Compare Kazantzakis's definition of civilization as a moment when σύνθεση (composition) and αποσύνθεση (decomposition) are balanced (Kaz. 1971a: 1259). This definition derives of course from Bergson.

43. We know that Kazantzakis resisted the argument that European civilization could regenerate itself if only it lived up to its own supposed principles of rationality and beauty (Hellenism) and compassionate nonviolence (Christianity). In his opinion, such principles had seen their day. Although once creative, they were no longer applicable to contemporary problems.

44. We know of course that Kazantzakis's approbation of war goes back much further in his career; it is part of his Nietzschianism. In the dissertation on Nietzsche he notes that "war, for Nietzsche, as for Pindar, is πάντων πατήϱ [father of everything], the strongest instrument of progress and selection." Kazantzakis also reminds us, however, that for Nietzsche "the use of violence by no means aims at the acquisition of material goods or the search for happiness"; rather, it is the means by which the ruling class achieves self-overcoming (Kaz. 1959c:84, 87).

45. The identifications are beyond dispute. In *Taksidévondas. Rusía* Kazantzakis speaks of Trotsky as flame, Stalin as soil or earth, and Lenin as light (Kaz. 1965c:211). This is repeated in the *Odyssey*, where Yérakas is associated with flame, Búrbulas with earth, and Neílos with light (Od. 10.432–454). Later, when they divide up tasks, Yérakas organizes the workers, Búrbulas rouses the peasants, and Neílos infiltrates the military (10.1229–1237). With allowance for poetic license, it is Bolshevism's inner circle transported to ancient Egypt. As an added touch, Kazantzakis gives Neílos Lenin's bald pate (10.494). He also reflects the rivalry between Stalin and Trotsky, the former accusing the latter of being a loose-tonged enthusiast (10.481–483). Lastly, Búrbulas mistrusts Odysséas for precisely the same reason—or pretext—that the Stalinists persecuted Roussakov. "He's not a worker," says Búrbulas; "he seems a smart-aleck shipowner" (10.485), that is, a capitalist in disguise.

46. At first "Lenin" graciously accepts Odysséas as a comrade despite their conflicting allegiances to materialism and idealism, respectively (Od. 10.565–572). Later, he chides Odysséas mildly for squandering his strength in an effort to find new gods or to mock old ones—"because the soul that mocks god is still god's slave" (11.728–732). Soon afterward, he becomes more antagonistic, as does Odysséas, who disparages the other's materialism: "I hate the virtue that eats and drinks . . ." (11.840). "Lenin" now grows abusive, while Odysséas is aghast

at his antagonist's harshness (11.988–1010). Finally, as they are about to part—Odysséas to begin the exodus, still in search of his gods—"Lenin" becomes more gentle, although remaining sarcastic: "Good luck to your castles in the air . . ." As for himself, he will one day "enjoy the great harvest, revenge," using the proletariat as his scythe (11.1344–1350).

47. For a survey of Kazantzakis's treatment of blacks, see Banks and Campbell 1964. The *Odyssey* is discussed on pp. 259–262. Their safe conclusion is that the symbolic black is used in the epic "to propel and power the universal man, Odysseus, toward his noble rendezvous with the Spirit" (259). This should be combined with Kazantzakis's approbation of the blood-curdling African "with the jaws of a gorilla" who dreams of massacres (Kaz. 1965e:231–232; 1989:223).

48. Nevertheless, I do wish to add here the remainder of Kazantzakis's own summary of his epic. Earlier, I translated this to the point where Kazantzakis writes: "Slowly, after a terrible internal struggle, [Odysséas's] mind is illuminated, his soul conquers, he stands up and resumes the march." This brings us to the end of Canto 17, just past the meditation on mind. Kazantzakis's summary continues as follows:

> He marches continually southward, meeting in his long journey all the great leaders who brought mankind a new religion, a chimera, a new world-view . . . He lives and talks with them, measures his soul against theirs, and leaves them one by one and continues his journey alone.
>
> He reaches the tip of Africa, his beloved sea. . . . He puts together his last boat, a small, narrow one, like a coffin. Bidding land goodbye, he leaves. He crosses the frozen ocean; a storm breaks out; the boat is smashed on wild snow-covered crags.
>
> Resuming his trek, he falls upon a village constructed of snow, where the wild seal-hunters receive him as a god. He spends one winter with them, and, in the spring, as the snow is melting, he slips into a sealskin kayak and sails out into the open sea again.
>
> He rows with the paddle toward the unsetting sun. Death comes quietly and sits opposite him, in the prow. . . . An iceberg emerges and overwhelms the vessel but Odysséas manages to scramble up onto it in time, and he sails along with it as though it were a ship.
>
> Odysséas senses that his last moments have come. He bids farewell to his five senses . . . and thanks them because they worked well for him: he has no complaints.
>
> Spreading his arms, he utters a cry and calls all his beloved companions—men and women whom he loved, and his faithful dog from Ithaca. They hear the master's voice. The former companions spring up out of their graves and arrive: Odysséas's boat fills once more with comrades. Odysséas is delighted. He receives them joyfully, raises his arm, and gives in a fearless, triumphant voice the signal for departure: "Luff, lads!" And death's breeze blows a fair wind. (Prev. 1965b:478–479)

References

Alexander, Ian W.

1957 *Bergson, Philosopher of Reflection*. London: Bowes & Bowes.

Alexiou, Christos

n.d. Η ποίηση του Σεφέρη από σκοπιά κοινωνική και ιστορική. Manuscript.

Alexiou, Elli

1966 Για να γίνει μεγάλος. Athens: Dorikos. (The third edition [Athens: Kastaniotis, 1981] is a photoreproduction with the identical pagination, but has an addendum on pp. 409–422.)

Alexiou, Elli, and Yiorgos E. Stefanakis

1977 Για το Νίκο Καζαντζάκη: είκοσι χρόνια από το θάνατό του. Athens: Kedros.

1983 Νίκος Καζαντζάκης: γεννήθηκε για τη δόξα. Athens: Kastaniotis.

Alexiou, Lefteris

1926 Ψυχολογικά σημειώματα για τις σύγχρονες ελληνικές προσωπικότητες. Α΄)Δραγούμης και Καζαντζάκης. Νεοελληνικά Γράμματα, Ηρακλείου, Κρήτης 1:77–82 (Nov.)

Anapliotis, Yannis

1960 Ο αληθινός Ζορμπάς κι ο Νίκος Καζαντζάκης. Athens: Difros.

Anayennisi

1926–1927 Αναγέννηση Α΄. September 1926–August 1927.

1927–1928 Αναγέννηση Β΄. September 1927–August 1928.

Androulidakis, Thrasivoulos

1958 Ο Καζαντζάκης στα χρόνια της κατοχής. Καινούρια Εποχή, Autumn 1958, pp. 268–279.

1978 Ο Καζαντζάκης στην Αίγινα το 1941. Καινούρια Εποχή, Autumn 1978, pp. 63–73.

Anemoyanni, Tea

1964a Μερικά γράμματα του Νίκου Καζαντζάκη προς την Τέα Ανεμογιάννη. Ηώς 7 (1964):492–493.

1964b Σκόρπιες θύμησες της Τέας Ανεμογιάννη. Ηώς 7: 490–491.

Anghelaki-Rooke, Katerina

1977 Ασκητική, ή ευθύνη η δεκάτη μούσα. Νέα Εστία 102, Christmas 1977, pp. 128–133.

Anorthosis

1925 Articles in the newspaper Ανόρθωσις (Iráklion, Crete). Editor: Andreas Zografos.

Aposkitou-Alexiou, Martha

1978 Τριάντα τέσσερα άγνωστα γράμματα του Νίκου Καζαντζάκη. Αμάλθεια [Agios Nikolaos, Crete], April–June 1978, pp. 117–164.

Athanasios of Syros, Bishop

1928 Υπόμνημα του Σεβ. Μητροπολίτου Σύρου προς την Ι. Σύνοδον της Εκκλησίας. Εκκλησία 6, 17 March 1928, pp. 81–86.

Augustinos, Gerasimos

1977 *Consciousness and History: Nationalist Critics of Greek Society, 1897–1914.* New York: Columbia University Press (distributor for *East European Quarterly*).

Avyeris, Markos

1939 Η νέα Οδύσσεια. Νέα Εστία 26:1247–1256, 1344–1349 (15 Sept. 1939 and 1 Oct. 1939). Reprinted in his Έλληνες λογοτέχνες (Athens: Themelio, 1966), pp. 213–256.

Ayer, Alfred Jules

1946 *Language, Truth and Logic.* 2nd ed., rev. London: Gollancz. First published in 1936.

Bailot, A.

1928 Bergson et Schopenhauer. *Mercure de France* 208:513–529 (15 Dec. 1928).

Banks, Arthur C., Jr., and Finley C. Campbell

1964 The Vision of the Negro in the Kazantzakian Universe. *Phylon, the Atlanta University Review of Race and Culture* 25:254–262.

Bastias, K.

1927 Το πολιτικό δεκαπενθήμερο. Ελληνικά Γράμματα Β΄. 15 Dec. 1927, p. 72.

Bataille, Georges

1983 *L'Expérience intérieure.* Paris: Gallimard. Originally published in 1943; revised edition 1954.

Bateson, F. W.

1954 *Wordsworth: A Re-interpretation.* London: Longmans, Green.

Berdyaev, Nicolas

1952 *The Beginning and the End* [Essay on Eschatological Metaphysics (Creation and Objectivisation)]. New York: Harper & Brothers.

Bergson, Henri

1907 *L'Évolution créatrice.* Paris: Félix Alcan.

1911 *Creative Evolution.* Translated by Arthur Mitchell. London: Macmillan.

1959 *Oeuvres.* Paris: Presses Universitaires de France.

1946 *The Creative Mind.* Translated by Mabelle Andison. New York: Philosophical Library. Translation of *La Pensée et le mouvant.* Paris: Alcan, 1934.

1960 *Time and Free Will, an Essay on the Immediate Data of Consciousness.* New York: Harper Torchbooks.

Bidal-Baudier, Marie-Louise

1974 *Nikos Kazantzaki. Comment l'homme devient immortel.* Paris: Plon.

Bien, Peter

1965 "Zorba the Greek," Nietzsche, and the Perennial Greek Predicament. *Antioch Review* 15/1 (Spring 1965): 147–163.

1972a *Kazantzakis and the Linguistic Revolution in Greek Literature.* Princeton: Princeton University Press.

1972b *Nikos Kazantzakis* [Columbia Essays on Modern Writers, no. 62.] New York: Columbia University Press. Reprinted in *Three Generations of Greek Writers* (Athens: Efstathiadis, 1983) and in *European Writ-*

ers: The Twentieth Century, ed. George Stade. Vol. 9. New York: Charles Scribner's Sons, 1989. Pp. 1067–1089. Issued in Greek translation by Kedros (Athens) in 1983.

1972c The Demoticism of Kazantzakis. In *Modern Greek Writers*, edited by Edmund Keeley and Peter Bien. Princeton: Princeton University Press. Pp. 145–169.

1972d Kazantzakis' Nietzschianism. *Journal of Modern Literature* 2/2 (1971–1972):245–266.

1980 Review of Nikos Kazantzakis, "The Suffering God: Selected Letters to Galatea and to Papastephanou." *World Literature Today*, Winter 1980, pp. 150–151.

1983 *Three Generations of Greek Writers: Introductions to Cavafy, Kazantzakis, Ritsos*. Athens: Efstanthiadis.

Bowra, C. M.

1959 Homer Redivivus. [Review of] "The Odyssey: A Modern Sequel." *The Observer* (London), 8 February 1959.

Breton, André

1972 *Manifestes du surréalisme*. Paris: Pauvert.

Bryer, Anthony

1965 The Great Idea. *History Today* [London] 15:159–168.

1975 Review of Michael Angold's "A Byzantine Government in Exile: Government and Society Under the Laskarids of Nicaea (1204–1261)." *Times Literary Supplement* (London), 5 Sept. 1975, p. 1005.

Buchheim, C. A., ed.

1894 *Goethe's "Dichtung und Wahrheit."* Oxford: Clarendon Press.

Campbell, John, and Philip Sherrard

1968 *Modern Greece*. London: Ernest Benn.

Camus, Albert

1956 *The Rebel*. With a Foreword by Sir Herbert Read. New York: Vintage.

1964 *The Myth of Sisyphus and Other Essays*. New York: Knopf.

Clogg, Richard

1979 *A Short History of Modern Greece*. Cambridge: Cambridge University Press.

Coomaraswamy, Ananda Kentish

1916 *Buddha and the Gospel of Buddhism*. New York: Putnam's.

Cossin, Jacques

1931 Enquête internationale sur le populisme. *La Grande Revue*, February 1931, pp. 587–622. A summary in Greek is printed in *Néa Estía*, 15 April 1931, p. 432ff.

Craft, Robert

1978 Stravinsky's politics: left, right, left. *Times Literary Supplement* (London), 26 May 1978, p. 579. Reprinted in Vera Stravinsky and Robert Craft, *Stravinsky in Pictures and Documents* (New York: Simon and Schuster, 1978), pp. 547–558.

Daoundakis, N.

1977 Interview with Mihalis Christodoulakis. Τα Νέα, 27 October.

Darakis, Loukas

1935 Μεγάλη έρευνα μεταξύ των λογίων μας. Μια ώρα με τον κ. Ν. Καζαντζάκη. Ἠχὼ τῆς Ἑλλάδος, 16 March 1935, p. 3.

Dialinas, Elias

1925 Το κοινωνικόν πρόβλημα. Νέα Εφημερίς [Iráklion], 17 Feb. 1925, p. 1; 20 Feb. 1925, p. 1; 23 Feb. 1925, p. 1.

Dianoümenon tis Athinas

1930 Έκκληση διανοουμένων της Αθήνας για την κατάδικη των φαντάρων του Καλπακιού. Ριζοσπάστης, 13 Dec. 1930. Reprinted in Γιατί, May 1987, pp. 41–42.

Dimakis, Minas

1975 Καζαντζάκης. Επιστολές Καζαντζάκη στον Μηνά Δημάκη. Athens: To Elinikó Vivlío. Reprints of the letters published in *Néa Estía* 91:237–244, 307–310 (Kaz. 1972), with additional scholia and general commentary.

1979 Ανέκδοτες επιστολές Καζαντζάκη από τα νεανικά έως τα ώριμα χρόνια του (1902–1956). Athens: Ékdosi Musíu Kazantzáki Kinótitos Barbáron Iraklíu.

Dimos Irakliu

1961 Δήμος Ηρακλείου Κρήτης. Αναμνηστικό λεύκωμα Νίκου Καζαντζάκη. Από το πρώτο φιλολογικό μνημόσυνό του στο Ηράκλειο στις 10 του Γενάρη 1960. Athens: Difros.

Dominique, Pierre

1929 Panaït Istrati chez les Soviets. *Les Nouvelles Littéraires*, 21 Dec. 1929, p. 7.

Dostálová, R., ed.

1985 *Nikos Kazantzakis. Beiträge zu seinem Werke und Leben*. Prague: Czechoslovakian Academy of Sciences.

Douglas, John Albert

1919 *The Redemption of Saint Sophia*. London: Faith Press.

Doulis, Thomas

1977 *Disaster and Fiction: Modern Greek Fiction and the Asia Minor Disaster of 1922*. Berkeley: University of California Press.

Dragoumis, Ion

1909 [Ίδα] Η μεγάλη ιδέα. Ο Νουμάς, 11 October 1909, p. 6.

1913 Ελληνικός πολιτισμός. Athens.

1926 Σαμοθράκη. In Έργα, 2nd ed. Athens.

Durrell, Lawrence

1977 *Sicilian Carousel*. London: Faber and Faber.

Eakin, Paul John

1985 *Fictions in Autobiography: Studies in the Art of Self-Invention*. Princeton: Princeton University Press.

Eleftheros Logos

1927 Kazantzakis's articles on Egypt (3 April–15 April) and Sinai (21 April–3 May).

Eleftheros Tipos

1926–1927 Kazantzakis's articles on Primo de Rivera's Spain, 12 Dec. 1926–7 Jan. 1927.

1927 Kazantzakis's articles on Italian fascism, 6 Feb.–28 Feb.

Evelpidis, C.

1958 Τα ταξίδια του Καζαντζάκη. Καινούρια Εποχή, Autumn 1958, p. 240.

Fanourakis, Yeoryios

1958 Ερμηνευτικές παρατηρήσεις στον "Καπετάν Μιχάλη." Καινούρια Εποχή, Autumn 1958, pp. 184–199.

Field, Frank

1975 *Three French Writers and the Great War; Studies in the Rise of Communism and Fascism.* Cambridge: Cambridge University Press.

Frangopoulos, T.D.

1977 Ο Καζαντζάκης και το ύψιστο "στοίχημα." Νέα Εστία 102, Christmas 1977, pp. 44–57.

Friar, Kimon

1977a Είκοσι δύο γράμματα του Νίκου Καζαντζάκη στον Kimon Friar. Τομές, October 1977, pp. 3–22.

1977b Review of Ofis ke Krino. *Néa Estía* 102, Christmas 1977, pp. 311, 313, 312.

1977c [Introduction to] Νίκου Καζαντζάκη "Κωμωδία: τραγωδία μονόπραχτη" και "Σόδομα και Γόμορα." Τομές, October 1977, pp. 26–29.

Friedman, Maurice

1967 The Modern Vitalist: Bergson and Kazantzakis. In his *To Deny Our Nothingness: Contemporary Images of Man.* New York: Delacorte Press. Pp. 63–79.

Frye, Northrop

1966 *Anatomy of Criticism.* New York: Atheneum.

Geblesco, Elisabeth

1983 Langue d'écriture et figures paternelles. *L'Arc,* nos. 86/87 (1983), pp. 57–72.

Geertz, Clifford

1966 Religion as a Cultural System. In *Anthropological Approaches to the Study of Religion,* edited by Michael Banton. New York: Praeger. Pp. 1–46.

Gelven, Michael

1976 Heidegger and Tragedy. *Boundary 2,* vol. 4, no. 2 (Winter 1976), pp. 555–568.

Georgopoulos, N.

1979 Kazantzakis, Bergson, Lenin and the "Russian Experiment." *Journal of the Hellenic Diaspora* 5/4 (Winter 1979):33–44.

Glinos, Dimitrios

1930 Letter to Grigorios Xenopoulos. Νέα Εστία 7:490 (1 May 1930).

Goudelis, Yannis

1978 Στοιχεία στη σύνθεση Καζαντζάκη. Καινούρια Εποχή, Spring 1978, pp. 7–57.

1987 Ο Καζαντζάκης ξανασταυρώνεται. Athens: Difros.

Gounelas, Haralambos-Dimitris

1977 Εισαγωγή στα τρία μονόπρακτα του Καζαντζάκη. Νέα Εστία 102, Christmas 1977, p. 166–182.

1982 Late Nineteenth-Century Views on Literature in Greece and the Periodical Ἡ Τέχνη. *Scandinavian Studies in Modern Greek*, no. 6:43–68.

1984 Η σοσιαλιστική συνείδηση στην ελληνική λογοτεχνία 1897–1912. Athens: Kedros.

Grammatas, Thodoros

1983 Η έννοια της ελευθερίας στο έργο του Ν. Καζαντζάκη. Athens: Dodoni.

Gregor, A. James

1979 *Young Mussolini and the Intellectual Origins of Fascism*. Berkeley: University of California Press.

Haïkalis, S.

1980 Ελλήνων λογοτεχνών βιογραφίες. 2 vols. Athens: Instituto Diadoseos Elliniku Vivliu.

Haravyi

1980 Ο Νίκος Καζαντζάκης μιλά στους εργάτες της Λεμεσού. Από το ανέκδοτο βιβλίο του Γιάννη Λεύκη Παπαγγέλου, "Οι Ρίζες." Χαραυγή [Cyprus], 26 May 1980.

Hardy, Sir Alister C.

1966 *The Divine Flame: an Essay Towards a Natural History of Religion*. London: Collins.

Haris, Manos, ed.

1961 Αναμνηστικό λεύκωμα Νίκου Καζαντζάκη. Athens: Difros.

Haris, Petros

1945 Η τέχνη και η εποχή. Νεα Εστία 38:511 (1 July 1945). Interview with Kazantzakis conducted in June 1945.

Hartocollis, Peter

1974 Mysticism and Violence: The Case of Nikos Kazantzakis. *International Journal of Psycho-Analysis* 55: 205–213.

Hatzinis, Yannis

1955 Review of Ο Χριστός ξανασταυρώνεται, Νέα Εστία 57:131–132 (15 Jan. 1955).

Hitchens, Christopher

1971 Review of Georg Lukács' "History and Class Consciousness" (London 1971). *The Times* [London], 11 March 1971, p. 12.

Hoberman, J.

1984 Who Is Victor Serge? (And Why Do We Have To Ask?). *Village Voice*. Literary Supplement no. 3. November 1984, pp. 12–17.

Hoffmann, Stanley

1987 Review of "Sartre: A Life," by Annie Cohen-Solal. *The New York Times Book Review*, 26 July 1987, pp. 3, 25.

Hollander, Paul

1981 *Political Pilgrims: Travels of Western Intellectuals to the Soviet Union, China, and Cuba 1928–1978*. Oxford: Oxford University Press.

Hopkins, Adam

1977 *Crete, Its Past, Present, and People*. London: Faber and Faber.

Hourmouzios, Emmanuel

1948 Ελληνικότητα και ξενηλασία. Νέα Εστία 44:819–825.

Istrati, Panaït

1928a Αι κοινωνικαί θεωρίαι. Μεταξύ της Δύσεως που πεθαίνει και της Ανατολής που γεννάται. Ελεύθερον Βήμα, 12 Jan. 1928, pp. 5–6.

1928b Notes et reportages d'un Vagabond du Monde. Parmi les gueux de Grèce, I, Nikos Kazantsaki. *Monde*, 23 June 1928, p. 3.

1929a *Vers l'autre flamme. Après seize mois dans l'U.R.S.S.* Paris: Rieder. (Vol. 1 of *Vers l'autre flamme.*)

1929b L'Affaire Roussakov ou l'U.R.S.S. d'aujourd'hui. *Nouvelle Revue Française* 33 (1929), 439–476 (1 Oct. 1929). Reprinted with some verbal changes in Istrati 1929a:207–280.

1931 *Russia Unveiled.* London: Allen & Unwin.

1983 Panaït Istrati–Nikos Kazantzaki. Correspondance inédite complète. *L'Arc*, nos. 86/87 (1983), pp. 21–35.

Izzet, Aziz

1964 Nikos Kazantzaki. *ahiers de Sud* [Marseilles] 57, no. 377:347–355.

1965 *Nikos Kazantzaki. Biographie.* Paris: Plon.

James, William

1890 *Principles of Psychology.* 2 vols. New York: Holt. The section translated by Kazantzakis (see James 1911) is vol. 2, pp. 383–441, Chapter 24: Instinct.

1909 *A Pluralistic Universe.* New York & London: Longmans, Green. Translated as *Philosophie de l'expérience* (Paris: Flammarion, 1910).

1911 Η θεωρία της συγκινήσεως. Translated by Nikos Kazantzakis. Athens: Fexis.

1920 *Le Pragmatisme.* Avec une introduction par H. Bergson. Paris: Flammarion. First published in 1911.

1955 *"Pragmatism" and Four Essays from the "Meaning of Truth."* New York: Meridian Books.

Janiaud-Lust, Colette

1970 *Nikos Kazantzaki: sa vie, son oeuvre* (1893–1957). Paris: Maspero.

Joll, James

1978 Review of Walther Rathenau's "Gesamtausgabe," vol. 2. *Times Literary Supplement* (London), 25 August 1978, pp. 942–943.

Jouvenel, Renaud de

1958 En souvenir de Kazantzaki. *Europe*, June 1958, pp. 85–105.

1962 Νίκος Καζαντζάκης, Νέα Εστία 72:1570–1585 (1 Nov. 1962). Translation of Jouvenel 1958.

Joyce, James

1947 *Finnegans Wake.* New York: Viking Press.

1959 *Stephen Hero.* New York: New Directions.

1986 *Ulysses* [The Corrected Text]. New York: Random House.

Kakridis, Yannis

1977 84 γράμματα του Καζαντζάκη στον Κακριδή. Νέα Εστία 102, Christmas 1977, pp. 257–300.

Kallen, Horace Meyer
1914 *William James and Henri Bergson, a Study in Contrasting Theories of Life.* Chicago: University of Chicago Press.
Karabasis, Ayisilaos S.
1924–1925 Letters to Νέα Εφημερίς regarding Το κοινωνικόν πρόβλημα. Νέα Εφημερίς [Iráklion], 1 Dec. 1924, p. 1; 14 May 1925, p. 1; 15 May 1925, p. 1; 16 May 1925, p. 1; 17 May 1925, pp. 1–2.
Karandonis, Andreas
1958a Εισαγωγή στη νεώτερη ποίηση. Athens: Difros.
1958b Η περίπτωση Καζαντζάκη. Καινούρια Εποχή, Autumn, 1958, pp. 265–267.
Karapanayiotis, E.
1913 Η φιλοσοφία του Μπέρξων. Ο Νουμάς, 9 Feb. 1913, pp. 29–30. Letter to the editor dated 31 Jan. 1913 regarding Kazantzakis's lecture on Bergson "the night before."
Karouzos, Ch.
1926 Απάντηση στον κ. Καζαντζάκη. Αναγέννηση Α΄:137–142 (Nov. 1926).
1927 Δευτερολογία. Αναγέννηση Α΄:267–271 (Jan. 1927).
Karyotakis, Kostas
1938 Άπαντα. Athens: Govostis.
Kasdaglis, Emmanuel
1986 Letter to Peter Bien, 19 May.
1987 Interview with Peter Bien. Athens, 28 April.
Katsimbalis, G. K.
1958a Βιβλιογραφία Ν. Καζαντζάκη Α΄, 1906–1948. Athens.
1958b Ο άγνωστος Καζαντζάκης: Ο πρωτομάστορας. Νέα Εστία 64:1558–1560 (15 October 1958).
1958c Ο άγνωστος Καζαντζάκης: οι πρώτες ταξιδιωτικές εντυπώσεις του. Νέα Εστία 64:1207–1208 (15 August 1958).
1958d Ο άγνωστος Καζαντζάκης: το πρώτο βιβλίο του, όπως το είδαν οι σύγχρονοί του. Νέα Εστία 63:612–615, 689–691 (15 April and 1 May 1958).
1958e Ο άγνωστος Καζαντζάκης: το πρώτο θεατρικό του έργο "Ξημερώνει." Νέα Εστία 63:745–756 (15 May 1958).
1961 Letter in Νέα Εστία 69:835 (15 June 1961).
Kazantzaki, Eleni N.
1938 [Eleni Samios] *La verdadera tragedia de Panait Istrati.* Santiago, Chile: Ercilla.
1968a [Helen Kazantzakis] *Nikos Kazantzakis, a biography based on his letters.* New York: Simon and Schuster.
1968b *Le Dissident: biographie de Nikos Kazantzaki.* Paris: Plon.
1969 Interview with Peter Bien, Algonquin Hotel, New York City, 17 April 1969.
1977 Νίκος Καζαντζάκης, ο ασυμβίβαστος. Athens: Eleni N. Kazantzaki.
1983 Δίχως οργή και με ντοκουμέντα. Το Βήμα της Κυριακής. 21 August 1983, p. 5.

Kazantzaki, Galatea
1957 Άνθρωποι και υπεράνθρωποι. Athens: Piksidia.
Kazantzakis, Nikos
Note: I do not include here the various holograph notebooks in Mrs. Kazantzakis's possession, because they are impossible to date.
1906 [Κάρμα Νιρβαμῆ] Όφις καί κρίνο. Athens. Reissued 1974, Athens: Ekdóseis Elénis Kazantzáki. Translated as *Serpent and Lily* by Theodora Vasils. Berkeley: University of California Press, 1980.
1907 [Ακρίτας] Χρονογραφήματα. Λέων Τολστόη. Ακρόπολις, 5 June 1907, p. 1.
1909a [Πέτρος Ψηλορείτης] Σπασμένες ψυχές. Ο Νουμάς 7 (1909) and 8 (1910). The serialization ran from 30 August 1909 until 7 February 1910. The novel has never been republished.
1909b Ὁ Φρειδερῖκος Νίτσε ἐν τῇ φιλοσοφίᾳ τοῦ δικαίου καὶ τῆς πολιτείας. Iráklion: Alexiou. For the reprint in *Kainúria Epohí*, see Kaz. 1959c.
1909c [Κάρμα Νιρβαμῆ] Φιλολογικαί Επιστολαί. Ελληνικά ποιήματα. Νέον Άστυ, 16 Feb. 1909. Reprinted in *Néa Estía* 64:1288–1290 (1 Sept. 1958).
1910a [Πέτρος Ψηλορείτης] Για τους νέους μας. Νέα Ζωή [Alexandria] 6/5–6–7 (Feb.–Mar.–Apr.):232–239. Excerpts in Yalourakis 1978: 59ff.
1910b [Πέτρος Ψηλορείτης] Jean Moréas. Νέα Ζωή [Alexandria] 6:353–360 (July–August–September 1910). Cited extensively in Yalourakis 1978:77ff.
1910c [Πέτρος Ψηλορείτης] Ο πρωτομάστορας. Athens: Panathinaion.
1910d [Πέτρος Ψηλορείτης] Οι Ραγιάδες. Ακρόπολις, 21 June 1910. Reprinted in *Néa Estía* 64:1563–1564 (15 Oct. 1958).
1912 H. Bergson. Δελτίο Εκπαιδευτικού Ομίλου Β':310–334 (October 1912). Reprinted in Καινούρια Εποχή, Autumn 1958, pp. 12–30, and in Alexiou and Stefanakis 1983:259–285. (Kazantzakis's lecture is dated 22 January 1913; the October 1912 issue of the *Bulletin of the Educational Association* must have been delayed and have actually appeared in 1913.)
1913a Γουσταύος Φλωμπέρ. Νέα Ελλάδα, 11 Sept. 1913, p. 3. Reprinted in *Kainúria Epohí*, Spring 1960, pp. 8–10, and in Alexiou and Stefanakis 1983:251–254.
1913?b Note to Manolis Triandafyllidis concerning the Σύλλογος Δημοτικιστών "Σολωμός." Αρχείο Μανόλη Τριανταφυλλίδη, Ινστιτούτο Νεοελληνικών Σπουδών, Πανεπιστημίου Θεσσαλονίκης. Drawn upon by Triandafyllidis in his Απολογία της δημοτικής, Δελτίο του Εκπαιδευτικού Ομίλου 4 (1914): 148.
1923 [Α. Γερανός]. Γράμματα στη γυναίκα μου. Ο Νουμάς, June 1923, pp. 402–406; October 1923, pp. 566–578.
1924 Diary entry for 15 July 1924. In Prevelakis 1965b:158–159; Mitsotakis 1972:116–117; and, with some differences, Eleni Kazantzaki 1977: 29–31; 1968a:26–27. French translation in Janiaud-Lust 1970:577.

1925a 'Ομολογία πίστεως. Νέα Εφημερίς (Iráklion), 16 Feb. 1925. Reprinted in Elli Alexiou 1966:297–300; Spanakis 1962:50–52. French translation in Janiaud-Lust, 1970:567ff.

1925b Το κοινωνικόν πρόβλημα. Νέα Εφημερίς (Iráklion), 19 Feb. 1925, p. 1.

1925c Το κοινωνικόν πρόβλημα [continued]. Νέα Εφημερίς (Iráklion), 22 Feb. 1925, p. 1. Reprinted in Mitsotakis 1972: 126–133.

1925d Μιχάλης Καλημεράκης. [Obituary.] Ανόρθωσις (Iráklion), 11 July 1925, p. 1.

1926a Προσεισαγωγικό σημείωμα. Αναγέννηση Α΄:136–137 (Nov. 1926).

1926b Συζήτηση μ'έναν αρχηγό. Αναγέννηση Α΄:19–24 (Sept. 1926). Expanded version in Ταξιδεύοντας. Ρουσία, pp. 217–226.

1926c Η νέα Πομπηία. Αναγέννηση Α΄:76–80 (October 1926). Reprinted in Ταξιδεύοντας. Ρουσία, pp. 259–267.

1926d Η έκτη επέτειος. Ίων Δραγούμης. Ελεύθερος Τύπος, 1 Aug. 1926. Reprinted in *Néa Estía* 68:978–980 (1 Aug. 1960).

1926e Δεύτερο σημείωμα. Αναγέννηση Α΄:203–204 (Dec. 1926).

1926f Φρειδερίκος Νίτσε. Ελεύθερος Τύπος, 22 Aug. and 26 Aug.

1927a Μία προφητεία του Σορέλ δια τον Μουσολίνι από το 1912. Ελεύθερος Τύπος, 7 Feb. 1927.

1927b Ο Γιάννης Σταβριδάκης. Νεοελληνικά Γράμματα [Ηράκλειο] May 1927, pp. 364–369.

1927c Η σταυρωμένη Ρουσία. Αναγέννηση Α΄:271–277 (January 1927). Reprinted in *Taksidevondas. Rusia*, pp. 251–259.

1927d Επισκόπηση της Σοβιετικής Ρουσίας. Αναγέννηση Α΄:349–352 (Feb. 1927). Reprinted in *Taksidevondas. Rusia*, pp. 267–270, much revised, under the title Γενική επισκόπηση.

1927e Παναΐτ Ιστράτι. Η Πρωΐα, 31 Dec. 1927, pp. 1–2.

1927f *Salvatores Dei*. Ασκητική. Αναγέννηση Α΄:599–631 (July–August 1927). This is the first version, unrevised.

1927g Νικηφόρος Φωκάς. Athens: Stohastis. Reprinted in Kaz. 1956c.

1927h Μία προφητεία του Σορέλ δια τον Μουσολίνι από το 1912. Ο Φασισμός καρπός εσωτερικής ιταλικής ανάγκης και όχι τυχαία έκρηξις βιαιότητος ή μεγαλομανίας. Ελεύθερος Τύπος, 7 February 1927.

1928a Βουδδισμός. Εγκυκλοπαιδικό Λεξικό Ελευθερουδάκη, vol. 3, pp. 445–446.

1928b Τί γίνεται στη Ρωσία. Αναγέννηση Β΄:193–198 (Jan. 1928). This is Kazantzakis's speech in the Alhambra Theater, 11 Jan. 1928. Reprinted in Elli Alexiou 1966:287–296.

1928c Εντυπώσεις από την Σοβιετικήν Ρωσσίαν. Στάλιν και Τρότσκη. Η Πρωΐα, 11 Jan. 1928.

1928d Εντυπώσεις από την Σοβιετικήν Ρωσσίαν. Το συνέδριον της Μόσχας. Η Πρωΐα, 10 Jan. 1928, pp. 1–2.

1930 Ιστορία της ρωσικής λογοτεχνίας. 2 volumes. Athens: Eleftheroudakis.

1931 Σοπενχάουερ. Εγκυκλοπαιδικό Λεξικό Ελευθερουδάκη. Vol. 11, pp. 618–619.

1936 Ο φόβος και η πείνα. Η Καθημερινή, 20 July 1936, p. 3. Reprinted in Vrettakos 1960:577–579.

1937 Letter dated 10 April 1937, to Lefteris Alexiou. Printed in Elli Alexiou, Για να γίνει μεγάλος, pp. 319–324.

1938 Νίτσε. [Terzina.] *Néa Estía* 24:1009–1013 (1 Aug. 1938). Reprinted in Kaz. 1960c.

1939a Ένα ανοιχτό γράμμα για την Κα Έλλη Λαμπρίδη. Νεοελληνικά Γράμματα, 25 March 1939, p. 13. (The Greek text is reprinted in Goudelis 1978:38–40. Kimon Friar translates most of it in Kaz. 1958f:823.)

1939b Ένα μικρό σχόλιο για την Οδύσεια. Νέα Εστία 26:1572 (15 Nov. 1939).

1941 Χαιρετισμός στον Ίωνα Δραγούμη. Νέα Εστία 29:223 (15 March 1941).

1942 Ταξιδεύοντας: παιδικά χρόνια στην Κρήτη. Νέα Εστία 31:344–348 (1 June 1942).

1943 Ένα σχόλιο στην Οδύσεια. Νέα Εστία 34:1028–1034 (15 August 1943).

1945a Interview in Ακρόπολις, 29 May 1945, p. 1, and 30 May 1945, p. 1.

1945b Introduction to S. Gopner's Η ορμητική άνοδος του πολιτισμού στην Ε.Σ.Σ.Δ. Athens: Papazisis. Pp. 3–6. Reprinted in Elli Alexiou 1966:242–244.

1945c Πώς πρωτοσυναντήθηκε ο Παναΐτ Ιστράτι με τον Γκόρκη. Νέα Εστία 38:934–936 (1 Nov. 1945).

1946 Speech welcoming Paul Eluard to Athens, 26 May 1946. Printed in Νέα Εστία 39:493 (15 April 1946); Ελεύθερα Γράμματα, 1 June 1946, p. 159; Elli Alexiou 1966:240–241.

1947 Ο θάνατος του παππού. Νέα Εστία 41:327–334 (15 March 1947).

1950 Unpublished letter to Apostolos Sachinis, 20 Nov. 1950.

1953 *Zorba the Greek*. New York: Simon and Schuster.

1954 Το δράμα και ο σημερινός άνθρωπος. Νέα Εστία 56:1636–1638 (15 Nov. 1954). For a partial recapitulation of the same ideas see Kaz. 1965a:227. For the translation of the essay see Kaz, 1976.

1955a Letter to Yannis Hatzinis. Νέα Εστία 57:202 (1 Feb. 1955).

1955b Οι δύο αδελφοί: τα ογδόντα χρόνια του Σβάιτσερ. Νέα Εστία 57:214–215 (15 Feb. 1955).

1955c Ο τελευταίος πειρασμός. Athens: Difros.

1956a *Freedom or Death*. New York: Simon and Schuster. Oxford: Cassirer (under the title *Freedom and Death*).

1956b Τόντα-Ράμπα. Translated by Yannis Manglis. Athens: Difros.

1956c Θέατρο Β΄. Athens: Difros.

1956d Ο φτωχούλης του Θεού. Athens: Difros.

1956e Θέατρο Γ΄. Athens: Difros.

1957 Οδύσσεια, 2nd ed. Athens.

1958a Επιστολές προς τη Γαλάτεια. Athens: Difros. Care should be taken in using this volume because of the editor's errors in dating the letters. The errors remain uncorrected in the second edition (Athens: Difros, 1984), which contains additional scholia by Elli Alexiou.

1958b H. Bergson. Καινούρια Εποχή, Autumn 1958, pp. 12–30. Reprinted from Δελτίο του Εκπαιδευτικού Ομίλου, October 1912.

1958c [Ακρίτας] Επιστολαί από το Παρίσι. Οι Έλληνες σπουδασταί. Νέα Εστία 64:1284–1285 (1 Sept. 1958). Reprinted from Νέον Άστυ, 8 March 1908.

1958d [Κάρμα Νιρβαμή] Ἡ ἀρρώστεια [sic] τοῦ αἰῶνος. Νέα Εστία 63:691–696 (1 May 1958). Reprinted from Πινακοθήκη 6, March–April–May 1906, pp. 8–11, 26–27, 46–47. Translation included in *Serpent and Lily* (Kaz. 1906). Another translation in *Ball State University Forum* 17/2 (Spring 1976):69–78.

1958e Η κραυγή της Ρόζας Λουξεμπούργκ. Καινούρια Εποχή, Winter 1958, pp. 171–175. Reprinted from Ηλύσια, 22 May 1927, pp. 12–15.

1958f *The Odyssey: a modern sequel.* Translated by Kimon Friar. New York: Simon and Schuster.

1958g Επιστολαί από το Παρίσι. Η ποικιλία παντού. Νέα Εστία 64:1210–1212 (15 Aug. 1958). Reprinted from Νέον Άστυ, 25 Oct. 1907.

1958h Η επιστήμη εχρεωκόπησε; Νέα Εστία 64:1374–1378 (15 Sept. 1958). Reprinted from Παναθήναια, 15 Nov. 1909, pp. 71–75.

1958i [Κάρμα Νιρβαμή] Τί μού λένε οι παπαρούνες. Νέα Εστία 64:1021–1022 (1 July 1958). Reprinted from Πινακοθήκη, August 1906, pp. 96–98.

1958j *Du Mont Sinaï à l'Île de Vénus: Carnets de voyage.* Paris: Plon.

1958k [Κάρμα Νιρβαμή] Νοσταλγία. Νέα Εστία 64:1081 (15 July 1958). Reprinted from Πινακοθήκη, June 1907, p. 73. Also published in Ακρόπολις 15 May 1907, signed "Akrítas."

1958l [Κάρμα Νιρβαμή] Χριστουγεννιάτικο. Νέα Εστία 64:1082–1083 (15 July 1958). Reprinted from Πινακοθήκη, Jan. 1908, pp. 172–173.

1958m [Ακρίτας] Χρονογραφήματα. Στην "Εστία." Νέα Εστία 63:753 (15 May 1958). Reprinted from Ακρόπολις, 8 May 1907.

1958n [Κάρμα Νιρβαμή] Ταξειδιωτικαί εντυπώσεις. Εις την Φλωρεντίαν. Νέα Εστία 64:1290–1292 (1 Sept. 1958). Reprinted from Νέον Άστυ, 10 April 1909.

1958o [Πέτρος Ψηλορείτης] Από τον Θεατρόκοσμον. Οι ραγιάδες. Νέα Εστία 64:1563–1564 (15 Oct. 1958). Reprinted from Ακρόπολις, 21 June 1910.

1958p [Ακρίτας] Παρισινά Γράμματα. Η εξέγερσις του σοσιαλισμού. Νέα Εστία 64:1212–1213 (15 August 1958). Reprinted from Νέον Άστυ, 6 Nov. 1907.

1958q Από το Παρίσι. Ο Έλλην γλύπτης. Νέα Εστία 64:1285–1288 (1 Sept. 1958). Reprinted from Νέον Άστυ, 26 June 1908.

1958r [Πέτρος Ψηλορείτης] Σπασμένες ψυχές [an article glossing the novel]. *Néa Estía* 64:1498–1501. Reprinted from Ο Νουμάς, 27 Sept. 1909, pp. 2–4.

1958s Credo. Written in 1953 for a proposed third volume of Edward R. Murrow's series *This I Believe* (New York: Simon and Schuster, 1952, 1954). English translation in Kimon Friar's introduction to the *Odyssey* (Kaz. 1958f:xxiii–xxiv). Greek text in Κρητικό Μέλλον (Haniá), 8 Dec. 1958, p. 1. An excerpt appears in Izzet 1965:63.

1958t Κωμωδία, τραγωδία μονόπρακτη. Νέα Εστία 63:616–625 (15 April 1958). Originally published in Κρητική Στοά (Iráklion), 1909, pp. 125–144, and concurrently in Σεράπιον (Alexandria), 1909, pp. 291–312. Reprinted in Προπύλαια (Zurich), 1969, with an introduction by Karl Kerényi. English translation by Kimon Friar, with introduction, in *The Literary Review* 18/4 (Summer 1975), pp. 417–454; reprinted in Kaz. 1982.

1959a Η Κρήτη. Νέα Εστία 66, Christmas 1959, pp. 39–42.

1959b *Le Jardin des rochers*. Paris: Plon, 1959.

1959c Ὁ Φρειδερῖκος Νίτσε ἐν τῇ φιλοσοφίᾳ τοῦ δικαίου καὶ τῆς πολιτείας. Καινούρια Εποχή, Summer 1959, pp. 34–89. (Originally published in 1909.)

1959d Βίος και πολιτεία του Αλέξη Ζορμπά. 5th ed. Athens.

1960a *The Last Temptation of Christ*. New York: Simon and Schuster.

1960b *The Saviors of God: Spiritual Exercises*. New York: Simon and Schuster.

1960c Τερτσίνες. Athens.

1962a Ασκητική, *Salvatores Dei*. 2nd ed. rev. Athens.

1962b Ταξιδεύοντας. Ισπανία, 3rd ed. Athens.

1962c *Toda-Raba: Moscou a crié*. Paris: Plon.

1962d *Saint Francis*. New York: Simon and Schuster. (Published in Great Britain under the title: *God's Pauper*.)

1963a *Japan China*. New York: Simon and Schuster.

1963b *The Rock Garden*. New York: Simon and Schuster.

1963c *Spain*. New York: Simon and Schuster.

1964a Αναφορά στον Γκρέκο. Athens: Eleni Kazantzaki.

1964b Ο Καπετάν Μιχάλης, 5th ed. Athens: Eleni Kazantzaki. (For pagination of the first two editions, add 6 pages to the page numbers in the third and subsequent editions.)

1964c Ταξιδεύοντας. Αγγλία. 5th ed. Athens: Eleni Kazantzaki.

1964d Ταξιδεύοντας. Ιαπωνία-Κίνα, 6th ed. Athens: Eleni Kazantzaki.

1964e *The Fratricides*. New York: Simon and Schuster.

1964f *Toda Raba*. New York: Simon and Schuster.

1965a *England*. New York: Simon and Schuster.

1965b *Journey to the Morea*. New York: Simon and Schuster.

1965c *Report to Greco*. New York: Simon and Schuster.

1965d Ταξιδεύοντας. Ιταλία, Αίγυπτος, Σινά, Ιερουσαλήμ, Κύπρος, Ο Μοριάς. 2nd ed. Athens: Eleni Kazantzaki.

1965e Ταξιδεύοντας. Ρουσία. 4th ed. Athens: Eleni Kazantzaki.

1971a Σκόρπιες σελίδες από τα τετράδια του Νίκου Καζαντζάκη. Νέα Εστία 90:1257–1261 (1 October 1971).

1971b Συμπόσιον. Athens: Eleni Kazantzaki.

1972 Γράμματα Νίκου Καζαντζάκη προς Μηνά Δημάκη. Νέα Εστία 91:237–246, 301–310. (15 Feb. 1972 and 1 March 1972). Reprinted in Dimakis 1975:13–33.

1974 *Symposium*. New York: Minerva Press.

1975 *Journeying: Travels in Italy, Egypt, Sinai, Jerusalem and Cyprus*. Boston: Little, Brown.

1976 Drama and Contemporary Man. *The Literary Review* 19 (1976):115–121.

1977a Δέκα επιστολές του Καζαντζάκη στον Χουρμούζιο. Τετράδια "Ευθύνης" Γ', pp. 180–195.

1977b Έξι γράμματα του Νίκου Καζαντζάκη στον Max Tau. Νέα Εστία 102, Christmas 1977, pp. 308–310.

1977c Φασγά. Νέα Εστία 102, Christmas 1977, pp. 236–256.

1977d Ξημερώνει. Νέα Εστία 102. Christmas 1977, pp. 182–210.

1977e Έως πότε; Νέα Εστία 102. Christmas 1977, pp. 211–235.

1979 *The Suffering God: Selected Letters to Galatea and to Papastephanou*. New Rochelle, N.Y.: Caratzas. (Unfortunately perpetuates the errors of dating and arrangement in Kazantzakis 1958a, and also omits large portions of the letters. See Bien 1980.)

1982 *Two Plays by Nikos Kazantzakis. "Sodom and Gomorrah" and "Comedy."* St. Paul, Minn.: North Central Publishing Co.

1983 *Buddha*. San Diego: Avant.

1985 Πέντε ανέκδοτες επιστολές προς τον Αλέξη Μινωτή. Η Λέξη, no. 42 (Feb. 1985), 114–118.

1989 *Russia*. Berkeley, Calif: Creative Arts Book Co.

Kerényi, Karl

1959 Νίκος Καζαντζάκης: συνεχιστής του Νίτσε στην Ελλάδα. Νέα Εστία 66, Christmas 1959, pp. 43–59.

Kierkegaard, Søren

1941 *Training in Christianity*. London: Oxford University Press.

1951 *A Kierkegaard Anthology*. Edited by Robert Bretall. Princeton: Princeton University Press. (Also issued by Random House in The Modern Library series, with identical pagination.)

Knös, Börje

1946–1960 Börje Knös brevsamling. University of Uppsala Library. (Unpublished letters to Knös from Nikos Kazantsakis and Eleni Kazantzaki.)

1977a Ανέκδοτα γράμματα του Ν. Καζαντζάκη στον Β. Knös. Νέα Εστία 102, Christmas 1977, pp. 301–303.

1977b Αποσπάσματα από ανέκδοτα γράμματα του Β. Knös στον Νίκο Καζαντζάκη. Νέα Εστία 102, Christmas 1977, pp. 304–307.

Knosos

1958 (Periodical publication of the Knosos Society of Crete). Vol. 5, no. 22. Athens, May 1958.

Knox, Benjamin D.

1977 A Comparison of the Russian Revolution of 1905 and a Scene from

Kazantzakis's Odyssey. Unpublished essay for Greek and Roman Studies 7, Fall 1977, Dartmouth College.

Kordatos, Yannis

1926 Φυσικοί και κοινωνικοί νόμοι. Αναγέννηση Α':199–203 (Dec. 1926).

1927 Οι επικριτές του Μαρξισμού. Αναγέννηση Α':259–264 (Jan. 1927).

1983 Ιστορία της νεοελληνικής λογοτεχνίας (από το 1453 ώς το 1961). 2 vols. Athens: Epikairotita. (Reprint of 1962 edition.)

Koumakis, Yorgos

1985 Νίκος Καζαντζάκης: Θεμελιώδη προβλήματα στη φιλοσοφία του. Athens: Estia.

Lagakos, E.

1927 Απάντηση στον κ. Καζαντζάκη. Αναγέννηση Α':552–555 (May–June 1927).

Laing, R. D.

1967 *The Politics of Experience*. New York: Ballantine Books.

Lambridi, Elli

1927 Προϋπόθεσες. Αναγέννηση Α':265–266 (Jan. 1927).

1939 Η "Οδύσσεια" του Ν. Καζαντζάκη. Η μεταφυσική της. Νεοελληνικά Γράμματα, 4 March, p. 11, and 11 March, p. 11.

Lambridis, Frixos

1947 [Λ. Τασολάμπρος] Η συμφιλίωση και οι πνευματικές ηγέτες: Ν. Καζαντζάκης, Α. Σικελιανός. Athens: Eleftheros Kratos.

Laourdas, Vasilios

1943 Σχόλιο σ' ένα κριτικό δοκίμιο. Νέα Εστία 34:1336–1341 (15 Nov. 1943).

1964 Η εποχή της "Τρισεύγενης." Thessaloniki. (No. 2 in the 1963–1964 lecture series of the Κρατικόν Θέατρον Βορείου Ελλάδος.)

Lawrence, D. H.

1966 *Apocalypse*. New York: Viking Press.

1981 *The Letters of D. H. Lawrence*. Vol. 2. Edited by George J. Zytaruk and James T. Boulton. Cambridge: Cambridge University Press.

Lea, James F.

1979 *Kazantzakis: The Politics of Salvation*. Tuscaloosa: University of Alabama Press.

Lebesgue, Philéas

1928 [Démétrius Astériotis] Lettres Néo-Grecques. *Mercure de France*, 15 Dec. 1928, pp. 721–726.

1930 [Démétrius Astériotis] Lettres Néo-Grecques. *Mercure de France*, 15 April 1930, pp. 484–490.

Lefèvre, Frédéric

1929 Une heure avec Panaït Istrati. *Les Nouvelles Littéraires*, 23 Feb. 1929, pp. 1, 9. Reprinted in Lefèvre's *Une heure avec . . .*, cinquième série (Paris: Gallimard, n.d. [1929]).

Leigh Fermor, Patrick

1978 The Landscape of Myth. *Times Literary Supplement* (London), 26 May 1978, p. 583.

Leontaritou, Kleopatra
1981 Η νεορομαντική βιοθεωρία του Καζαντζάκη. Athens: Themelio.
Levitt, Morton P.
1972 The Cretan Glance: The World and Art of Nikos Kazantzakis. *Journal of Modern Literature* 2/2 (1971–1972): 163–188.
Lewis, Wyndham
1927 *Time and Western Man*. London: Chatto and Windus.
Lossky, Vladimir
1957 *The Mystical Theology of the Eastern Church*. London: James Clark. (Translation of *Essai sur la théologie mystique de l'Eglise d'orient*. Paris, 1944.)
Lucretius
1925 *On the Nature of Things*. Translated by Sir Robert Allison. London: Hatchards.
Lukács, Georg
1962 *The Meaning of Contemporary Realism*. London: Merlin Press.
Macdonald, Graham, and Crispin Wright
1986 *Fact, Science and Morality: Essays on A. J. Ayer's "Language, Truth and Logic."* Oxford: Blackwell.
McDonough, B. T.
1978 *Nietzsche and Kazantzakis*. Washington, D.C.: University Press of America.
Mackridge, Peter
1980 Review of "Serpent and Lily." *Times Literary Supplement* (London), 4 July 1980, p. 749.
1985 European Influences in the Greek Novel During the 1930s. *Journal of Modern Greek Studies* 3:1–20.
Makriyannis, Yannis
1965 Απομνημονεύματα. Athens: Galaksia.
1966 *The Memoirs of General Makriyannis 1794–1864*. Translated by H. A. Lidderdale. London: Oxford University Press.
Mann, Thomas
1963 *The Magic Mountain*. New York: Knopf.
Manolikakis, Ioannos G.
1971 (See Venizelos 1971, for which Manolikakis provided notes, apparatus, and a Chronicle of the Revolution of 1889.)
Manousakis, G.
1977 Τα πρόσωπα του "Καπετάν Μιχάλη": μια καζαντζακική ανθρωπολογική κλίμακα. Τετράδια "Ευθύνης" Γ΄, 118–153. (Translated in *The Charioteer*, nos. 22–23 [1980–1981], 66–102, under the title, "The Characters in *Freedom or Death*: A Kazantzakean Anthropological Scale."
Markakis, Petros
1959a Κ. Ουράνης και Νίκος Καζαντζάκης. Δημιουργοί της ταξιδιωτικής μας λογοτεχνίας. Καινούρια Εποχή, Autumn 1959, pp. 40–43.
1959b Ανέκδοτα γράμματα του Νίκου Καζαντζάκη: το περιοδικό "Πινακοθήκη" κι ο Δημ. Καλογερόπουλος. Καινούρια Εποχή, Autumn 1959, pp. 30–38.

Martinescu, P.

1958 Νίκος Καζαντζάκης και Παναΐτ Ιστράτι. Αθήναι, 12 Oct. 1958, pp. 9–10.

Megas, Georges

1953 La Prise de Constantinople dans la poésie et la tradition populaires grecques. In *L'Hellénisme Contemporain, le cinq-centième anniversaire de la prise de Constantinople*. Athens: Imprimerie Nationale.

Merrill, Reed B.

1975 "Zorba the Greek" and Nietzschean Nihilism. *Mosaic* 8/2 (Winter 1975): 99–113.

Mitsotakis, Kyriakos

1972 Ο Καζαντζάκης μιλεί για Θεό. Athens: Minoas. The Papastefanou letters are translated, in part, in Kazantzakis 1979, *The Suffering God*. Mrs. Kazantzakis warns against Mitsotakis's errors regarding the genesis of *Askitkí*, owing to his ignorance of Papastefanou's letters to Kazantzakis (Eleni Kaz. 1977:77, fn.1); on this, see Stamatiou 1975.

Monde

1928 Istrati's series: Notes et reportages d'un Vagabond du Monde, 9 June–21 July. This weekly periodical was published by Henri Barbusse. The editorial committee included A. Einstein, M. Gorki, Upton Sinclair, Manuel Ugarte, and M. de Unamuno!

Monod, Jacques

1971 *Chance and Necessity: An Essay on the Natural Philosophy of Modern Biology*. New York: Knopf.

Mousopouolos, Athanasios

1972 Η επίδραση των ιδεών του Νίτσε στην ελληνική διανόηση και η υπέρβασή τους από τον Καζαντζάκη. Ξάνθη: Έκδοση "Θρακικών Χρονιών," July 1972.

Myrivilis, Stratis

1936 Ο καλλιτέχνης και ο κομμουνισμός. Η Εθνική, 29 July 1936, p. 3.

Nea Efimeris

1924–1925 Editorials, articles, letters, and announcements in the newspaper Νέα Ἐφημερίς (Iráklion, Crete). Editor: Elias Dialinas.

Nehamas, Alexander

1985 *Nietzsche: Life as Literature*. Cambridge, Mass.: Harvard University Press.

Nemoianu, Virgil

1984 Review of Istrati's "Le Pèlerin du coeur," edited by Alexandre Talex—an anthology of recollections, fragments, lectures. *Times Literary Supplement*, 5 Oct. 1984, p. 1133.

Nicolopoulos, John

1985 From Agathangelos to the Megale Idea: Russia and the Emergence of Modern Greek Nationalism. *Balkan Studies* 26: 41–56.

Nietzsche, Friedrich

1910 *The Joyful Wisdom* (La Gaya Scienza). *The Complete Works of Friedrich Nietzsche*. Vol. 10. Edinburgh: Foulis.

1913 *The Genealogy of Morals. The Complete Works of Friedrich Nietzsche.* Vol. 13. Edinburgh: Foulis.

Nordstrom, Louis, ed.

1976 *Namu Dai Bosa: A Transmission of Zen Buddhism to America*, by Nyogen Senzaki, Soen Nakagawa, Eido Shimano. The Bhaisajaguru Series. New York: Theatre Arts Books.

Nye, Robert

1965 Review of "Report to Greco." *The Scotsman* [Edinburgh], 11 Dec.

Oikonomidou, Eleftheria

1985 Ο Νίκος Καζαντζάκης και το αντικείμενο αναζήτησής του. Iráklion: Dimos Irakliou.

Orwell, George

1961 *Collected Essays.* London: Secker & Warburg.

Pachter, Henry M.

1978 Walther Rathenau, Musil's Arnheim or Mann's Naphta? *Boston University Journal* 25/3:17–28.

Palamas, Kostis

1911 Το κλειδί του σπιτιού. Ακρόπολις, 1 January.

1969 *The Twelve Lays of the Gypsy.* Translated with an introduction, by George Thomson. London: Lawrence & Wishart.

Palamas, Leandros

1921 Ίων Δραγούμης. Δελτίο του Εκπαιδευτικού Ομίλου 9:99–108.

Papahatzaki-Katsaraki, Theodora

1985 Το θεατρικό έργο του Νίκου Καζαντζάκη. Athens: Dodoni.

Papathanasopoulos, Thanasis

1985 Γύρω στον Καζαντζάκη. Athens.

Paraschos, Kleon

1927 Ν. Καζαντζάκη "Salvatores Dei." Νέα Εστία 2:889–891 (1 November 1927).

1956 Το ρεύμα της απαισιοδοξίας στη νέα Ελληνική λογοτεχνία. Καινούρια Εποχή, Spring 1956, pp. 142–145.

Pashley, Robert

1837 *Travels in Crete.* 2 vols. London. (1970 reprint by Adolph Hakkert, Amsterdam.)

Peñuelas, Marcelino C.

1968 *Jacinto Benavente.* New York: Twayne.

Petritakis, Yannis, and Frofo Hatzini

1984 Ο Γιάννης Χατζίνης & τα νεοελληνικά γράμματα. Athens.

Politis, Fotos

1927 Μια κραυγή. (Πέρα από τον κομμουνισμό). Πολιτεία, 16 October 1927, p. 2, and 18 October 1927, p. 1.

Politis, G. N.

1927 Ο δρόμος της καρδιάς. Ελληνικά Γράμματα 1:440–443 (15 October 1927).

Popper, Karl L.

1982 *The Open Universe: An Argument for Indeterminism.* Edited by W. W. Bartley III. London: Hutchinson.

Poulakidas, Andreas K.
1972 Kazantzakis and Bergson: Metaphysic Aestheticians. *Journal of Modern Literature* 2/2 (1971–1972): 267–283.
1975 Kazantzakis' "Spiritual Exercises" and Buddhism. *Comparative Literature* 27/3 (Summer 1975):208–217.
Pouliopoulos, Nikos D.
1972 Ο Νίκος Καζαντζάκης και τα παγκόσμια ιδεολογικά ρεύματα. Vol. 1. Athens.
1975 Ο Νίκος Καζαντζάκης και τα παγκόσμια ιδεολογικά ρεύματα. Vol. 2. Athens.
Prevelakis, Pandelis
1927 Δύο έργα του Νίκου Καζαντζάκη. Αναγέννηση Β΄:177–180 (December 1927).
1958 Ο ποιητής και το ποίημα της Οδύσσειας. Athens: Estia.
1961 Nikos Kazantzakis and His "Odyssey": A Study of the Poet and the Poem. New York: Simon and Schuster.
1965a Ο Κρητικός: Το δέντρο, Η πρώτη λευτεριά, Η πολιτεία. Athens: Galaksia.
1965b Τετρακόσια γράμματα του Καζαντζάκη στον Πρεβελάκη. Athens: Eleni N. Kazantzaki.
1969 Παντέρμη Κρήτη, χρονικό του σηκωμού του 66. 2nd ed. Athens: Estia.
1975 Interviewed by Peter Bien, Athens, 9 April 1975.
1977 Ο Καζαντζάκης, βίος και έργα. Τετράδια "Ευθύνης" Γ΄, 9–45.
1981 Kazantzakis: Life and Works. *The Charioteer*, nos. 22–23: 23–65.
1983 Kazantzakis-Sikelianos: The Chronicle of a Friendship. *Journal of the Hellenic Diaspora*, Winter 1983, pp. 5–20. Greek text in *Néa Estía* 114 (1983): 976–987 (15 Aug. 1983).
1984 Το αγιορείτικο ημερόλογιο του Σικελιανού. Νέα Εστία 115: 352–377 (15 March 1984).
1985 Δείχτες πορείας. Athens: Estia.
Proïa
1928 Kazantzakis's articles based on his third trip to Russia. 8 January–14 January. Also, four articles were published in Alexandria in Athanasios Marselos's periodical *Ermis*.
Psilakis, Vasilios
1909 Ιστορία της Κρήτης. 3 vols. Hania, Crete.
Quiller-Couch, Sir Arthur
1922 *Studies in Literature*, Second Series. Cambridge: Cambridge University Press.
Raftopoulos, Dimitris
1958 Τα πρόσωπα της "Ασκητικής" του Καζαντζάκη. Καινούρια Εποχή, Autumn 1958, pp. 331–347.
Raydon, Edouard
1968 *Panaït Istrati, vagabond de génie*. Paris: Les Editions Municipales.
Renan, Ernest
1867 *The Life of Jesus*. New York: Carleton.

Renault, Mary

1965 Review of "Report to Greco." *The New York Times Book Review*, 15 August 1965, p. 1.

Rose, Steven

1980 Essay-review of Gregory Bateson's "Mind and Nature: A Necessary Unity." *Times Literary Supplement* (London), 21 Nov. 1980, p. 1313.

Rotas, Vassilis

1927 Ενα μετακομουνιστικό "Πιστεύω." Αναγέννηση Β′:172–176 (December 1927).

Sachinis, Apostolos

1967 Πεζογράφοι του καιρού μας. Athens: Estia.

Sadoul, Robert

1955 Rencontré à Antibes. *Les Nouvelles Littéraires*, 17 March, p. 5. Greek translation in *Néa Estía* 57 (1955): 545.

Salter, William Mackintire

1917 *Nietzsche the Thinker*. New York: Henry Holt.

Schubert-Soldern, Rainer

1962 *Mechanism and Vitalism: Philosophical Aspects of Biology*. Edited by Philip G. Fothergill. London: Burns and Oates. Notre Dame, Ind.: University of Notre Dame Press.

Seferis, George

1967 *On the Greek Style*. London: Bodley Head.

1974 Δοκιμές. 3 vols. 3rd ed. Athens: Ikaros.

1977 Μέρες Γ′, 16 Απρίλη 1934–14 Δεκέμβρη 1940. Athens: Ikaros.

1983 Υστερόγραφο στη δοκιμή "Κ. Π. Καβάφης, Θ. Σ. Έλιοτ· παράλληλοι." Η Λέξη, March–April 1983.

Serge, Victor

1951 *Mémoires d'un révolutionnaire 1901–1941*. Paris: Éditions du Seuil.

1963 *Memoirs of a Revolutionary 1901–1941*. London: Oxford University Press.

Sfakianakis, Yannis

1958 Ο Νίκος Καζαντζάκης και ο "Καπετάν Μιχάλης". Καινούρια Εποχή, Winter 1958, pp. 224–234.

Sherrard, Philip

1959 *The Greek East and the Latin West*. Oxford: Oxford University Press.

Shestov, Lev

1920 *All Things Are Possible*. Forword by D. H. Lawrence. New York: McBride. (Translation of *Apotheosis of Groundlessness*, 1905.)

Sipriot, Pierre

1957 Dialogue avec Nikos Kazantzaki. *Lettres Etrangères*, 5 June 1957, pp. 3–4. Also published in the French periodical *Arts*, 5 June 1957. Excerpts in Eleni Kaz. 1968a:527–530. Based on six radio programs (see Prev. 1965b:719, 725).

Smith, Warren Sylvester

1963 *The Religious Speeches of Bernard Shaw*. University Park: The Pennsylvania State University Press.

Sorel, Georges
1941 *Reflections on Violence*. New York: B. W. Huebsch. (Translation of *Réflexions sur la violence*, first published in 1908.)
Spanakis, Stergios G.
1962 Η πολιτική διαθήκη του Νίκου Καζαντζάκη. Κρητική Πρωτοχρονιά 2 (Athens 1962): 49–50.
Spengler, Oswald
1922–1923 *Der Untergang des Abendlandes*. 2 vols. Munich: Beck. In this edition, vol. 1 (1923) is "völlig umgestaltete" (fully revised). Vol. 1 was originally published in 1918 and vol. 2 in 1922.
1980 *The Decline of the West*. 2 vols. New York: Knopf.
Stamatiou, Yeorgios
1971 Καζαντζάκης: ένας αξεδίψαστος της ελευθερίας. Athens: Karavias.
1975 Οι αληθινές θεολογικές σχέσεις Ν. Καζαντζάκη και Εμμ. Παπαστεφάνου. Νέα Εστία 98:960–966, 1032–1039 (15 July and 1 August 1975).
Stanford, W. B.
1963 *The Ulysses Theme*. 2nd ed. Oxford: Blackwell.
Stefanakis, Yiorgos E.
1973 Ο Νίκος Καζαντζάκης πλάϊ στον Ελευθέριο Βενιζέλο (άγνωστα στοιχεία κι επιστολές από την ελλαδική περίοδο 1912–1922 του Νίκου Καζαντζάκη). Κατάθεση '73. Αθήνα: Μπουκουμάνης. Pp. 207–220. Reprinted in Alexiou and Stefanakis 1977:46–56; 1983:127–138.
Talex, Alexandre
1983a Une Amitié retrouvée: Istrati-Kazantzaki. *L'Arc*, nos. 86/87 (1983), pp. 15–19.
1983b Repères bibliographiques. *L'Arc*, nos. 86/87 (1983), pp. 173–179.
Talvart, Hector, and Joseph Place
1950 *Bibliographie des auteurs modernes de langue française (1801–1949)*. Vol. 2. Paris: Horizons de France.
Terzakis, Angelos
1972 Ένας νεανικός Καζαντζάκης. Το Βήμα της Κυριακής, 2 July 1972.
Theotokas, Yorgos
1939 Παρατηρήσεις στο περιθώριο των γεγονότων. Νεοελληνικά Γράμματα, 2 Dec. 1939, pp. 1–2. Reprinted in his Πνευματική πορεία, pp. 365–373.
1955 The Modern Greeks. An Interpretation of National Characteristics. *The Atlantic Monthly*. June 1955, pp. 101–105.
1958 Τα ελληνικά ιδανικά στον 20όν αιώνα. Το Βήμα, 21 Sept. 1958, p. 1. Reprinted in his Πνευματική πορεία, pp. 113–118.
1961 Πνευματική πορεία. Athens: Fexis.
1965 Νεοελληνικό λαϊκό θέατρο. Athens: Estia.
Tillich, Paul
1952 *The Courage to Be*. New Haven: Yale University Press.
Trilling, Lionel
1976 Why We Read Jane Austen. *Times Literary Supplement* (London), 5 March 1976, pp. 250–252.

Tsiropoulos, Kostas E.

1977 Νέα ανάγνωση της "Ασκητικής." Τετράδια "Ευθύνης" 3. Athens. Pp. 162–179.

Tziovas, Dimitrios

1986 *The Nationism of the Demoticists and Its Impact on Their Literary Theory (1888–1930).* Amsterdam: Hakkert.

1989 Residual Orality and Belated Textuality in Greek Literature and Culture. *Journal of Modern Greek Studies* 7/2 (October, 1989): 321–336.

Varnalis, Kostas

1928 Νίκου Καζαντζάκη "Χριστός." Αναγέννηση Β':494–499 (July–Aug. 1928).

1947 Ο υπαρξισμός: φιλοσοφία και φιλολογία της αντίδρασης. Ριζοσπάστης, 18 Sept. 1947, p. 2.

1984 Αισθητικά-Κριτικά. Athens: Kedros.

Veï, Mairi

1963 Δύο επιστολές του Νίκου Καζαντζάκη προς τον Νίκο Βέη. Νέα Εστία 74:1688–1691 (15 Nov. 1963).

Venezis, Elias

1943 Η προσφυγιά του 1922 στην Ελληνική Λογοτεχνία. Προσφυγικός Κόσμος, 24 Jan. 1943, pp. 1–2. Cited in Doulis 1977, pp. 281–282.

1964 In: Ακρόπολις, 24 May 1964, p. 5.

Venizelos, Eleftherios

1971 Η κρητική επανάσταση του 1889. Edited by Ioannos G. Manolikakis. Athens: Aptera.

Vita-Finzi, P.

1968 Italian Fascism and the Intellectuals. In *The Nature of Fascism*, edited by S. J. Woolf. London: Weidenfeld and Nicholson.

Vitti, Mario

1977 Η γενιά του τριάντα: ιδεολογία και μορφή. Athens: Ermis.

Voutieridis, E.

1911 Ο "Τριτομάστορας." Interview in Αθήναι, 4 June.

Voyatzidis, G. K.

1953 La Grande Idée. In *L'Hellénisme Contemporain, le cinq-centième anniversaire de la prise de Constaninople.* Athens: Imprimerie Nationale. Pp. 279–287. Reprint of Γ. Κ. Βογιατζίδη, Η αρχή και η εξέλιξις της Μεγάλης Ιδέας. Ημερολόγιο Μεγάλης Ελλάδας, 1923.

Vrettakos, Nikiforos

1960 Νίκος Καζαντζάκης, η αγωνία του και το έργο του. Athens: Sypsas.

1977 Ο Καζαντζάκης και η "Ασκητική" του. Νέα Εστία, Christmas 1977, pp. 36–40.

1983 Η περίπτωση της "Οδύσσειας" του Νίκου Καζαντζάκη. Σύγχρονοι Καιροί 5:209 (May–June 1983).

Wellek, René

1968 The Name and Nature of Comparative Literature. In *Comparatists at Work*, edited by Stephen G. Nichols, Jr., and Richard B. Vowles. Waltham, Mass.: Blaisdell.

Whitman, Cedric
1965 *Homer and the Heroic Tradition*. New York: Norton.
Wilson, Edward O.
1978 *On Human Nature*. Cambridge: Harvard University Press.
Woodhouse, C. M.
1948 *Apple of Discord*. London: Hutchinson.
1976 *The Struggle for Greece 1941–1949*. London: Hart-Davis, MacGibbon.
Yalourakis, Manolis
1958 Ο Καζαντζάκης μου είπε . . . Καινούρια Εποχή, Autumn 1958, pp. 154–162.
1970 Καζαντζάκης-Μυριβήλης, κριτικά δοκίμια. Athens: Ptolemaios.
1978 Ο κριτικός Νίκος Καζαντζάκης. Athens: Diodos.
1983 Ο Καζαντζάκης και η Αίγυπτος. Νέα Εστία 113:729–732 (1 June 1983).
Yeorgoulis, K.
1927 Και πάλι οι κοινωνικοί νόμοι. Αναγέννηση Α΄:266–267 (Jan. 1927).
1948 Η φαινομενολογική οντολογία του Martin Heidegger. *Νέα Εστία* 44:833–837 (1 July); 911–916 (15 July); 976–983 (1 August).
Zambelis, E.
1936 Ἐξ ἀφορμῆς ἑνός ἄρθρου. Ἡ Καθημερινή, 27 July 1936, p. 4.
Zervos, Ioannis
1909 [Αρέτας] Τά βιβλία: Ὁ Φρειδερῖκος Νίτσε ἐν τῇ φιλοσοφίᾳ τοῦ δικαίου καί τῆς πολιτείας, ὑπό Ν. Μ. Καζαντζάκη. Παναθήναια, 15 Oct., 1909, pp. 25–26. Reprinted in *Νέα Εστία* 64:1373–1374 (15 Sept. 1958).
Zografou, Lili
1960 Νίκος Καζαντζάκης, ένας τραγικός. Athens: Kedros. (The fourth edition [Athens: Asteri, 1981] is a photo-reproduction, but with slightly different pagination. Add 2 pages to the 1960 edition to get the 1981 pagination.)
Zweig, Stefan
1925 *Der Kampf mit dem Dämon. Hölderlin, Kleist, Nietzsche*. Leipzig: Insel-Verlag.

Index